RODALE'S
No-Fail
Flower Garden

RODALE'S
No-Fail
Flower Garden

How to Plan, Plant and Grow a Beautiful, Easy-Care Garden

Edited by:
Joan Benjamin and Barbara W. Ellis

Rodale Press, Emmaus, Pennsylvania

Our Purpose

*"We inspire and enable people to improve
their lives and the world around them."*

If you have any questions or comments concerning this book, please write to:
  Rodale Press, Inc.
  Book Readers' Service
  33 East Minor Street
  Emmaus, PA 18098

"Soil Health Makes Good Scents" on page 262 adapted from *Start with the Soil* by Grace Gershuny (Emmaus, Pa.: Rodale Press, 1993). Reprinted by permission of the author.

Executive Editor: Margaret Lydic Balitas
Managing Editor: Barbara W. Ellis
Editor: Joan Benjamin
Contributing Editors: Fern Marshall Bradley,
  Deborah L. Martin, Ellen Phillips
Copy Editor: Barbara M. Webb
Copy Manager: Dolores Plikaitis
Senior Research Associate: Heidi A. Stonehill
Administrative Assistant: Susan Nickol
Office Manager: Karen Earl-Braymer
Editorial Assistance: Deborah Weisel
Indexer: Ed Yeager

Art Director: Michael Mandarano
Cover and Interior Designer: Linda Jacopetti
Front and Back Cover Photographer: Ed Landrock
Interior Illustrators: Robin Brickman, Pamela Carroll,
  Frank Fretz, Patricia Kay, Kathryn D. Kester

Library of Congress Cataloging-in-Publication Data

Rodale's no-fail flower garden : how to plan, plant,
  and grow a beautiful, easy-care garden / edited by
  Joan Benjamin and Barbara W. Ellis.
    p.   cm.
  Includes bibliographical references (p.   )
  and index.
  ISBN 0–87596–606–3 hardcover
  ISBN 0–87596–954–2 paperback
  1. Flower gardening. 2. Gardens—Design. 3.
Flowers. 4. Low maintenance gardening.   I.
Benjamin, Joan. II. Ellis, Barbara W. III. Rodale
Press. IV. Title: No-fail flower garden.
SB405.R683 1994
635.9—dc20   93–48200

Distributed in the book trade by St. Martin's Press

  2 4 6 8 10 9 7 5 3   hardcover
  2 4 6 8 10 9 7 5 3   paperback

Contents

Credits vi
What Is a No-Fail Flower Garden? viii

PART 1: DESIGNING A NO-FAIL FLOWER GARDEN
    Chapter One: Where Should Your Garden Grow? 2
    Chapter Two: Choose the Flower Garden That's Right for You 27
    Chapter Three: No-Fail Plant Combinations 63
    Chapter Four: Design Your Own No-Fail Garden 104
    Chapter Five: A Gallery of Easy Garden Designs 143
    Chapter Six: Great Ideas and Finishing Touches 211

PART 2: NO-FAIL FLOWER GARDENING TECHNIQUES
    Chapter Seven: Planting and Propagating No-Fail Flowers 238
    Chapter Eight: Taking Care of Your Garden 277
    Chapter Nine: Keeping Your Garden's Good Looks 322

A Plant-by-Plant Guide to No-Fail Flowers.. 340
Sources 358
Recommended Reading 359
USDA Plant Hardiness Zone Map 360
Index 361

Credits

Writers

Marianne Binetti is a landscape designer and award-winning syndicated garden columnist who lives in Enumclaw, Washington. She designed the Garden for a Sunny Slope and the Fragrant Heirloom Garden in this book, and she is the author of *Tips for Carefree Landscapes* and *Shortcuts for Accenting Your Garden.*

C. Colston (Cole) Burrell is a garden designer, writer, and photographer whose Minnesota-based design business, Native Landscapes, specializes in the use of native plants and perennials. Burrell designed the Hardy Northern Garden for this book, and he is co-author of *Rodale's Illustrated Encyclopedia of Perennials.*

Nancy Drushal teaches landscaping at Columbus State Community College, in Columbus, Ohio. She has a B.S. in agriculture from Ohio State University.

Erin Hynes is a freelance garden writer from Austin, Texas, and is the author of *Rodale's Successful Organic Gardening: Improving the Soil.* She has a B.S. in agronomy from the University of Illinois and an M.S. in weed science from Pennsylvania State University.

Nancy J. Ondra is an associate editor of garden books at Rodale Press, in Emmaus, Pennsylvania. She has a B.S. in agronomy from Delaware Valley College. Ondra designed the Color Theme Garden for this book, which includes some of the many perennials she grows and propagates at her home.

Garden Designers

Pamela Allenstein is a gardener at Longwood Gardens in Kennett Square, Pennsylvania. She has a B.S. in horticulture from Michigan State University and an M.S. in public horticulture administration through the University of Delaware's Longwood Graduate Program.

Sue Bartelette is a freelance garden designer who specializes in flower gardens. She owns and operates a greenhouse in Lupus, Missouri, where she, her husband, and five children grow perennials organically.

Joan Benjamin is an associate editor of garden books at Rodale Press in Emmaus, Pennsylvania. She has a B.S. in agriculture from the University of Missouri and an M.S. in public horticulture administration through the University of Delaware's Longwood Graduate Program.

LuAnn Craighton is an Interpretive Naturalist at Callaway Gardens in Pine Mountain, Georgia. She enjoys experimenting with and teaching about wildlife gardening techniques.

Barrie Crawford is the author of *For the Love of Wild Flowers* and co-author of *The Gardens of Two Sisters*. She gives workshops on wildflowers at Callaway Gardens in Pine Mountain, Georgia.

Neil Diboll designs native plant gardens and landscapes at Prairie Nursery in Westfield, Wisconsin. He has a B.S. in plant ecology from the University of Wisconsin.

Edith R. Eddleman is a garden designer, writer, and lecturer from Durham, North Carolina. Her designs have been featured in Pam Harper's *Designing with Perennials* and *Perennial Portraits 1991* and in *Rodale's Illustrated Encyclopedia of Perennials.*

Douglas H. (Scottie) Garrett was born and educated in Scotland. While manager of buildings and grounds for Shelter Insurance Companies in Columbia, Missouri, he designed and constructed their award-winning gardens. Garrett now works as a private landscape consultant. He and his wife, Miriam (also an avid gardener), experiment with new and different plant materials in their Scottish-style garden.

Ellen Phillips is an editor of garden books at Rodale Press, in Emmaus, Pennsylvania. She has an M.S. in horticulture from the University of Kentucky and an M.S. in creative writing from Indiana University.

Phillips is co-author of *Rodale's Illustrated Encyclopedia of Perennials.*

Cynthia Woodyard is a garden photographer and designer from Portland, Oregon. Her photos have appeared in many horticulture magazines and books, including Allen Lacy's *The Garden in Autumn* and *Gardening with Groundcovers and Vines.*

Interior Photographers:

Patricia J. Bruno/Positive Images: page 61.
C. Colston Burrell: pages 55, 81, 87, 89, 101, 105, 135. **R. Todd Davis:** pages 103, 232.
Carl Doney/Rodale Stock Images: page 15.
Edith R. Eddleman: pages 111, 216.
Stan Green: page 91. **T. L. Gettings/Rodale Stock Images:** pages 3, 17, 48, 71, 137, 224, 229. **John P. Hamel/Rodale Stock Images:** page 110. **Pamela J. Harper:** pages 25, 33, 42, 47, 52, 57, 67, 97, 113, 118, 120, 121, 140.
Margaret Hensel/Positive Images: pages 7, 18, 218. **Jerry Howard/Positive Images:** pages 5, 93, 128. **Dwight R. Kuhn:** page 49.
Ed Landrock/Rodale Stock Images: pages x–1, 236–237. **Peter Lindtner:** page 230.
Mitch Mandel/Rodale Stock Images: pages 77, 95. **Nancy J. Ondra:** page 35. **Jerry Pavia:** pages 9, 11, 29, 31, 37, 40, 43, 45, 50, 54, 56, 69, 75, 79, 83, 99, 115, 234. **Joanne Pavia:** pages 30, 212, 221. **Rodale Stock Images:** page 142.
Susan A. Roth: pages 65, 73, 85, 126.
Marilyn Stouffer/Rodale Stock Images: pages 53, 227, 235. **Sally Ann Ullman/Rodale Stock Images:** page 59. **Cynthia Woodyard:** pages 112, 114, 116.

What Is a No-Fail Flower Garden?

That's an easy question. A no-fail flower garden is one that looks great and grows well for you. Here's what makes a no-fail flower garden work:

- It pleases you. If you don't like the flowers, the colors, the size, or the shape, it's not a no-fail garden.
- It uses low-maintenance plants. With the right plants in the right place, there's relatively little weeding, staking, or watering.
- It brightens and improves the appearance of your home and yard.
- It's colorful through several seasons, not just for a few weeks in spring or summer.
- It's generally pest- and disease-free.
- It takes only as much time and money as you want to spend.

Does that sound like a lot to ask of a garden? Maybe, but it's what you can expect if you use the no-fail techniques, plants, and garden designs included in this book.

We've divided the no-fail process into two simple steps. Part 1, "Designing a No-Fail Flower Garden," starts on page 1. It helps you choose the right garden site and design the perfect garden for you. To inspire you, we've included dozens of color photos of no-fail gardens and plants to choose from. Chapter 3 features great plant combinations that you can use alone as focal points, in groups as simple garden designs, or with other combinations for spectacular effects. And for even more inspiration, we've devoted

Chapter 5 to foolproof flower garden designs. Page through the color drawings and garden plans and choose your favorites. We've included all the information you'll need to create each garden. We've even added ideas for phasing gardens in and finding great but inexpensive plants so that lack of time or money won't stand in your way.

Part 2, "No-Fail Flower Gardening Techniques," begins on page 237 and gives you the nitty-gritty details of soil preparation, planting, and plant care. You'll learn how to avoid pest and disease problems, how to reduce watering, weeding, and other chores—even easy ways to make more plants for free.

For quick access to all the plant information you need, we've included a special section, "A Plant-by-Plant Guide to No-Fail Flowers," which starts on page 340. There you'll find descriptions of dozens of no-fail plants. We've made it easy to find the best flowers for your garden.

What is a no-fail flower garden? With the colorful, easy designs, outstanding plant combinations, and no-nonsense gardening expertise in this book, you'll be able to answer this question yourself: "It's *my* garden!"

PART 1

DESIGNING A NO-FAIL FLOWER GARDEN

CHAPTER 1

Where Should Your Garden Grow?

No-fail flower gardens don't start with wild shopping sprees at the local garden center, late nights ordering every plant in your favorite mail-order catalogs, or even hours of dedicated digging in the backyard. Why not? Because the best gardens start out in your imagination, and they're firmed up with a little basic planning. Fortunately, in this case, that doesn't mean spending hours measuring your yard to the last quarter inch or slaving away over detailed drawings. After all, you can create a great-looking garden without knowing exactly how big it is. Instead, it means asking yourself two basic questions: What do I want the garden to do, and what flowers do I want to grow? Once you've answered these questions, you'll use the information you've gathered to pick the best site for your garden.

Asking yourself what you want a garden to do may seem odd at first, but it's the key to planning a garden that's successful and that you'll enjoy—and that's what no-fail flower gardening is all about. For example, say you want a colorful flower garden that you can enjoy from your patio but that also screens an unattractive view of your neighbor's trash cans. A garden that fills the bill will not only feature plants that are tall enough to screen the trash cans, it will also be the right size and shape so you can enjoy it from

Combine a garden full of colorful, easy-care annuals and perennials with a site that's visited daily, and what do you have? A recipe for a no-fail garden that will provide loads of enjoyment. Here, a path through the bed to the lawn beyond directs traffic and allows visitors to enjoy the flowers up close.

WHAT CAN GARDENS DO?

The most effective flower gardens are pretty, to be sure, but they're also hardworking parts of a well-planned landscape. Here are some ways you can use flowers to get the most out of your yard.

- Create a colorful, shady retreat under trees.
- Enclose or surround a patio or deck.
- Provide an attractive view from inside the house.
- Replace a lawn area with blooming groundcovers.
- Screen an unsightly view in neighboring yards.
- Create an island of color in a green sea of lawn.
- Dress up a fence or hedge to add color and interest.
- Add color to a boring foundation planting.
- Reduce maintenance by replacing lawn on hard-to-mow slopes or under trees.
- Attract wildlife like butterflies or birds.
- Provide flowers for cutting or drying.

anywhere on the patio. On the other hand, if your heart is set on growing your favorite flowers, you'll want to look for a site that provides the amount of sun or shade they thrive in.

In this chapter, you'll find a host of ideas, suggestions, and simple exercises that will help you decide just what you want your no-fail flower garden to do and where you want it to be. You can also use this information if you already have a garden. Just use the suggestions that follow to help you evaluate the gardens you already have. For information on enhancing an existing garden, see Chapter 6. For information on changing or rearranging an existing garden, see "Renewing Existing Gardens" on page 322.

What Do You Want Your Garden to Do?

Before you buy a plant or turn a shovelful of soil, take time to walk around your yard and look at it carefully. Think about the places you would like to have a flower garden. Would you like to have islands of flowers in the lawn to stroll around? A colorful, low-maintenance planting to clothe a tough-to-mow slope? Something other than scraggly grass and weeds under the trees? Colorful foliage and bright blooms at the front door to dress up the house and welcome visitors? Less lawn to mow and water? You should also take time to walk through your house and look out through the windows. Are there any places you'd especially enjoy a colorful flower garden from indoors? These observations will help you decide what you want your garden to do for you. For more ideas to consider, see "What Can Gardens Do?" on this page. Just remember, the more ideas you have at the outset, the better your garden will be.

Dreaming about the garden you'd like to have is another great place to start. Get a cup of coffee, find a comfortable chair, and sit down with a notepad. Write down whatever ideas come to mind. Think of gardens you have visited, seen in books, or admired while walking through your

Whether lining a driveway, a front walk, or a sidewalk, flowers can add color and excitement to any front yard. Who wouldn't be welcomed by this planting of climbing roses and heat-tolerant perennials including coreopsis (*Coreopsis* sp.), lavender cotton (*Santolina* sp.), and lavender?

WHAT DO YOU LIKE?

A list of elements you find most appealing in other gardens will help you plan your own garden. As you think about gardens you like, use the following questions to help analyze just what it is you most admire. Then try to incorporate those elements in your own garden.

Do the individual plants in a garden appeal to you most, or is it the way they're combined? Do the colors of the flowers attract you first, or is it their fragrances? Maybe you notice foliage textures, colors, and shapes before flowers. Do you like many colors and shapes or just a few?

Think about the position of the garden and how it relates to the house. Is it in the middle of a large lawn or in the cool shade of trees? Does it surround a terrace or deck? Border a fence or driveway? Is the design uniquely suited to the style of the house?

Does the design of the garden encourage you to stroll through it, sit in it, or walk around it to see it from all sides? Or do you simply view it from afar?

neighborhood. Try to imagine how you'd like to use a garden, too. Would you like to view it from afar? Stroll through it? Sit in the middle of it to enjoy its color and fragrance? "What Do You Like?" on this page will help you decide what gardens especially appeal to you. See Chapter 6 for easy ways to collect ideas from other gardens that you can use in yours.

At this point, don't think too much about the style of garden you'd like—you'll find plenty of information on that in Chapter 2, "Choose the Flower Garden That's Right for You." You also shouldn't worry about exactly how you'll design the garden or pick the plants. You'll find that information in Chapter 4, "Design Your Own No-Fail Garden." For now, concentrate on more general considerations like adding a bright spot of color you can enjoy from your kitchen window, making room for your grandmother's peonies, or hiding something you don't want to look at every day.

Garden Options

As you look at your yard and think about where you'd like to plant a garden, it may help to keep in mind the different types of gardens you can plan. Depending on what size and shape of yard you have, what plants you'd like to grow, or what you'd like your garden to do, each type of garden has advantages.

Flower Beds

A flower garden placed around the edge of the lawn or along a patio or building is generally called a bed. Beds are usually designed to be viewed from several sides and are also usually seen close-up. This means they're a great option if you'd like to collect lots of different plants, because you'll be able to enjoy them at close range. It also means details really matter: For best results, carefully select the plants you'll include. Ideally, you'll want flowers that have a long season of bloom and foliage that's attractive all season. Flower beds are great for almost any site—from sun to shade. If you have a shady yard, look for sites where you can make beds that encompass trees and shrubs.

Island Beds

Island beds are flower gardens surrounded by a sea of grass. They are generally first viewed from across a lawn, but they can be enjoyed from all sides. Use island beds to break up a large lawn or add color under trees. Try to place them so they have visual prominence from popular viewing spots such as your kitchen windows, deck, or breakfast nook.

Choose your spot and the shape of the garden carefully. Misplaced island beds can be awkward looking and unnatural. Think of them as a pool of water on the landscape, and look for sites that suggest a natural shape—around sev-

FOUNDATION FLOWERS

Why not replace those boring, overgrown foundation plantings with a colorful flower bed? It may seem like a drastic step, but what better way to welcome visitors and decorate the front of your house? By replacing prickly junipers and bowling-ball yews with a selection of colorful and fragrant annuals and perennials, you'll create a garden to enjoy from indoors and out. Also add some flowering shrubs to provide structure and interest in the winter.

A bed full of flowers makes an effective, low-growing foundation planting that can be enjoyed from either outdoors or in. Here, bellflowers (*Campanula* sp.), peonies, and astilbe provide a blue and white theme.

━━━━━━━ ➻ · ➸ ━━━━━━━

PLACES FOR FLOWERS

All too often, flowers and shrubs are pushed up against the edges of a yard, like furniture against the walls of a room. Yet a flower garden can add much more to the landscape than just a spot of color against the back fence. Here are some suggestions to help you find just the right place for your flowers.

• Line the driveway with a border of perennials and shrubs to welcome you home each day.

• Replace the lawn next to the curb with a colorful planting of drought-tolerant perennials.

• Welcome visitors with beds of flowers and herbs on each side of the front door.

• Create a screen of tall perennials and shrubs to enclose a patio or terrace and provide a private sitting area.

• Add flowers for cutting to your vegetable garden.

• Join clumps of trees and shrubs with a bed of shade-loving flowers and groundcovers—instead of tough-to-trim lawn.

━━━━━━━ ➻ · ➸ ━━━━━━━

eral trees or along a dip or rise in your landscape, for example. The most effective island beds are oval or free-form in shape with graceful, sweeping curves.

One common mistake is to make an island bed that is too small. Small size coupled with plants that are too large makes a very unbalanced picture indeed. Plan on a garden that is at least twice as wide as the tallest plant to help keep things in scale. If you have a small yard, island beds may not be the best option. Your yard will look larger with the flower beds off to the sides and a central area of lawn.

You can use island beds to screen or block views by using tall plants in the middle, such as Japanese silver grass (*Miscanthus sinensis*), foxgloves (*Digitalis* spp.), cleomes (*Cleome hasslerana*), or sunflowers (*Helianthus* spp.). Use shorter plants such as yarrows (*Achillea* spp.) and cranes-bills (*Geranium* spp.) in the middle of the island if you'd like to see what is behind the bed. You can also design island beds around trees and shrubs on a shaded site. Making beds around trees not only makes for an attractive garden, it also reduces maintenance because you no longer need to trim or mow around individual trees.

Borders

Borders run lengthwise along a drive, walk, or fence. They are much longer than they are wide and are often designed to be viewed from one side, with the tallest plants at the back and shorter ones near the front.

Use borders to direct where people walk or to enliven a dull wall or fence. You can also use a border to enclose an area to create an outdoor room. For example, you could use one to separate your lawn from the vegetable garden. Borders fronting walls and fences have a long tradition—they're the classic image of the English perennial garden. They're ideal for jazzing up an uninspired fence erected by a neighbor or for decorating a blank wall you look at every day from your dining room or kitchen. Don't limit your plant choices when you design a border—it's for more than just perennials. You can plant annuals, perennials, bulbs, and flowering shrubs together to create a border filled with bloom from spring until frost.

A flower border is a great way to dress up a less-than-attractive fence. Annual candytuft (*Iberis umbellata*) and poppies add vibrant pinks and reds to this scene, turning an eyesore into a garden backdrop.

➙ · ᐸ

PLANT FOR ENJOYMENT

The site you pick can have a lot to do with how much you enjoy your garden. So when you're looking for a site, think about where you'll see it most. You'll get much more enjoyment from a garden that you see every day from the kitchen window than one along the side yard where you rarely venture. Here are some suggestions to help you look for a spot you'll enjoy.

Look out your windows. Ask yourself which sites you'd see most often from indoors, and where you'd most enjoy seeing a garden.

Walk frequently traveled paths. Would you enjoy flowers on your way out to the car each morning? On the path you use to take out the garbage?

Sit outdoors. Would you enjoy flowers near a terrace? By the front or back stoop? If you don't have a spot to sit outdoors, consider including plans for one in your no-fail flower garden.

➙ · ᐸ

Pick the Right Garden Spot

If there's a golden rule of no-fail flower gardening, it is "right plant, right place." Basically, there are two ways to use this rule to guide you in planning your no-fail garden. If your heart is set on growing a garden full of peonies, irises, daylilies, and asters, let the plants determine the right place for your garden. For these sun lovers, for example, you'd want a spot that receives six or more hours of sun a day. If your yard is shaded by a mature canopy of trees, however, it's time to think again: You simply don't have the right place for sun-loving plants to thrive. That doesn't mean you can't have a gorgeous garden, though. You just need to create one with shade-loving plants that will thrive in the conditions your yard has to offer. See "Shade Gardens" on page 34 for suggestions of plants to consider.

Let the place choose the plants, on the other hand, if you have a small yard with only one really good site for a garden. That's also the best option if you want a garden that serves a particular purpose—to screen a garage or surround a patio, for example. That means you'll want to look carefully at the site, especially its exposure and soil type, and select plants that will thrive there. No matter what your site offers—sun, shade, sand, clay, wet spots, or hot spots—there are many beautiful plants from which to choose.

Later in this chapter, you'll find complete information on learning more about your site—its climate, soil, and other conditions that determine which plants will thrive best there.

Placement Practicalities

In most yards, there are a number of places you can plant a garden, but practical matters should always come first in no-fail flower gardening. One time-honored axiom you should keep in mind is that a bed or border should be no farther from the house than the longest hose. Within hose-reach, however, you have the opportunity to place the garden where it shows off to best advantage. Here are some other practical matters to keep in mind.

Whatever type of site you have—hot and dry or cool and moist—
your best bet for success is to match plants to the conditions of the
site. Sedums, pink baby's-breath, pinks (*Dianthus* sp.), and bellflowers (*Campanula* sp.) thrive in this well-drained site.

Traffic Flow and Circulation

When you are looking for the perfect site, think carefully about how you move through your yard. Do you walk from the driveway to the front of the house? Do you cross the backyard to get to a garden shed? Where is your compost pile? Is there a play area for the kids? Where does the mail carrier walk? Do you need to be able to get a garden cart around to the vegetable garden—right though the site you're thinking about planting flowers in?

Traffic patterns are strong organizing factors in any yard. You don't want to locate your flower garden smack in the middle of the path everyone uses to take the trash out or run next door. Placing a flower bed right next to the lawn that the kids use for football practice probably isn't a good idea, either.

Fighting established patterns is a losing battle. Either

When you add a flower bed to a new yard, site it where it will fulfill your needs. Opportunities for this property include flower beds to dress up the front of the house, island beds to eliminate mowing around trees, and a border to beautify the lot line fence.

keep your flower garden clear of established routes or work them into your design. To accommodate an established path, for example, you could add a stepping-stone path through a bed. Just be sure it's wide enough and clearly marked to direct the flow of traffic. To separate a flower bed from the backyard football field, you could use a hedge, a fence, or clumps of sturdy Japanese silver grass (*Miscanthus sinensis*) along the back of the bed.

Picking the Best Site

Whether you're starting with a list of plants you'd like to grow or with a site you'd like to transform with a garden, it pays to visualize the garden you're planning. That way you can double-check to be sure it will be an effective addition to your yard and will accomplish the purpose you intended. Happy accidents are great when they happen. But more

Solve maintenance problems in established yards with flower beds. On this site, you could replace the sparse lawn grass under the mature trees with groundcovers, or convert the weedy, difficult-to-mow site at the bottom of the slope into a moist-meadow garden.

→ ⋅ ←

SEE THE GARDEN BEFORE YOU PLANT

Use these techniques to visualize your garden before you decide where to plant it. They'll help you make sure you have just the right spot.

Draw the outline. Outline the garden with a hose, rope, or sprinkling of flour to visualize its general shape.

See the size. Pile garbage bags full of leaves on the site (or cover lawn chairs with sheets) to see how big the garden will seem. If you're trying to screen an unsightly view, this will help you see how tall the plants need to be.

Walk around it. Examine your "garden" from all sides and look at it from windows you hope to view it from. Will you be able to enjoy it from where you hoped to? Does it hide what you hoped to hide?

Work around it. Before you dismantle your leaf-bag or lawn-chair garden, wheel your wheelbarrow or garden cart around it to make sure it doesn't block access to other parts of your yard.

→ ⋅ ←

often than not, impetuous placement makes a sure-fail garden instead of a no-fail garden.

Some gardeners are blessed with the ability to envision a garden in their mind's eye. They can imagine how tall it needs to be, imagine where they'll be able to see it from, and think through all of the practicalities about how they'll be able to care for it. As you think about sites for your garden, try to visualize what that garden might look like. Think of seeing it across the lawn or walking out onto a patio surrounded by flowers. Which scenario suits your needs? Which works best in your yard? If you have trouble visualizing the garden—and most of us do—don't hesitate to try some of the tricks listed in "See the Garden Before You Plant" on this page. They'll help you make sure it will be in the right place.

While you plan, try to think of your garden as an extension of your house. Your flower garden can be something you enjoy from indoors while visually drawing you out of the house into an outdoor room, such as a hedge-enclosed herb garden or a brick terrace patio under the canopy of a shade tree. For more on creating garden rooms, see "Outdoor Living Areas" on page 26.

Get to Know Your Garden Spot

Once you have thought about the aesthetics and logistics of the garden, it's time to take a close look at your site. Remember "right plant, right place"? Site characteristics such as temperature, rainfall, patterns of sun and shade, soil type, and other environmental factors will determine which plants will thrive in your site. (If you're starting with a list of plants you want to grow, you'll use these same factors to identify which site is best.) The more you know about your site and the more closely you can match the plants to it, the more successful your garden will be.

Climate and Microclimate

Climate refers to the overall environmental conditions that affect broad regions of the country. Temperature, rain-

A bed of yellow daylilies and purple gayfeathers (*Liatris* sp.) frames the view out the windows of this sun space. The bed also doubles as a foundation planting, which softens the outline of the house.

⇢•⇠

MORE ON MICROCLIMATES

A microclimate is the climate of a very small area such as your yard or a small part of your yard. For example, a south-facing wall can create a protected pocket with its own microclimate by storing and reflecting the sun's heat and blocking cold winds. Plants that are normally not quite hardy in your region may thrive there. Spring bulbs and other flowers may bloom extra-early when planted on a protected site because it warms up on sunny winter days.

A location on the north side of a wall or building doesn't receive direct winter sun, so plants growing there will start to grow later in the spring. This may help prevent frost damage to tender flower buds such as those of magnolias. North-facing sites also tend to be cooler in summer than south-facing ones.

⇢•⇠

fall, and prevailing winds are the primary climatic factors to consider.

Once you have an understanding of the general climatic conditions in your area, strike out into your own yard to investigate its unique environment. Wind, sun, soil, and moisture are important variables that can change from site to site. See "More on Microclimates" on this page and "Map Your Microclimates" on page 18 for details on investigating the microclimates in your yard.

Temperature

Most gardeners are familiar with the USDA plant hardiness zone map and how it's used to determine which plants will be hardy in a given region. (You'll find the map on page 360.) You can use hardiness zones to pick plants for your area, but keep in mind that they're only a starting point. That's because most maps (including the USDA one) reference only minimum winter temperatures. But the maximum and minimum temperatures *in the summer* also affect how plants perform. In fact, summer heat may be a more limiting factor in some areas than winter cold. For example, USDA Zone 8 stretches from Virginia and North Carolina through Texas and up the West Coast to British Columbia. A whole range of environmental conditions lie within this zone, which has only one common factor—minimum winter temperature. A plant that performs well in the summer heat and humidity of the Southeast may not thrive in the cool summers of the Pacific Northwest, and vice versa. That's why looking around locally to find plants that do well in your area is such a good idea.

Rainfall

Within any plant's hardiness range, rainfall is the single most limiting factor. If a plant doesn't get enough water, it won't survive. It's that simple. True, you can plant flowers that need weekly watering to survive in your area, but hauling hoses creates extra work for you and indicates you don't have the best plant match for the site. You'll ultimately have a much more successful garden if you select flow-

Why struggle to grow grass on a shady site when you can have flowers—and no more mowing! The azaleas (*Rhododendron* spp.), lilies-of-the-valley, bleeding hearts (*Dicentra* sp.), and for-get-me-nots (*Myosotis* sp.) in this shady garden will be much more colorful than lawn would ever be, and they require much less maintenance.

MAP YOUR MICROCLIMATES

Patterns of sun and shade, rainfall, and exposure create different microclimates in your yard. Use the exercises below to find and map your microclimates.

Catch the rain. On a rainy day, put jars around your yard to see how much rain reaches the ground. Find out and record which spots are too wet or too dry.

Find breezy spots. Place small flags around your yard, and watch them wave to find still and breezy spots.

Test temperature. Use your skin to find warm and cool spots; feel the heat from a south-facing wall, or where trees cool your yard.

If summer or winter winds threaten the survival of your flower bed, block them with an attractive fence. Here, a white picket fence protects and shows off a planting of yellow daylilies, heliopsis (*Heliopsis* sp.), and purple clematis.

ers that will grow well with the natural amount of rainfall your area receives. Soil, discussed in "Sizing Up Your Soil" on page 21, also determines how much water your plants will need.

Exposure

Prevailing winds also affect plant growth. Hot, dry summer winds or cold winter winds can dry out the soil, damage plant stems, and desiccate foliage. If you have a site where winds are a problem, select plants that can withstand wind and dry soil. Stay away from ones that have brittle stems or that need staking—delphiniums, for example.

Another alternative is to provide screens in the form of fences, hedges, shrub borders, or rows of trees to break the force of the wind. Keep in mind that winter winds come from a different direction than summer winds, and plan your windbreaks accordingly. Your local weather bureau is

a good source of information on seasonal variations in direction, intensity, and duration of winds.

On the other hand, if your yard doesn't receive even a breath of air, you'll want to keep that in mind. Still air—especially if it is humid—increases the chances that fungal diseases will be a problem. You may want to stay away from plants like roses and garden phlox (*Phlox paniculata*) that are subject to fungal diseases, or look for disease-resistant cultivars of plants you especially want to grow.

Map Your Sun and Shade

The amount of sunlight a site receives is an all-important environmental factor. Look at sun and shade patterns to determine how much light you have, or don't have. If you want to grow sun-loving plants, for example, you must find the sunniest spot in the yard. If your yard is a featureless plain or is covered entirely with mature trees, it's probably easy to decide which sites are sunny and which are shady.

A fence can block fierce winds that freeze plants in winter or scorch them in summer. But if you want a windbreak that provides cover and food for wildlife, too, add fruiting trees and shrubs. Plant evergreen trees to block winter winds and deciduous trees to slow summer blasts.

NW WINDS

―――――――――― ⇢ · ⇠ ――――――――――

REGIONAL RAINFALL

Consult the local Cooperative Extension Service, state university, or local weather bureau for annual rainfall information for your area. Annual rainfall varies from 45 inches in the mid-Atlantic, 32 inches in the Great Lakes region, and 110 inches in the Pacific Northwest to 9 inches or less in the desert Southwest. Monthly distribution of rain is as important as annual accumulation. You can always augment natural water with a hose during dry spells, but a true no-fail flower garden matches plants to naturally available moisture.

―――――――――― ⇢ · ⇠ ――――――――――

But it's easy to make incorrect assumptions if you have a mixture of open areas, trees, and buildings to deal with. To get a clear picture of the amount of sunlight a site receives, you'll need to observe it throughout the day as well as throughout the year, since the position of the sun changes.

To understand sun and shade patterns better, try a fun and simple mapping exercise. You will need graph paper with ¼- or ½-inch squares, a ruler, a 100-foot tape measure, and a compass. First, make a map of your property to scale using graph paper. (Your title company or the developer who built your house may be able to provide you with a scale drawing of your house and property.) Use a convenient scale such as one square equals 10 feet to represent your property on the graph paper. Measure the length and width of the lot and draw the property lines on your paper. Use the compass to figure out which way is north. Orient the drawing on your paper with north at the top. Next, measure the size of your house and the distances from your property lines. Place the house on the plan. Add any other buildings. Also add sidewalks and paths. Then draw in the trees. Try to represent the size of the tree canopy, not just the trunk. Also add in any hedges or fences.

Once you have your rough plan complete, make nine copies of it. Label three copies April 15, three copies June 15, and three copies August 15. Within each month, label the three pages 10:00 A.M., 1:00 P.M., and 5:00 P.M.

When April 15 arrives, pull out your plans and start mapping. Draw the patterns of sun and shade cast by trees, buildings, and fences at 10:00 A.M. The most legible technique is to darken in the shaded areas and leave the sunny areas blank. You may want to distinguish between deep shade and lighter shade—the deep shadows cast by the center of a tree canopy as opposed to the lighter shade around its perimeter, for example.

Repeat the process at 1:00 and 5:00 P.M. using the other two sheets. This gives you a clear indication of which areas receive the most sun and which are always in shade.

Repeat the mapping process on June 15, as the summer sun rises high into the sky. The changing position of the sun will change the light and shadow patterns in your yard. Since summer sun is hot, it is important to know where summer shade is if you want to grow woodland plants. Repeat the exercise on August 15. Now you have a complete picture of sun and shade patterns on your property. Use it to match plants to the available light for no-fail results.

Sizing Up Your Soil

Good soil is the backbone of a good garden. The type of soil you have determines not only what plants you can grow easily and well but also how easy it will be to dig your garden bed and manage your soil. It pays to take a good look at the soil in your proposed garden site and learn about the type of soil you'll be working with. This is especially true if your soil is hard to work or drains too

The patterns of sun and shade in your yard change from season to season as the sun changes position in the sky. Map the location of sunny and shady areas throughout the year to help you identify which sites will provide the right amount of sun or shade for your flower garden.

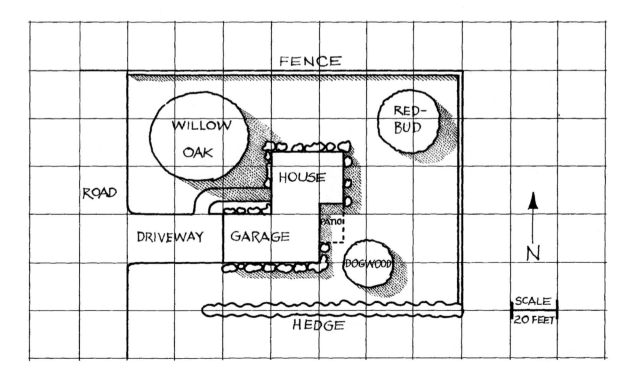

SIMPLE TEXTURE TEST

Use this at-home test for soil texture to find out what kind of soil you have. Squeeze a handful of moist but not soggy soil from the site where you want your garden. Then open your hand. Watch how the soil crumbles, and also rub it between your fingers.

If the ball disintegrates instantly and either sifts through your fingers or you can see and feel gritty particles in it, it's a sandy soil.

Silty soils also fall apart immediately. They have some texture, but you can't feel particles. Silty soils are often described as feeling mealy or greasy.

If you open your hand and the ball holds together, stay hopeful. Push the ball with your finger. If it falls apart with pressure, you've got loam. A clay soil is sticky and smooth like peanut butter when it's wet, and it's hard as a rock when it's dry. It will hold together no matter how you massage it.

quickly or too slowly, or if plants in your yard aren't as healthy as they should be.

Read Your Weeds

Surprisingly enough, a quick assessment of the weeds on your proposed garden site can tell you volumes about the soil beneath it. Here are some weeds to look for and the problems they indicate:

Annual sow thistle (*Sonchus oleraceus*): heavy clay soil

Canada thistle (*Cirsium arvense*): heavy clay soil

Coltsfoot (*Tussilago farfara*): heavy clay soil; waterlogged or poorly drained

Dandelion (*Taraxacum officinale*): compacted or heavy clay soil

Docks (*Rumex* spp.): waterlogged or poorly drained soil

Field bindweed (*Convolvulus arvensis*): compacted soil; low organic matter

Mosses (Musci class): waterlogged or poorly drained soil

Plantains (*Plantago* spp.): heavy clay soil; waterlogged or poorly drained

Quackgrass (*Agropyron repens*): compacted soil; a hardpan or crusty surface; low organic matter

Silvery cinquefoil (*Potentilla argentea*): dry soil, often with thin topsoil; acidic or low lime level

Soil Basics

Next, it's time to get up close and personal with your soil. Soil is a fascinating mix of fine rock particles, organic matter, water, air, microorganisms, and other animals. By volume it is 45 percent rock particles—the sand, silt, and clay portion of soil—and 50 percent space between particles. The space between particles is filled with air and water, which plant roots need to grow. Organic matter and soil organisms make up the remaining 5 percent.

You'll want to get an idea of the soil texture you'll be working with on your site. Soil texture refers to the relative percentages of sand, silt, and clay in the soil. Of the three types of particles, sand is the most coarse; clay, the finest. Silt is in between. Most soils contain a mixture of sand, silt, and clay. The sand portion of soil encourages good drainage, while the clay and silt help to hold nutrients and some moisture for good root growth. See "Simple Texture Test" on the opposite page for an easy way to determine soil texture.

Most soils in residential areas are loams—soils with moderate amounts of clay, silt, and sand. The ideal garden soil is said to be a loam made up of 20 percent clay, 40 percent silt, and 40 percent sand. While soils in most residential areas are loams, they may have higher or lower percentages of clay, silt, and sand than the ideal. Your soil may be classified as a clay loam, a silty loam, or a sandy loam, depending on which soil particle you have the most of.

The next important attribute, soil structure, refers to how the individual particles are combined and arranged in the soil. Soil structure determines how well soil retains water and how quickly or slowly it drains. It also determines how much air is available in the soil and how easily nutrients

You can learn a lot about the condition of the soil on your site by looking at the plants that grow there. Patchy lawn and the presence of dandelions and plantains on this site indicate infertile, heavy clay soil.

——————— ➡•⬅ ———————

THE WATERING TEST

When you're watering the garden, does the water disappear so fast that it seems only the leaves have gotten wet, rather than the soil surface? Do you have to water frequently to keep plants from wilting? If so, you have very sandy soil.

Or does water puddle up and take forever to sink into the soil? If that's the case, you have a high percentage of clay. Clay soil may dry and crack apart in clods between rains, and it becomes sticky or slippery when it's wet.

If you aren't sure how well your soil drains, use this simple test to find out. Start by watering a small area of your yard very thoroughly. Two days later, dig a small hole 6 inches deep where you watered. If the soil already is dry to the bottom of the hole, your soil probably doesn't hold water well enough for good plant growth.

Whether you have soil that drains too quickly or too slowly, adding organic matter to your soil will improve the way that it handles water.

——————— ➡•⬅ ———————

are released for uptake by plant roots. For a simple test that will help you learn more about how well your soil drains, see "The Watering Test" on this page.

You can't change the texture of the soil on your site, but you can improve its structure—and therefore its fertility, how well it drains, and how easily plant roots can grow through it—by adding organic matter. You can also destroy soil structure by working soil when it's too wet or too dry. Walking on beds or driving heavy equipment over them can have a similar effect: It compacts the soil and eliminates the spaces between soil particles (50 percent of its volume) that hold water and air for plants. If the site you're looking at has compacted soil, you can still have a good flower garden, but you'll need to prepare the site carefully or plant in raised beds, or both. For one approach to a site with poor soil, see "A Mulch-and-Grow Garden" on page 152. For information on improving your soil before you plant, see Chapter 7.

If you have good soil to begin with and you use sound gardening techniques like mulching, composting, and adding organic matter to your garden beds, you are well on your way to a great flower garden. You'll find information on caring for and improving your soil in Chapter 8. Ideally, your goal is a bed with soil that is fluffy and loose, so that water, air, and nutrients can filter down easily and so that roots have room to stretch.

Topography and Soil Moisture

While you're looking at potential sites, you'll also want to determine where the wet, dry, and in-between spots are. After a rain, look for sites where water stands as well as sites where water sheets off the land, flattening all the plants in its wake. While you can grow moisture-loving plants in sites where water tends to puddle up, it's best to avoid planting a flower garden in the middle of a drainage area.

Topography, exposure, and soil type can also affect moisture. If you have sandy soil, you'll find that spots high on a ridge or hill will dry out more quickly. Clay soils are

Great soil makes a great garden. The flowers in this vibrant foundation planting, including tiger lilies (*Lilium lancifolium*), phlox, dahlias, feverfew (*Chrysanthemum parthenium*), and heliopsis (*Heliopsis* sp.), all thrive on deep, well-drained soil that is rich in organic matter. An edging strip around the bed keeps the lawn from invading the space that's reserved for flowers.

➝ ∙ ⬅

OUTDOOR LIVING AREAS

To enjoy your yard to the fullest, think about it as an extension of your home. You can use plants to create garden rooms for the outdoor activities you enjoy, and they can have floors, walls, and ceilings just like indoor rooms. The floors are areas of lawn and groundcovers. Shrubs, hedges, and fences are walls; canopy trees and archways, the ceilings. The flowers are like the carpet and furnishings.

You could create a private sitting "room," for example, by placing a bench in a shady flower bed and screening it from view with small trees and shrubs. A small wood-chip path could serve as the "corridor" leading to this secluded spot. Or, use a colorful flower bed around a terrace to create a cheerful scene that will beckon you to come outdoors when you're in the house. If you'd like to add privacy to such an area, incorporate shrubs in the bed or add a "wall" of shrubs behind the flowers to set them off and screen the area from the rest of the yard.

➝ ∙ ⬅

especially slow to dry out in low spots. You can amend your soil with organic matter to help it hold more moisture or drain more quickly, but it's best to try working with what you've got. There are beautiful plants to meet every combination of sunlight, soil, and moisture. For great plant ideas for your site, see Chapter 3 and "A Plant-by-Plant Guide to No-Fail Flowers" on page 340. And take a look at "Special Considerations and Challenging Situations" on page 133 for even more inspiration.

Putting It All Together

Whether you're picking plants, fine-tuning your design, or planning a new garden for a year or two from now, use the information you've gathered on your site to guide you. You'll want to keep the details handy, so jot down a list of the major points you need to remember. You may want to start a notebook for all your garden plans, plant orders, and so forth. Or keep notes on a bulletin board that you'll see just as you go out to the garden center. From start to finish, you'll find it's the key to a no-fail flower garden.

CHAPTER 2

Choose the Flower Garden That's Right for You

There are as many types of flower gardens as there are flowers to put in them. Dreaming and scheming about what you want your garden to do sets you up for success, but deciding what type and size garden you want can be a challenge. So where do you start? If you can't decide whether you want a formal rose garden or an informal cottage garden, read on. The first section below will help you decide. If you already know exactly what kind of garden you want but don't know whether you can afford it, turn to "Stop Dreaming and Face Reality" on page 50 for tips and hints on gardening with a budget.

If you have an existing garden that's not as satisfying or successful as you had hoped, you can use the ideas below to figure out what changes you'd like to make. For information on enhancing an existing garden, see Chapter 6. For information on changing or rearranging an existing garden, see "Renewing Existing Gardens" on page 322.

Picture-Perfect Flowers

One good place to start is to think about the kinds of flowers you like best. Do you know whether you prefer annuals or perennials? Garden styles may use one or both types of flowers, so it's a good idea to be familiar with the features of each. You'll also find that a host of other types of plants make fine additions to flower gardens. Glance through Chapter 5, for example, and you'll find that many

—→ · ←—

BEGINNER BASICS: FLOWER TYPES

Do you mix up the terms annual, perennial, and biennial? Use these hints to keep them straight:

Annuals. These are just like high school annuals or yearbooks: A new one comes out each year. Annuals live and flower for a season and must be replaced each year. Reseeding annuals will come back year after year from self-sown seed.

Perennials. Perennials like daylilies and peonies come back each year. The tops of the plants may die to the ground in winter, but new growth sprouts from the roots each spring. Bulbs, like daffodils and tulips, are a type of perennial. Tender perennials are plants that die when exposed to cold winter temperatures.

Biennials. Biennials produce only foliage the first year after they are planted from seed. They flower the second year, set seed, and then die. Many biennials—like foxgloves and hollyhocks—will come back from self-sown seed.

—→ · ←—

of the garden designs include herbs, trees, shrubs, and even vegetables.

If you're a fair-weather gardener and only like to putter during the summer months, then a garden of annuals might be perfect for you. You can purchase a wide variety of annuals as plants, instead of growing them from seed, and get an instant shot of color for your garden. For frugal gardeners, annuals are still the best landscaping bargain around. For little more than a dollar you can buy a six-pack of petunias, marigolds, or impatiens. Split up the plants, spacing them 6 to 12 inches apart; with proper care you'll enjoy an explosion of color all summer long. Annuals are also great for a quick burst of color in a newly planted perennial bed or around a new house. They provide a season-long blanket of color that basically doesn't change. What's the downside? These plants live life in the fast lane, and they require lots of food and water to bloom continuously. Most will need to be deadheaded (have their spent flower heads removed) to encourage repeat blooming. Although most annuals must be planted every year, there are reseeding annuals such as cleomes (*Cleome* spp.) that will come back year after year.

If you prefer a garden that changes color and appearance throughout the season, perennials may be just the ticket. Although most perennials don't bloom for more than a few weeks each year, by combining them you can have a planting that changes from week to week. For example, you can design a flower bed with perennials like irises, columbines, and peonies that bloom in spring or early summer, and lilies, daylilies, mums, and asters that bloom in midsummer or fall. Perennials increase in size and beauty over the years as the clumps of flowers grow and multiply. You won't have to replant them every spring, but most perennial plants need to be dug and divided every two or three years to produce the best blooms and healthiest growth.

Picture Your Perfect Garden

Think about all the gardens you've seen. Is there a certain type of garden you dream about? Do you have a

Choosing which plants to grow is as much fun as growing them. Make a list of your favorite flowers whenever you visit gardens, and imagine them in your own yard. Just for practice, picture the everchanging colors and textures of foxgloves (*Digitalis* spp.), bellflowers (*Campanula* spp.), blanket flowers (*Gaillardia* spp.), pinks (*Dianthus* spp.), and evening primroses (*Oenothera* spp.) in your garden.

EXTRA-EARLY FLOWERS

It's easy to add some extra-early color to your flower garden: Just plant hardy spring-blooming bulbs. You can plant annuals right over a bed that's brimming with bulbs. Or tuck bulbs in between clumps of perennials.

For the longest season of color, choose a mixture of bulbs that bloom in early, mid-, and late spring. (Reputable nurseries indicate this for each cultivar.) Snowdrops (*Galanthus* spp.), squills (*Scilla* spp.), reticulated iris (*Iris reticulata*), and crocuses (*Crocus* spp.) bloom earliest, followed by daffodils (*Narcissus* spp.) and tulips (*Tulipa* spp.).

Anything goes in an informal herb garden. Stately pink foxgloves (*Digitalis* sp.) and a tree rose in a pot blend happily with more relaxed flowers and vegetables. Pinks (*Dianthus* spp.), leaf lettuce, and a variety of herbs spill over garden edges and into each other with enthusiasm.

favorite style? What exactly do you want your garden to look like? Just for a moment, forget about budget constraints, size restrictions, and any insecurities about growing unusual plants. Imagine yourself in front of an easel, and fill up the canvas with a painting of your dream garden.

There is no wrong way to picture your perfect flower garden. If you're a romantic at heart and love old-fashioned flowers and picket fences, choose a casual flower garden. Imagine a cottage or heritage garden filled with easy-to-grow flowers such as irises, daylilies, and foxgloves (*Digitalis* spp.). Or picture a shade garden with pastel pink and blue wildflowers. If your taste runs more toward neatly trimmed borders and carefully pruned plants, try a formal garden of perennials, roses, or herbs. And if your personality has both a casual and a formal side, your garden can,

Formal herb gardens are all neatness and order. Constant attention, training, and pruning keep lavender cotton (*Santolina* spp.) in tight mounds, boxwoods (*Buxus* spp.) in tidy low hedges, and rose flowers perfectly placed. Geometrically shaped plantings contribute to the formal look.

too. There's a style to fit every personality. On the pages that follow, you'll explore some of the most popular garden styles, just for starters. See if you recognize your dream garden there, but don't let this list limit you. You'll find garden ideas in every photograph in this book as well as in the garden designs in Chapter 5.

Cottage Gardens

Even if you don't live in a cottage, you might want your own cottage garden—the cheerful disorder of this garden style looks surprisingly contemporary. Cottage gardens originated during the Middle Ages, when people grew patches of flowers and other plants outside their doorsteps. They feature a patchwork of herbs, flowers, vegetables, and fruit trees. The style has an air of country casualness; instead of plants arranged from tallest to smallest and in distinct groups (as a traditional perennial border would have), cottage garden plants are mixed together like an exuberant bouquet. You can locate a cottage garden anywhere in your yard; but for the most authentic look, choose a sunny plot surrounding a path to the front or kitchen door, and enclose the yard, or part of it, with a rustic fence.

The flowers in a cottage garden are the sturdy plants passed from neighbor to neighbor and handed down through generations of gardeners. Cottage garden plants aren't fussy; most prefer full sun and average soil. They include biennials such as foxgloves, hollyhocks (*Alcea* spp.), and honesty (*Lunaria annua*). Irises, peonies, daylilies, lilies, and daisies, as well as bee balm (*Monarda didyma*), pinks (*Dianthus* spp.), lavender, and thyme, are among the best perennials for cottage gardens. Many reseeding annuals, which return to the garden each year via self-sown seed, are also popular cottage garden plants.

Also included are flowering shrubs and trees. Shrub roses usually bloom along a wall or fence or may sprawl beside the front door. Old-fashioned flowering shrubs or small trees, including crab apples, lilacs, hydrangeas, European cranberrybush viburnum (*Viburnum opulus*) and mock

ANNUALS FOR COTTAGE GARDENS

Add some of these reseeding annuals to your cottage garden. To get them started, prepare a seedbed where you want the plants to grow, and scatter the seeds.

- Baby-blue-eyes (*Nemophila menziesii*)
- Cleome (*Cleome hasslerana*)
- Cornflower (*Centaurea cyanus*)
- Flowering tobacco (*Nicotiana alata*)
- Four-o'clock (*Mirabilis jalapa*)
- Johnny-jump-up (*Viola tricolor*)
- Love-in-a-mist (*Nigella damascena*)
- Pot marigold (*Calendula officinalis*)
- Rocket larkspur (*Consolida ambigua*)
- Sweet alyssum (*Lobularia maritima*)

Don't forget to add some reseeding herbs to your cottage garden. Dill bears pretty yellow flowers, feathery foliage, and ornamental seed heads. Coriander bears white flowers; its foliage is the herb cilantro, used in Mexican cooking.

In cottage gardens, common old-fashioned plants like 'Silver King' artemisia (*Artemisia ludoviciana* 'Silver King'), blanket flowers (*Gaillardia* spp.), sneezewort (*Achillea ptarmica*), and orange daylilies mingle freely. In this planting they've teamed up with more unusual perennials like yellow-flowered olympic mullein (*Verbascum olympicum*) and 'Blue Charm' veronica (*Veronica grandis* 'Blue Charm') for a bold effect.

MADE FOR THE SHADE

To brighten up a shady spot, try featuring the perennials listed below. To add extra color to your shade garden, add hardy spring bulbs such as crocuses and daffodils, plus begonias and impatiens for annual color.

Bethlehem sage (*Pulmonaria saccharata*): In spring, pink buds open to blue flowers; silver-spotted foliage.

Coral bells (*Heuchera × brizoides*): Clusters of tiny white, pink, or red flowers on 1- to 2-foot stalks in summer; heart-shaped evergreen foliage.

Fringed bleeding heart (*Dicentra eximia*): Clusters of pink, heart-shaped flowers on 2-foot plants; blue-green, fernlike foliage.

Hellebores (*Helleborus* spp.): Clusters of bell-like flowers borne in very early spring on 2-foot plants; evergreen foliage.

Hostas (*Hosta* spp.): Broad-leaved foliage plant with spikes of white or lavender flowers; height ranges from 6 inches to 3 feet or more. Leaves may be green, yellow, or blue and may have white, yellow, or green variegations.

orange (*Philadelphus coronarius*), are popular choices. Wooden trellises, picket fences, birdbaths, sundials, and other garden features add to the look of an old-fashioned flower garden.

Shade Gardens

If your garden spot is located on the north or east side of your house, or if tall trees and neighboring buildings hide the sun, consider a garden in the shade. You'll find there are plenty of flowers that light up shady spots. Spring bulbs such as daffodils are a perfect choice, as are perennial wildflowers such as columbines (*Aquilegia* spp.) and Virginia bluebells (*Mertensia virginica*). Brightly colored annuals such as impatiens and begonias insist on blooming in even the darkest gardens. Plan to feature foliage in your shade garden for extra splashes of color. Try hostas with gold- or cream-variegated leaves and lungworts (*Pulmonaria* spp.) with silver-spotted foliage to make your garden glow. Blooming groundcovers like wild blue phlox (*Phlox divaricata*), creeping phlox (*Phlox stolonifera*), and foamflower (*Tiarella cordifolia*) brighten plantings in light to deep shade. And don't forget about flowering shrubs like rhododendrons and azaleas that love spots with filtered shade. You'll find more great combinations for shade in Chapter 3 and in "A Plant-by-Plant Guide to No-Fail Flowers" on page 340. If you're not sure how much shade you have, or which sites in your yard are most shady, see "Map Your Sun and Shade" on page 19.

A shade garden can be woodsy and casual with wood chip or pine needle paths and a variety of flowering and foliage plants. For a more formal and elegant feel, try planting white-blooming shade lovers, like goat's beard (*Aruncus dioicus*), and elegant foliage plants, like epimediums (*Epimedium* spp.).

Once you've started experimenting with shade plants, you'll never want to stop. And after all, where would you rather spend your summer afternoons—tending plants in a cool, shady spot or out in the hot summer sun?

The dappled shade beneath this large pine tree makes a perfect planting site. The tree's needle-like leaves give honesty (*Lunaria annua*) and garden forget-me-not (*Myosotis sylvatica*) relief from the afternoon sun and let in enough light for these and other spring-blooming perennials to thrive.

→ · ←

BALANCE YOUR FLOWERS

Combining trees and shrubs with flowers can be a balancing act. It's all too easy to end up with an awkward-looking mixture of giant trees and tiny flowers. To make sure your mixed beds are balanced-looking, keep these hints in mind:

• For every tree, plan on three shrubs grouped around the base. Group large shrubs around tall trees and smaller shrubs around shorter trees.

• For every shrub, add at least five perennials or annuals. Choose some with a tall, spiky form, some medium-sized plants, and some low-growing groundcovers.

• Strive for a smooth transition from tall trees to large and medium-sized shrubs down to taller perennials, then mid-sized blooming plants, and finally groundcovers.

→ · ←

Mixed Beds

If the cottage garden style appeals to you but you also like shade garden plants and want to grow a few herbs, don't despair. Mixed beds have everything you're looking for. Just as their name suggests, mixed beds combine a little of everything—perennials, annuals, roses, herbs, rock garden plants, and even trees and shrubs. They usually are casual in design, with rounded corners and gentle curves that complement a bed of trees, billowing shrubs, and flowers.

If you're one of those gardeners who want to try one of everything, a mixed bed makes a good experimental garden. When the urge strikes you to plant one of every kind of plant you can get your hands on, you'll find that a mixed bed has places for shade- and sun-loving plants. It's easy to add plants without disrupting the design.

A mixed flower garden is a good choice if you have an established landscape. You can quickly create a flower garden by removing several feet of sod from around existing trees and shrubs to create a bed. Prepare the new space by adding compost, then plant it with flowers. Try not to disturb the roots of trees and shrubs when you work in the bed. There's no need to plant right up to their bases. As the plants in your garden grow, they'll fill in the gaps. To fight off weeds in the meantime, you can add patches of quick-growing groundcovers like common periwinkle (*Vinca minor*), or spreading annual flowers like edging lobelia (*Lobelia erinus*), and cover bare areas with mulch.

There's a double benefit to including existing trees and shrubs in the flower bed. They provide an instant backdrop for flowers, and it's easier to mow around them as a group than as individual plants in the lawn.

To get the best results, repeat flower colors, shapes, and forms throughout your mixed bed. Also pay attention to what type of tree dominates the garden or what shade of green the largest shrub wears. Whatever makes the strongest statement in your mixed bed sets the tone for the whole garden. Paying attention to design will give your garden a unified, finished look rather than the choppy, thrown-together feel of a tossed green salad.

Mixed beds combine the best features of trees and shrubs with the showy drama of flowers. The trees provide a dark backdrop that makes the leaves of curled leaf hosta (*Hosta crispula*) and the flowers of spurge (*Euphorbia* sp.) glow. Flowering shrubs like rhododendron fill in with huge clusters of flowers until the hosta opens its deep-lilac blooms in midsummer.

ROSE CARE REVIEW

To grow a rose garden that starts out healthy and stays that way, follow the guidelines below.

• Roses require a site in full sun for best performance.

• Fertile, well-drained soil that is rich in organic matter is ideal. Work the soil to a depth of 1 foot when planting.

• Don't let your roses go thirsty; it invites problems with diseases and insects. Install a soaker hose around the plants and cover it with a layer of organic mulch. Water deeply, at least once a week in dry weather.

• Mulch roses with composted bark or another organic mulch in spring to help keep down weeds, retain moisture in the soil, and prevent any disease-causing fungal spores from being splashed up on the foliage when it rains. Remove the mulch and replace it annually.

• Fertilize at least every six weeks with a balanced organic fertilizer containing nitrogen, phosphorus, and potassium.

Rose Gardens

Do you dream of a garden filled with roses? Fortunately, there's a type of rose that will please almost everyone and a spot in almost every garden that can accommodate a rose. It is also possible to have a rose garden that requires a minimum of pruning, spraying, and other care. If you're not sure you have the right conditions or the patience to grow roses, see "Rose Care Review" on this page.

Selecting No-Fail Roses

For an easy-care, successful rose garden, the best roses are the toughest, most adaptable ones you can find. Three types of shrub roses are among the top choices available: rugosa roses (*Rosa rugosa* and its cultivars), Meidiland series shrub roses, and English roses. All three types are long-blooming, disease-resistant, and generally easy to grow. They also require little pruning.

Rugosa Roses. Rugosas are large, vigorous plants that reach 6 feet; red-, white-, and yellow-flowered cultivars are available. The flowers are fragrant and are followed by showy rose hips that provide winter interest. Good cultivars include 'Frau Dagmar Hastrup' (light pink), 'Blanc Double de Coubert' (white), and 'David Thompson' (pink).

Meidiland Shrub Roses. Of the Meidiland roses, probably best known is the All-America Rose Selections winner 'Bonica', with pink, 3-inch blooms. Like the other Meidiland roses, it is hardy in Zones 4 to 9, has attractive foliage and abundant bloom, and makes a spectacular hedge or specimen. 'Carefree Wonder' (pink) and 'Alba Meidiland' (white) are other disease- and insect-resistant cultivars.

English Roses. Also called David Austin roses, these combine the vigor, disease resistance, hardiness, and lush appearance of old roses with the everblooming character of modern roses. They bear intensely fragrant, many-petaled blooms on 4- to 8-foot plants. Cultivars to look for include 'Graham Thomas' (yellow), 'Fair Bianca' (white), and 'Mary Rose' (pink).

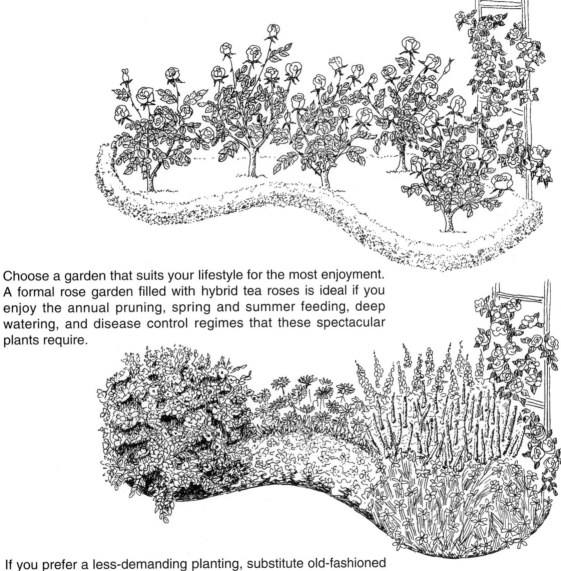

Choose a garden that suits your lifestyle for the most enjoyment. A formal rose garden filled with hybrid tea roses is ideal if you enjoy the annual pruning, spring and summer feeding, deep watering, and disease control regimes that these spectacular plants require.

If you prefer a less-demanding planting, substitute old-fashioned shrub roses and perennial flowers for hybrid teas and neatly trimmed borders. You'll have a garden that's just as colorful but a lot less trouble.

DISEASE-RESISTANT ROSES

An American Rose Society survey found the following rose cultivars to be among the best for disease resistance.

Miniature Roses. 'Baby Betsy McCall', 'Gourmet Popcorn', 'Little Artist', 'Rose Gilardi'

Grandiflora. 'Queen Elizabeth'

Floribundas. 'Impatient', 'Sunsprite'

Shrub Roses. 'All That Jazz', 'Carefree Wonder'

Hybrid Teas. 'Duet', 'Olympiad', 'Smooth Lady'

Other disease-resistant roses include the rugosa, Meidiland, and English roses on page 38; 'The Fairy', a polyantha rose; and miniatures 'Avandel', 'Magic Carrousel', and 'Pacesetter'.

Choose More Than Pretty Flowers

When you look for roses to buy, don't be seduced by the first pretty flower you see. You want to look for roses that will grow well in your yard, fit in with your design, and not require more maintenance than you can handle. The following questions will help you choose a garden full of no-fail roses. Use them when you look at mail-order catalog listings or shop at your local nursery or garden center.

Is it hardy in my area? If you don't want to spend time protecting your plants from freezing temperatures, make sure the plants you select are hardy in your area without winter protection. Your local nursery or garden center should be able to recommend choices for your area.

Is it disease-resistant? Hybrid tea roses may be America's best-loved flower, but most are too disease-prone

Pink rugosa roses and hardy daylilies make a great low-maintenance combination. Shrub roses like the rugosas are more disease-resistant than modern hybrid tea roses.

to make them good choices for no-fail gardens. Fortunately, hybridizers have been working hard to develop disease-resistant cultivars. See "Disease-Resistant Roses" on the opposite page for a list of hybrid teas and other roses recommended by the American Rose Society. Check with local rose growers, too, since disease resistance may be better or worse depending on your climate. Garden club members, neighbors, and horticulturists at public gardens can help you make good choices. And when you visit gardens and evaluate roses, don't rely on looks alone. Ask whether the plants must be sprayed constantly, or if they can fend for themselves. Also be aware that large plantings of roses may concentrate disease problems, so try planting just one or two.

Is it once-blooming or repeat-blooming? Modern roses such as hybrid teas, floribundas, grandifloras, miniature roses, and some climbing roses bloom repeatedly throughout the summer. Many old-fashioned roses bloom once, generally in June. If you want summer-long color from your roses, make sure you select ones that are described as repeat-bloomers.

What is its size and habit? The best roses for you will depend on your site and the size and style of your garden. If you have a fence along one side of your garden, a climber might be perfect. Miniature roses are great for small gardens and are delightful mixed into a perennial bed. Shrub roses are great for the back of a mixed border or planted in a garden unto themselves. There are also roses that make ideal blooming groundcovers.

Will it require lots of pruning? Many shrub roses need very little pruning; hybrid teas, on the other hand, require severe annual pruning for best performance. If you hate pruning or don't have time for it, stick to roses that will perform well with minimal pruning.

What other features does it have? If your dream garden features fragrant roses, be sure to look for cultivars having that characteristic. Many hybrid tea roses don't have any fragrance, for example; English roses, on the other hand, are intensely fragrant. Also find out whether the plants you're considering have unusually attractive foliage or bear showy hips, which add fall and winter interest.

RESISTANT CLIMBERS

There's a place for a climbing rose in nearly every garden—especially a disease-resistant one. In a survey conducted by Maggie Oster, author of *The Rose Book,* consulting rosarians recommended the following disease- and insect-resistant roses that can be used as climbers or shrubs. All have attractive foliage, are hardy to −40°F, and are repeat-blooming unless otherwise noted.

'Constance Spry': Fragrant, double, 3-inch pink blooms on 10-foot plants; hardy to −30°F. Once-blooming; an English rose.

'Dortmund': Fragrant, single, 3-inch, bright red blooms with white eye on 10-foot plants; hardy to −20°F.

'John Cabot': Double, 3-inch, deep pink-red blooms on 8-foot plants.

'John Davis': Fragrant, double, 3-inch pink blooms on 6-foot plants. Use as a trailing shrub or small climber.

'William Baffin': Semi-double, 3-inch, deep pink blooms on 8-foot plants.

━━━━━━━ ➔·➔ ━━━━━━━

RAISED-BED ROCKS

If you don't have a slope or a rocky site but you love rock garden plants, don't despair. You can transform even a pancake-flat yard with a raised-bed rock garden. Select a site in full sun, and create a low mound of well-drained soil. (You don't want a pointed volcano; a gently mounded hill looks more natural.) Then place rocks in the mound, let the soil settle for a few weeks, and plant. Rock garden plants will thrive in the perfect drainage your raised bed garden provides.

━━━━━━━ ➔·➔ ━━━━━━━

Rock Gardens

It may seem that rock gardens are only for very experienced specialist gardeners, but they can be as easy to care for as you'd like them to be. In fact, they're great for solving problems in the landscape. You can transform a hot, rocky site or a difficult-to-mow slope with a colorful carpet of plants and rocks that needs very little maintenance. If you have an already-rocky site, incorporating rocks into your design is an obvious choice; but you can also purchase rocks to use. Visiting a local rock quarry or outcropping will show you what's available in your area and give you some great ideas for placing rocks. If you use locally found rocks, your garden will fit more naturally into your

Remember rock garden plants if you need flowers for a well-drained site. Raised planting areas, like this sunny wall, provide the perfect growing conditions for rock garden plants like purple rock cress (*Aubrieta deltoidia*), wall rock cress (*Arabis caucasica*), and basket-of-gold (*Aurinia* spp.).

If you don't have a rock wall, a sunny hillside has what it takes to make low-growing rock garden plants feel at home: plenty of sunlight and good drainage. The bountiful number of blooms show that this site agrees with bellflowers (*Campanula* sp.), pinks (*Dianthus* sp.), swordleaf inula (*Inula ensifolia*), and the small, pink-flowered shrub, *Bruckenthalia spiculifolia*.

Mimic Mother Nature when you place stones in a rock garden. Use the same color and type of stones throughout the garden, and bury them at least halfway underground so they'll sit securely and look natural. Place smaller rocks off to the sides of large ones as if they'd broken away from a main outcropping. And make sure you place the largest rocks near the bottom so the garden won't look top-heavy. Tilt the stones so that rainwater will run into the garden, not down the hill.

landscape. And since they don't have to be hauled long distances, local rocks are cheaper. Most rock gardens have a natural-looking style that's determined to a large extent by the rocks used in them. You can design a more formal-looking rock garden around patio pavers or above a low wall.

Most rock garden plants are sun-loving and require good air circulation and well-drained soil. Perennial candytuft (*Iberis sempervirens*), basket-of-gold (*Aurinia saxatilis*), hens-and-chickens (*Sempervivum* spp.), and moss pink (*Phlox subulata*), along with low-growing sedums (*Sedum* spp.) and thymes (*Thymus* spp.), are among the most tolerant rock garden plants. Ajugas (*Ajuga* spp.) make fine rock garden plants, but they can be too vigorous and swallow up slower-growing plants. Dwarf, needle-leaved evergreens like dwarf Alberta spruce (*Picea glauca* 'Conica') can supply evergreen color in a border of rocks, and spring-blooming bulbs will thrive in little pockets of soil baked hot by the summer sun. Choose bulbs such as dwarf daffodils, crocuses, and Kaufmanniana tulips that are short, tough, and adaptable to the rocky life of a garden among the stones.

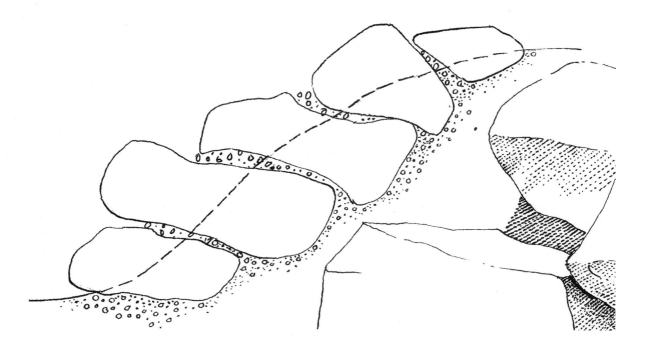

Herb Gardens

Nearly every gardener grows some herbs (or wants to), whether in the vegetable garden, in mixed beds with flowers, or alone in a traditional herb planting. A garden that features herbs can be formal or informal and as simple or as complicated as you choose to make it. Although most gardeners would love to have an exquisitely groomed formal herb garden, these aren't for everyone, since the neatly trimmed, geometric arrangements they feature require lots of time to keep them looking their best. Informal gardens can be just as lovely and require a lot less maintenance. (See the photos on pages 29 and 30 for a comparison between these two styles.)

Since herbs are such useful plants, one good way to decide which ones to grow—and how to incorporate them into your design—is simply to pick the ones you'd like to

FLOWERS FOR HERB GARDENS

Well-known herbs such as catnip, chives, dill, lavender, sage, and thyme add colorful blooms and delicious fragrances to your herb garden. There are many more flowers that are perfect for herb gardens. Try feverfew (*Chrysanthemum parthenium*), florist's carnation (*Dianthus caryophyllus*), foxgloves (*Digitalis* spp.), both green- and gray-leaved lavender cotton (*Santolina* spp.), and aromatic yarrows (*Achillea* spp.). Be sure to add blue-flowered perennials, too, including blue flax (*Linum perenne*), catmint (*Nepeta* spp.), and Russian sages (*Perovskia* spp.).

Herb gardens often feature soft, subtle colors, and this one is no exception. It combines soothing shades of green and silver foliage with the pale lavender flowers of common chives (*Allium schoenoprasum*), and the dark purple leaves of purple sage (*Salvia officinalis* 'Purpurea') and feathery bronze fennel (*Foeniculum vulgare* var. *purpureum*).

—→ · ←—

HERB THEME GARDENS

If you can't decide on a design for your herb garden, spark your imagination with a theme. Here are two ideas to get you started.

Spicy Italian herb garden. Form a circle with bricks or rocks and divide it into even wedges just as you would cut up a pizza. Plant each wedge of your pizza garden with a different herb used in Italian cooking. Include marjoram, oregano, parsley, rosemary, sage, and thyme.

Plant a crescent-shaped moon. Fill a crescent-shaped garden with silver- and gray-leaved herbs. These plants are drought-resistant and tolerate infertile soil. There are many herbs with distinctive silver foliage from which you can choose, including artemisias, lavender, lavender cotton (*Santolina* spp.), sage, savory, and sweet marjoram. Several thymes also have silver foliage.

—→ · ←—

use. If you like to make potpourris, you could plan a garden of fragrant roses and flowering herbs to cut and use. For other ideas, see "Herb Theme Gardens" on this page.

Perhaps the easiest and most rewarding way to use herbs in the landscape is in an informal herb garden. It can be a free-form island bed, or more like a perennial border and set against a wall, hedge, or fence. (Generally, herbs need a site in full sun with well-drained soil, so choose your site accordingly.) So many flowering plants have been used as herbs that even the most rigid purist—one who wants a garden of only traditional herbs—could create an herb garden with plenty of color. And, of course, herb gardens feature an abundance of fragrances, plus the bonus of plenty of herbs to use in wreaths, potpourris, or other projects. See "Flowers for Herb Gardens" on page 45 for some of the best plants to consider including.

Specialty Gardens

Don't let these descriptions of garden styles limit your imagination. No two gardeners are exactly alike and neither are their gardens. Great gardens are an expression of their owners' personality and interests. If one of the garden types listed here doesn't strike your fancy, combine the elements of two or more that you like and create your own style. You may want to create your own specialty garden, perhaps to suit very specific growing conditions in your yard—an unusually wet or dry site, for example. You'll find more ideas for specialty gardens below. See "Recommended Reading" on page 359 for books on different types of specialty gardens.

Water Gardens. Picture a pool filled with waterlilies, brightly colored fish, and a small fountain or waterfall, and you'll know why water gardens fascinate many gardeners. Installation takes time, but with modern pool liners and the many companies that sell water garden supplies to support you, it's fairly foolproof. If you have your heart set on blooming water lilies, select a site in full sun. You can easily incorporate a water garden in a rock garden or mixed bed.

Butterfly and Wildlife Gardens. Gardens can be

When presented with an unusual garden site, like a wet spot, don't panic. Instead, create a specialty garden that fits your needs and growing conditions. For a garden lining a stream or drainage area, grow moisture-loving shield ferns (*Polystichum* sp.), forget-me-nots (*Myosotis* sp.), and azaleas (*Rhododendron* sp.), as shown here.

THEME GARDENS

If you want a garden bursting with personality, think of a theme and use it to plant a garden.

For a patriotic touch, why not plant a red, white, and blue flagpole garden? Arrange red geraniums, white petunias, and blue lobelia (*Lobelia* spp.) in the shape of a flag or as a colorful circle around a flagpole.

How about a carpet garden? Look for low-growing plants and arrange them in an oriental rug–style pattern. Start with low-growing groundcovers like sedums and thymes, then add dwarf conifers for year-round interest.

If you like rock garden plants and water lilies, build a specialty garden that combines your interests. Colorful rock garden plants thrive in this stone wall, while goldfish act as festive "flowers" among the water lily leaves.

designed to provide a happy home to butterflies, birds, toads, and other creatures. A bird lover's garden might feature flowers that produce edible seeds, roses that bear an abundant crop of rose hips, plus a birdbath, nesting boxes, and feeding stations. A butterfly garden would include plants such as butterfly weed (*Asclepias tuberosa*) and butterfly bush (*Buddleia* spp.).

Theme Gardens. Ever hear of a Bible Garden? It's composed only of plants mentioned in the scripture. Think of lilies and mustard seeds. Or, you could plan a Shakespeare garden. The themes and interests of gardeners are as individual as plants themselves. Don't be afraid to think up your own theme gardens celebrating your personal or pet plants. You can plan them for any size and shape of bed you want. If you work long days and only get to enjoy your garden at night, consider a garden of night-blooming

---◆·◆---

PLANT A SUNNY THEME

For a garden guaranteed to cheer you up every time you look at it, plant a golden sunset. In a sunny site, cut a half-circle into the lawn. Divide it into rays that radiate outward in the shape of a setting sun. Plant each ray with either yellow or gold marigolds. (You'll need several different cultivars for this garden.) Alternate yellow and gold rays or start with light colored shades then plant darker ones as you move across the bed. Position the tallest plants in the center of the half-circle and smaller plants on each side.

---◆·◆---

Discover the brilliant colors and fascinating lifestyle of butterflies, and you'll never go back to gardening without them. When a silver-spotted aphrodite butterfly, like this one, stops to take a sip of nectar from your black-eyed Susan (*Rudbeckia hirta*), you'll find yourself planting violets and other caterpillar food plants so she'll stay and lay her eggs.

→ · ←

GROW A FLOWER "BED"

Here's a theme garden for anyone who refuses to take home landscaping too seriously. Dig a rectangular bed and position the headboard and footboard of an old metal bedstead at each end. Plant soft-looking flowers such as petunias or impatiens to make a comfy-looking blanket. Or arrange a quilt-inspired pattern using blocks of low-growing alyssum and pansies. Plant the pillow section on a slightly higher level and use all white flowers. For a dreamy final touch, grow morning glories on the headboard.

→ · ←

Are you a plant collector at heart? Why not build a specialty garden to showcase your collection? This compartment garden gives each hens-and-chickens (*Sempervivum* spp.) plant the attention it deserves. The mixture of textures, colors, and growth habits creates delightful contrasts.

plants. (There are more of them than you'd think!) Or consider a garden with a fragrant-flowers theme. Who could resist a garden of lavender, English roses, and other flowers with wonderful aromas? Color theme gardens are also popular—with a collection of all blue or all white flowers. (See "A Color Theme Garden" on page 144 for a plan for this type of garden.)

Stop Dreaming and Face Reality

Once you have your dream garden in mind, it's time to face the facts. Choosing the flower garden that's right for you means acknowledging your interests and striving for your dream garden, but it also means taking your time and your budget into account. The right garden is a good compromise between what you can grow and what you dream of growing.

First, review your answers to the question posed in

Chapter 1, "What do you want your garden to do?" Will your dream garden accomplish your objectives? Will it grow well on the site you decided on? Is there a way you can make it hide that ugly view you want to cover up? If your answer to any of these questions is "no," you'll need to reconsider. For example, say your heart is set on growing a collection of shrub roses, but the site you selected is shady. You'll need to change the site or decide on new plants. The same is true if you have an extremely small yard, because you may not have room for more than one of these large plants. In that case, maybe a garden that features one shrub rose, or climbing roses all around the edges, may be a good compromise. The objective is to match your garden dreams to your site.

Budgeting Your Gardening Time

Next, ask yourself how much time you have for a flower garden. If you're not sure, it's best to start small. You can always make a garden bigger, or trade in your low-maintenance groundcovers for more exotic flowers later. Digging out a huge garden and then finding you don't have the time to weed and water it is a hard row to hoe. If you've made this mistake in the past, remember that there are ways to cut back on the maintenance needs of your existing flower beds. Look for these tips in "Tame the Maintenance Monster" on page 331.

The size of a flower garden is not a good indicator of the maintenance required to keep it attractive. That's because it's not the square feet of space that determines the maintenance, it's the types of plants, the style of the garden, exposure of the site, and how well you've matched the soil, sunlight, and available water to your plants. Plants in a flower garden can range from low-maintenance groundcovers that bloom beautifully every spring and lie dormant during the summer months to high-maintenance hybrid tea roses. You'll find that a small formal rose garden can require much more care than a large rockery filled with sedums, phlox, and dwarf evergreens.

➨ • ⬅

EXPLORE PLANT OPTIONS

If time, money, or difficult growing conditions stand between you and the flowers of your dreams, try alternative plants. Many flowers can give you the same effect with less cost or fuss.

For example, perhaps you crave hybrid tea roses but your site is just too dry, wet, or shady for them to thrive. Try substituting one of the wild roses listed below, or other plants with showy flowers.

Arkansas rose (*Rosa arkansana*) has lovely white to medium-pink flowers on even the driest sites. For wet sites, try swamp rose (*Rosa palustris*) or pasture rose (*Rosa carolina*). Both have fragrant, medium-pink, single blooms. Many native species, and some of the shrub roses, tolerate some shade.

On sites too dry for any roses, try the new rose-of-Sharon (*Hibiscus syriacus*) cultivars: pink-flowered 'Aphrodite', white 'Diana', or lavender 'Minerva'.

➨ • ⬅

When water features or slopes make mowing difficult, remove the problem by planting low-maintenance perennials. A combination of blue false indigo (*Baptisia australis*), fluffy pink peonies (*Paeonia* spp.), perennial candytuft (*Iberis sempervirens*), threadleaf coreopsis (*Coreopsis verticillata*), and violet sage (*Salvia* × *superba*) makes living easy.

Maintenance—Lots or Little?

Here are some guidelines on garden features that will help you determine whether your dream garden would require lots of maintenance or just a little. Keep them in mind as you develop your plan.

Consider how design styles can dictate maintenance. Formal design doesn't have to mean high maintenance, but it can. Closely clipped hedges surrounding flower beds and geometric-shaped beds can require frequent pruning and edging. Choose naturally dwarf plants for hedges, and opt for natural shapes instead of clipped squares and rectangles to reduce pruning. To retain the

→ · ←

GET TO KNOW
THE NATIVES

Native plants can give you great ideas for low-maintenance additions to your garden. Check nearby roadsides and meadows for plants adapted to your climate, soil conditions, and pests.

For example, if goldenrod thrives in a field or vacant lot near your home, try non-invasive species in your garden like stiff goldenrod (*Solidago rigida*) or showy goldenrod (*S. speciosa*). Avoid aggressive spreaders like Canada goldenrod (*S. canadensis*), and substitute well-behaved cultivars like 'Golden Baby' and 'Peter Pan'.

→ · ←

Flower beds can actually lower yard maintenance if they are placed properly and have simple shapes. These gardens help keep lawn grass away from the fence and hedge, saving hours of tedious grass trimming. Their gently curved borders are easier to mow around than beds with sharp angles.

Bulbs bring easy-care color to sunny sites. Create a spring spectacular with pink and red tulips and a white-flowered lilac. Underplant the lilac with shade-loving forget-me-nots (*Myosotis* sp.) and the tulips with red English daisies (*Bellis perennis* 'Pomponette') to extend the bloom season when tulips fade.

crisp, geometric bed shapes with the least effort, use mulch and edging strips to keep weeds at bay.

Informal design generally means low maintenance. Plants are allowed to grow in their natural shapes, without rigid staking or excessive pruning.

Plan an efficient bed shape. Beds with sweeping curves are easy to mow around just by circling the bed. Circular beds are just as easy, and squares and rectangles just require turns at the corners. Complicated bed shapes (with fluted edges, for example) require more back-and-forth mowing.

Reduce site preparation and watering with raised beds. Building a raised bed over a site with poor or com-

FLOWERS FOR DRY SITES

For low-maintenance color in spots the hose can't reach, try these tough but beautiful perennials. All need well-drained soil but tolerate heat and drought. They may take over rich, moist sites or fade in high humidity.

Baptisias (*Baptisia* spp.), blanket flower (*Gaillardia* × *grandiflora*), coneflowers (*Rudbeckia* spp.), coreopsis (*Coreopsis* spp.), goldenrods (*Solidago* spp.), lamb's-ears (*Stachys* spp.), pinks (*Dianthus* spp.), salvias (*Salvia* spp.), sedums (*Sedum* spp.), spurge (*Euphorbia* spp.), yarrows (*Achillea* spp.).

Tired of trying to deal with that shaded strip of lawn next to the driveway? Plant shade-loving groundcovers like ostrich fern (*Matteuccia struthiopteris*) and Celandine poppy (*Stylophorum diphyllum*) beneath your trees, and store the mower.

—❯·❮—

FLOWERS
FOR SHADY SITES

Don't let a shady spot stand in the way of your flower gardening goals. Although most plants bloom better with a little sunlight, the woodland perennials listed below will produce colorful flowers and interesting foliage even in deep shade.

Alumroots (*Heuchera* spp.), bugbanes (*Cimicifuga* spp.), epimediums (*Epimedium* spp.), hostas (*Hosta* spp.), lungworts (*Pulmonaria* spp.), Siberian bugloss (*Brunnera macrophylla*), Solomon's seals (*Polygonatum* spp.), Virginia bluebells (*Mertensia virginica*).

—❯·❮—

Some soils are poor and others are downright impossible. If your soil won't even grow weeds, consider a raised bed. You'll be able to grow the flowers you want, including airy favorites like Brazilian vervain (*Verbena bonariensis*), white gaura (*Gaura lindheimeri*), clary (*Salvia sclarea* var. *turkestaniana*), and blue oat grass (*Helictotrichon sempervirens*).

pacted soil is often easier than struggling to dig the site and improve the soil. On sites with very sandy or very shallow soil, or sites with hard clay or rocks, raised beds are an easy way to give plants a deep soil, rich in organic matter. Root systems will have a chance to grow large and healthy, and the amended soil will hold water better.

Match plants to your site. Selecting the wrong plants for a given site can have a major effect on maintenance. Planting moisture-loving plants on a dry site will increase watering chores; growing sun-loving plants in the shade will not only reduce bloom, it will open plants up to diseases and insects that might not affect them in a sunny site. Your best bet for low maintenance is to select plants that will thrive in the conditions you have, not the conditions you wish you had.

Choose the best plant for the job. If you don't want to water, look for drought-tolerant plants. If you hate staking, stay away from delphiniums and other perennials that need

Match your plants to your site, and problems disappear. Watch moisture-loving blue flag iris (*Iris versicolor*) turn a drainage ditch into a garden that's rich with flowers. Use honeysuckle to line the bank for a sweet-scented hummingbird haven.

—◆·◆—

BEAUTY ON A BUDGET

The lavish flower garden of your dreams can look like a million bucks without costing you a fortune. Use the tips below to build cost savings into garden plans and purchases.

Buy in bulk. To take advantage of volume discounts and save on shipping costs, combine plant orders with those of other gardeners. Buy annuals by the flat, then split them with neighbors to get a variety of plants. Look for wholesale growers who sell to the public.

Explore alternative outlets. Shop at local botanic gardens, arboretums, and garden club plant sales. You'll often find great bargains on plants that are just right for your area.

Make your own compost. Compost is a free source of mulch and plant food, and it's a great way to recycle yard waste.

Garden more efficiently. Careful plant selection and good maintenance reduce the amounts of water, fertilizer, time, and replacement plants your garden will need.

—◆·◆—

to be staked to look their best. And to minimize pruning, look for plants that mature at the size you'd like to have. Don't buy something that's too big and hope to prune it into submission.

Mulch, and use edging strips. Whatever style of garden you select, nothing beats a layer of organic mulch for reducing weeding chores. Organic mulches like chopped leaves or composted bark also are a low-maintenance way to improve the soil. They'll add nutrients as they break down and protect the soil from erosion during hard rains.

Edging strips—either those constructed of bricks set side by side around the bed, or plastic or metal ones available commercially in rolls or strips—keep lawn grasses out of your beds.

Set edging strips at least 4 inches deep in the ground to discourage grass roots and to keep them from heaving out of the ground when the soil freezes and thaws. Unless you are using the edging as a decorative border, set it flush with or just barely above ground level. That way you can also eliminate trimming since you can mow with one wheel in the bed and one in the lawn.

Select low-maintenance plants. Here, the best rules to keep in mind are to look for disease resistance or insect resistance when you are selecting plants to buy, stay away from plants that need staking or excessive pruning to look their best, and look for plants that are generally tough and uncomplaining. See "A Plant-by-Plant Guide to No-Fail Flowers" on page 340 for some of the best low-maintenance plants.

If your dreams are bigger than your time budget, it's time to face facts. Gardens that are too big or that have too many high-maintenance plants will have you playing catch-up until you give up. If you are in doubt about how much garden you can handle, reduce the size before you plant. It's much easier to cut down on the size of a garden while it's still on paper. You can always add plants later. Also keep in mind that new gardens generally require more work than established ones. A newly planted perennial garden, for example, will require extra weeding and watering until the plants are well established.

Herb gardens and flower borders provide months of blooms and pleasure. Plan ahead to spend those months enjoying your flowers instead of maintaining them. Use simple shapes like rectangles to make your bed easy to mow around. Plant drought-tolerant spreading herbs and use mulch to reduce watering and keep weeds at bay. Choose two or three easy-care perennial flowers like peonies and clustered bellflower (*Campanula glomerata*) for spring and summer color.

→ · ←

THE BEST BARGAIN PLANTS

When you're faced with an empty flower bed, a long wish list of plants, and a limited budget, free plants from friends and neighbors can be tempting.

While it's not polite to look a gift horse in the mouth, it is prudent to examine gift plants carefully. Before adding a plant to your garden, ask if you can see it growing in your friend's garden. As you admire it aloud, review this mental checklist:

- Do you like it?
- Will it fit into your garden design/color scheme?
- Is it healthy and free of pest and disease symptoms?
- Is it too invasive?

Ask your friend:
- How long has he or she grown the plant?
- Does it grow well in your area's climate?
- Have there been any problems with it?
- Does it need special care?

If the answers to these questions satisfy you, then accept the best kind of bargain plant—a garden-tested one.

→ · ←

Flowers on a Budget

Filling a garden with flowers takes more than knowledge, soil improvement, and maintenance. It also takes money. Every gardener knows how quickly a visit to the local garden center can eat into the budget. Fortunately, you don't need $10,000 to plant a great garden. But while the success of your garden isn't determined by the size of your budget, it is a good idea to try to choose a flower garden that's a good fit with your paycheck as well as your personality.

Tips for a Low-Cost Flower Garden

If you have more dimes than dollars in your flower budget, use these tips to stretch them as far as they'll go.

Grow plants from seed. Choose plants that are easy to grow from seed. Annuals like marigolds, nasturtiums, and zinnias are a natural choice from seed, but many perennials are equally easy. See "Easy Annuals from Seed" on page 242 and "Perennials for First-Season Flowers" on page 249.

Propagate your own. If your heart is set on an expensive hosta or daylily, buy one and plan to dig and divide it annually to build up a stock of plants to fill your garden. Many perennials are also easy to grow from cuttings. See "Multiplying by Division" on page 254 and "New Plants from Cuttings" on page 256.

Plant old-fashioned flowers. Perennials that have been around since Grandmother's time are good bargains, since you're not paying for a patent or promotional fees. Old-fashioned perennials that are easy to start from divisions include daylilies, irises, and poppies. See "Multiplying by Division" on page 254.

Look carefully at bargain plants. They may cost a bit more, but healthy, well-grown plants from a reputable nursery are generally better bargains than neglected, unhealthy ones from a discount store. With good-quality plants, you have a better chance of getting them established quickly. You'll also probably get blooms and a plant that's large enough to divide sooner.

The difficult hill below your house becomes a place with style and grace when you plant and propagate perennial flowers from friends and neighbors. See Chapter 7 for tips on growing perennials from seed or division.

DIVIDE GARDENS INTO EASY-TO-PLANT PIECES

When you don't have the time or money to install a garden all at once, divide it into four pieces. Assign each piece a different season of bloom and plant them one at a time.

1. Fill a back corner of your flower bed with spring blooms. Use shrubs like forsythia plus crocus and daffodil bulbs and spring-blooming perennials like violets.

2. Group summer-blooming annuals and perennials together at the front of the bed where their colors will hide fading spring flowers.

3. Beside the summer section, plant fall flowers and foliage. Use small shrubs, bulbs like autumn crocus (*Colchicum autumnale*), and annual and perennial flowers like flowering cabbage and 'Autumn Joy' sedum.

4. Plant a winter section as a backdrop, using evergreens like holly plus other fruiting trees and shrubs. Add winter-blooming perennials like Christmas rose (*Helleborus niger*) and bulbs like snowdrops (*Galanthus* spp.).

Look for plant donations. Friends and neighbors generally have an abundance of plants that grow well. Graciously accepting cast-off or recycled plants is the easiest cost-cutting measure a new gardener can take. Beginning gardeners often turn down sickly-looking iris divisions or small and insignificant bulbs because the plant names may not be familiar and the present appearance is depressing. Take such plants home and tuck them into your garden beds anyway. You can always dig them up and throw them out if you absolutely hate the flowers. Even if the plants die, you will be out nothing. Keep in mind also that up until a generation ago, most Americans spent very little on flowering plants and grew only the flowers that were shared among family and friends.

Consider your garden style. Some types of flowers and plants are just more expensive than others. A rose garden is more expensive to install than a small annual garden or a cottage garden, for example. Rock gardens can be very expensive if you need to purchase and install the stone, but the plants themselves will cost just a few dollars each.

Phase Your Garden In

Not many gardeners have both unlimited time and money to plant their gardens. But gardening with a budget—whether one that's dictated by time or money—doesn't have to be a disaster; it can be a creative challenge. If you don't have the money to buy all the plants you want to grow this year, make a plan to plant your garden over several years. If you want an island bed with trees and shrubs, you might want to outline the bed, plant the trees and/or shrubs, and fill in the rest with annuals the first year. Or you could plant one of each perennial you'd like to have in a border, and systematically divide them until you have enough to fill the space.

No matter what size garden you're working with, take a look at "Develop Large Gardens in Phases" on page 138. You'll find that ideas for phasing in large gardens work just as well for small ones. There's no need to let budgets get in the way of planning and planting your dream garden.

CHAPTER 3

No-Fail Plant Combinations

A beautiful flower garden is like an exquisite painting, with contrasting and complementary colors, shapes, and textures. But unlike a painting, a garden is continually changing, as temperatures rise and fall through the year and plants go in and out of bloom. Part of the pleasure of gardening is creating little plant "portraits"—or combinations—to admire as you walk through the garden in different seasons.

A great plant combination can be as simple or as detailed as you want it to be. The one thing that all good groupings have in common is plants with compatible growth needs. Identifying the conditions that your site has to offer, and choosing plants that are adapted to those conditions, is a key step in this whole process. The right plants in the right place will naturally look good, because they'll be healthy and vigorous without a lot of fussing on your part.

In this chapter, you'll find a gallery of inspiring combinations to try in your own garden. Each grouping has a full-color photograph, along with a discussion of the highlights of the combination, and tips for customizing it to fit your needs. The "Growing Guidelines" is where you'll find a summary of the growing conditions, along with a brief description of each plant's vital statistics (like height, bloom time, and hardiness zones). Browse through this section when you want a solution for a particular site, or when you are just scouting for new ideas to pep up an existing bed.

...s
...e
...venly
...-drained soil.
... bulbs need spring sun,
but the perennials prefer
shade in summer.

'Krossa Regal' hosta
(*Hosta* 'Krossa Regal'):
Height and spread to 30
inches. Summer blooms
on 5- to 6-foot stems.
Zones 3 to 8. Remove
flower stalks after bloom.

Grape hyacinth (*Muscari
armeniacum*): Height to 6
inches; spread to 4 inches.
Early-spring blooms. Zones 3
to 9. Goes dormant soon
after bloom.

Tulips (*Tulipa* spp.):
Height to 12 inches;
spread to 6 inches. Spring
flowers. Zones 3 to 8. Go
dormant a few weeks after
flowering.

Astilbe (*Astilbe* × *arendsii*): Height to 4 feet;
spread to 3 feet. Summer
blooms. Zones 4 to 8. Will
flower less in deep shade.

Japanese pachysandra
(*Pachysandra terminalis*):
Height and spread to 8
inches. All-year foliage
interest; late-spring flowers. Zones 4 to 9. Can
adapt to deep shade.

Spring Fling for a Shady Spot

Early spring has to be one of the greatest times in the garden. You've survived another long winter, and you're ready
for some colorful flowers. What could be better than a planting of fast-growing bulbs to chase off those winter blues?

This combination is an ideal solution for gardens under
deciduous trees. The tulips and grape hyacinths (*Muscari
armeniacum*) bloom in the early spring sunshine, before
the trees have produced their new leaves. The remaining
astilbe, hosta, and Japanese pachysandra plants
(*Pachysandra terminalis*) will thrive in the cool summer
shade once the overhanging trees leaf out.

This gardener has chosen a glowing magenta-red double
early tulip that harmonizes beautifully with the blue-purple
spikes of grape hyacinth. The lacy astilbe in the foreground, the glossy pachysandra behind, and the bold hosta
leaves emerging on the upper right provide a green frame
for this colorful combination.

As the season progresses, the bulbs will finish their
show, leaving their foliage behind to produce and store
food for the following year. Combine spring bulbs with
perennials and groundcovers to mask the yellowing bulb
foliage and to fill in when the bulbs go dormant. Hostas
and astilbes are great for this purpose, and their summer
flowers are an extra benefit. Japanese pachysandra offers a
year-round backdrop of evergreen foliage as well as late-
spring flowers of its own.

It's easy to translate the basic parts of this combination to
your own site. Choose any combination of spring bulbs that
you enjoy—maybe yellow daffodils and pink hyacinths, or
white crocus with yellow reticulated iris (*Iris reticulata*).
Then surround it with leafy perennials like hostas, cranesbills (*Geranium* spp.), or even ferns. Add a patch of evergreen groundcover, like pachysandra or periwinkle (*Vinca*
spp.), and you've got a low-maintenance planting that
looks good all year long.

Bright spring bulbs are a great antidote to the winter blues. Start with a splash of early tulips and grape hyacinths for surefire color. Add bushy, shade-loving perennials such as hostas and astilbes for a summer show, and a dash of evergreen pachysandra for year-round interest.

GROWING GUIDELINES

Try these moisture lovers for a site that stays wet all season. Partial shade is ideal, although they can take more sun in northern gardens.

Japanese primrose (*Primula japonica*): Height to 2 feet; spread to 1½ feet. Late-spring and early-summer flowers. Zones 5 to 8. Plants will self-sow.

Sensitive fern (*Onoclea sensibilis*): Height and spread to 2 feet. All-season foliage interest; spore cases appear in midsummer. Zones 3 to 8.

Skunk cabbage (*Symplocarpus foetidus*): Height to 3 feet; spread to 2 feet. Large, attractive leaves appear after the flowers. Late-winter and early-spring flowers. Zones 3 to 9. This plant has a skunklike scent and is best used in moist areas away from the house.

Primroses Transform a Soggy Site

Have a soggy spot in your garden that just never seems to dry out? Tired of sinking in up to your ankles every time you try to slog through on your way to other parts of the yard? Turn that trial into a triumph with a selection of plants that thrive in moist soil.

This combination highlights Japanese primrose (*Primula japonica*), skunk cabbage (*Symplocarpus foetidus*), and sensitive fern (*Onoclea sensibilis*)—just a few of the easy-care plants that can take constantly moist soil. Partial shade is ideal, especially in hot southern summers, but these plants will take more sun as long as their roots can get plenty of water.

Peak season for this grouping is late spring to early summer, as the Japanese primroses burst into bloom in shades of pink, magenta, and white. The light green fronds of sensitive fern and glossy green leaves of skunk cabbage provide a background for this tapestry of color.

While the primroses are the real highlight, the other plants in this combination help to extend the season of interest for many months. The excitement begins in late winter (usually around February), as the curiously spotted and hooded flowers of the skunk cabbage emerge from the cold ground, several weeks before the leaves. In early spring, the foliage of the primroses, sensitive ferns, and skunk cabbage begins to poke up into the cool spring sunshine. After the primroses bloom and go to seed, the mature skunk cabbage and sensitive fern foliage expand to form a carpet of contrasting textures in varying shades of green. In midsummer, the sensitive fern sends up stalks with beadlike green spore cases that age to dark brown and last well into fall.

While all of these plants demand a constant supply of moisture, you could create a similar effect in a better-drained spot with a combination of primroses, hostas, and ferns. Steady soil moisture would still be helpful, but it's not quite as critical, especially on a shady site.

Don't struggle with that soggy spot—turn it into a showplace with
moisture-loving Japanese primroses, sensitive ferns, and skunk
cabbage. Even after the primroses fade, the contrasting foliage
colors and textures give this combination season-long impact.

—→·←—

GROWING GUIDELINES

Try these great shade plants for a fabulous foliage combination. They will thrive in a spot with evenly moist but well-drained soil. All three prefer partial to full shade, but they can take a few hours of direct morning sun.

Maidenhair fern (*Adiantum pedatum*): Height and spread to 1½ feet. Foliage provides all-season interest. Zones 3 to 8. Steady soil moisture is critical for healthy foliage.

Solomon's seals (*Polygonatum* spp.): Height to 3 feet; spread to 1 foot. Late-spring bloom, followed by blue-black berries. Zones 3 to 9. Tolerate dry shade.

Hostas (*Hosta* spp.): Height and spread to 3 feet (varies by species and cultivar). Summer or fall bloom. Zones 4 to 9. Remove spent flowerstalks after blooming.

—→·←—

Lush Leaves for a Shady Site

Shade gardens don't have to be dull and boring! Even without flowers, you can create subtle but beautiful borders with a variety of foliage colors and textures. Throw in a few plants that do produce flowers as well as good-looking foliage, and you've got a no-fail combination.

This grouping is a great example of what you can do with a partially to fully shaded site. Hostas, maidenhair fern (*Adiantum pedatum*), and Solomon's seals (*Polygonatum* spp.) can all thrive with no direct sun. Try them along a wall in a shady urban garden, under shrubs and trees, or on the cool north side of the house.

In this planting, the bold, medium green leaves of the hostas contrast beautifully with the frothy, yellow-green fronds and black stems of the maidenhair fern. Behind these, Solomon's seal arches gracefully over the maidenhair, creating a "frame" for the fern foliage. The bell-shaped greenish white blooms of the Solomon's seal dangle beneath the arching stems in late spring, completing this combination.

Throughout the season, these plants continue to add interest with their beautiful textures and forms. Over the summer, the older maidenhair fronds age to a darker green, which provides extra contrast to the newest light-colored foliage. The lavender or white funnel-shaped flowers of the hostas add excitement in mid- to late summer. And the Solomon's seal flowers are followed by dangling blue-black fruit in late summer or fall.

If you have a shady spot with evenly moist soil, try this combination as is, or jazz it up with variegated foliage. Instead of a plain green Solomon's seal, consider variegated fragrant Solomon's seal (*Polygonatum odoratum* var. *thunbergii* 'Variegatum'), with reddish stems and green leaves edged with ivory white. Or try a different type of hosta. Hundreds of cultivars are available, differing in leaf size, shape, and color—you're sure to find one you like. Whichever you choose, you'll appreciate the value of long-lasting foliage as an important part of your no-fail garden.

Brighten up a shady area with fantastic foliage in a variety of shapes, textures, and colors. Combine fine-textured maidenhair ferns, bold hostas, and arching Solomon's seals for a pleasing show you'll enjoy all season long.

—→·←—

If you've got a sunny site with evenly moist but well-drained soil, these plants could be perfect for your garden.

Hostas (*Hosta* spp.): Height and spread to 3 feet (varies by species and cultivar). Summer or fall bloom. Zones 4 to 9. Evenly moist but well-drained soil in partial to full shade; some can take full sun, especially with a steady supply of soil moisture.

Daylilies (*Hemerocallis* spp.): Height to 3 feet; spread to 2 feet. Summer bloom. Zones 3 to 9. Well-drained soil in full sun to partial shade.

Lilies (*Lilium* spp.): Height to 5 feet; spread to 6 inches. Summer bloom. Zones 4 to 8. Well-drained soil in full sun to partial shade.

Alliums (*Allium* spp.): Height to 3 feet; spread to 4 inches. Spring, summer, or fall bloom. Zones 3 to 9. Well-drained soil in full sun.

—→·←—

Cheerful Color with Easy-Care Perennials

One of the greatest rewards of gardening is having your yard filled with masses of beautiful blooms all summer. It's easy with no-fail perennials and bulbs—just plant them once and let them reward you with years of easy-care enjoyment.

Lilies, daylilies, alliums (*Allium* spp.), and sun-tolerant hostas are easy-to-grow garden plants for a sunny spot with average soil. Their bold, bright flowers are natural choices for surefire summer color. Try them in a formal border, or in sweeps of a wide open area for a meadowlike effect.

The grouping shown here starts with a mixture of yellow, golden, pink, and peach-colored hybrid daylilies. In the back, clumps of orange and yellow lilies add broad bands of easy-care color. The huge purple-flowered hosta in the foreground is echoed by the soft purple-pink heads of an allium in the back. All together, these different colors complement each other in a glorious display of floral abandon.

Summer is when this combination really shines. The daylilies will bloom over several weeks; some cultivars are rebloomers that can produce new flowerstalks throughout the season. Lilies are usually reliable for several weeks of bloom in midsummer. Hostas generally bloom around midsummer, but they have the benefit of beautiful foliage that looks great all season. The big, broad hosta leaves also contrast nicely with the narrow grassy leaves of the daylily clumps. Remove the spent flowerstalks, and you'll enjoy the foliage into fall.

If you live in a hot-summer climate where a hosta would fry in the sun, consider planting another bold-leaved perennial—perhaps bear's-breeches (*Acanthus* spp.)—instead. In most climates, the original combination could grow well with a few hours of shade each day; in fact, the hosta would likely prefer some shade.

Add masses of summer color to your yard with these easy-care perennials. Enjoy weeks of beautiful blooms from hostas, daylilies, alliums, and lilies with minimal maintenance.

————— ⇀·↼ —————

GROWING GUIDELINES

Turn a partially shaded corner with evenly moist but well-drained soil into a showplace with these colorful plants.

Azaleas (*Rhododendron* spp.): Height and spread to 6 feet. Spring bloom. Zones 5 to 9.

Avens (*Geum* spp.): Height to 2 feet; spread to 1½ feet. Spring and early-summer bloom. Zones 4 to 7. Full sun to partial shade.

Hostas (*Hosta* spp): Height and spread to 3 feet (varies by species and cultivar). Summer or fall bloom. Zones 4 to 9. Partial to full shade.

Bearded iris (*Iris* spp.): Height to 3 feet; spread to 2 feet. Early-summer flowers. Zones 4 to 9. Full sun to light shade.

Basket-of-gold (*Aurinia saxatilis*): Height and spread to 1 foot. Spring bloom. Zones 3 to 7. Well-drained soil in full sun.

————— ⇀·↼ —————

Bountiful Blooms in a Sunny-Shady Garden

Combining plants that look good together is a mixture of art and science. The science is figuring out what plants will grow on a particular site, based on their light and soil needs. The art is grouping plants that will complement each other in some way—by color, texture, or growth habit. Part of the fun of gardening is trying out new combinations in your own garden and seeing what pleases your eye.

This beautiful border shows one way you can mix flowers and foliage to create great combinations that suit particular sites. On the lightly shaded left side, there's a classic combination of green and white, with a white-flowered azalea (*Rhododendron* sp.), white bearded iris, and white-variegated hosta. In the sunnier middle to right side, colorful scarlet-flowered avens (*Geum* sp.) and bright yellow basket-of-gold (*Aurinia saxatilis*) create an eye-catching mix of their own. The striking contrast between the greens and whites and the scarlet adds excitement and ties the two parts of the planting together. If you look closely, you'll also see that the white iris flowers have a scarlet center "beard" that picks up the color of the avens flowers.

While you could reproduce this planting exactly in your own garden, you may not have just the right site to fill the needs of all these plants. But you definitely could use the same principles that this gardener used to create a pleasing garden setting of your own. First, think of your garden as a series of small settings—a shady, moist patch here, a sunnier, drier spot there. Find the plants that suit each site, and group them together in some way that pleases you—perhaps by flower color, or by complementary foliage textures. Then link the combinations by repeating some feature in both combinations (as this gardener did by planting the scarlet-centered white iris near the scarlet-flowered avens). Simple visual clues like this are the chains that link otherwise separate settings into a coherent and pleasing garden design.

Brighten up a partially shaded border with white-variegated hostas, white azaleas, and cool white bearded irises. Add a splash of scarlet-flowered avens and bright yellow basket-of-gold to the sunnier side, and you've got a combination that's sure to please.

→ · ←

GROWING GUIDELINES

These fantastic foliage plants will all thrive in evenly moist but well-drained soil in full sun to light shade.

Variegated Japanese silver grass (*Miscanthus sinensis* 'Variegatus'): Height and spread to 6 feet. All-season foliage interest; late-summer flowers. Zones 5 to 9. Tends to flop in too much shade.

'Carol Mackie' Burkwood daphne (*Daphne × burkwoodii* 'Carol Mackie'): Height and spread to 3 feet. Early-summer flowers. Zones 4 to 8. Slow-growing but worth the wait.

Cranesbills (*Geranium* spp.): Height and spread to 3 feet. Late-spring to early-summer bloom. Zones 3 to 8.

→ · ←

Fabulous Foliage for a Season-Long Show

Who needs flowers when you can have beautiful foliage? Flowers come and go, but you have the leaves to look at from spring through fall, and perhaps through the winter. Long or short, fine or coarse, glossy or dull, foliage plays an starring role in a garden planned for season-long interest.

This combination offers great-looking foliage for a sunny or lightly shaded spot. Variegated Japanese silver grass (*Miscanthus sinensis* 'Variegatus'), 'Carol Mackie' Burkwood daphne (*Daphne × burkwoodii* 'Carol Mackie'), and cranesbills (*Geranium* spp.) all thrive in evenly moist but well-drained soil. Try this combination near a door, in a foundation planting, or as part of a larger bed or border.

Wherever you place it, there's nothing quite like variegated foliage for adding a dramatic touch to your garden. But this grouping has extra appeal thanks to the variety of foliage forms. The long, narrow leaves of the grass and the short, narrow leaves of the daphne are perfectly complemented by the rounded, lobed, bright green cranesbill leaves.

While the foliage looks great all season, each of these plants offers a bonus of attractive flowers. In early summer, the daphne will produce masses of fragrant, pale pink flowers. Cranesbills also bloom in late spring to early summer in shades of blue, purple, pink, or white. In late summer, the grass will send up showy flower plumes that add interest well into fall. Over winter, the cranesbill will go dormant, but the grass foliage can be attractive until you cut it down the following spring. The daphne is semi-evergreen, so in most climates you'll get to enjoy the foliage through the winter.

Try this combination in your own garden, or substitute other plants to fit your particular conditions. Many perennials and grasses are available in white- or yellow-variegated foliage forms. Once you start using these plants, you're liable to become a foliage fanatic!

Light up your landscape with this striking combination of variegated Japanese silver grass, 'Carol Mackie' Burkwood daphne, and cranesbills. These plants all thrive in full sun to light shade.

GROWING GUIDELINES

Sun and well-drained soil will provide the right conditions for a cheerful cottage-garden combination.

Rocket larkspur (*Consolida ambigua*): Height to 4 feet; spread to 1 foot. Summer flowers. Annual. Thrives in cool summers; has a shorter bloom period in areas with hot summers.

'The Fairy' rose (*Rosa* 'The Fairy'): Height and spread to 3 feet. Summer flowers. Zones 4 to 9. Steady soil moisture is a plus. Prune in early spring if the plant needs shaping or to remove dead branches.

Honesty (*Lunaria annua*): Height to 2½ feet; spread to 1 foot. Late-spring to early-summer bloom. Biennial. May self-sow.

The Casual Cottage-Garden Look

There's something romantic about a cottage garden, where shrub roses, annuals, and biennials mingle to create a scene of casual elegance. As a bonus, the informal style of a cottage garden is the essence of low maintenance: easy-care roses and self-sowing flowers that look great each year without replanting, dividing, deadheading, or staking.

Start a cottage garden of your own with this charming combination of roses (*Rosa* 'The Fairy'), larkspur (*Consolida ambigua*), and honesty (*Lunaria annua*). All of these plants will thrive in full sun with average, well-drained soil. Try this grouping for easy-care color in a sunny side yard, along a garage, or in an unused corner of your property.

Early summer is the peak season for this show, with the larkspur and roses in full flower. In cool climates, larkspur will keep flowering throughout the summer; in hot-summer areas, it will start blooming in spring and keep going until the high temperatures arrive. Deadheading may help prolong the bloom, but for the ultimate in low maintenance, let the plants go to seed and self-sow for next year.

Early summer is traditionally the best time for shrub roses, though some cultivars may take a short rest after the first flush of bloom and continue to flower sporadically into fall. 'The Fairy' is a dwarf shrub rose known for the large quantities of double pink blooms it produces. Other shrub roses, like the rugosas, also form showy fruits (hips) that add interest later in the season. Honesty is a biennial that produces tidy clumps of foliage the first year. In its second year it offers three seasons of interest, with rosy-purple flowers in spring and flattened round seedpods that turn from green in summer to silvery in fall.

These three plants form a great basis for a cheerful cottage garden, but you don't have to stop there. Add extra interest with other easy-care plants that will grow in your conditions. Poppies, hollyhocks (*Alcea* spp.), cosmos, and cranesbills (*Geranium* spp.) are just a few of the flowers that look good together in an informal planting.

Celebrate summer with this lush, informal grouping of pale pink roses, bright purple-blue larkspur, and light green honesty seedpods. They'll grow happily in a well-drained spot with plenty of sunshine.

GROWING GUIDELINES

Start your colorful mixed border in a sunny spot with well-drained soil.

Lamb's-ears (*Stachys byzantina*): Height to 1 foot; spread to 2 feet. Late-spring bloom. Zones 4 to 8.

Wallflowers (*Cheiranthus* spp.): Height to 2 feet; spread to 1½ feet. Spring bloom. Perennials usually grown as annuals or biennials.

Armenian cranesbill (*Geranium psilostemon*): Height and spread to 4 feet. Midsummer bloom. Zones 5 to 8. Appreciates some extra moisture.

Spurges (*Euphorbia* spp.): Height and spread to 3 feet (varies by species and cultivar). Spring to early-summer bloom. Zones 3 to 9.

'Nevada' rose (*Rosa* 'Nevada'): Height and spread to 7 feet. Summer into fall bloom. Zones 4 to 9.

'Baggesen's Gold' boxleaf honeysuckle (*Lonicera nitida* 'Baggesen's Gold'): Height and spread to 5 feet. Spring flowers are insignificant. Zones 7 to 9.

→•←

A Mixed Border for All-Season Interest

With so many beautiful flower colors to choose from, it can be hard to decide which ones to put in your garden. If possible, resist the urge to buy one of each and stick them all together in one border. A multicolored garden may sound nice in theory, but in practice it can look like a real jumble. A border based on two or three colors has a much more coherent and elegant feel.

This planting is a perfect example of what you can do with a restrained color scheme. Magenta-flowered Armenian cranesbill (*Geranium psilostemon*) and wallflowers (*Cheiranthus* spp.) accent the soft yellows of 'Nevada' rose (*Rosa* 'Nevada'), 'Baggesen's Gold' boxleaf honeysuckle (*Lonicera nitida* 'Baggesen's Gold'), and a mounding spurge (*Euphorbia* sp.). These are highlighted by the soft, silvery flower spikes of lamb's-ears (*Stachys byzantina*). This grouping would be great as an accent for a deck or foundation planting or as a basis for a larger bed. All of these plants thrive in sun and average, well-drained soil.

The early-blooming spurge and wallflowers start the color theme in early to mid-spring. If temperatures stay cool, the wallflowers will hang on to usher in the peak bloom season with the roses, cranesbill, and lamb's-ears. After its main flush of flowers in early summer, the 'Nevada' rose will keep blooming off and on through fall.

It would be an easy matter to expand this color-theme planting to fill a whole border. For spring flowers, repeat clumps of the spurges and wallflowers, and add chartreuse-yellow lady's-mantle (*Alchemilla mollis*) and clumps of purplish 'Violacea' tulip (*Tulipa pulchella* 'Violacea'). For mid- to late summer excitement, add a few bulbs of violet-purple giant onion (*Allium giganteum*). End the season with a bright combination of yellow patrinia (*Patrinia scabiosifolia*) and rosy-pink 'Alma Potschke' New England aster (*Aster novae-angliae* 'Alma Potschke').

Start a colorful mixed border with this cheerful combination of pale yellow 'Nevada' rose, yellow-leaved 'Baggesen's Gold' boxleaf honeysuckle, and chartreuse spurge. Add magenta-flowered wallflowers and Armenian cranesbill, as well as silvery lamb's-ears, for some contrast. All of these plants will thrive on a sunny site with well-drained soil.

GROWING GUIDELINES

Plants with unusual foliage textures add interest to a sunny or lightly shaded site with average, well-drained soil.

Curled parsley (*Petroselinum crispum* var. *crispum*): Height to 8 inches; spread to 1 foot. Attractive foliage all season. Biennial usually grown as an annual.

'Vera Jameson' sedum (*Sedum* 'Vera Jameson'): Height and spread to 1 foot. Fall flowers. Zones 5 to 9. Well-drained soil in full sun to light shade.

Lamb's-ears (*Stachys byzantina*): Height to 1 foot; spread to 2 feet. Late-spring bloom. Zones 4 to 8. Moist but well-drained soil in full sun to partial shade.

Foliage for the Front of the Border

Tall, brightly colored flowers often get most of the attention in a garden, but low-growing foliage plants have their own important role to play in creating a coherent garden scene. Tucked in an odd corner or skirting a large border, compact plants with beautiful leaves create a soothing backdrop for the sunny beauty of showier blooms.

This clever combination of foliage colors and textures showcases fuzzy, silver lamb's-ears (*Stachys byzantina*), crinkly, bright green curled parsley (*Petroselinum crispum* var. *crispum*), and succulent blue-purple 'Vera Jameson' sedum (*Sedum* 'Vera Jameson'). These easy-to-grow plants can thrive in average, well-drained soil on any sunny to lightly shaded spot. The grouping would look great planted along a wall or walkway or as an all-season edging for a bed or border.

While the foliage of all three plants looks terrific from spring through fall, late summer spotlights the rosy-pink blooms of the sedum. The lamb's-ears will send up fuzzy silver bloom stalks, topped with tiny purple-pink flowers, in early summer. Some gardeners like the flower stalks; others don't. If you don't like them, it's easy to snip them off at the base.

Parsley's beautiful rosettes of lush green leaves have long been admired in the herb garden, and more and more gardeners are appreciating the plant's value as an ornamental edging plant. Though commonly grown as an annual, parsley is really a biennial, and it will send up stalks of flowers that aren't particularly showy its second summer. Unless you want to collect the seed, pull the plants out at the end of the season and replace them with new transplants each year.

Try this simple grouping in your flower garden, or use it as an inspiration for your own foliage combinations. Don't forget that some of our most beloved herbs—including sage, thyme, and oregano—have lovely leaves that look as good in the flower border as in the herb garden!

Plan your garden around good-looking foliage, and your flowers will be like icing on a cake. If you've got a sunny or lightly shaded spot with well-drained soil, try this simple but striking mixture of silver lamb's-ears, curly parsley, and purple-leaved 'Vera Jameson' sedum.

GROWING GUIDELINES

Find a sunny or lightly shaded spot with average soil, and you've got the right conditions for an eye-catching combination of the following plants.

Red valerian (*Centranthus ruber*): Height to 3 feet; spread to 2 feet. Summer bloom. Zones 4 to 8. Well-drained soil in full sun. Variable from seed; buy plants in bloom to get the flower color you want.

'Moonshine' yarrow (*Achillea* 'Moonshine'): Height to 2 feet; spread to 1½ feet. Summer bloom. Zones 3 to 8. Well-drained soil in full sun.

'Johnson's Blue' cranesbill (*Geranium* 'Johnson's Blue'): Height and spread to 1½ feet. Late-spring into summer bloom. Zones 4 to 8. Well-drained soil in full sun to light shade.

Combining Compatible Colors

Ask anyone to describe a flowering plant, and the person will probably start by telling you the flower color. Color is one of the most obvious features of any combination, and it's one of the most fun to work with. You can create an exciting or calm mood just by the colors you choose. You may prefer a combination of warm, electric colors like orange, red, and yellow, or a grouping of cool, soothing blues, greens, and purples. Mix warm and cool colors together to show each other off to best advantage. No matter what colors you like, or what growing conditions your garden has to offer, you can find plants that will make a pleasing grouping.

If you've got a sunny to lightly shaded spot with average, well-drained soil, consider this eye-catching combination of red valerian (*Centranthus ruber*), 'Moonshine' yarrow (*Achillea* 'Moonshine'), and 'Johnson's Blue' cranesbill (*Geranium* 'Johnson's Blue'). Try them spilling over a wall, along a favorite path, or as part of a more formal border planting.

This grouping really glows in midsummer, as all three plants burst into bloom that lasts for several weeks. Part of the charm of the combination is the way the blooms mingle as the plants lean on each other for support. The casual look is one benefit of not restricting plants with rigid staking.

While the planting shown here has a soft, pastel feel, it would be a snap to pep it up by simply selecting different cultivars. Instead of the soft yellow 'Moonshine' yarrow, try a golden yellow like 'Coronation Gold'. Or replace the cool-colored 'Johnson's Blue' cranesbill with a vibrant violet like 'Kashmir Purple' (*Geranium clarkei* 'Kashmir Purple'). Red valerian comes in many shades of red, so buy plants when they are in bloom. Look for the brightest red-flowered form for a real riot of color.

Replace one, two, or even all three of the soft-colored plants with their brighter counterparts, and you'll get a completely different feel. You could create a whole garden just around variations of this one simple grouping. No matter what cultivars you try, you'll enjoy the long-lasting beauty of these colorful, no-fail flowers.

Enjoy the surefire summer color of rosy red valerian, pale yellow 'Moonbeam' yarrow, and 'Johnson's Blue' cranesbill. All of these easy-to-please plants will grow in a sunny to lightly shaded spot.

—→·←—

GROWING GUIDELINES

A sunny site with average, well-drained soil is ideal for a colorful combination of flowers and foliage plants.

Purple coneflower (*Echinacea purpurea*): Height to 4 feet; spread to 1½ feet. Summer flowers. Zones 3 to 8. Well-drained soil in full sun.

'Royal Purple' purple smoke tree (*Cotinus coggygria* 'Royal Purple'): Height and spread to 15 feet. All-season foliage interest; summer flowers on mature wood. Zones 4 to 9.

Wild rye (*Elymus* spp.): Height and spread to 3 feet. All-season interest from foliage; summer bloom. Zones 4 to 10.

Peonies (*Paeonia* spp.): Height and spread to 3 feet. Spring to early-summer bloom. Zones 3 to 8.

—→·←—

Add Excitement with Contrasting Textures

Want to reduce maintenance but still have a garden that looks super all season? Start with shrubs and grasses for long-lasting foliage interest, add some no-fail flowers for spots of seasonal color, and you've got the formula for a high-performance planting.

This easy-care combination is an excellent choice for a sunny, well-drained site. Peonies, purple coneflower (*Echinacea purpurea*), 'Royal Purple' purple smoke tree (*Cotinus coggygria* 'Royal Purple'), and wild rye (*Elymus* spp.) are all tough, dependable choices.

Throughout the season, the rounded, rich purple leaves of the purple smoke tree and spiky, silvery foliage of the wild rye foliage form a striking scene. In the foreground, the mounded form of the peony is topped with colorful flowers in late spring; in mid- to late summer, the spiky blooms of purple coneflower add a cheerful note. As the plants grow through the season, you can enjoy the changing show of blooms against the beautiful backdrop of the contrasting textures and foliage colors.

More and more gardeners are beginning to appreciate the value of purple smoke tree in the garden. When allowed to grow naturally, the plant tends to form a small multi-stemmed tree and eventually produces showy clusters of flowerstalks on the mature wood. To get the best foliage color, though, you can cut the stems to the ground each winter. You won't get flowers then, but the young stems will produce larger, more deeply colored leaves. The rounded leaves are a perfect contrast for all kinds of spiky ornamental grasses.

Try this pink, purple, and silver combination as it is, for a cool, soothing look, or you could echo the colors along the front of the border with the grouping of lamb's-ears (*Stachys byzantina*), curled parsley (*Petroselinum crispum* var. *crispum*), and 'Vera Jameson' sedum (*Sedum* 'Vera Jameson') shown in the photo on page 81.

Want a low-maintenance garden? Start with easy-care plants like 'Royal Purple' purple smoke tree and silvery wild rye. Peonies and purple coneflowers add splashes of seasonal color.

➛ · ↚

GROWING GUIDELINES

These no-fail flowers will thrive in any sunny spot with average, well-drained soil.

'Carmen' showy stonecrop (*Sedum spectabile* 'Carmen'): Height and spread to 1½ feet. Late-summer bloom. Zones 3 to 9.

'Goldsturm' black-eyed Susan (*Rudbeckia fulgida* var. *sullivantii* 'Goldsturm'): Height to 2 feet; spread to 1½ feet. Summer bloom. Zones 3 to 9. Leave the seedheads for winter interest, or cut them off to prevent self-sowing.

➛ · ↚

Surefire Late-Summer Flowers

After a long, hot summer, your flower garden can start to look drab and tired. But this is just the time you need some cheerful color to celebrate the arrival of cooler fall temperatures. Try a selection of late-blooming flowers to keep your garden looking great through the end of the season.

For a simple but smashing planting, combine 'Goldsturm' black-eyed Susan (*Rudbeckia fulgida* var. *sullivantii*) and 'Carmen' showy stonecrop (*Sedum spectabile* 'Carmen'). These two dependable performers are a perfect solution to that hot, dry, sunny site. Try them as part of a large bed or border for late-season interest, or just use them together to spotlight a feature like steps or a deck.

The show begins in mid- to late summer, as the black-eyed Susans send up their sturdy flowerstalks. At the same time, the showy stonecrop is starting to form its broccoli-like heads of tightly packed flower buds over tidy mounds of succulent green leaves. As the black-eyed Susans begin to bloom, the stonecrop's flower heads start to stretch upward and eventually burst into rosy-pink bloom by early fall.

These surefire flowers will continue to bloom into the cooler fall season, but the show doesn't stop there. Both the black-eyed Susans and the showy stonecrop produce attractive seed heads that can add garden interest well into winter. The color of the seed heads will fade as they weather, but they'll hold their shape even in snow. If they start to look too ratty by midwinter, cut the stems to the ground and toss them on the compost pile.

Alone or together, black-eyed Susans and showy stonecrop are super selections for late-season color. As you plan your flower beds and borders, don't forget to include these dependable plants to prolong the summer show. Boltonia (*Boltonia asteroides*), Joe-Pye weed (*Eupatorium purpureum*), goldenrods (*Solidago* spp.), asters, and ornamental grasses are other excellent choices for extending interest into the fall season.

Add some excitement to your late-summer garden with this easy-care pairing of 'Goldsturm' black-eyed Susans and 'Carmen' showy stonecrop. As a plus, you'll be able to enjoy their showy seed heads well into the winter season.

GROWING GUIDELINES

A combination of the following two plants would be great in a sunny or lightly shaded spot with average, well-drained soil; some extra soil moisture will keep the bee balm looking its best.

Bee balm (*Monarda didyma*): Height to 3 feet; spread to 1½ feet. Summer bloom. Zones 4 to 8.

Daylilies (*Hemerocallis* spp.): Height to 3 feet; spread to 2 feet. Summer bloom. Zones 3 to 9.

Pastels for Romantic Plantings

Creating great plant combinations doesn't take lots of complicated planning. It can be as easy as putting two plants next to each other and seeing what happens. Sometimes the plants won't bloom at the right times, or in compatible colors; if they don't work, they're easy to move. But often, you'll find that plants go together in the garden even better than they did on paper.

If you have a sunny or lightly shaded spot with average, well-drained soil, try this simple summer combination of bee balm (*Monarda didyma*) and daylilies (*Hemerocallis* spp.). These tall beauties are ideal for the back of a small to medium-sized border or the middle of an island bed. Or group them in front of even-taller shrubs and ornamental grasses.

The grouping shown here highlights a soft pink-flowered cultivar of bee balm and a very pale peach daylily. Bee balm is a dependable summer-bloomer, with strong-stemmed blooms that are great for cutting; it's a real favorite with hummingbirds, bees, and butterflies. Sturdy daylilies are a natural choice for a no-fail combination. Established clumps can produce hundreds of flower buds and bloom for weeks from mid- to late summer. The soft color combination adds a restful tone to the garden all summer.

Both bee balm and daylilies are available in many different colors. If pastels aren't in your plan, consider grouping vibrant red 'Cambridge Scarlet' bee balm with lemon yellow 'Hyperion' daylily, or white 'Snow Queen' bee balm with raspberry pink 'Cherry Cheeks' daylily. If powdery mildew turns the leaves of your bee balm dusty white, try planting the new mildew-resistant cultivars, like long-blooming bright pink 'Marshall's Delight'. 'Mahogany' and 'Gardenview Scarlet' are also reported to have some mildew resistance. Thinning the stems of crowded bee balm clumps in early spring will also promote better air circulation and keep your combination looking good all summer.

Pale peach daylilies and soft pink bee balm make a no-fail combination for a sunny or lightly shaded spot. Both plants come in
a range of colors, so you can personalize your grouping by picking the cultivars with colors that you like best.

GROWING GUIDELINES

A grouping of these three plants would be a good choice for a sunny site with moist to well-drained soil.

Bee balm (*Monarda* spp.): Height to 4 feet; spread to 2 feet. Summer bloom.

Golden marguerite (*Anthemis tinctoria*): Height and spread to 3 feet. Summer bloom. Zones 3 to 8. Best in cool climates.

Hibiscus (*Hibiscus* spp.): Height to 8 feet; spread to 5 feet. Summer bloom. Grows tallest with moist soil.

Bright Blooms for Bountiful Borders

What could be more rewarding than strolling through your own garden surrounded by exuberant masses of colorful flowers? Choose fast-growing, no-fail plants, set them in the right conditions, and step back! You'll be bowled over by the resulting bunches of blooms.

If you have a sunny spot with average, well-drained soil, you've got what it takes to create a great combination like the one shown here. Hibiscus (*Hibiscus* spp.), bee balm (*Monarda* spp.), and golden marguerite (*Anthemis tinctoria*) are all adaptable, easy-to-grow perennials.

All three of these plants will bloom together for weeks in mid- to late summer. Their relative heights can vary widely, depending on how much moisture they get. To suit all the plants' needs, an evenly moist to well-drained soil is best. In very moist soil, some species of hibiscus can reach 8 feet; in drier soil, they'll flower well but grow shorter. Bee balm will take short dry spells, but very dry soil shortens the bloom season and causes leaf drop. If your site is fairly dry, consider planting wild bergamot (*Monarda fistulosa*), which is more drought-tolerant than other species.

Good drainage is usually recommended for golden marguerite, since it encourages compact growth. Extra moisture promotes longer stems, which tend to sprawl into neighboring plants. (Depending on how you look at it, this habit could be either charming or annoying!) After the first flush of bloom, cut plants back to just above ground level to promote a new batch of foliage. Golden marguerite grows best in cool climates; in the heat of Zones 7 and higher, it may bloom in early spring and then collapse. If you live in a warm climate, replace the golden marguerite with a coreopsis (*Coreopsis* spp.) for summer-long yellow blooms.

Tailor this pink-and-yellow combination to fit into a different color scheme by choosing different species and cultivars of bee balm and hibiscus. Besides lavender-pink, bee balm comes in red, violet-blue, white, and bright pink. Hibiscus is available in shades of red, pink, or white.

Enjoy this colorful combination of bright pink hibiscus, lavender-pink bee balm, and golden marguerite in your own garden. Just give them a sunny spot with average soil, and watch them thrive.

➡️ · ⬅️

GROWING GUIDELINES

Highlight a sunny, well-drained spot with this no-fail combination.

Bearded iris (*Iris* spp.): Height to 3 feet; spread to 2 feet. Early-summer flowers. Zones 4 to 9.

Snow-in-summer (*Cerastium tomentosum*): Height to 10 inches; spread to 2 feet. Late-spring and early-summer bloom. Zones 3 to 7.

English ivy (*Hedera helix*): Height to 8 inches as a groundcover; spread indefinite. All-year foliage interest. Zones 5 to 9. May be damaged by full sun, especially in winter.

➡️ · ⬅️

An Elegant Mix for Late-Spring Color

You don't need a large garden to create great plant combinations. Make the most of your available space by planning layered plantings. Surrounding taller plants with medium-sized and groundcover companions helps to visually anchor the larger plants to the site. Carefully chosen companions can also extend the season of interest by producing beautiful flowers or foliage that looks good even when the taller plants aren't blooming.

This stunning mixture features bearded iris, snow-in-summer (*Cerastium tomentosum*), and English ivy (*Hedera helix*). All three of these plants grow well in average, well-drained soil. Full sun is ideal for the iris and snow-in-summer; if possible, site the English ivy to the north or east side, where the taller iris foliage can provide a bit of shade. If your soil isn't particularly well drained, a raised bed or rock wall can provide the ideal growing conditions.

Late spring to early summer is really the peak time for this grouping. Established iris clumps can bloom for several weeks. The snow-in-summer bursts into bloom at the same time, creating a cloud of snowy white blooms that perfectly highlights the irises.

After the bloom season, take a few minutes to snip off the spent iris flower stalks, and give the snow-in-summer an overall trim to promote bushy growth. Then just step back and enjoy the contrast between the delicate, silvery snow-in-summer foliage and the bold, blue-green iris leaves. The bright green leaves of the English ivy provide a tidy-looking "skirt" that looks good all year long.

Whether you plant this or another combination, remember the value of low-growing perennials and groundcover plants to hide the "bare ankles" of taller-growing companions. Try cranesbills (*Geranium* spp.) below garden phlox (*Phlox paniculata*), or low-growing sedums with asters. In a shady spot, use the same idea by underplanting lilies with hostas or lungworts (*Pulmonaria* spp.).

Add a touch of class to a sunny, well-drained spot with this elegant grouping of bearded iris, snow-in-summer, and English ivy. Enjoy the blooms in early summer, then admire the contrasting foliage colors and textures for the rest of the season.

—→• •←—

GROWING GUIDELINES

A sunny, well-drained site is all you need for a striking mix of hot-colored flowers.

Corn poppy (*Papaver rhoeas*): Height to 2 feet; spread to 1 foot. Summer bloom. Annual. Direct-sow seed the first year; usually self-sows for following years.

Yarrows (*Achillea* spp.): Height to 4 feet; spread to 3 feet. Summer bloom. Zones 3 to 9.

Golden ginger mint (*Mentha × gentilis* 'Variegata'): Height to 1½ feet; spread to 2 feet. All-season foliage interest. Zones 5 to 9.

—→• •←—

Color Contrasts for Maximum Impact

When subtle just won't cut it, shocking may be the answer. Some people may cringe at an intense combination like yellow and red or purple and orange, but it's a sure way to draw attention to your garden. Bright colors give your yard a fresh, cheerful look that you just can't get with soft pastel shades.

This simple but surefire combination features bright yellow yarrows (*Achillea* spp.) and brilliant scarlet corn poppy (*Papaver rhoeas*) underplanted with low-growing golden ginger mint (*Mentha × gentilis*). These plants are perfect for any sunny spot with well-drained soil. Try them in masses for broad sweeps of stunning color.

Yarrows are dependable bloomers for late-spring to summer color. The bloom season for corn poppies depends on the climate; they tend to bloom in late spring in hot climates and early to midsummer in cooler areas. Either way, the bloom times should overlap for at least a few weeks of eye-catching color. Both yarrows and poppies make great cut flowers, too. (To help poppies last, hold the base of the stems over a flame or in boiling water for a few seconds as soon as possible after picking.)

After the poppies have bloomed, let them go to seed, and they'll self-sow in the spots that suit their needs. The yarrow will probably continue to bloom for several more weeks, creating a charming combination with the yellow-splashed foliage of golden ginger mint at its feet.

If you like this combination but want to extend the season of interest, you could interplant with fall-flowering selections. For bright yellow color, try cultivars of common sneezeweed (*Helenium autumnale*) or species of sunflowers (*Helianthus* spp.). Zinnias are no-fail flowers for color from summer through fall. Choose cultivars like 'Big Red', 'Scarlet Ruffles', or 'Firecracker' to echo the scarlet of the earlier corn poppies, or try a different color for contrast.

Paint an unforgettable garden picture with this combination of scarlet corn poppies, yellow yarrows, and golden ginger mint. These dependable, easy-care flowers will provide you with weeks of summer enjoyment for minimal work.

—→·←—

These wildflowers will thrive on a hot, dry, sun-baked site.

Prickly pear (*Opuntia humifusa*): Height to 6 inches; spread to 3 feet. Early-summer bloom. Zones 4 to 9.

Butterfly weed (*Asclepias tuberosa*): Height to 3 feet; spread to 1½ feet. Summer bloom. Zones 3 to 9.

—→·←—

Wildflowers for a Hot, Dry Site

Hot, dry spots can be one of the toughest gardening challenges. Flower borders near pools, sidewalks, and driveways often have to cope with relentless sun and reflected heat and light from the adjacent pavement. Don't despair of finding a solution—look to the natural environment to find plants that have become adapted to just those sorts of tough sites.

This combination of butterfly weed (*Asclepias tuberosa*) and prickly pear (*Opuntia humifusa*) is one super solution to a hot, dry site. These drought-tolerant perennials will grow just fine in loose, well-drained soil and all the sunshine you can give. Try them in the front of a full-sun border or as an edging for paved areas.

Butterfly weed is a tough, showy plant native to dry fields and prairies. The common name reflects the fact that butterflies are quite attracted by the showy orange, yellow, or reddish flowers. (You can prolong the blooming season by deadheading the first set of flowers.) Butterfly weed's drought tolerance is due to long taproots that can reach water resources deep in the soil. Those taproots also make it difficult to transplant butterfly weed successfully. For best results, start with young container-grown specimens, or grow them yourself from seed and transplant the seedlings to their final spot when they have developed their second set of true leaves.

Prickly pears aren't a common choice for flower borders, but they certainly have the features of a great ornamental: a unique growth habit, showy yellow early-summer flowers, and attractive greenish or purplish fruits. True, the spines can be a disadvantage, but the plant needs so little maintenance that you'll only rarely need to work around it. Gloves are, of course, a sensible precaution.

Let these two tough perennials solve that troublesome dry, sunny spot in your garden. For extra color, combine them with other adaptable, dependable bloomers like sedums and evening primroses (*Oenothera* spp.).

If you've got a garden near a street, sidewalk, driveway, or pool,
you need plants that laugh in the face of heat and drought.
Butterfly weed and prickly pear are two natural choices.

GROWING GUIDELINES

A grouping of these three plants would be great for any sunny, well-drained spot.

Purple sage (*Salvia officinalis* 'Purpurescens'): Height to 2 feet; spread to 3 feet. All-season foliage interest. Zones 3 to 9.

Comfrey (*Symphytum officinale*): Height to 3 feet; spread to 2 feet. Early-summer bloom. Zones 5 to 9. Grows best with extra moisture, but then may become invasive.

'Superba' littleleaf lilac (*Syringa microphylla* 'Superba'): Height to 6 feet; spread to 9 feet. Summer bloom. Zones 5 to 8. Resistant to powdery mildew (a common lilac disease).

Herbs and Shrubs for Easy Care

Don't relegate your herbs to a separate corner of the yard—mix them into your flower beds and borders for all-season interest. These tough, adaptable plants are the epitome of low maintenance: Give them the right site, and they'll thrive with little extra help from you. For good-looking foliage and seasonal flowers, it's smart to incorporate at least a few herbs into your ornamental gardens.

This combination highlights two easy-care herbs: purple sage (*Salvia officinalis* 'Purpurescens') and comfrey (*Symphytum officinale*). Behind these, a low-growing 'Superba' littleleaf lilac (*Syringa microphylla* 'Superba') forms a colorful backdrop. All three will thrive in well-drained soil in full sun. This grouping would be ideal as part of a larger bed or border or even in a foundation planting.

Early summer is the time to see this combination in its full glory. The lilac produces its main flush of fragrant, rosy pink bloom in late spring through early summer. The comfrey sends up its bloom stalks at the same time, clad in coarse, bright green leaves and topped with tiny, bell-like rosy pink to purplish flowers.

Even after the main bloom season, though, this combination still holds its own. The purple sage foliage looks great all season long, and the lilac may continue to bloom sporadically until fall. If you cut the comfrey stalks to the ground after bloom, you'll get a new clump of leaves that will look respectable for the rest of the season.

If you want to add on to this combination to fill a larger area, consider mixing in more herbs and shrubs to continue the theme and to keep maintenance to a minimum. The combination of sedum, parsley, and lamb's-ears shown in the photo on page 81 would make a super front-of-the-border grouping. A purple smoke bush (*Cotinus coggygria*) could be an excellent choice for the back of the border, to echo the dusty purplish sage foliage.

Easy-to-grow herbs and shrubs are great choices for a no-fail
garden. The sun lovers shown here are purple sage, comfrey,
and pink-flowered 'Superba' littleleaf lilac.

GROWING GUIDELINES

Add an elegant touch to a sunny, well-drained spot by creating a cool-color combination with the plants below.

Common thrift (*Armeria maritima*): Height and spread to 1 foot. Late-spring to early-summer bloom. Zones 3 to 8.

Lamb's-ears (*Stachys byzantina*): Height to 1 foot; spread to 2 feet. Late-spring bloom. Zones 4 to 8.

Common chives (*Allium schoenoprasum*): Height to 1½ feet; spread to 2 inches. Summer bloom. Zones 3 to 9.

Violet sage (*Salvia × superba*): Height to 3½ feet; spread to 2 feet. Early to midsummer bloom. Zones 4 to 7.

Artemisias (*Artemisia* spp.): Height to 3 feet; spread to 2 feet. All-season foliage interest. Zones 3 to 9.

Yarrows (*Achillea* spp.): Height to 4 feet; spread to 3 feet. Summer bloom. Zones 3 to 9.

A Soothing Silver Garden

What could be more refreshing on a hot summer day than a cool-colored garden? Blues, soft pinks, and silvers have a calming, restful look that can provide visual relief from the heat and glare of the scorching summer sun.

This carefully planned combination is an inspired example of using soft colors in a small border. Full sun and average, well-drained soil suit this grouping of artemisias (*Artemisia* spp.), lamb's-ears (*Stachys byzantina*), violet sage (*Salvia × superba*), yarrows (*Achillea* spp.), common chives (*Allium schoenoprasum*), and common thrift (*Armeria maritima*). A green hedge makes a perfect backdrop for the pale flower and foliage colors.

Late spring to early summer is peak bloom time. On the right side, the cheery pink blooms of common thrift are echoed by the shorter-stalked, lavender-pink flowers of common chives. In the center, a clump of violet sage is topped with spikes of densely packed purple-blue blooms. At its base, low-growing lamb's-ears sends up its fuzzy silver stalks with tiny purple-pink flowers. A few weeks later, the yarrow will produce flattened heads of pale yellow blooms.

By mid- to late summer, the violet sage is past its first show. Cut off the spent bloom stalks to promote a new flush of leaves and flowers for late summer into fall. You may also want to trim off the spent chive flowers to prevent self-sowing. Prune the lamb's-ears flowerstalks to the ground, too; this will encourage a tidy mat of soft, silvery foliage that looks great with the lacy silver-gray leaves of the artemisias all season long.

It would be easy to extend this border with other compatible plants. Pale yellow 'Moonbeam' coreopsis (*Coreopsis verticillata* 'Moonbeam') and spiky blue fescue (*Festucea cinerea*) are natural choices. For extra color, consider adding pale yellow 'Moonshine' yarrow (*Achillea* 'Moonshine'), soft blue 'Johnson's Blue' cranesbill (*Geranium* 'Johnson's Blue'), and rosy red valerian (*Centranthus ruber*), featured in the photo on page 83.

Soothing silvers, pinks, and blues create a lovely combination for a sunny, well-drained site. This grouping features silvery artemisia and lamb's-ears, blue-purple violet sage, yarrow, and pinkish common chives and common thrift.

❖ · ❖

GROWING GUIDELINES

A sunny spot with evenly moist soil is ideal for a low-maintenance grouping of the following plants.

Sargent juniper (*Juniperus chinensis* var. *sargentii*): Height to 2 feet; spread to 9 feet. All-year foliage interest. Zones 3 to 9.

Fountain grasses (*Pennisetum* spp.): Height and spread to 3 feet. Summer bloom. Zones 5 to 10. Can take fairly dry conditions in northern climates.

Zinnia (*Zinnia angustifolia*): Height and spread to 1 foot. Summer bloom. Annual.

❖ · ❖

Maximum Impact with Minimal Work

Low-maintenance doesn't have to mean no-color. With a little planning, you can have a garden that looks good in every season with just an hour or two of work per year. Sound too good to be true? It isn't. Just choose the right plants, put them in the right conditions, and enjoy their year-round beauty.

This combination is a perfect example of an easy-care planting. Sargent juniper (*Juniperus chinensis* var. *sargentii*), fountain grass (*Pennisetum* sp.), and zinnias (*Zinnia angustifolia*) all thrive in full sun and average, evenly moist soil. (They'll take some drought, but the juniper and grass really prefer supplemental water when growing in well-drained soil.) This grouping is a natural choice for a tough site: on a slope, in a foundation planting, or along a driveway or paved area.

On the left, the Sargent juniper contributes soft-looking evergreen needles on gently curved, layered branches for year-round interest. On the right, mounded green clumps of fountain grass are topped with spikes of fuzzy-looking flowers in summer. Later on, the flowers give way to equally attractive seedheads that can last well into winter. (Cut plants to the ground in late winter to make room for new growth.)

For color power alone, the real star of this combination is the underused *Zinnia angustifolia* (also sold as *Z. linearis*). This easy-to-grow annual is becoming more popular for its dependable bloom, disease resistance, and excellent tolerance of heat, humidity, and drought. The bright orange flowers of the species look great against the green juniper and fountain grass shown here, but they can be tricky to mix well with other colors. For a different look, you could try *Zinnia angustifolia* 'Star White', with creamy white, yellow-centered blooms. Or, if perennials are more to your liking, replace the zinnias with a perennial coreopsis, like soft yellow 'Moonbeam' or golden yellow 'Zagreb' (*Coreopsis verticillata* 'Moonbeam' or 'Zagreb').

No-fuss, no-fail plants are the way to go if you want low-mainte-nance plantings. Try this dependable combination of Sargent juniper, fountain grass, and annual narrowleaf zinnia for surefire, easy-care color all season long.

CHAPTER 4

Design Your Own No-Fail Garden

Some people compare garden making to cooking. All you need is a great recipe and the right ingredients. Fortunately, with both gardening and cooking, you're free to be as creative as you like. You can improvise and come up with a recipe that suits your own personal taste.

In Chapter 1, "Where Should Your Garden Grow?" you chose some of the ingredients for your no-fail garden. You decided what you want your garden to do for you and which site is best for your garden. In Chapter 2, "Choose the Flower Garden That's Right for You," you explored a variety of different garden styles. You either chose one of the garden styles, adapted a style to suit your taste, or decided to keep looking for other ideas. It's just like choosing the recipe you want to use for dinner: If you don't see what you want, you keep looking at recipes or adapt one to fit your taste. If you need more garden "recipes" to look at, turn to Chapter 3, "No-Fail Plant Combinations," or Chapter 5, "A Gallery of Easy Garden Designs." You can pick out one or more plant combinations that fit your site and mix and match them to create a very personal garden design. Even if you're working with a tiny yard, dry clay, soggy shade, or some other challenging garden site, a good design can solve your problems; it's your personal recipe for a no-fail garden.

Use sidewalks and driveways to help you determine the best size and shape for your flower beds. The curving walkway to this house doesn't leave much room for lawn, but it makes a tidy border for a showy entrance planting of perennial flowers and ornamental grasses.

—◦→ · ◦←—

FIT FLOWERS TO YOUR HOUSE

The architecture of some houses cries out for gardens that respect their history and style. A traditional herb garden is a perfect match for a colonial-style house, for example. For ideas on what style garden might best suit your house, see the list below.

Ranch or Cottage-Style House. The casual country look goes well with cottage or heritage gardens. Plant blooming shrubs and flowers around the perimeter of the house in beds with rounded corners and smooth lines.

Modern, Contemporary Home. The angular lines of modern homes look best with beds shaped to complement their sharp corners. Try beds with straight lines and right angles like triangles and octagons. Flowers with stiff, compact growth habits match the clean contemporary lines.

Traditional or Colonial House. Symmetrically placed flower beds complement colonial or formal homes. Beds shaped like squares, rectangles, octagons, or circles look especially formal around a birdbath or sundial.

—◦→ · ◦←—

In this chapter, we'll show you how to tie together all of the information in Chapters 1, 2, and 3. We'll take you through the design process step by step so you'll know exactly how to create a garden with a pleasing shape, size, and arrangement of plants. We'll lay out the design ingredients that make each garden style work and invite you to get growing.

What Shape Will Your Garden Take?

Once you've considered your site and what style your flower garden will be, it's time to think about the size and shape of the flower bed. Often, it's easy to determine a flower garden's size because of limits imposed by property lines, driveways, and walkways. The lines or shape of your flower garden, however, should fit the style of the plants you are growing as well as the style of your house and your personality. In certain situations the shape of the bed is what will give a garden a formal, tidy appearance or a casual-country look. Some flower beds can be so unusually shaped that it is the outline of the bed, rather than the flowers themselves, that draws the eye, brings a smile, or creates a memory.

A formal flower bed is usually more difficult to maintain than a rounded one, because crisp corners are difficult to mow around. And as border plants grow, they blur the distinct lines of straight boundaries and require more clipping and trimming to keep them in place.

A flower garden with curved corners and gentle curves is the easiest to maintain and mow around, and it's also the best suited to casual, sprawling plants such as those used in perennial gardens, in shade gardens, and around rockery plants. Edging the curved bed is more difficult, however. While landscape timbers, railroad ties, and other wood can be used to define the border in a straight-edged bed, a flower garden with curves needs to have bricks, poured cement curbing, metal, or thin, flexible wood or plastic borders installed around the edge to define the shape.

Remember that removing the grass to create a shapely flower bed is not permanent. The lawn will grow back or the flowers will grow into the lawn unless the grass is edged at least once during the growing season. Mulch will help keep plants and lawn separated, but installing a permanent barrier is the only way to eliminate time-consuming edge maintenance.

The shape of the flower garden that runs alongside the house can be straight, curved, or even scalloped or zigzag. Keep in mind that any unusual treatment of garden shape will draw attention to that area. Use this fact to draw the eye to a bay window by making the foundation planting around this architectural feature echo the curved shape of the bay. Palladian windows or those with a half-circle on top of a rectangular window can also be echoed with a curving half-circle garden directly below. Contemporary

Flower beds come in as many sizes and shapes as people do. Choose the size and shape that suits your site and personality. Fit a corner of your yard with a flower bed to make the best use of limited space. Use gently curving lines for easy mowing around an island bed set in your lawn, or try a long, straight-edged bed for a showy foundation planting between your house and sidewalk.

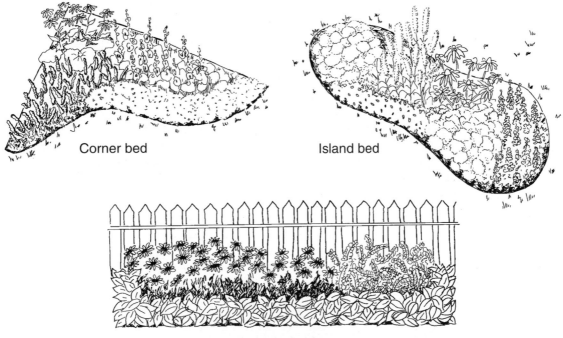

Corner bed

Island bed

Foundation planting

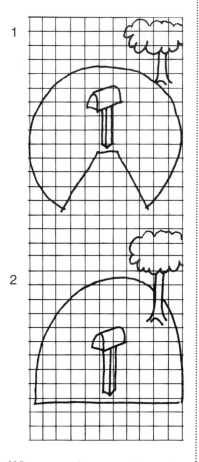

When you choose a shape for your flower bed, think about how it functions.

1. For example, a circular bed around a mailbox works fine if you add a path to reach the mail.

2. Consider maintenance, too. Using a straight border and including nearby trees or shrubs in the bed will simplify mowing.

homes with sharp angles and clean lines can be played up with sharply zigzag flower bed shapes, while Victorian homes look best adorned with scalloped edgings.

The flow of the beds around the house is important when deciding on a shape. The best way to play with creative ideas such as how wide or how long the beds should be is to draw out several versions on paper.

Gardening with a Pencil

Don't start tensing up at the thought of measuring your home, drawing everything to scale, and sketching a perfect design on paper. Perfectly lovely landscapes are designed by people who can't draw, don't own a tape measure, and think diet as soon as they hear the word scale. Use your pencil to design the shape of your bed in much the same way you would doodle an idea on a cocktail napkin.

For now, don't worry about measurements, grades, or size restrictions. Just draw the outline of your flower bed. If your garden is located next to your house, include it in the drawing, too. It may help to draw your house as a rectangle or a square instead of trying to put all the angles and pathways in their proper place. The idea is to imagine the look of your garden with both straight and curved lines, wide and narrow beds, traditional and whimsical patterns.

Once you've decided on a shape you like, it's time to check the size of your garden. First, head outside and pace off or measure the length and width of the area you want your garden to fit into. Next, get a piece of graph paper and assign it a simple scale. One inch equals a foot is an easy scale to work with, but use whatever scale you need to fit your entire garden design on the piece of graph paper. Write the scale on the graph paper so you won't forget it, then transfer your design to the graph paper. When your design is drawn to scale, it's easy to figure out the number of plants you'll need to fill it. You'll find details on counting plants in "How Many Plants Do You Need?" on page 132.

If the details of scale, proper spacing, and accuracy of

measuring are difficult for you to accomplish, then chances are your strengths lie in being a creative thinker. Picturing how your garden will look may be easier for you than for a more detailed personality type who will matter-of-factly measure the property and use the squares on a piece of graph paper to get the proper perspective. For more ideas on visualizing your flower bed, read "See the Garden Before You Plant" on page 14.

Garden Design Principles

With a style and shape in mind, you can use a design to turn your garden dream into a reality. Even though most gardens look natural, as if they just "happened," you can bet they started with a design. If you're trying to redesign an existing garden, don't worry. The design ideas listed here work just as well for straightening out old gardens as they do for new gardens.

Garden design is based on a set of tried and true principles, and you don't have to be a landscape architect to understand them. They are mostly commonsense rules for how to arrange and combine plants. These principles are employed in all successful gardens. They help you create a garden of nonstop interest and excitement by balancing drama with restfulness, and order with disorder. Let's explore them. Once you are comfortable with the garden design principles, you can use them to create your own no-fail design.

Scale or Proportion

Gardens are in scale or proportion when the size of the plants fits well with the size of the flower bed as well as the surrounding area and features. For example, if you have a large house and yard, you would choose a larger flower bed and plants than you would for a small cottage-style house with a postage stamp–sized yard. A huge, 15-foot-tall clump of bamboo (*Phyllostachys* spp.) may be just the thing for a garden located behind or beside a two-story

EVALUATING EXISTING GARDENS

When you move to a house with existing gardens, you inherit opportunities and problems. Use these tips to decide which plants to keep and which to take out.

Watch and wait. Let the garden grow for a year, see what comes up, and write down plant locations and names. Give dormant perennials and bulbs a chance to show themselves.

Ask, "Who is it?" When unknown flowers raise their heads, find out who they are before moving them. Check your local library for easy plant identification books.

Hold them over. If you can't wait a year to start rearranging flowers, move existing plants to a nursery bed. Once you see how they perform, you can move them back to the spot you want.

Don't judge too quickly. Sickly flowers may simply be overcrowded. If you see puny daylilies, irises, or daffodils, dig up and divide the plants after the flowers fade. See Chapter 9, "Keeping Your Garden's Good Looks," for details.

Keep your flowers and garden features in scale with each other for a comfortable, inviting feeling. The tall zinnias, cleomes (*Cleome hasslerana*), and cosmos surrounding this bench look just right because they're big enough to provide a colorful backdrop but not so large that they dwarf the bench or hide the view.

Large plants can make gardens lopsided unless you balance them. Here, giant Joe-Pye weed (*Eupatorium* sp.) is balanced by a group of three smaller plants: fall-blooming reed grass (*Calamagrostis arundinacea* var. *brachytricha*), 'Golden Fleece' goldenrod (*Solidago* 'Golden Fleece'), and purple New England aster (*Aster novae-angliae*).

SET YOUR GARDEN'S SCALE

If you aren't sure how to keep your garden in scale with your yard, try these sizing tricks.

Make flower borders half the width of your lawn. A 40-foot-wide yard calls for a 20-foot-wide border on one side or else two 10-foot-wide borders, one on each side of the lawn. The split arrangement is often better since a narrow border is easier to manage.

Use viewing distance to set bed size. Flower beds may be located anywhere in your yard, so instead of basing their size on your lawn width, make them half as wide as the distance from which you view them. If you're 20 feet from the bed, make it 10 feet wide.

---

house, but it would overwhelm a small patio garden just outside a bungalow's kitchen door.

Balance

Balance gives the garden a comfortable feeling when you look at it. An unbalanced design feels lopsided and unsettled. In a formal design, symmetry gives the garden balance. For example, you can place matching flower pots or clumps of daylilies on either end of your formal bed.

In informal designs, asymmetry creates balance. Rather than using identical plants, you can provide balance by

While a variety of colors, textures, and shapes creates excitement in the garden, too much variety may prove tiring. In this planting, a clever gardener repeated the pink color of the Iceland poppies (*Papaver nudicaule*) with pink-flowered phlox. The pink color ties the design together and gives your eyes a place to rest after viewing violet violas and yellow pansies.

matching the visual weight of different plants. For example, you can place two or more smaller plants on one end of a flower bed and balance them with one larger plant on the opposite end.

Repetition

Repetition unifies a design. If every plant in your garden is different, the result can be confusing to look at. Your eyes will jump from tall to small plant and from yellow to pink to purple flower with nowhere to rest. But if you repeat plants now and then—or at least use some plants with similar shapes, colors, or textures—your eyes will pick up the pattern and you can relax. Next time you look at a flower garden, notice the order in which you look at plants. What do you see first? second? third? You'll find you have a practiced eye at picking out similarities.

FUN WITH FOLIAGE

Leaf color plays a big role in successful garden design. Judy Glattstein, author of *Garden Design with Foliage,* uses unusual leaf colors to set off flowers. She loves stunning combinations such as purple-leaved perilla (*Perilla frutescens* 'Atropurpurea') with the bright rose-purple blooms of purple coneflower (*Echinacea purpurea*). Another favorite combination mixes the lavender flowers of alliums (*Allium* spp.) with the purple leaves of 'Rose Glow' barberry (*Berberis thunbergii* var. *atropurpurea* 'Rose Glow').

Warm-colored flowers catch your eye, which makes even distant plantings seem close at hand. The warm yellow flowers of these black-eyed Susans (*Rudbeckia hirta*) jump up and say "Here we are!" whether they're planted nearby or far away.

Cool colors seem to lower the temperature on warm days. Here, soothing lavender pansies and violets blend with the cool green and white leaves of hosta and variegated giant dogwood (*Cornus controversa* 'Variegata').

---- →・← ----

FUN WITH COLOR

Rainbow-colored flowers and foliage grab your attention. But neutral colors—white, cream, green, and gray—will also show off your plantings.

Use white and gray foliage to accentuate colors. The pale yellow flowers of 'Moonbeam' threadleaf coreopsis (*Coreopsis verticillata* 'Moonbeam') look brighter next to the silver-gray leaves of lamb's-ears (*Stachys byzantina*).

Use cream flowers or foliage, or green or gray leaves, to tone down clashing colors. Even a jarring planting of orange butterfly weed (*Asclepias tuberosa*) and bright red bee balm (*Monarda didyma*) will look pleasing if separated by the silvery foliage of white sage (*Artemisia ludoviciana*) or by the cream-striped leaves of variegated sweet iris (*Iris pallida* 'Variegata').

---- →・← ----

Designing with Flowers

Now that you understand the design principles that make a successful garden bed, it's time to put them to work arranging the flowers. Mixing and matching flowers can make you feel like the sorcerer's apprentice. There are so many choices, it's easy to get swept away in a whirlwind of colors, shapes, sizes, and textures. Keep your perspective and make the best choices by using the simple hints listed below.

Set the Mood with Color

Color is a powerful part of a design. You can determine the mood of your garden by using colors that are bright and showy or pale and subtle. Bright yellows, oranges, reds, and deep magentas are called warm or hot colors. Visually they are very exciting. They are festive, summer

A garden that mixes vertical plant shapes with rounded ones creates a sense of movement and excitement. Here, the strong upright lines of Siberian iris (*Iris sibirica*) leaves and flowerstalks provide a lively contrast to the rounded forms of trees and shrubs in the background.

When you use plants with contrasting leaf and flower shapes, it's easy to create an interesting look. Here, deeply divided peony leaves provide a dramatic difference beside puffy round peony flowers and the rounded leaves and flowers of lilac cranesbill (*Geranium himalayense*).

colors. Use them to create excitement in the garden. In mass or as accents, warm colors attract your eye and seem closer than they really are. In contrast, shades of purples, blues, and greens, as well as pale pinks and light creamy yellows, are referred to as cool colors. They have a soothing effect on the eye. View a garden of cool colors on a hot summer day and you'll say "ahh." Visually, cool colors retreat from the eye. In other words, they look farther away from you than they really are. This is especially true of blues and purples. They're good choices if you want to make a small garden seem bigger.

Highlight Plant Forms and Habits

Form and habit are terms that refer to the overall shape and growth patterns of plants—whether they are spiky or spear-shaped, rounded or mounded, or flat and prostrate. Mixing plant shapes highlights the differences between them and creates interest. A plant like Siberian iris (*Iris sibirica*), with spear-shaped leaves, provides your garden with an upright or vertical look and feeling. Mix it with fluffy mounded plants like garden phlox (*Phlox paniculata*) to create a strong contrast. Add some low, spreading plants like wall rock cress (*Arabis caucasica*) to change your garden's profile even more. Just remember to repeat a few plants or use a few with a similar look to unify the design.

Mix Heights for Maximum Interest

The size of plants helps you determine their place in the flower bed. If you're planting against a wall or fence, you'll want to keep the tallest plants in the back of your garden. It's just common sense. If you plant all the tall plants in front, you won't be able to see the shorter plants. As you move toward the front of the bed, plant shorter and shorter plants, with the lowest-growing ones at the front edge.

To make your garden more interesting and avoid the stair-step look of high school bleachers, pull a few tall plants forward. This works especially well with spiky plants. Place a bold clump of iris near the front edge of the

---

HINTS ABOUT HEIGHT

In a flower border, it's a good basic rule to keep short plants in front and tall plants in back. But don't be rigid about it, says Sarah Price, curator of Central Park's Conservatory Garden. She explains how to make your garden's profile more interesting and dramatic by mixing plants of different heights together.

Place some taller flopping plants at the front of the border to avoid a regimented series of low mounds. Use catmint (*Nepeta* spp.), speedwells (*Veronica* spp.), and cranesbills (*Geranium* spp.) to create a pleasant undulating rhythm and blur the line between the border and lawn.

In the middle of the border, plant airy plants around the bases of taller ones to create a tiered effect. Purple coneflower (*Echinacea purpurea*) looks stunning when surrounded by the airy foliage of white sage (*Artemisia ludoviciana*).

In the middle or back of the border, let some tall plants flop among the mounds at the front.

An intriguing mixture of short and tall leaf heights brings you back to this garden for a second look. The smooth yellow and green leaves of 'Variegata' yellow flags (*Iris pseudacorus* 'Variegata') stand out like soldiers above the crinkled, deep-green leaves of Japanese primroses (*Primula japonica*).

bed with low mounded plants around it for contrast. Or, for a really different look, place a stately rhubarb plant at the front of your garden where the bold texture of its large, coarse leaves will attract your attention. You can even pull some tall, airy plants such as white gaura (*Gaura lindheimeri*) and Brazilian vervain (*Verbena bonariensis*) to the front edge of the border to create a veil through which you view other plants. These see-through plants are effective in both large and small gardens.

Add Appeal with Varied Textures

Texture refers to the way the surface of leaves and flowers look or the way they might feel. Textures are described as fine, medium, or coarse. When you think of fine textures, think of cotton candy and fern fronds. They are light and airy, appear soft to the touch, and might be described as lacy, open, or delicate. Yarrows (*Achillea* spp.) and threadleaf coreopsis (*Coreopsis verticillata*) have narrow, fine-textured foliage. Dainty flowers, like coral bells (*Heuchera sanguinea*) and baby's-breath (*Gypsophila paniculata*), are also fine-textured. Most ornamental grasses have both fine-textured foliage and fine-textured flowers.

Many popular annuals and perennials have medium-textured foliage and flowers. Think of plants that are average-sized, with leaves or flowers that are neither too big nor too small. Flowering tobacco (*Nicotiana alata*), bee balm (*Monarda didyma*), marigolds (*Tagetes* spp.), and primroses (*Primula* spp.) fall into this group. Medium textures show up well in the garden. They form the backbone of any well-designed planting scheme, providing contrast for bold textures and a background for fine ones.

Use coarse or bold textures to wake up a dull, monotextured garden. Large-sized leaves and flowers are considered coarse. They stand out just as an elephant does in the animal world. Try planting a clump of 'Big Mama' hosta in a shade garden and you'll get the idea. The huge leaves demand attention and are hard to resist. Large flowers have the same effect. The dinner plate–sized flowers of bright-red hibiscus or dahlias are showstoppers.

→ · ←

TRICKS WITH TEXTURE

Does your garden seem too small or big? Then consider what texture can do to create a feeling of more or less space.

Make your garden seem bigger by placing bold-textured plants like hostas toward the front of beds or borders, and fine-textured plants like ferns behind them. The fine-textured plants appear to be farther away because of the stark contrast with the bold leaves. In tiny gardens, avoid huge leaves and gaudy flowers. They are out of scale and will make the garden's size seem even smaller. Choose medium- and fine-textured plants instead.

Texture can help at the large end of the scale, too. Make a big garden feel more intimate by framing the view out over it with fine- or medium-textured trees like thornless honey locust (*Gleditsia triacanthos* var. *inermis*) or downy serviceberry (*Amelanchier arborea*). Bring a distant planting closer by massing one or more bold-textured plants. The mass of foliage rushes to meet your eye as you view the garden.

→ · ←

DON'T FORGET FOLIAGE

When you choose garden plants, look as closely at the leaves as at the flowers. Judy Glattstein, author of *Garden Design with Foliage,* thinks foliage is great for enhancing flowers and creating drama. For a sunny spot Judy recommends a mix of three distinct foliage textures: lacy peonies, spiky Siberian irises (*Iris sibirica*), and a large-leaved perennial like bear's-breeches (*Acanthus* spp.) or bergenias (*Bergenia* spp.). The lush foliage, in contrasting textures, keeps the display attractive from spring through fall.

Small leaves can have a coarse texture if their surface area looks unusual. Imagine fuzzy leaves or leaves with textures like corduroy and seersucker cloth. As soon as you see them, you'll want to reach out and touch them. Coarse textures focus attention in your garden. Make sure you place these plants where you want people to look. Dancing the textural two-step is fun. Mix and match various sizes, shapes, and colors of both flowers and foliage to create a garden that is both beautiful and exhilarating.

Flowers for Four Seasons

No matter which garden style and shape you choose, you'll want to plan for several seasons of color. But what's

Plan on late-season color with combinations that flower in fall. The rosy-pink blooms of 'Autumn Joy' sedum peak in late summer and early fall along with the soft lavender flowers of asters and the pale pink to tan flowers of fountain grass (*Pennisetum alopecuroides*).

Choose carefully and you can have color in your garden in late fall and early winter. The flowers of 'Autumn Joy' sedum turn brick-red as they mature and make a showy contrast against the tan stems and seed heads of fountain grass (*Pennisetum alopecuroides*). These lavender asters will keep blooming until a hard frost reminds you and them that it's winter.

FOUR SEASONS OF FRUIT...AND BIRDS

Add year-round color to your garden with fruiting shrubs and trees. Choose plants with showy fruits for extra pizzazz, but don't ignore ones with dull seeds and berries. They add color bursts to your garden by attracting songbirds.

Joan Feely, curator of native plants at the U.S. National Arboretum, recommends planting many different shrubs and trees to provide a sequence of fruits for birds from spring through winter. Trees such as ashes (*Fraxinus* spp.), elms (*Ulmus* spp.), and maples (*Acer* spp.) provide an abundance of seeds in spring. For summer fruit, plant elders (*Sambucus* spp.), serviceberries (*Amelanchier* spp.), and shrub dogwoods (*Cornus* spp.).

In late summer and autumn, snowberries (*Symphoricarpos* spp.) and chokeberries (*Aronia* spp.) produce fruit.

In winter, after several hard freezes, the fruits of crab apples and hollies are more desirable to birds and are greedily devoured by waxwings, bluebirds, and robins.

a gardener to do? Plants that bloom in the spring, such as tulips and daffodils, rest in the summer. Annual flowers that are colorful all summer disappear with the first frost. Fall-blooming chrysanthemums and asters take all summer to get to that stage, and shrubs with bright red berries in the winter lose their attractive fruits by the start of spring.

The reality and the challenge of gardening is that no single plant can offer flowers year-round, so you must learn to mix and match flowering plants to produce a show with four seasons of color. Just because you choose to grow a bright and sun-loving bed of annuals doesn't mean you have to look at bare-naked earth in winter, spring, and fall. Think of your annual bed as four separate gardens, one for each season of the year.

Add some spring-blooming bulbs to the back of the bed. When they are done blooming, their dying foliage will be camouflaged by the growing annuals in early summer. (Once the bulb leaves turn brown you can pull them out of the ground easily, but leave them in place until they do, so they can produce food for next year's blooms.) Use the middle section as a place to plug in chrysanthemum plants or flowering cabbage once frost has nipped the tips of the most cold-sensitive annual flowers. In winter, imagine the flower bed lying peacefully in the snow, with a small grouping of dwarf evergreen shrubs in one corner. Mother Nature doesn't limit her beauty to one season of the year, and there's no need for you to let your garden lie fallow and vacant either.

In a formal garden of roses or herbs, group the seasonal flowers in the corners of the bed or line them up in a row along the back of the bed. For a very sophisticated look, space the blooming plants evenly apart and keep like colors together. A rose garden won't have much color in early spring unless you light it up with groups of yellow daffodils in each corner of the bed. Extend the spring season into May with a double row of red tulips across the back of the garden. The roses will carry the show through summer and into fall, when you can brighten the corners again—this time with chrysanthemums or ornamental cabbages.

Give a casual flower garden a long season of bloom by placing pockets of flowering bulbs and plants randomly throughout the planting. Accent the bed with small evergreen shrubs, fall crocuses, and blooming Christmas roses (*Helleborus niger*) for winter interest. Use a large boulder or two to mark these winter-color areas. Dress the boulders up in front with small bulbs such as 'Tête-à-tête' daffodils or low-growing Grecian windflowers (*Anemone blanda*), and you won't forget where your winter bloomers are and dig them up by mistake.

With bulbs and a variety of perennials, you'll weave a tapestry of blooming flowers that ebbs and flows depending on the season. If you plant just one type of plant—all roses or only herbs—they won't give you a four-season show. Imitate Mother Nature and mix trees, shrubs, perennials, annuals, and bulbs together for a garden of year-long interest.

Identify the design principles that make gardens successful, and you're well on your way to creating your own no-fail design. This garden combines a diverse mix of plant textures, colors, shapes, and sizes for interesting viewing; but the use of scale, balance, and repetition keeps it from turning into chaos.

Plan Your Flower Bed the Easy Way

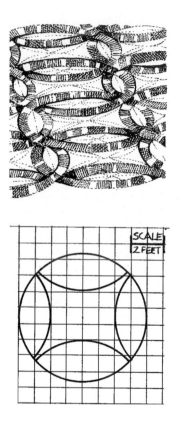

Simple patterns found in everyday objects make outstanding garden designs. One circle from the wedding ring pattern of a quilt (*top*) neatly divides a round flower bed into five planting areas (*bottom*).

Now, with visions of warm and cool color schemes and a variety of plant sizes and shapes running through your head, you need to decide which plants to use, how to arrange them, and how many you need. Putting it down on paper will help you sort out your ideas. The rest of this chapter tells you all you need to know to bring your garden to full flower.

Flower garden designs are as individual as the people who create them. So it's not surprising that there's more than one way of coming up with a design. Choose the method that suits your personality, likes, and dislikes best. If the arrangement of your plants is more important to you than the individual flowers, plan your garden design first and then pick the flowers that go with it. But if the specific flowers you grow are more important to you than the design, choose all of your flowers first and then decide how to arrange them.

If you prefer the flowers-first method, start with "Create a Design with Plants" on the opposite page. Choosing plants first and then creating combinations can be more complicated, however, so let's start the simple way by creating shapes or patterns and then adding the plants you want. This method is especially useful when you want to have large blocks of a single plant. You can use patterns to help you organize annual bedding flower schemes and simple perennial garden designs.

Familiar Patterns Make Great Garden Designs

Start with the outline of your flower bed that you drew for "Gardening with a Pencil" on page 108. Then get out your pencil again, because it's time to come up with a design.

Even experienced designers sometimes lack a starting point when it's time to arrange the flowers. An easy way to get over the first hump and get your design started is to create your design from a familiar pattern. Your clothes, house, and the everyday items around you are great sources of inspiration.

Look for Design Patterns Close to Home

It's not always easy to come up with the perfect garden design. But patterns are easy to find, and they make great garden designs. The striped pattern on your sweater or the simple design embroidered on your tablecloth may be all you need. Try searching for design patterns all over your house. Here are some places to look to get you started:

• Plow through the closet. Or, search all your drawers to find a shirt that has a pattern you love.
• Examine the wallpaper if your wardrobe offers no inspiration. Head for the den or bathroom and look for patterns on those walls.
• Check the windows and floors if the walls don't give you any good ideas. And look for patterns on the curtains and rugs.

Choose a simple shape that is easy to transpose. Intricate designs like stained glass windows, while beautiful in a chapel, are much too complicated to translate to the garden. Look at the pattern in the illustration on the opposite page to see how to turn a simple quilt pattern into a garden design. Then translate your own pattern into a design for your garden.

Trace your pattern onto the drawing you made of your flower bed shape. Use the lines of the pattern to divide the flower bed into sections. Then, using a variety of colors, forms, textures, and heights, choose different plants for each section of the pattern. Don't worry if you can't recognize the original pattern once the plants are established. The most important duty for the pattern is to help you get organized. Skip to "Picture-Perfect Plans" on page 132 to learn how to visualize your garden design, or read on to explore another method of designing your garden.

Create a Design with Plants

There are no wrong ways to plan a bed or border—just different ways. You learned how to create a design and

DESIGN PATTERNS

If you use a pattern for your garden design, you'll need a way to transfer the design from paper onto the ground. Try this easy method suggested by Wayne Ambler of Ambler's Flower Farm in Ashland, Virginia.

1. Rake the surface of your planting area smooth.

2. Use two stakes and a piece of string to mark off one end of the garden.

3. With a yardstick, and using the string as a starting point, measure out a grid made of squares 1 to 3 feet wide, depending on the size of the garden and the intricacy of the pattern. An intricate pattern needs a smaller grid.

4. Trace the outline of the squares in the soil using a rake handle or trowel. Be sure to cover the entire garden with the grid.

5. Next, "draw" the shape of the pattern on your garden spot with cupfuls of sand, using the grid to get the spacing right.

6. Transpose the entire pattern onto the bed so you can do all the planting at once. Wayne says to make a thick line so you don't erase it while planting.

Patterns like this one make it easy to organize the flowers in your garden. The S-shaped curve of French marigolds (*Tagetes patula*) is much more pleasing to look at than a straight line of plants. And it sets off the taller purple-flowered mealy-cup sage plants (*Salvia farinacea*) and low creeping zinnias (*Sanvitalia procumbens*) to best advantage.

then choose plants in "Familiar Patterns Make Great Garden Designs" on page 124. An equally rewarding but perhaps more challenging method starts by choosing plants first and then weaving them into a design. There are no preconceived patterns or shapes. The only predetermined conditions are soil, light, and moisture.

Start by making a list of all the plants you want to grow. For ideas, look through the designs in Chapters 3 and 5 and the plant lists in "A Plant-by-Plant Guide to No-Fail Flowers" on page 340. If you still can't decide which flowers you want, turn to Chapter 6, "Great Ideas and Finishing Touches," or order and look through the plant and seed catalogs under "Sources" on page 358. You're sure to find inspiration as you flip through pages of plant lists, color drawings, and color photos; maybe too much inspiration. Make sure you are practical and realistic. Choose only the plants that thrive under your soil, moisture, and light conditions. If you have several different beds or borders with different conditions, list the plants for each bed separately. Make each list as complete as you can. You can always pare it down later using the hints in "Evaluate Your Choices" on this page.

Once your list is done, look up the color, bloom time, height, and spread of each plant. Make a chart with columns across the top for characteristics like color, and list the names down the side of the page. A completed chart is a valuable design tool. You will have all the information you need at your fingertips. For quick reference, see the chart of plant characteristics in "A Plant-by-Plant Guide to No-Fail Flowers" on page 340.

Evaluate Your Choices

Now that you've made a list of plants you want to grow, think about how they'll work together. Use the design hints listed below to narrow your list down to ten or fewer plants and determine the best way to combine them.

Limit your color choices. Too many colors in a small garden are dizzying, not restful. Avoid a riot of shades and

---

EASY-CARE ANNUALS

If you love colorful annual flowers, you'll want to grow every one you can find. Sooner or later, however, you'll have to narrow your choices. To help you decide which plants are right for you, Brenda Skarphol, horticulturist at Green Spring Gardens Park in Alexandria, Virginia, suggests you consider plants that don't need pampering.

Choose showy, drought-tolerant annuals that bloom all season without the need for deadheading. You'll save hours of garden maintenance. Some of Brenda's favorite workhorses are red-orange Mexican sunflowers (*Tithonia rotundifolia*), red, purple, or white globe amaranths (*Gomphrena globosa*), and nonstop-blooming 'Italian White' sunflowers (*Helianthus annuus* 'Italian White').

Bold Shasta daisies (*Chrysanthemum* × *superbum*) elbow their way into the neighboring planting in this informal garden. Well-mannered rose campion plants (*Lychnis coronaria*) support the flopping flowers with their silvery stems and leaves, eliminating the need for stakes.

tints by choosing a cool or warm color scheme (as described in "Set the Mood with Color" on page 114), and stick to your choices once you have made them. Avoid the temptation to throw in just one more old favorite.

Sort out plant shapes. Think about the shapes of the plants. Remember unity and variety. Put rounded forms next to spiky plants, and place some trailers along the edge. Don't place too many similar shapes together. Keep the tallest plants toward the back unless they are see-through plants.

Consider plant performance. Some plants are refined, with neat and tidy habits. They maintain a tight shape, never drop their petals, and always look fresh. Other, more vulgar garden denizens make outrageous displays of foliage and flowers, drop their spent blooms wherever they like, and flop shamelessly in wind or rain. Greedy types

such as bee balm (*Monarda didyma*) seem to want every inch of the garden for themselves. They spread around wantonly, over and through their neighbors without the slightest bit of remorse. Yet a garden would be incomplete without these characters and all those in between.

So, what's a designer to do? Love it! The plant personalities make garden design interesting. With aggressive plants, proper spacing is important. Give them plenty of room to spread. Also, you may need to divide them every two to three years to keep them in check.

What about the shameless floppers? Love them or stake them! If your style is informal, a little flopping is hardly noticed. Just make sure delicate plants are out of the shade of the sprawling masses. If your style is more controlled, use individual stakes or wire supports to keep the plants upright. Another way to help is to place taller plants in groups. You will get a more dramatic display, and the plants will hold each other up.

Turn shrinking violets into showy groups. Small and delicate plants are often outshone by more dazzling neighbors. To really make them count, plant in groups of three to five of the same kind. Plant them close enough together so they fill in quickly. Place such groupings at the front of the border, along paths, or at corners to soften hard angles.

Putting Your Plant Choices Together

A list of your plants' characteristics—bloom time, color, height, and shape—helps you arrange your plants so they look good together. If you aren't familiar with the plants, though, it can be hard to make decisions, even with the design hints listed above. Here's an easy way to combine and design a garden with perfect plant placement. If you aren't sure which plants on your list go well together, pick a favorite grouping from a neighbor's garden or from one of the no-fail plant combinations in Chapter 3. Or choose three to five plants from one of the garden designs in Chapter 5 and rearrange them to suit your site. Use this plant combination as a building block for creating a series of new combinations. Make sure you choose only plants that will grow well together.

WORKING WITH FUSSY FLOWERS

Some plants need much more care than others to look their best. Sarah Price, curator of Central Park's Conservatory Garden, avoids fussbudgets when she can, but when she can't, she relies on plant selection and maintenance tricks.

• Avoid plants that need staking unless they are real beauties. If plants do need staking, wire cages require less maintenance than staking individual plants.

• If you love peonies but tire of seeing them face down in the mud after every storm, try the single-flowered types. Many single peonies have short, stout stems and the single flowers aren't as heavy. See "Low-Flop Peonies" on page 300 for good cultivars to try.

• Instead of deadheading floriferous plants like catmint (*Nepeta* spp.), violet sage (*Salvia* × *superba*), and cranesbills (*Geranium* spp.), rejuvenate them by shearing. As blooms fade, cut the entire plant to the ground. You'll get repeat flowering plus fresh, compact growth.

CHOOSE TO AVOID PEST AND DISEASE PROBLEMS

You can grow healthy plants even if they're disease- and insect-prone, if you make good choices. Janis Kieft, garden columnist for the *Minneapolis Star Tribune* newspaper, offers the following suggestions.

Choose disease- and pest-resistant cultivars. For example, powdery mildew is particularly worrisome on garden phlox (*Phlox paniculata*) and bee balm (*Monarda didyma*). New cultivars are resistant to this disease, so check nursery catalogs for resistant cultivars before you buy.

Plan on proper spacing. Plants need good air circulation to help them dry off quickly. Crowded plants are susceptible to foliage disease, and a tangled thicket of leaves is sure to harbor pests. Check catalogs or "A Plant-by-Plant Guide to No-Fail Flowers" on page 340 to determine proper spacing before you plant. Believe what you read: The tiny plants you bring home from the nursery really do get that big. Space them accordingly.

The secret to success lies in choosing and combining plants to maximize their attributes. Use one plant to show off another or to fill a space left when one goes dormant. Link plants in a logical sequence. Choose low, spreading plants in front of mounded or grassy ones, and use large mounds to complement tall spikes. Combine billowing, airy plants with bold-textured ones. Make each plant you choose pay its rent and do its duty.

For example, if you have a sunny, well-drained site and you want to grow fernleaf yarrow (*Achillea filipendulina*) and 'Autumn Joy' sedum, use them as the start of the garden. Both plants have rounded forms, but their flower colors and bloom times are different. Fernleaf yarrow's yellow flowers appear in early summer, while the pink blooms of 'Autumn Joy' sedum don't peak until fall. To fill out your planting, think of a few plants that bloom at the same time as these two but with different forms and colors. Glance through the plant list in "A Plant-by-Plant Guide to No-Fail Flowers" on page 340 for some good choices. You'll find blood-red cranesbill (*Geranium sanguineum*) and blue false indigo (*Baptisia australis*) for contrasting with fernleaf yarrow's yellow flowers. Place the sedum behind the cranesbill so it can take over the show when the cranesbill is finished. Add a patch of lamb's-ears (*Stachys byzantina*) at the front of the garden for its fuzzy foliage texture. Use plants like ornamental grasses and yuccas for vertical form, and 'Goldsturm' black-eyed Susans (*Rudbeckia fulgida* var. *sullivantii* 'Goldsturm') and threadleaf coreopsis (*Coreopsis verticillata* 'Moonbeam') to keep the flowers going through the summer and fall. Choose asters or chrysanthemums to bloom with the sedum for late-autumn interest. The seed heads of the sedum and grasses will make the winter scene interesting.

There are no right or wrong combinations. Everyone's taste is different. Just make sure all the plants you choose need the same conditions. Keep linking pleasing, varied combinations until you have filled your garden space. Be sure to repeat one plant or at least a color or form throughout the garden to

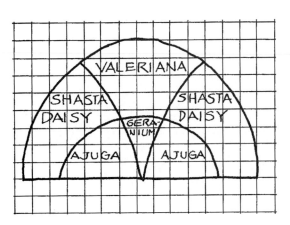

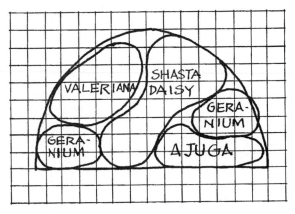

maintain unity and create rhythm. A unified design is important to make the garden look and feel right.

Putting It Down on Paper

Once you've decided on the plants or plant combinations you want to use, it's time to record them on paper and see how they look together. Make several copies of your flower bed outline, drawn to scale (see "Gardening with a Pencil" on page 108), or buy some sheets of tracing paper to use for design experiments. Using a copy of your outline or a piece of tracing paper placed over your original outline, divide the drawing into the same number of areas as the number of plants you want to grow. Use blocks, rectangles, ovals, circles, or squares to divide your drawing into sections. Decide which direction you will usually view the garden from, and choose plants for each spot based on color, shape, and size to make an interesting but unified composition.

There are as many ways to design gardens as there are gardeners, so choose the method that you are most comfortable with. You could divide your flower bed into sections, using a love-knot pattern (*left*), then choose plants to fill in each section. Or choose the plants first, then divide the bed into planting areas of various shapes that show off each flower to best advantage (*right*).

→·←

LOSE BAD-DRAINAGE BLUES

Sites that are soggy in winter and spring and bone-dry in summer make gardening a real trial. Wayne Ambler of Ambler's Flower Farm in Ashland, Virginia, found success with proper soil preparation and plant selection.

Amend the soil. Add to your soil 4 inches of a mix of 1 part sand to 3 parts rotted sawdust, rotted manure, or compost. Mix the amendment into the soil 15 inches deep, using a garden fork, and let the soil settle for three weeks. Level the bed with a rake, and slope the edges gradually down to meet existing grades. Your bed will be 2 to 3 inches higher than the lawn, which improves winter drainage.

Use tough perennials. On sunny sites, try swamp sunflower (*Helianthus angustifolius*), scarlet rose mallow (*Hibiscus coccineus*), and great blue lobelia (*Lobelia siphilitica*). In shade, use Chinese astilbe (*Astilbe chinensis*), fringed bleeding heart (*Dicentra eximia*), and interrupted fern (*Osmunda claytoniana*).

→·←

Picture-Perfect Plans

Cutouts are an easy and fun way to help you visualize how your colors, forms, and textures will look together. Once you've chosen your plants and design, cutouts bring the garden to life. Clip pictures of your plants from nursery catalogs. Fasten the pictures to their chosen places in the design using tape or rubber cement. If you don't like a flower's position, peel it off and try it in another spot. Do your rearranging and fine-tuning now. Changes are troublesome and costly once plants are in the ground. Designing on paper is the easiest and least expensive way to plan a successful flower garden.

How Many Plants Do You Need?

Once all the planning, designing, and soil preparations are done, it's time to buy plants. Determining how many plants you'll need to fill your design is easy. All you'll need is a drawing of your plan on graph paper (like the one on the opposite page) and the spacing requirements for each of the plants you want to grow. To calculate the number of plants, follow the steps below:

1. Draw your plan with a scale that's easy to work with, such as one square equals 1 square foot. For large gardens, you may need to work in increments of one-quarter squares (for example, one-quarter square equals 1 square foot).

2. Estimate the number of square feet allotted for each plant by counting the squares in each area. Approximate square footage is fine. (In the example on the opposite page, the area for daylilies occupies about 8 square feet.)

3. Write the square footage for each plant on your plan.

4. Next, determine how many square feet each plant needs by multiplying the linear spacing for each plant by itself. (For the daylily example, that's 1½ feet times 1½ feet equals 2.25 square feet per plant.)

5. Finally, to determine how many plants you'll need, divide the total number of square feet by the square feet for

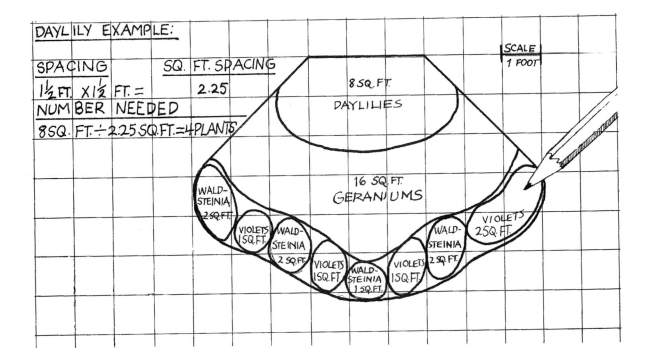

DAYLILY EXAMPLE:

SPACING | SQ. FT. SPACING
1½ FT. X 1½ FT. = | 2.25
NUMBER NEEDED
8 SQ. FT. ÷ 2.25 SQ.FT. = 4 PLANTS

SCALE
1 FOOT

8 SQ. FT.
DAYLILIES

16 SQ. FT.
GERANIUMS

WALD-STEINIA 2 SQ. FT.

VIOLETS 1 SQ. FT. WALD-STEINIA 2 SQ. FT.

VIOLETS 1 SQ. FT.

WALD-STEINIA 1 SQ. FT.

VIOLETS 1 SQ. FT.

WALD-STEINIA 2 SQ. FT.

VIOLETS 2 SQ. FT.

each plant. Round the result to the nearest whole number to find the number of plants you need. (In the daylily example, 8 square feet divided by 2.25 equals 3.55. Rounding to 4, this means you'll need four plants.)

Special Considerations and Challenging Situations

Exposure, temperature, soil, and water do not always combine in the way you wish they would. In addition, your garden space may be smaller or larger than you want. More often than not you are faced with one or more challenging garden situations that require special consideration. You can have a beautiful, healthy garden anywhere if you know how to turn liabilities into assets. Success depends on proper plant selection and placement. You can find plants for every spot, no matter how challenging. Match your plants

Figuring out how many plants you need is a simple process if you draw your garden plan to scale on graph paper. Follow the steps listed under "How Many Plants Do You Need?" on the opposite page to calculate the number of plants that will fit in your garden space.

→ · ←

GRASSES GROW WHERE WINDS BLOW

Wind is often considered an enemy to flower gardens since it dries out the soil and sucks moisture from leaves. Wayne Ambler of Ambler's Flower Farm in Ashland, Virginia, suggests using tall ornamental grasses on windy sites. Plant them on the west and/or north side of flower beds. In summer, they'll break the wind and protect your flowers from the hot afternoon sun. Grasses also serve as a backdrop for beds and borders to set off the plants growing in front of them.

In winter, grasses offer a thick and effective windbreak against which snow collects and stays, insulating the garden. Even the most fierce wind will not harm the grasses because their aboveground parts are already dry and dead. In the spring, use strong clippers or a weed whip to cut them to the ground.

→ · ←
---

to your site and you will have a bountiful, colorful, no-fail flower garden. Read on for creative solutions to small and large sites, and challenging growing conditions. And consult "Stop Dreaming and Face Reality" on page 50, Chapter 3, and "A Plant-by-Plant Guide to No-Fail Flowers" on page 340 for plants that thrive on difficult sites, from sun-baked clay to dry shade.

Work with the Natives

Native flowers, shrubs, and grasses growing in the woods, fields, and wetlands around your home can help you choose the right plants for your challenging garden spot. Take a look around and you'll find natives that thrive under the very conditions your yard offers. Choose a good field guide to help you identify your wild neighbors. Keep lists of the plants you like that grow on sites similar to yours. Then look at your yard with a critical eye. Was your house built in a wooded area? If so, were the trees preserved? If not, the best plants for your garden will be the ones growing in the fields. Construction alters sites so much that a once-wooded lot may soon resemble a wheat field. Be sure to match plants to the conditions as they are now, not as they once were. You'll find that native plants make tough and beautiful solutions to most problem sites. For sources, check the list of wildflower and native plant nurseries listed in "Sources" on page 358.

Small Sites

If you have a small garden, the challenge is to make the best use of the area you have. Since space is limited, you will have to limit your plant choices. Why not consider a theme garden? How about using only white and silver flowers, using only dwarf plants, putting foliage first, or planting only native plants?

Make every plant contribute as many of the following special features or design options to the garden as possible. **Look for good foliage, flowers, and fruit.** Why settle for a plant with nice flowers when you can have one with

Limited garden space means fewer plants, but there's no need to limit the beauty of your design. Try a garden based on two or three colors and a variety of textures. The white flowers of 'Album' showy autumn crocus (*Colchicum speciosum* 'Album') light up this small corner and set off the fine, gray foliage of *Artemisia canescens*, and the green and white leaves of licorice plant (*Helichrysum petiolare* 'Variegatum').

SURVIVING SALTY SITES

Many plants are sensitive to salt. It dries out roots, crisps leaves, and may even kill plants. Sea air and the spray from high-speed highways brings in salt that settles on leaves. Use a steady, forceful stream of water to wash off plants in spring before buds break and during the growing season.

Many plants are naturally adapted to high-salt areas. Try blanket flowers (*Gaillardia* spp.), common thrift (*Armeria maritima*), daylilies, and bigleaf hydrangea (*Hydrangea macrophylla*).

---

great foliage and fruits, too? Leaves and fruits come in a variety of textures and colors and will add seasons of interest to your flower garden.

Find fragrant flowers. Pleasing scents are particularly appreciated in a small garden. You're close enough to the flowers to notice even mild fragrances.

Maximize bloom with bulbs. Plant lots of bulbs for early-spring color that will be covered over by later-blooming plants.

Plant under shrubs and trees. Prune shrubs and small trees up so you can grow herbaceous plants beneath them and maximize your use of space. Use shrubs to fill in with bloom while flowers take a rest. Shrubs like orange-eye butterfly bushes (*Buddleia davidii*), roses, mock oranges (*Philadelphus* spp.), and azaleas (*Rhododendron* spp.) are perfect companions for annuals and perennials. Their com-

—→·←—

SHRUBS FOR ALL SEASONS

Flowering shrubs enhance gardens with much more than bright blooms. Here are a few reasons why Brenda Skarphol, horticulturist at Green Spring Gardens Park in Alexandria, Virginia, recommends planting them for year-round interest.

Winter. Bare branches provide a framework for the garden and a background for early bulbs. Try witch hazels (*Hamamelis* spp.) for blooms even in bitter cold.

Spring. New leaves, like the "praying hands" of oak-leaf hydrangeas (*Hydrangea quercifolia*), are as handsome as any flowers. Try native deciduous azaleas (*Rhododendron* spp.) for some of spring's earliest blooms.

Summer. Add spicy fragrance to sun or light shade with summersweet (*Clethra alnifolia*). Its cultivar 'Hummingbird' stays under 3 feet tall.

Fall. For showy fruits and foliage, shrubs with red fruit, like winterberry holly (*Ilex verticillata*), or red leaves, like sweetspire (*Itea virginica*), can't be beat.

—→·←—

pact growth, prolific flowers, and wide color ranges allow for varied and exciting combinations.

Use single specimens. You don't need to plant in drifts since you are so close to the plants. Single plants show up just fine.

Create unity with repetition. There's no need to use the same plant over and over again; instead, repeat the color, form, or texture to tie your planting design together.

Expand your space with flower pots. When you have filled every available space, try pots. A few flower pots on the terrace will allow you to grow seasonal plants that would take up too much valuable space in the ground.

Reach for the sky. Many small gardens are enclosed by walls or fences. Make use of the vertical space by growing vines or attaching hanging containers.

Large Sites

Large gardens present endless possibilities but pose many challenges. Wide open spaces can be intimidating. You may not know where or how to start turning a large space into a garden space. Try the following tips to get a grip on your site.

Divide and conquer with paths. Dividing a large space into smaller, more intimate areas is the first order of business. Use pathways to create smaller areas of interest and to turn your attention from one direction to another.

Flowering trees guide the way. You can also use trees to direct what you will or will not see. They're great for blocking unwanted views and creating interesting backdrops for flowers. Use flowering trees as a screen along your property line. Try airy serviceberries (*Amelanchier* spp.) to provide fluffy white flowers in spring, neat rounded foliage, edible blue-black berries in summer, and brilliant red-orange color in fall. Many other attractive small trees such as crab apples (*Malus* spp.), white fringe trees (*Chionanthus virginicus*), golden-rain trees (*Koelreuteria paniculata*), dogwoods (*Cornus* spp.), and magnolias (*Magnolia* spp.) offer variety in flower, foliage, or fruit.

Large garden sites can overwhelm your senses unless you find
ways to divide the space. Trees and shrubs create an enclosed,
intimate feeling in this sprawling hillside garden. A winding path
hides the view, so as you turn each corner, new vistas open up
and hold your interest.

Flowering shrubs and trees make a showy backdrop for flowers. Choose early bloomers like Carolina all-spice (*Calycanthus floridus*) and white fringe tree (*Chionanthus virginicus*) to brighten your garden in spring. Pick shrubs with long bloom seasons and attractive foliage, like St.-John's-wort (*Hypericum* spp.), to fill large garden spaces and add color when perennials are finished blooming.

Evergreens create a sense of privacy. Evergreen trees provide a consistent, year-round green backdrop and privacy screen for your garden. American arborvitaes (*Thuja occidentalis*), yews (*Taxus* spp.), junipers, and hollies are just a few of the trees available to gardeners. Evergreens add interest to the garden in winter and early spring, when flowers are absent or scarce.

Fill up the space with shrubs. Large gardens need lots of plants, but too many flowers can create a maintenance nightmare. Use plantings of shrubs for neat, low-maintenance fillers. A few shrubs planted in a mass can fill the same space as a dozen or more perennials.

Develop Large Gardens in Phases

If a lack of time or money keeps you from planting your garden all at once, develop it in phases. You can divide the work by plant type and size as described below, or by bloom times, as explained in "Divide Gardens into Easy-to-

Plant Pieces" on page 62. No matter which method you use, a step-by-step approach makes even the largest garden more manageable.

Plant trees and shrubs first to enclose garden spaces, establish views, or create a backdrop for flowers. Pick flowering shrubs such as hydrangeas, viburnums, lilacs, and spireas to contribute to the colorful display. For a more restful, static background, try evergreen plants such as hollies. Woody plants grow more slowly than flowers, so get them in first. Keep in mind your views to the larger garden, though, and don't block them with plantings.

Next, plant the trees and shrubs that form the edges of the garden. Build in from the outside edges with large trees, small flowering trees, and then shrubs. These larger plants divide the planting into smaller areas and create a sense of privacy and intimacy. As these plantings mature, add flowers and groundcover plantings in front of the shrubs. When time and budget permit, plant borders and beds to complete the garden. Use big drifts of plants and bold textures to make the garden stand out.

What If the Plants You Like Don't Like Your Site?

Dreams are the seeds from which gardens grow. We all have ideas about what kind of garden we want and what plants we wish to grow. When the time comes to reconcile dreams with realities, some disappointments are inevitable. You just can't grow everything. Sometimes you even find you can't grow the plants you want most. What's to be done? Get creative! Let's look at a specific example.

Turn a Shady Plight into a Perfect Garden Site

Suppose you want a sunny perennial border and you have mostly shade. What can you do? First off, think of ways to bring more light into your garden. Paint nearby walls with reflective colors and remove lower limbs from trees. If you have a tangled cluster of trees, consider removing a weak or misshapen one. Next, acquaint yourself with the many beautiful plants that thrive in a partially shaded situation. You won't be able to grow bearded irises,

---

NURSERY BEDS BEAT BUDGET WOES

Buying plants can be hard on the wallet. One way to increase your supply of plants inexpensively is to build a nursery bed. Here's how.

1. Select a site that gets afternoon shade and is near a water source. If you don't have shade, stretch wood lath, shade cloth, or fine window screening over the bed to shield plants from the sun and heavy rains.

2. Prepare the soil by digging to at least a spade's depth and amending with plenty of compost. Or build a raised bed with landscape timbers and fill with amended soil.

3. Mulch to control weeds.

4. Buy or ask friends for plants of easy-to-propagate perennials like daylilies, hostas, and groundcovers.

5. Set the plants in the bed and divide them regularly to fill your garden. See "Multiplying by Division" on page 254 for division tips.

6. You can also use your nursery bed for growing seedlings until they are big enough for the garden.

Sunny sites offer lots of flower options, but shady sites have their own rewards. Foliage plants and shade-loving perennials can compete with the brightest perennial border when it comes to texture and color combinations. It's hard to find a more inviting sight than this planting of feathery ostrich ferns (*Matteuccia struthiopteris*) and colorful Japanese primroses (*Primula japonica*).

but you can grow Siberian irises (*Iris sibirica*), roof irises (*I. tectorum*), and crested irises (*I. cristata*).

Many shade and woodland plants bloom in the spring, leaving summer to the foliage. Make the best of leaves. They come in all colors, sizes, shapes, and textures. A carefully planned foliage garden can have a dramatic impact without the need for flowers. Use bold leaves as focal points, brightly colored leaves for dramatic effect, silver and variegated leaves to brighten a dull spot, and fine-textured leaves such as ferns for the background. Foliage gardening is fun and rewarding. Spring flowers are a bonus that almost seems of secondary importance.

Another way to enliven the shade garden is to plant summer-blooming perennials. Bloom in the woodland garden need not end in spring. There are many plants that flower in the summer, and some are quite dramatic. The tall candelabra spikes of black snakeroot (*Cimicifuga racemosa*) are dramatic swaying above the neat foliage clumps in May and June. Other species of snakeroot bloom in autumn, such as *Cimicifuga simplex* var. *ramosa* 'Atropurpurea', which produces delightfully scented flowers. Hostas are another group with good summer flowers. The fragrant white bells of August lily (*Hosta plantaginea*) are particularly handsome. Choose great blue lobelia (*Lobelia siphilitica*) for its tall spikes of true-blue summer flowers or its cousin, cardinal flower (*Lobelia cardinalis*), if you want red flowers.

If you have light shade, some of the old-fashioned daylilies will bloom well. Choose tawny daylily (*Hemerocallis fulva*) and hybrid cultivars such as 'Hyperion' (*Hemerocallis* × *hybrida* 'Hyperion'). With a little sun, fringed bleeding heart (*Dicentra eximia*) will produce mounds of pink or white flowers all summer. Bellflowers (*Campanula* spp.), astilbes, and lilies all extend the blooming season well into summer. Toad lilies (*Tricyrtis* spp.) bloom from late summer through frost to finish off the season.

You can always add annuals! Impatiens, flowering tobacco (*Nicotiana alata*), wish-bone flower (*Torenia fournieri*), begonias, and Madagascar periwinkle (*Catharanthus rosus*)

CAN PRUNING SOLVE YOUR PROBLEM?

Trees and shrubs can grace gardens with flowers and shade or choke them with dense growth. If thick growth is stifling your flowers, check the list of solutions below.

Remove low tree limbs. It's hard to grow flowers beneath large trees that branch low to the ground. Consider removing a few of the lowest limbs. You and your flowers will be amazed at how much light comes in.

Restart big shrubs. Do you have huge, healthy shrubs such as spireas and lilacs that overpower your flowers? Chop them to the ground in early spring to renew their growth. They'll use the energy stored in their roots to bounce back with fresh growth.

Thin branches for better flower health. When small multi-stemmed trees and flowering shrubs grow into tangled masses of branches, nearby flowers suffer. Increase air circulation and light by thinning the stems. Choose the best three to five stems for trees and five to seven for shrubs. Remove the rest of them at ground level.

—➤·➤·—

FLOWER-FRIENDLY TREES

Before you add trees to your garden, make sure your flowers will grow with them. Phil Normandy, curator of Brookside Gardens in Wheaton, Maryland, suggests small, fine-textured trees that cast only light shade. Some of Phil's favorites are sweet bays (*Magnolia virginiana*), 'Okame' cherries (*Prunus 'Okame'*), Sargent crab apples (*Malus sargentii*), serviceberries (*Amelanchier* spp.), and crape myrtle (*Lagerstroemia indica*).

—➤·➤·—

all bloom tirelessly until frost cuts them down. So the shade garden need not be a second choice to a billowing border but can instead be a prized garden of delightful flowers, foliage, and fruits.

Design Time Is a Fine Time

No matter what challenges you face in your new or existing garden site, a good design is your recipe for success. Chapter 5 offers 16 foolproof garden designs to inspire you if you haven't already come up with a plan. Design is the most exciting part of creating a garden, so there's no need to rush it. Out of your imagination will spring a garden of earthly delights if you plan ahead and match your plants to your site. Once the planning is done, you can head outside and prepare your site. Before you do, look over Part 2, "No-Fail Flower Gardening Techniques." It has all the details you'll need for digging in the dirt.

A large, shady site won't eat up all your time or money if you develop it in stages. Fill in gaps with bright but inexpensive annuals, like the variegated coleus shown here, until you're ready to add perennials and groundcovers.

CHAPTER 5

A Gallery of Easy Garden Designs

Garden daydreaming is a pleasant diversion in mid-winter, when the only thing growing is the size of the heating bill. We can close our eyes and remember the beauty of last year's garden, or hungrily eye the technicolor catalog pictures of plants we'd like to grow.

Daydreaming eventually organizes itself into bona fide planning for the season to come. You'll begin making garden sketches and looking for combinations or garden themes to try.

This chapter presents 16 gardens designed by professional horticulturists and garden writers. Each designer limited the number of plants he or she used so that the gardens would be easy and affordable. On your daydreaming days, you'll enjoy browsing through the garden descriptions and watercolor views. Once you switch to planning mode, focus on the planting plans and plant lists to find ideas that you can try in your own garden.

With each of these gardens, you have the choice of planting the design exactly as presented or else adapting all or part of it to suit your needs. Look in the garden descriptions for suggestions on how to adapt the garden for larger or smaller sites.

➡ · ⬅

NO-FAIL FEATURES

Refreshing Simplicity. This color-themed flower garden blends shades of a single bloom color and provides interest by changing the predominant shade from season to season. Pink spring flowers, followed by blues and greens in summer and white in the fall, provide a pleasing feature for gardeners who prefer simple, classic design.

Casual Charm. The corner of a fence is an abrupt cut in a landscape. This casual mix of plant heights and groupings masks the fence and creates a softer edge and a more relaxed feel to the yard.

Grows in Shade or Sun. This planting will work for a sunny or shady corner. The plants chosen can all tolerate light shade. And the design allows for planting in full sun, as tall plants on the south side of the garden will protect shade-loving plants from the full heat of afternoon sun.

➡ · ⬅

A Color Theme Garden

Picket fences have charm, but a white fence and green grass alone make for a monotonous view. Highlight a fence by adding a corner perennial bed. This design by Nancy Ondra uses color as its theme and offers an element of surprise—the color theme changes with the season!

In spring, the theme is a warm, rosy pink, as deep pink heartleaf bergenia and rose-colored fringed bleeding heart blooms appear. The pink flowers of spotted lamium carpet the front of the bed.

Early summer brings cool blue and lavender colors. Willow blue star's icy blue flowers, the puffy violet-blue buds of balloon flower, and the lavender-blue of 'Johnson's Blue' cranesbill call attention to the center of the bed. The large, glossy leaves of 'Royal Standard' hosta add soothing green to the scene.

In fall, when many flower gardens are winding down for the winter, this flower border is painted anew with the white blooms of the boltonia 'Snowbank' and Japanese anemone, highlighted by bright yellow leaves of the blue star and balloon flower. The foliage of the bergenia and hosta takes on added richness in the cool autumn air, adding to the change in color in this chameleon garden.

This garden is a mix of sun- and shade-loving plants. The shade lovers—bleeding heart, hosta, and lamium—are grouped along the right-hand side of the garden, as pictured on the opposite page. One way to ensure that these plants are protected from afternoon sun is to orient the garden with the heat haters to the north side. The tall blue star and boltonia will cast shade on the northern side in the afternoon. Siting the garden under a tree will also provide shade. In warmer climates, all the plants in this design would benefit from light shade. If there's no existing tree, a good choice to plant is sourwood, a hardy and beautiful tree native to the eastern and southeastern United States. The addition of its white flowers, cream-colored fruit capsules, and brilliant red fall foliage will bring another highlight to the theme garden.

Use color to unify the plants in perennial beds. The blue blossoms of willow blue star, balloon flower, and cranesbill blend beautifully during the summer. An added feature of this design is the way the color theme changes with the season: White boltonia, hosta, and Japanese anemone blooms dominate in fall as blue flowers fade, and pink blooms appear in spring.

—❧ · ❧—

BLOOMING IN TANDEM

To make a color theme garden work, you need plants that bloom at the same time. Don't rely on books or plant labels for this information. Instead, find out when various species and cultivars actually bloom in your area. Do some research! Take pencil and paper along so you can note dates and ranges of time that different plants are in flower.

Check out neighboring gardens. If the daylilies in your neighbor's yard are in full bloom every Fourth of July, you can bet the same cultivar would bloom with a bang on the Fourth in your yard, too.

Visit local public parks. Many parks have name tags on their plants. Ask a caretaker to identify any unmarked plants.

Check nursery display gardens. Nurseries often have container-grown plants shipped in or sell blooming plants that have been greenhouse forced. But the plants in demonstration gardens probably have been growing on the property for several seasons.

—❧ · ❧—

Creating a Color Theme Garden

All of these perennials thrive in Zones 4 through 8, except for the anemone, which is hardy only from Zones 5 through 8.

The plants in this design grow best in average soil with plenty of organic matter. When you plant, leave 12 to 18 inches between the fence and the plants that abut it, so you'll have room to get at plants for maintenance chores. For directions on planting perennials, see "Problem-Free Planting" on page 271.

Every year, spread a 1- to 2-inch layer of organic mulch such as bark chips or compost; this will conserve moisture as well as discourage weeds. Irrigate during summer dry spells.

Plants for a Color Theme Garden

Balloon flower (*Platycodon grandiflorus*): Perennial, 2 to 3 feet tall. Toothed, oval leaves. In mid- to late summer, globe-shaped blue flower buds appear that open to form a cupped, five-pointed star. Space 3 feet apart. Plant is slow to emerge; mark location of plants in fall to avoid damaging roots in spring.

Boltonia (*Boltonia asteroides* 'Snowbank'): Perennial, 4 to 5 feet tall and 2 to 3 feet wide. Blue-green leaves; white, daisylike flowers bloom from late summer into fall. Space 3 feet apart. In early summer, cut back foliage by about 4 inches to encourage bushy growth.

Cranesbill (*Geranium* × 'Johnson's Blue'): Perennial, 1 to 2 feet tall. Mounded growth habit and 2-inch-wide blue flowers that bloom all summer. Space 2 feet apart. Trim plants to ground level after blooming to encourage flush of new leaves in late summer.

Fringed bleeding heart (*Dicentra eximia*): Perennial, 1 to 2 feet tall. Delicate ferny foliage; pendulant, heart-shaped pink blooms in spring. Space 1 foot apart. Cut back foliage if it yellows in summer heat.

Heartleaf bergenia (*Bergenia cordifolia* 'Perfecta'): Perennial, 1½ feet tall. Large, round leaves that turn from green to bronze in winter; pink flowers borne on stiff stems in spring. Space 2 feet apart.

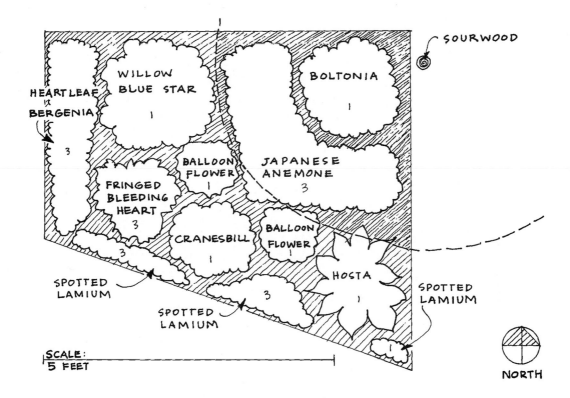

Hosta (*Hosta* 'Royal Standard'): Perennial, 2 feet tall. Large, handsome blue-green leaves; spikes of fragrant white flowers in late summer. Space 3 feet apart.

Japanese anemone (*Anemone* × *hybrida* 'Honorine Jobert'): Perennial, 3 feet tall. Dark green, lobed leaves. Yellow-centered white flowers appear from late summer into fall. Space 2 feet apart.

Sourwood (*Oxydendrum arboreum*): Deciduous tree, 25 to 30 feet tall with a 20-foot spread. Dark green leaves turn bright red to purple in fall; white, fragrant flowers in summer, with cream-colored fruit capsules in fall.

Spotted lamium (*Lamium maculatum* 'Beacon Silver'): Perennial, 6 to 12 inches tall. Silver green foliage; rose-pink flowers in spring. Space 2 feet apart. Trim back growth that overgrows other plants.

Willow blue star (*Amsonia tabernaemontana*): Perennial, to 3 feet tall and 2 feet wide. Light blue flowers in early summer; lance-shaped leaves turn bright yellow in fall. Space 3 feet apart.

➡ · ⬅

NO-FAIL FEATURES

Spectacular Fall Color. Brilliant purple asters are the focal point in fall, complemented by the yellow of dwarf goldenrod. Oxeye daisies add white clouds of blooms, and sedum contributes red and rust.

Early Spring Color. You'll know winter has ended when this garden bursts out in cheerful color. Siberian iris and blue star fill the bed with blues. Adam's-needle leaves and phlomis flowers add a touch of yellow against contrasting shades of green foliage.

Plants That Handle the Heat. In hot-summer areas, even dedicated gardeners would rather avoid working outdoors. This garden is drought-tolerant and can thrive without any special care in hot weather.

➡ · ⬅

A Garden for Spring and Fall

Hot midsummer days are great for vacations, picnics, and playing at your local pool or park. They're not the time to be worrying about garden maintenance. With this garden, your summer days will be free for fun, and you'll enjoy breathtaking color during the spring and fall bloom seasons.

In the spring, the garden comes to life early with a blue and yellow color scheme. During the quiet summer months, there are plenty of great foliage textures that provide seasonal interest but don't require any time investment for deadheading. Plus, all the plants in this garden are drought-tolerant. Once established, this garden can easily survive a couple of weeks of neglect—good news for gardeners off for weekend jaunts or a full-fledged vacation.

The fall colors in this bed go beyond the usual rust and yellow color scheme, as shown on the opposite page. Don't be alarmed by the presence of dwarf goldenrod in the garden. Contrary to popular belief, goldenrod pollen is not the cause of hayfever—it's the yellow flowers of ragweed that make many of us sniffle and sneeze.

Adapt the garden for a smaller space by using only the spring- or fall-blooming plants. For example, you could create a small spring garden by combining the cushion spurge, oxeye daisies, Siberian iris, and columbine. For a fall garden, choose the New England aster, dwarf goldenrod, sedum, and Adam's-needle.

For a larger garden, designer Edith Eddleman suggests duplicating this plan end to end. She also points out that you can play with the shape of this design. For example, try creating a curving sweep to the corners for a more casual look. For more formality, add a stepping stone pathway through the middle. The pathway could lead to a garden focal point in the center of the bed, such as a wishing well or sundial. Or it could invite visitors to a bench where they could appreciate the spring sunshine and enjoy the rich colors on a crisp autumn day.

Crisp white oxeye daisies set off the intense purple flowers of 'Purple Dome' New England aster as fall arrives in this garden. Warm yellows fill the bed when the foliage of the willow blue star turns in autumn and brings out the golden color of the Adam's-needle leaves and dwarf goldenrod blooms. Sedum 'Autumn Joy' adds a rusty rose to the composition.

ADDING A FOCAL POINT

A focal point is a plant or object in a flower garden that attracts attention and acts as a centerpiece. Choose the right one and you can add year-round interest without any extra maintenance. Garden centers are full of beautiful and traditional birdbaths, sundials, and benches, but the frugal gardener can improvise and come up with imaginative and inexpensive garden focal points. Consider these options if you have a limited budget, or as temporary stand-ins until you find that perfect piece of garden artwork.

• A rusty antique plow: Surround it with some low-growing flowers such as alyssum.

• An old metal milk can: Paint it or use it as a container garden.

• A cast-off metal headboard or footboard of a bed: Turn it into a garden gate or arbor.

• A wooden post: Nail a collection of bird houses to it.

• A mailbox: Paint or decorate it and use it to hold gloves, a hand trowel, and seed packets.

Creating a Garden for Spring and Fall

These plants thrive in Zones 4 through 8. All like full sun and grow best if watered deeply once a week. They can tolerate less watering once established.

For directions on planting perennials, see "Problem-Free Planting" on page 271. Keep the bed well weeded during the first year after planting.

In the fall, cut foliage to the ground after it dies back. Apply compost around the plants each fall to maintain soil fertility. In areas where the soil freezes during the winter, cover the plants with a mulch of shredded leaves or pine needles after the soil has frozen.

Plants for a Garden for Spring and Fall

Adam's-needle (*Yucca filamentosa* 'Golden Sword'): Evergreen perennial. Stiff yellow and green swordlike leaves 2½ feet long; flowerstalks reach 5 feet and are covered with white, bell-shaped blooms in spring. Space 3 feet apart.

Columbine (*Aquilegia vulgaris* 'Hensol Harebell'): Perennial, 2 feet tall. Lacy foliage and deep blue nodding flowers in spring. Space 1 foot apart. Plants self-sow, but seedlings will not come true; pull them out as they appear.

Cushion spurge (*Euphorbia epithymoides*): Perennial, 2 feet tall. Chartreuse bracts in early spring; red and orange leaves in fall. Space 1 foot apart.

Dwarf goldenrod (*Solidagao sphacelata*): Perennial, 18 inches tall. Heart-shaped green leaves; golden flowers in the fall. Space 1 foot apart.

New England aster (*Aster novae-angliae* 'Purple Dome'): Perennial, 2 to 3 feet tall. Deep purple mounds of blooms in fall. Space 2 feet apart. Shear lightly in early summer. Stake tall or floppy plants in early autumn.

Oxeye daisy (*Chrysanthemum leucanthemum* 'May Queen'): Perennial, 2 feet tall. Deeply toothed foliage topped by daisylike white flowers. Space 1 foot apart. Cut back in early summer after first flush of blooms. Plants will continue flowering as long as spent blossoms are removed.

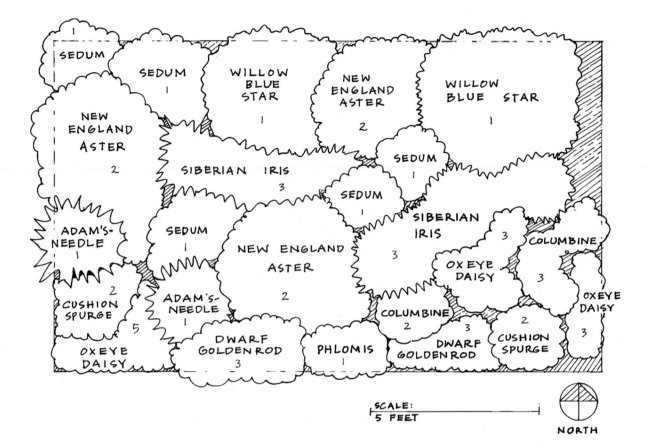

Phlomis (*Phlomis russeliana*): Perennial, 2 to 3 feet tall. Bold olive green leaves and whorls of soft yellow spring flowers. Space 3 feet apart.

Sedum (*Sedum* 'Autumn Joy'): Perennial, 2 feet tall. Thick stems and rounded, waxy leaves. Pink flowers in late summer turn deep rose and then bronze in late fall. Leave dried seed heads on plants for winter interest.

Siberian iris (*Iris sibirica* 'Sky Wings'): Perennial, 2 to 3 feet tall. Grassy leaves with sky blue flowers in spring. Space 2 feet apart.

Willow blue star (*Amsonia tabernaemontana*): Perennial, to 3 feet tall and 2 feet wide. Light blue flowers in early summer; lance-shaped leaves turn bright yellow in fall. Space 3 feet apart.

———————— ➪·← ————————

NO-FAIL FEATURES

Lovely Flowers in Lousy Soil. You can have a no-fail flower garden even if the ground has never been worked or is compacted and infertile.

A Simple Soil Fix. Making good soil from poor soil can mean heavy-duty digging to break up soil and work in amendments. By mulching and by spreading the work over three years, the task of improving soil becomes a low-input, more passive process.

Three Seasons of Color. Annual flowers appear in vivid shades of pink, red, purple, and white all summer. Over time, they're replaced with perennials for a glowing display of yellow, gold, and purple from spring until late fall.

Flowers for Arranging. Globe amaranth 'Buddy', 'East Friesland' sage, artemisia foliage, and seedpods of Missouri primrose make wonderful additions to dried flower arrangements. All of the annual flowers have a long vase life. You can also use many of the perennials for fresh indoor bouquets.

———————— ➪·← ————————

A Mulch-and-Grow Garden

Does your garden site looks like a weed patch, or a barren moonscape? Bring it back to life with a thick layer of mulch and annual flowers. You'll discover that conscientious mulching with compost and straw can revive compacted, unhealthy soil in two or three years.

Soil packed down by heavy foot or vehicle traffic doesn't have the network of tiny spaces, called pores, that hold air and water. Compacted soil also may be low in organic matter. As discussed in "Improving Your Soil" on page 261, if you try starting a flower bed in poor soil like this, you'll probably end up with a poor garden.

Designer Joan Benjamin's plan for a mulch-and-grow garden lets you restore soil fertility and grow flowers at the same time. Her design calls for a three-year phase-in of the garden. It begins as an annual garden, with flowers growing in a layer of compost on top of the poor soil. As compost and a mulch cover, heal, and feed the soil, the garden shifts to a mix of perennials and annuals, and finally to all perennials. If your soil is extremely compacted, mulch and grow annuals for two or three growing seasons before adding perennials.

For fast color the first season, try "planting" pots of spreading annuals such as petunias and vinca in the bed, pot and all. Buy six-packs of annuals, and pot them up in 6- or 8-inch pots (put two or three plants in each pot). Tuck the flower pots in the mulch throughout the garden so the pots are hidden. Cover the straw mulch with bark chips for a finished look. Remember to check the moisture content of the soil in the pots frequently, and water whenever the top inch feels dry. In the fall, remove the pots and lay down more straw or hay mulch.

If you'd like to mulch-and-grow a bed that's a different shape, just remember this simple principle: taller plants to the back, shorter ones in front.

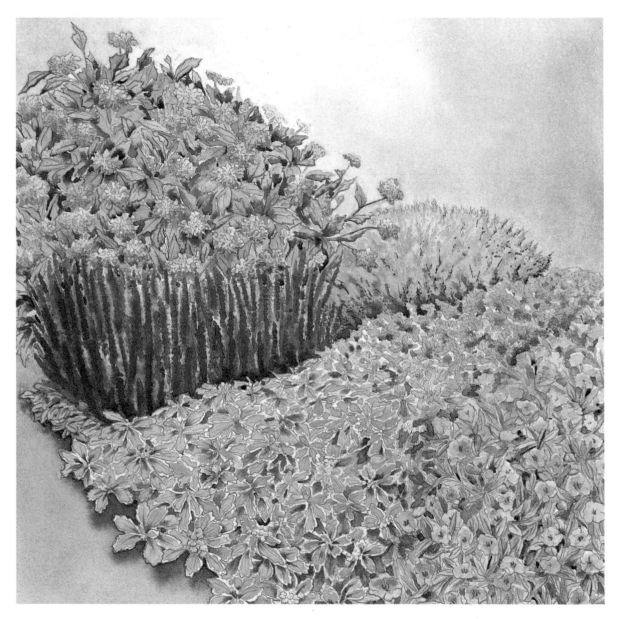

Two years of mulch, compost, and vigorous annuals can work wonders on even the most infertile site. In its third year, with soil fertility and good drainage restored, this garden welcomes a variety of showy perennials like shining coneflower, 'East Friesland' sage, artemisia, and Missouri primrose.

→ · ←

CREATING GREAT SOIL

The secret to changing a wasteland into a floral wonderland is to start with the soil. And the first step in improving garden soil is to get the soil surface covered. Spread your future garden site with a 10-inch layer of organic mulch. You can use straw or spoiled hay, mixing in leaves or grass clippings if you have them.

After laying the mulch, add some earthworms to hurry the improvement process along. Dig worms from a nearby site with good soil, and tuck groups of four to eight earthworms under the mulch in two or three places. Moisten the mulch lightly if it's dry.

If your site has grass or weeds growing on it, first cover the area with thick cardboard or several sections of newspaper. Then layer the straw or hay on top. The cardboard or paper barrier will block and eventually smother out the weeds. By the following year, it will have broken down sufficiently that you can plant right through it.

Creating a Mulch-and-Grow Garden

This is a garden for a sunny site in Zones 4 through 7. Gold-and-silver chrysanthemum needs winter protection in Zone 4. You'll need to get a head start on soil improvement by mulching the season before you plant your troubled site. See "Creating Great Soil" on this page for more information.

Year 1: In the spring, spread a layer of compost 2 to 3 inches thick over the straw mulch covering your garden site. As the season progresses, plant cleome, cosmos, and globe amaranth seeds in the compost. The annual flowers will bloom from summer until frost. Collect cosmos seeds when they dry in late summer or fall. After frost, remove and compost the plants. Move the mulch aside and plant daffodil bulbs before a hard freeze. Then cover the entire garden with 3 to 4 more inches of mulch.

Year 2: In the spring, plant cosmos seed saved from last fall, and set out shining coneflower and artemisia plants. For instructions on planting perennials, see "Problem-Free Planting" on page 271. Move mulch aside for planting, then pull it back close to plants to discourage weeds. Remove and compost the cosmos after frost; cut back perennials if they look ratty, or leave them for winter interest.

Year 3: In the spring, after danger of frost is past, plant out salvia, Missouri primrose, and gold-and-silver chrysanthemum plants. Keep spent flowers cut for summer-long show. After a frost, cut most plant stems back to 4 or 5 inches; leave those like artemisia that have winter interest.

Plants for a Mulch-and-Grow Garden

Artemisia (*Artemisia ludoviciana* 'Silver King'): Perennial, 2 to 3 feet tall. Silvery foliage is showy from spring through winter. Space 2 feet apart.

Cleome (*Cleome hasslerana* 'Ruby Queen'): Annual, 3 to 4 feet tall. Airy pink flowers from summer until frost; bean-like seedpods in fall; strong herbal fragrance. Space 2 feet apart. Plant seeds in cool soil in early spring.

Cosmos (*Cosmos bipinnatus* 'Early Wonder'): Annual, to 3½ feet. Pink, red, and white daisylike flowers, fine foliage. Space 8 to 10 inches apart. Plant seeds when danger of frost is past.

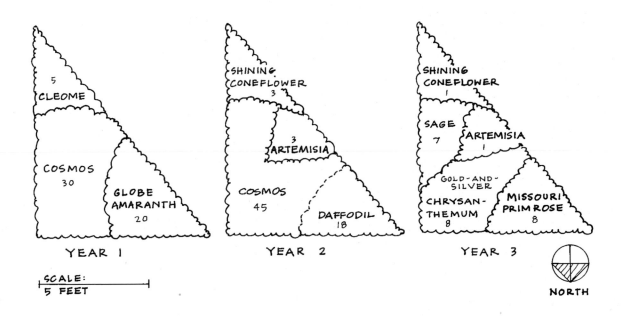

CLEOME 5

COSMOS 30

GLOBE AMARANTH 20

YEAR 1

SHINING CONEFLOWER 3

ARTEMISIA 3

COSMOS 45

DAFFODIL 18

YEAR 2

SHINING CONEFLOWER 1

SAGE 7

ARTEMISIA 1

GOLD-AND-SILVER CHRYSANTHEMUM 8

MISSOURI PRIMROSE 8

YEAR 3

SCALE: 5 FEET

NORTH

Daffodils (*Narcissus* spp.): Bulb. Straplike foliage. Yellow, white, and orange spring-blooming cultivars. Plant bulbs in fall. Space 6 to 8 inches apart.

Globe amaranth (*Gomphrena globosa* 'Buddy'): Annual, 8 to 10 inches tall. Purple cloverlike blooms in summer and fall. Space 8 to 10 inches apart. Plant seeds in warm soil after danger of frost is past.

Gold-and-silver chrysanthemum (*Chrysanthemum pacificum*): Perennial, to 1 foot tall. Green leaves edged with white; yellow flowers in late fall. Space 1 foot apart.

Missouri primrose (*Oenothera missouriensis*): Perennial, to 1 foot tall. Trailing plant with lemon-yellow flowers in summer; winged seedpods. Space 1 foot apart. Also known as Ozark sundrops.

Shining coneflower (*Rudbeckia nitida* 'Goldquelle'): Annual, to 3 feet tall. Double yellow flowers in summer; bright green foliage. Space 1½ to 2 feet apart.

Sage (*Salvia × superba* 'East Friesland'): Perennial, 1 to 1½ feet tall. Purple-blue spikes bloom in summer on stiff, clump-forming plants. Space 1 to 1½ feet apart.

NO-FAIL FEATURES

No More Mowing. This design mixes low-maintenance shrubs, trees, and perennials to put an end to difficult mowing chores.

No More Washouts. These tough plants have vigorous spreading roots that anchor soil, or creeping foliage that protects soil from the impact of heavy rains and runoff. They're drought-tolerant and rarely need supplemental watering, so there's also no worry about runoff from sprinklers or hand-watering.

Steps for Easy Care. Wooden or stone steps make it easier to reach plants for occasional weeding and pruning. The steps also break up the steep face of the slope and invite visitors to walk through the garden.

Pinks and Purples. The dominant pink and purple color scheme is punctuated with the gleam of orange daylilies to make a unique and delightful feature out of a "garden trouble spot." Evergreen plants with colorful berries and rose hips lend four-season interest.

A Garden for a Sunny Slope

Pushing and pulling a lawnmower across a rough slope can provoke muttered curses from the most temperate gardener. If you're among those who struggle to maintain a grass-covered bank, you'll love this design. It will turn that difficult-to-maintain slope into a low-maintenance, colorful planting. The plants are all tough survivors that can succeed despite the dry and infertile conditions often found on sloping sites. Some have strong, spreading root systems that hold soil in place, while others put out creeping runners that provide a dense cover of leaves that prevents runoff and erosion. This planting is generally drought-tolerant, a desirable feature for a site where watering can be an unpleasant chore and can worsen erosion problems.

Designer Marianne Binetti chose purple, gray, and pink to dominate the summer color scheme. The tones are set by the foliage of the purple smoke tree and the gray leaves and hot pink flowers of rose campion. Wooden stairs or stepping stones allow you to take a cool stroll through your sloping garden, instead of a sweaty climb. They also provide access for the occasional chores of weeding, pruning, or dividing needed to keep this garden at its best. For tips on building a path along your slope, see "Steps and Stones" on page 226.

Adapt this design to suit your site. If you have a very long slope, you may want to repeat elements of the design. For example, you could plant additional bearberries and perennials to the right of the rugosa rose. For a small site, just pick one section of the design to plant. On a small site, you can keep the purple smoke tree in proportion by cutting it to the ground each year in late winter. If you do, it will grow as a shrub. The new growth will be deep purple, but the plant will not produce any showy plumes, because it blooms only on three-year-old wood. If you have a gentle slope, you can put in a mulched trail with a switchback instead of building in steps.

Why struggle with a difficult-to-mow slope when you can turn it into a colorful, low-maintenance garden that's attractive year-round? Purple smoke tree and bearberry are tough, drought-tolerant survivors that thrive even in the hot, dry conditions on a sunny slope. Rose campion enjoys a protected niche behind a rock outcropping in the shade of the smoke tree.

———— ⇢·⇠ ————

PLANTING POCKETS

Here's how to create a planting pocket on a steep slope:

1. Dig a shovel or two of earth from the planting site, piling the excavated earth just downhill from the hole it came out of. This forms a miniature terrace.
2. Stabilize this terrace with a rock. Scoop away some soil, and place the rock with its exposed face slanting outward so that rainwater can flow down into the pocket. Then replace the soil so that at least half of the rock is buried.
3. Sculpt the terrace so that it slopes slightly down into the hillside.
4. Dig a planting hole straight down into the terrace.

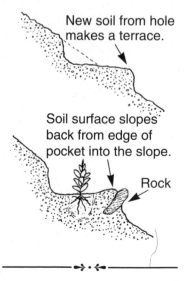

New soil from hole makes a terrace.

Soil surface slopes back from edge of pocket into the slope.

Rock

———— ⇢·⇠ ————

Creating a Garden for a Sunny Slope

These hardy plants thrive in Zones 5 through 8 and request only good drainage and four or more hours of sun per day. While they all tolerate infertile soil, it's important to clear weeds or sod from the planting site before you plant. Refer to "Clearing Your Site" on page 260. Also refer to the illustration on page 275 for instructions on planting the purple smoke tree and rugosa rose. If your soil is very sandy, add compost to areas where you'll plant perennials to get the best bloom.

The flowering perennials have higher water requirements than the other plants in this garden and can be prone to washing out. Plant them in planting pockets, which will trap water and direct it to the plants, and also provide a protective cradle for the plants until they become firmly rooted. See "Planting Pockets" on this page for instructions.

Plants for a Sunny Slope

Bearberry (*Arctostaphylos uva-ursi*): Broad-leaved evergreen groundcover, spreads to 15 feet. Small, white to light pink, urn-shaped flowers appear in spring; red berries cling through the winter. Space plants 3 feet apart. Cut back growth that overtakes neighboring plants.

Candytuft (*Iberis sempervirens*): Perennial, 1 foot tall and wide. Narrow, dark green, evergreen leaves; white flowers in spring. Space 10 to 12 inches apart. Shear off one-third of the plant after bloom.

Crocuses (*Crocus* spp.): Corm, grows 4 to 6 inches tall. Purple, yellow, or white flowers appear in early spring. Plant 3 inches apart in fall. Allow grassy foliage to yellow after flowering; pull it out after it has dried.

Kaufmanniana tulip (*Tulipa kaufmanniana*): Bulb, grows 6 to 9 inches tall. Leaves are mottled purple; starlike flowers in white, salmon, and red appear in early spring. Plant 6 inches apart in fall. Leave foliage to yellow after flowering; pull it out after it has dried.

Moss pink (*Phlox subulata*): Perennial, 6 inches tall and 2 feet wide. Semi-evergreen, needle-like leaves. Pink, white, or lavender blooms in spring. Space 1 foot apart. Shear off one-third of the plant after bloom.

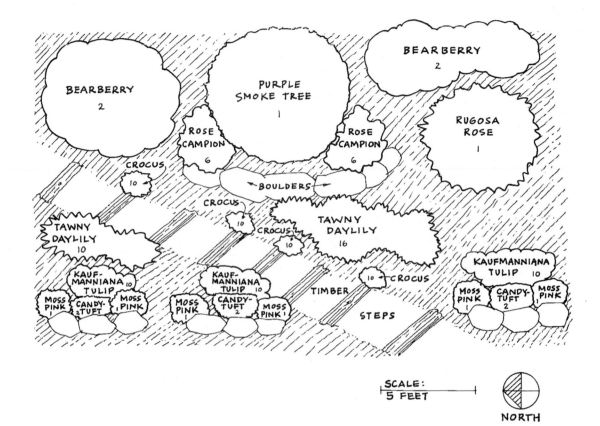

Purple smoke tree (*Cotinus coggygria* 'Royal Purple'): Deciduous shrub or tree, 15 feet tall and wide. Has rounded purple leaves; purplish green plumes appear in summer and last into the fall. Plant 10 feet apart.

Rose campion (*Lychnis coronaria*): Perennial, 2 feet tall, 1½ feet wide. Forms a rosette of silvery gray leaves, with hot pink blossoms appearing on branched stems in spring. Space 1 foot apart. Tends to reseed.

Rugosa rose (*Rosa rugosa* 'Alba' or 'Rubra'): Decidous shrub, 6 feet tall and 8 feet wide. Single, old-fashioned white or red flowers appear in June and are followed by large, bright red rose hips that last through the winter. Space 5 feet apart. Prune as needed to remove dead wood.

Tawny daylily (*Hemerocallis fulva*): Perennial. In late spring to early summer, bloom stalks reach to 3 or 4 feet above 2½-foot, straplike leaves. Space 1 foot apart. Divide clumps after four to six years.

ROCK OUTCROPPINGS

To imitate the look of a natural rock outcropping, use two or three large boulders emerging from the hillside with smaller rocks off to the sides. Try to position the small rocks so they look as if they broke away naturally from the main outcropping. For the most natural look, don't mix different types of stone in a group.

NO-FAIL FEATURES

Low-Maintenance Color. These densely planted prairie gardens are designed so that their root systems will crowd out unwanted weeds. Once established, these gardens require no additional irrigation or fertilizing.

A Mini Wildlife Refuge. Some of the native wildflowers that butterflies and birds depend on are becoming increasingly difficult for these creatures to find as our wildlands vanish. Winter-feeding birds and a wide variety of butterflies will soon discover these treasured plants in your prairie garden.

Surprising Changes. Prairie gardens evolve and change from day to day and month to month. In a few years the color and placement of the plants will be new, fresh, and totally different from what you planted. Mother Nature is your partner in designing these gardens, as seeds are blown about by the wind and carried by the wildlife and as unseen spreading root systems lead plants to new places in the garden.

Two Native Prairie Gardens

Lawns seem like the all-American landscape feature, but in many parts of North America, prairies and meadows of native wildflowers are the true native landscape. Our native prairies and meadows are naturally diverse plant communities composed of wildflowers and grasses. Converting part of your lawn to a small natural prairie garden is an exciting project that will make your home landscape more colorful and diverse and will reduce the time and trouble of lawn maintenance.

Controlled chaos is the best way to describe a prairie garden. To create one, you'll scatter the plants throughout the garden in a random fashion, just as they might occur in nature. Some are grouped together to provide a sense of unity, but generally the wild feeling is kept intact. When possible, plants with dense, fibrous roots are planted beside flowers with deep taproots. Together they fill the available root space and squeeze out weeds.

Native wildflower gardens are dynamic entities that defy the status quo. They change throughout the seasons in a constant parade of color, and they vary from year to year depending upon growing conditions. Don't expect these plants to stay put! They will seed into one another and move around over time. The garden gradually evolves as the plants respond to the specific conditions of each site. Some will thrive and spread, and others will bloom once and never return, as you observe a real-life struggle of survival of the fittest in your own hand-planted prairie.

Designer Neil Diboll has created two plans for prairie gardens: one for dry soil and one for average soil. You'll find the planting plan for the dry garden on page 163; the planting plan for the garden for average soil is on page 165. Notice that the shapes of these two plans differ. One is a rectangle, the other is a sweeping arc. You can also create a crescent-shaped bed. To adapt either plan to a different bed shape, make an outline of the shape you want, then draw the plants on the new plan, keeping them in the same parallel rows.

Soft pastel and rich jewel colors flow effortlessly into one another in a garden of native prairie wildflowers. Although prairie gardens work well on flat sites, they adapt well to slopes like this one, too. Orange butterfly weed blossoms mingle with purple prairie clover and cheerful black and orange black-eyed Susans.

⇢·⇠

THE PRAIRIE LOOK

Prairie gardens offer a fascinating jumble of colors and textures that change with the seasons. As fall progresses and the prairie plants dry out and die, you may be tempted to tidy up the garden. However, it's important to leave the plants standing all winter. No matter how bad you think it looks, remember that birds and butterflies use the garden for food and shelter through the winter. Birds will visit in search of seeds and overwintering insects. Butterflies and other beneficial insects commonly spend the winter as chrysalises and pupae attached to plants, or leave behind eggs that will hatch in spring.

Once you give your winter prairie garden a chance, you may find that its browned stems and seed heads are quite beautiful. And when spring arrives, you can indulge your complusion to clean house, either by burning the garden off or by cutting and raking off the previous year's growth.

⇢·⇠

Creating a Prairie Garden for Dry Soil

These hardy native plants grow in full sun in Zones 3 through 8. They do best in areas that average at least 25 inches of rain per year.

For directions on planting perennials, see "Problem-Free Planting" on page 271. In this design, all plants are spaced 1 foot apart at planting.

During the first year of growth, this garden will need weeding and watering to ensure that the plants become well established. Mulching between transplants helps to keep weeds down, but some will come up through the mulch. This first-year weeding is crucial to the long-term success of these gardens.

Plants for a Prairie Garden for Dry Soil

Azure aster (*Aster azureus*): Perennial, 2 feet tall. Tiny, daisylike, blue flowers cover plant in early fall.

Black-eyed Susan (*Rudbeckia hirta*): Annual or biennial, 2 feet tall. Daisylike flowers bloom in summer. Self-seeds.

Butterfly weed (*Asclepias tuberosa*): Perennial, 2 to 3 feet tall, 2 feet wide. Bears flat-topped orange flowers atop stiff stems in midsummer.

Button gayfeather (*Liatris aspera*): Perennial, 3 to 6 feet tall. Tall flowerstalks covered with small pink flowers in late summer, followed by fluffy white seeds.

Heath aster (*Aster ericoides*): Perennial, 2 feet tall. Small, white, daisylike flowers in early fall.

Large-flowered beardtongue (*Penstemon grandiflorus*): Perennial, 3 feet tall. Tubular lavender flowers on upright flower stems appear in late spring.

Little bluestem (*Schizachyrium scoparium*): Perennial, to 3 feet tall. Blue-green grass with tiny flowers in late summer.

Ohio spiderwort (*Tradescantia ohiensis*): Perennial, 1 to 3 feet tall. Spiky blue-green foliage; deep blue flowers open in the morning and close by early afternoon. Blooms in late spring and early summer.

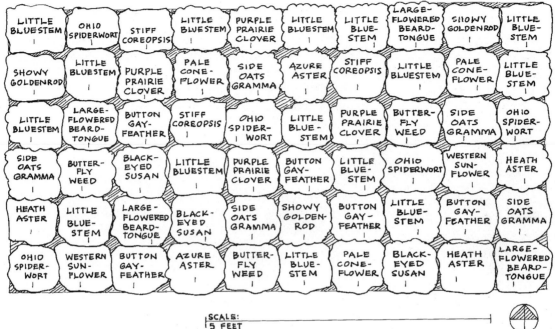

SCALE: 5 FEET

NORTH

Pale coneflower (*Echinacea pallida*): Perennial, to 4 feet tall. Purple flowers with drooping petals in early summer.

Purple prairie clover (*Petalostemon purpureum*): Perennial, 2 feet tall. Bright purple and yellow flower heads in midsummer.

Showy goldenrod (*Solidago speciosa*): Perennial, 2 to 3 feet tall. Foot-long clusters of bright yellow flowers in early fall provide much-needed nectar for butterflies.

Side oats gramma grass (*Bouteloua curtipendula*): Perennial, 2 feet tall. Golden grass with purple and orange flowerstalks in late summer, followed by small seeds, similar to oats, in fall.

Stiff coreopsis (*Coreopsis palmata*): Perennial, 3 feet tall. Delicate foliage; yellow daisylike flowers in midsummer.

Western sunflower (*Helianthus occidentalis*): Perennial, 3 feet tall. Starlike flowers have yellow petals and dark centers. Blooms in late summer.

—➔·←—

ESTABLISHING YOUNG PLANTS

When a plant is described as care-free or low-maintenance, it doesn't mean that you can just plant it and forget it. Every plant deserves to be pampered a bit with extra water and protection for at least the first month of growth. A light mulch right after planting will help these wildflowers compete with aggressive non-native weeds.

Once a plant is obviously growing and looks vigorous, you can consider it "established." From then on, extra water, weeding, and mulching are not as crucial.

Each plant has different requirements to get it to the care-free, established stage. A newly planted prairie garden usually needs one month to settle down after being planted, and then the native plants will fend for themselves beautifully.

—➔·←—

Creating a Prairie Garden for Average Soil

These hardy native plants grow in full sun in Zones 3 through 8. They do best in areas that average at least 25 inches of rain per year.

For directions on planting perennials, see "Problem-Free Planting" on page 271. In this design, all plants are spaced 1 foot apart at planting.

During the first year of growth, this garden will need weeding and watering to ensure that the plants become well established. Mulching between transplants helps to keep weeds down, but some will come up through the mulch. This first-year weeding is crucial to the long-term success of these gardens.

Plants for a Prairie Garden in Average Soil

Azure aster (*Aster azureus*): Perennial, 2 feet tall. Tiny, daisylike, blue flowers cover plant in early fall.

Black-eyed Susan (*Rudbeckia hirta*): Annual or biennial, 2 feet tall. Daisylike flowers bloom in summer. Self-seeds.

Butterfly weed (*Asclepias tuberosa*): Perennial, 2 to 3 feet tall, 2 feet wide. Bears flat-topped orange flowers atop stiff stems in midsummer.

Foxglove penstemon (*Penstemon digitalis*): Perennial, 2 to 5 feet tall. Clusters of white tubular flowers in summer.

Kansas gayfeather (*Liatris pycnostachya*): Perennial, 3 to 5 feet tall. Spikes of magenta flowers bloom in midsummer. Makes an excellent cut or dried flower.

Little bluestem (*Schizachyrium scoparium*): Perennial, to 3 feet tall. Blue-green grass with tiny flowers in late summer. Leaves turn red in fall.

Ohio spiderwort (*Tradescantia ohiensis*): Perennial, 1 to 3 feet tall. Spiky foliage; deep blue flowers open in the morning and close by early afternoon. Blooms in late spring and early summer.

Nodding wild onion (*Allium cernuum*): Perennial bulb, to 2 feet tall. In midsummer, produces white, globe-shaped flowers that later turn pink.

Pale coneflower (*Echinacea pallida*): Perennial, to 4

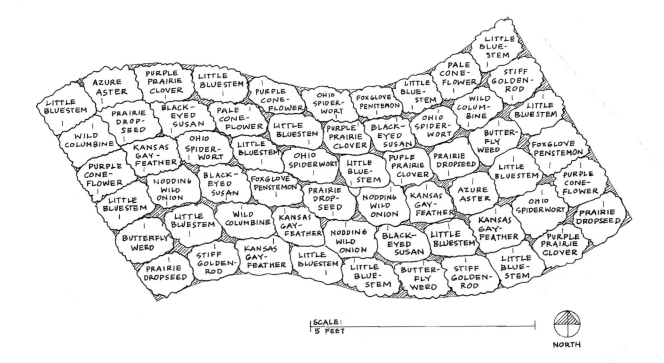

SCALE:
5 FEET

NORTH

feet tall. Purple flowers with dark cones and drooping petals in early summer.

Prairie dropseed (*Sporobolus heterolepis*): Perennial, 3 feet tall. Fine green grass with small flowers and fall seed heads.

Purple coneflower (*Echinacea purpurea*): Perennial, 2 to 4 feet tall. Daisylike flowers have purple petals with pointed orange centers. Blooms in summer.

Purple prairie clover (*Petalostemon purpureum*): Perennial, 2 feet tall. Bright purple and yellow flower heads in midsummer.

Stiff goldenrod (*Solidago rigida*): Perennial, 2 feet tall. Yellow flat-topped flower clusters in early fall.

Wild columbine (*Aquilegia canadensis*): Perennial, to 1½ feet tall. In early spring, red and yellow blossoms borne above delicate, lobed foliage.

—➔·←—

Fills a Soggy Spot. All the plants in this garden are moisture lovers. This garden can turn a low spot that's too wet for lawns or a conventional flower border from a problem into a highlight of your yard.

Colorful Natives. Native wildflowers are tough, adaptable, and beautiful. They are also a food source for many of our native birds and butterflies, so your moist meadow may well become a wildlife habitat, too.

Unique Bouquets. With this garden, you can create lovely and unusual fresh flower arrangements to bring some of the natural beauty indoors. Try a lovely fall arrangement of New England asters, obedient plant, and sweet coneflower.

—➔·←—

A Moist Meadow Wildflower Garden

"This plant doesn't like wet feet" is a nearly ubiquitous phrase in garden books and catalogs. It applies to most vegetables and herbs, lawn grasses, and many perennials, shrubs, and trees. So what *can* you plant by a stream, or in that low spot where runoff keeps the ground wet? How about a collection of moisture-loving native wildflowers with lovely pink, blue, and white blossoms?

There is a range of native flowering perennials that are happiest growing in soil that is constantly very moist. And maintaining a moist meadow garden is a snap, because you won't need to water or to lay mulch to conserve moisture. And the dense planting scheme of this garden helps ensure that once the garden is established you'll have minimal weeding to do.

The first blooms in this garden bud out in June when the white flowers of purple meadow rue burst open, along with the pink queen-of-the-prairie and spikes of white false indigo. In July, pink swamp milkweed and white Culver's root bloom on 5-foot-high stems. The tall, broad foliage of pale Indian plantain and clumps of blue wild iris complete the composition.

By August, the meadow is turning pink, blue, and red as the towering pink Joe-Pye weed and red western ironweed start to bloom. Great blue lobelia fills in the front of this crescent-shaped bed. September color ends the summer season with the lovely combination of blue New England asters, pure yellow black-eyed Susans, and pink obedient plant.

Neil Diboll designed this flower garden as a crescent to fit around the edge of a small pond or in a low spot in a field. You can adjust the shape to be more rectangular or to make a sweeping curve. For ideas on how to make a planting with either of these shapes, refer to the planting plans in "Two Native Prairie Gardens" on page 160.

Moisture-loving meadow flowers make a reflected rainbow in the waters of a small stream or pond. Spotted Joe-Pye weed, Culver's root, and sweet coneflower all carry blossoms close to eye level for a breathtaking effect in late summer.

MEADOW MANAGEMENT

Manage your meadow the way Mother Nature manages her gardens: Let nature take its course.

You may find that one or two plants in your meadow suffer from a heavy infestation of insects or a serious bout of disease. Your inclination might be to apply an organically acceptable pesticide to save the day. But hold back—these pesticides could have harmful effects on the birds, butterflies, and beneficial insects that have made your meadow their home. And in turn, killing beneficials that are eating pest insects could result in yet another pest problem in your meadow.

Let the infected plant die out naturally. Perhaps a few hardier strains of the infected plant will survive and regrow. Plants that are struggling because the site is too dry or too wet should also be allowed to die out. What will take over the garden are only the strong, pest-free plants that can survive on their own.

Creating a Moist Meadow Wildflower Garden

These hardy native plants grow in full sun in Zones 3 through 8. They do best in soils that are constantly very moist but not waterlogged.

For directions on planting perennials, see "Problem-Free Planting" on page 271. In this design, all plants are spaced 1 foot apart at planting.

During the first year of growth, this garden will need careful weeding to ensure that the plants become well established. Mulching between transplants helps to keep weeds down, but some will come up through the mulch. This first-year weeding is crucial to the long-term success of these gardens. In very dry seasons, these plants may also need supplemental water if the soil in which they are growing dries out.

For information on caring for an established wildflower meadow, see "The Prairie Look" on page 162.

Plants for a Moist Meadow Wildflower Garden

Culver's root (*Veronicastrum virginicum*): Perennial, 5 feet tall. Showy spikes of white flowers in midsummer.

Great blue lobelia (*Lobelia siphilitica*): Perennial, 2 to 3 feet tall. Deep blue, buck-toothed flowers in midsummer.

Kansas gayfeather (*Liatris pycnostachya*): Perennial, 3 to 5 feet tall. Spikes of magenta flowers bloom in midsummer. Makes an excellent cut or dried flower.

New England aster (*Aster novae-angliae*): Perennial, 3 to 6 feet tall. Small, sky blue, daisylike flowers in fall.

Obedient plant (*Physostegia virginiana*): Perennial, 3 to 4 feet tall. Spikes of pink or white flowers in late summer.

Pale Indian plantain (*Cacalia atriplicifolia*): Perennial, flowerstalks to 7 feet. Broad, bluish green, long-lasting leaves; clusters of white flowers in late summer.

Prairie wild indigo (*Baptisia leucantha*): Perennial, 3 to 5 feet tall. Erect spikes of white flowers in late spring.

Purple meadow rue (*Thalictrum dasycarpum*): Perennial, 5 feet tall. Attractive, lacy leaves; white flowers in late spring.

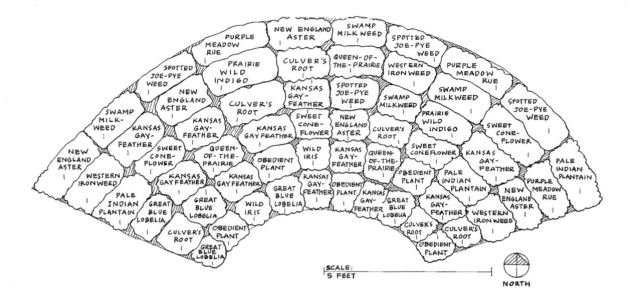

SCALE:
5 FEET

NORTH

Queen-of-the-prairie (*Filipendula rubra*): Perennial, 5 feet tall, spreads to form a large clump. Frothy pink plumes top bold foliage in summer.

Spotted Joe-Pye weed (*Eupatorium maculatum*): Perennial, 4 to 6 feet tall. Flat-topped clusters of red to purple flowers in late summer.

Swamp milkweed (*Asclepias incarnata*): Perennial, 3 to 5 feet tall. Flat clusters of pale rose to rose-purple flowers in summer. Attracts monarch butterflies, who lay their eggs on the leaves. Monarch caterpillars feed on milkweeds exclusively.

Sweet coneflower (*Rudbeckia subtomentosa*): Perennial, to 5 feet tall. Flowers have yellow petals around a reddish brown center. Blooms in fall.

Western ironweed (*Vernonia fasciculata*): Perennial, 6 feet tall. Clusters of red flowers in late summer.

Wild iris (*Iris shrevei*): Perennial, 2 feet tall. Grassy foliage; blue-violet flowers in late spring.

NO-FAIL FEATURES

Dual-Purpose Plants. The edible plants in this garden are attractive and produce tasty vegetables, fruits, and seasonings, too.

An Outdoor Retreat. The vine-covered trellis and rugosa roses serve as walls for the patio, creating a sense of privacy without blocking fresh air and cooling breezes.

Easy Harvesting. Dinner is literally right outside the door with this garden. Trellised beans are easy to pick, and the container of herbs on the patio provides a quick supply of fresh flavors to enhance your cooking. The ingredients for a fresh salad are a few quick steps away.

Color and Contrast. Edibles add beauty to this yard. From the rippling form of rhubarb leaves to the brilliant shades of ripe tomatoes and crab apples, there's a wonderful variety of color and texture.

An Incredible Edible Garden

If your yard is too small for a separate vegetable garden, try creating an edible landscape. You'll find the leaves and edible fruits of vegetables, shrubs, and trees can add as much beauty to your plantings as inedible ornamentals. This garden uses basic design principles for combining color, form, and texture to make a lovely landscape that doubles as a food garden. Red rhubarb stalks and tomato fruits provide bursts of color, and their fountain-shaped and bushy plant forms contrast with the strict upright shape of leeks. A vine-covered trellis creates a strong vertical accent and a shady nook for relaxing; it also makes for easy pickings, because the vine bears string beans. Vegetable leaves add delightful texture differences, ranging from the smooth look of leeks to rhubarb's broad and crinkled foliage, to the tightly curled leaves of parsley.

Pam Allenstein has included plenty of floral display in her design, including crab apple blossoms in spring and roses and nasturtiums in summer. After flowering, these plants offer secondary benefits as well. Crab apples that form after blossoms have fallen make wonderful jelly and will attract birds. The roses produce rose hips for tea, and the nasturtium blossoms make a colorful and unusual addition to summer salads.

It's easy to adapt this design to include your favorite vegetables. Just substitute the crop you'd like to grow for a plant with similar form. For example, if you're not a rhubarb fan, grow in its place an annual vegetable with bold foliage, such as zucchini or swiss chard. You can grow peppers or eggplant instead of tomatoes (or some of all three). Onions or dill can fill the spots designated here for leeks.

For even more diversity, you can grow two crops in succession in one bed. For example, try planting lettuce or radishes in early spring in the spaces where you'll plant tomatoes and leeks later on. The early crops will be ready to harvest just about the time the tomato transplants should be put into the ground.

A crab apple tree bearing flowers or fruit makes a perfect focal point in a compact edible landscape. Border plantings of lettuce and gold and orange nasturtiums add color and foliage interest. Stocky tomato bushes hold bright splotches of ripening fruit. Leeks displayed against a fence or wall provide strong vertical accents.

EDIBLES
IN THE LANDSCAPE

When substituting edibles for ornamentals in a garden or landscape planting, make your selections based on plant shape and form. For example, peas or pole beans can substitute well for clematis, because all three are climbing vines. However, lettuce wouldn't fill the bill as a clematis substitute. Here are some other suggestions for edibles in the landscape:

• Plant carrots or herbs as a low border for a rose garden.

• Plant a blueberry hedge to screen the edge of your property.

• Create a formal flower bed with globular heads of purple cabbage, and border it with pink petunias.

• Lavender makes a wonderful low, fragrant hedge alongside a walkway or bordering a sunny patio.

• An invasive herb like mint can serve as a groundcover in areas where you want a natural, wild look.

➼ · ↢

Creating an Incredible Edible Garden

Provide these incredible edibles with sun and well-drained soil in Zones 5 through 8. Establish the perennial crops in the first year. Planting the annual vegetables will be a yearly ritual. For information on planting trees, such as the crab apple, see the illustration on page 275. Plant rugosa roses and rhubarb crowns as you would other perennials as illustrated on page 274.

Most vegetables and herbs grow best in well-drained, loamy soil. Mix compost or well-rotted manure into the beds each spring before planting. Start early-spring crops like lettuce, peas, and radishes from seed. When warm weather arrives, plant beans and nasturtiums from seed, but buy tomato and parsley transplants from a local nursery or garden center. You may want to substitute cultivars well suited to your local growing conditions for the ones listed below. Whenever possible, select disease-resistant cultivars.

Plants for an Incredible Edible Garden

Crab apple (*Malus* 'Dolgo'): Deciduous tree, reaches 20 feet in ten years, ultimately to 40 feet tall. White blossoms in early spring; small, edible crab apples in fall. Reddish green, dense foliage. Space 20 to 30 feet apart. Prune suckers from base of tree in spring.

Curly parsley: Biennial, 10 to 12 inches tall. Dark green, very textured foliage. Space 6 inches apart. Pick leaves as needed, or harvest whole plants. Freeze or dry leaves for later use.

Leek ('Titan'): Annual, 12 to 14 inches tall. Produces spiky, upright leaves with swollen base. Sow seeds indoors in flats two to three months before last average frost. Thin seedlings as they grow to avoid crowding. Space 6 inches apart. Pile soil or mulch around lower stems to blanch, if desired.

Lettuce ('Burpee's Salad Garden'): Annual, to 6 inches tall. Crisp, lobed, red or green leaves. Broadcast seeds and rake lightly to cover. Thin seedlings to 8 inches apart.

Nasturtium ('Fordhook Favorites Mixed'): Annual vine climbs to 6 feet. Round, flat leaves and gold, orange, and

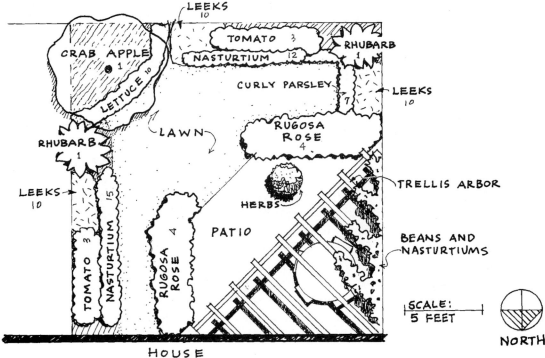

red edible flowers that have a peppery flavor. Direct-seed into warm soil; space seeds 6 to 8 inches apart.

Rhubarb: Perennial, 2 feet high and 3 feet wide. Ruffled leaves on long green or reddish stalks. Space crowns 3 to 4 feet apart. Harvest stems in spring; don't harvest in first year of growth. Leaves are poisonous.

Rugosa rose (*Rosa rugosa* 'Alba'): Shrub, 3 to 4 feet tall. White, open, fragrant flowers in summer; red rose hips in fall. Disease- and insect-resistant. Space 2 feet apart. Prune lightly in spring.

Runner bean: Annual vine, reaches 10 feet. White or red flowers attract hummingbirds. Plant seeds 10 to 12 inches apart.

Tomato ('Burpee's Big Girl'): Perennial grown as annual, 4 feet tall. Scarlet fruits; deep green, bushy plants. Space plants 3 feet apart. Stake or cage to keep plants from sprawling and to help prevent fruit rot.

NIBBLING ON NASTURTIUMS

Nasturtiums are easy to grow, and they make a great addition to salads. The leaves are peppery but not irritating to sensitive stomachs. Try them in place of lettuce to give crunch to a sandwich. The flowers are edible, too. Stuff the open florets with cream cheese and walnuts for a beautiful and healthful appetizer.

Fresh Flavors. Nothing adds zest to a meal like fresh herbs. Having a backyard herb garden makes this special treat an easy one, too! The wonderful flavors of Italian parsley, sage, and winter savory enhance even the most simple dishes. As with most herbs, the leaves from these plants are easy to dry and store.

Herbs for Crafts. Purple basil adds unusual texture and color to floral bouquets. The germander and thyme are both used in making wreaths; their flowers are easy to dry for indoor arrangements.

Formal Charm. The brick patio and pathways enhance the formal layout of this herb garden and contrast nicely with the subtle greens and grays of the herb foliage. The brick also matches the terra-cotta pots that hold the lemon trees and annual flowers.

A Corner Herb Garden

Herb gardens satisfy both our practical bent and our aesthetic sense. We can use herbs to season our food and also to create a pleasant garden that offers beautiful sights and enticing fragrance.

Herbs love the heat and sunshine of this south-facing corner garden against a house. Cynthia Woodyard's design combines elements of the old-fashioned kitchen garden with the elegance of a formal herb garden.

In the inner circle of this garden, pots of colorful annuals accent a beautiful herbal tapestry of textures and scents. Pathways through this area make it easy to gather sprigs of sweet marjoram, Italian parsley, thyme, and other fresh herbs for cooking. The outer circle lends the character of a formal herb garden, with lemon trees in Italian terra-cotta pots sitting amidst a sea of blue-green chamomile groundcover surrounded by a germander hedge.

The fan shape of this garden fits neatly into the corner of a building, but if that won't suit your site, you can move sections around. The three beds beside the terrace or the outer bed of lemon trees can be laid out in a row against a flat wall or up against a south-facing fence.

If you'd like to install this garden in stages, start with the three beds closest to the terrace. Instead of brick edgings and pathways, line the beds with edging strips, and use gravel and stepping stones in the paths. If you don't have an existing terrace, you can create a simple temporary sitting area of crushed rock. Later, when budget and time allow, you can convert the sitting area and paths to brick and then install the outer bed.

Use your imagination when choosing plants for the pots near the terrace. Try sweet-scented annuals like heliotrope, or one of the many scented geraniums. Avid cooks may want to use the containers to grow vegetables like lettuce, carrots, bush cucumbers, cherry tomatoes, and peppers.

For more early-spring color, try underplanting the chamomile and marjoram with crocuses, dwarf daffodils, and tulips.

Hearty, pungent fragrance fills this herb garden in summer. Pathways invite visitors to explore, and they provide easy access for snipping bits of winter savory, thyme, cilantro, chives, and parsley. The bricks, together with potted lemon trees and a germander hedge, add a traditionally formal air to the garden.

———————— ❧ · ☙ ————————

POTTED LEMON TREES

Whether you winter potted lemon trees over in a sunroom or in a greenhouse, you'll need to be sure they have good ventilation, high humidity, and at least half a day of full sun. Temperatures should be between 70° and 75°F during the day and from 45° to 55°F at night.

'Meyer Improved' lemon trees will grow well in a 5-gallon pot. Plant them in a loose, well-drained potting mix. Don't let the potting mix dry out. Water whenever the top ½ inch of potting mix starts to dry out, and then water thoroughly until water drains from the bottom. At least once a month, water with liquid fertilizer such as seaweed extract. Mist leaves frequently and group plants to conserve humidity.

Your trees will need a light yearly pruning. Thin out branches rather than shortening them, or you'll get a flush of new branches sprouting below the cut.

———————— ❧ · ☙ ————————

Creating a Corner Herb Garden

All of these plants are hardy in Zones 4 through 8, except for the potted lemon trees. These trees are hardy only to 20°F and must be overwintered indoors. See "Potted Lemon Trees" on this page for details.

Full sun and good drainage are crucial. Adding humus can help improve drainage of heavy soils; for very heavy soils, consider installing drainage tiles.

Plant herb seeds and plants as you would other annuals and perennials. See "Starting Flowers from Seed" on page 241 and "Problem-Free Planting" on page 271. Mulch the garden after planting to help control weeds, but avoid heavy mulches that can retain too much moisture and lead to rot.

Plants for a Corner Herb Garden

Chamomile (*Chamaemelum nobile*): Perennial, to 4 inches. Evergreen, matlike foliage; lavender blooms in spring. Space 8 inches apart. Trim with pruning shears after first and second round of bloom.

Chives (*Allium schoenoprasum*): Perennial, to 1 foot tall. Grassy, tubular foliage; pink, globe-shaped flowers in spring. Space 1 foot apart. Cut tops frequently to maintain production.

Cilantro (*Coriandrum sativum*): Annual, to 2 feet tall. Ferny, delicate foliage. Grown for the seeds and leaves. Seed 4 inches apart in rows 1 foot apart.

Germander (*Teucrium chamaedrys*): Perennial, to 2 feet tall. Shrubby, dense, richly scented foliage. Space 1 foot apart. Prune in spring and again in midsummer.

Italian parsley (*Petroselinum crispum* var. *neapolitanum*): Biennial, to 1 foot tall. Flat, sharply lobed leaves. Space 6 inches apart. Soak seeds in warm water overnight before planting. Harvest greens to thin.

Lemon (*Citrus limon* 'Meyer Improved'): Evergreen tree, to 6 feet in containers. Thick leaves and spiny branches. Requires winter protection. One tree per pot.

Purpleleaf basil (*Ocimum basilicum* 'Dark Opal'): Annual, to 2 feet tall. Dark purple leaves; small white or purple flowers. Thin seedlings to 9 inches apart.

Sweet marjoram (*Origanum majorana*): Perennial

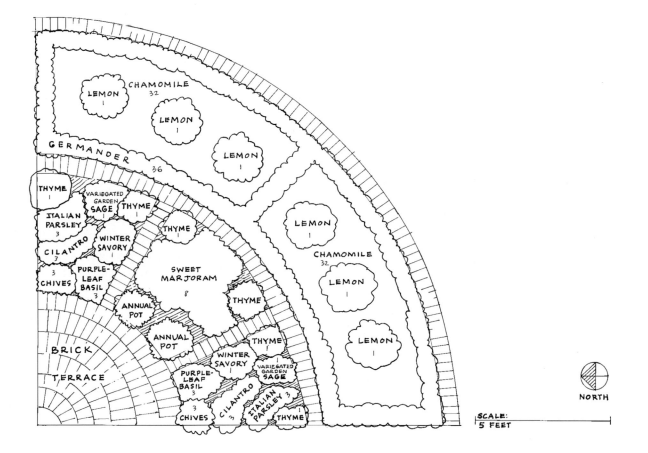

grown as annual, to 2 feet tall. Pointed leaves and small white or purple flowers. Space 12 inches apart in rows 18 inches apart. Cut back flowers after bloom, or allow them to ripen on plants, and collect them for crafts.

Thyme (*Thymus vulgaris*): Perennial, 1 foot tall. Tiny, gray-green, pointed leaves and small lavender blossoms. Space 1 foot apart.

Variegated garden sage (*Salvia officinalis* 'Icterina'): Perennial, to 3 feet wide. Green leaves with a yellow edge; may lose variegation if exposed to harsh winter conditions. Space plants 3 feet apart.

Winter savory (*Satureja montana*): Perennial, 6 to 12 inches tall. Woody herb with fine gray leaves and tiny white flowers. Space 1 foot apart.

NO-FAIL FEATURES

A Compatible Combo. This garden blends trees, shrubs, perennials, and annuals for a garden with great variety in shapes and sizes. The Persian lilac helps to balance the small redbud tree. The combination of annuals and perennials gives this bed a long season of color that starts with the daffodils and ends when the yarrow blooms dry in late fall.

Romantic Spring Color. Pink-flowered moss pinks bloom in spring, joined by the redbud blossoms. The Persian lilacs start their fragrant bloom as well, and delphiniums finish up the spring display as they welcome summer in shades of purple and blue.

Classic Dried Flowers. Sea lavender and yarrow are excellent flowers for drying. Cut them on a dry day when they are slightly past the bud stage. Bind the stems with a rubber band, and hang the clusters upside down to dry in a cool room.

A Marvelous Mixed Garden

Many flowering plants are compatible souls that mix well with shrubby plants and small trees. This mixed flower garden features an eastern redbud tree and a Persian lilac, bridged by a combination of perennial and annual flowers. This grouping succeeds because all of these plants do well in full sun and well-drained soil. The daylilies and moss pinks can also tolerate the filtered shade under the branches of the redbud.

Designer Scottie Garrett has planned this combination to provide color from early spring, when the daffodils bloom, until first frost, when the zinnias and daylilies are winding down. The garden provides flowers from toe level, where the moss pinks spread a pink carpet, to bird's-eye level when the redbud blooms.

Summer color is easy-care and drought-tolerant with sun-loving orange and red zinnias, orange daylilies, golden yarrow, and red and yellow blanket flowers. These bright hot colors will show up well in the summer sun, especially since they're given a gray-green backdrop from the summer foliage of the redbud and Persian lilacs. Delphiniums add spectacular blue flower spikes. Most delphiniums need staking to support their heavy, tall flowerstalks; however, the Connecticut Yankee hybrids selected for this design are stockier bush-type plants that are more reliable and easier to care for.

You can repeat this garden plan down the length of a driveway or along a fence line using a row of flowering trees. As the trees and shrubs grow larger over time, move the daylilies more toward the front of the bed. If the delphiniums and blanket flowers become shaded out as the tree grows large, try replacing them with shade-tolerant hostas and astilbe.

Don't plant this garden under an existing shade tree unless it's a deeply rooted tree such as an oak. Digging in the area covered by the drip line of a tree can damage delicate surface tree roots.

Friendly zinnias line the edge of a mixed planting that show-cases an eastern redbud tree and Persian lilac. Blanket flow-ers, daylilies, and delphiniums create a bold sweep of color that links the shrub and tree.

DESIGNING MIXED PLANTINGS

These tips will help you combine trees, shrubs, and flowers without turning your garden into an overgrown jungle.

Remember that trees grow. Even so-called small trees (15 to 25 feet when mature) can double in size in less than three years. Plant shrubs at least 8 feet away from the tree's trunk, or they'll end up crowding one another.

Plant more small plants to balance the bulk of the large plants. For example, plant two or three shrubs to balance one small tree. Three to five large blooming perennials, such as delphiniums or foxgloves, will balance one shrub.

Play up the flowering tree. Add at least one annual, bulb, or perennial flower to your mixed bed that flowers at the same time as the tree. Choose a shrub or flower that is in the same color family as the blooming tree or that has a color that contrasts beautifully.

Creating a Marvelous Mixed Garden

These plants are hardy from Zones 3 through 8, with the exception of delphiniums, which won't tolerate summer heat south of Zone 7, and sea lavender, which is hardy only to Zone 4. All like full sun and need average, well-drained soil.

For instructions on planting trees and shrubs, see the illustration on page 275. You'll find general planting instructions in "Problem-Free Planting" on page 271. Keep plants well watered and free of weeds during the first few months of growth. Once the garden is established, it needs little seasonal care.

Prune any dead, diseased, or crossing branches off the Persian lilac after it has finished blooming in spring. Avoid pruning in summer because it will prevent the plant from setting next year's buds, resulting in fewer flowers. Shear back moss pinks immediately after they bloom in spring to encourage them to flower again in summer. Remove the spent blossoms from the blanket flowers and zinnias to keep them blooming all summer long.

Plants for a Marvelous Mixed Garden

Blanket flower (*Gaillardia* × *grandiflora* 'Goblin'): Annual, 1 foot tall. Red blooms with yellow edges in summer. Space 1 foot apart. Deadhead to encourage repeat blooming.

Daffodils (*Narcissus* spp.): Bulb, 12 to 15 inches tall. Yellow or orange trumpet flowers in spring. Space bulbs 6 inches apart.

Daylily (*Hemerocallis* 'Toyland'): Perennial, 2 feet tall. Straplike leaves and orange blooms in early to midsummer. Space 2 feet apart.

Delphinium (*Delphinium* Connecticut Yankee series): Perennial, to 30 inches tall. Showy blue flowers all summer. Space 2 feet apart. Add extra humus around plants for best performance.

Eastern redbud (*Cercis canadensis*): Deciduous tree, 25 to 35 feet tall. Rich green, heart-shaped leaves; small, rosy pink flowers in early spring.

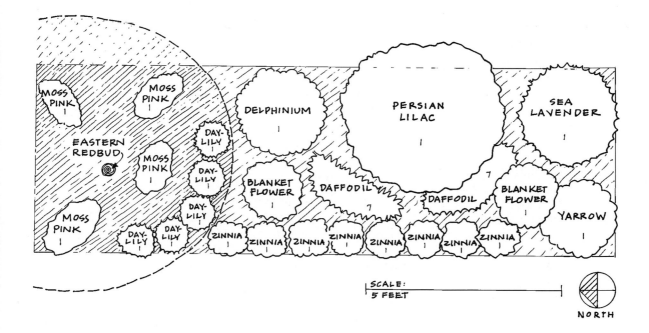

Moss pink (*Phlox subulata* 'Emerald Cushion Pink'): Perennial, less than 6 inches tall; tiny evergreen leaves. Pink spring flowers. Space 3 feet apart. Shear after spring bloom to encourage reblooming.

Persian lilac (*Syringa* × *persica*): Deciduous shrub, 4 to 5 feet tall. Graceful clusters of lilac-colored, fragrant blooms in spring. Space 6 feet apart. Prune immediately after bloom.

Sea lavender (*Limonium latifolium*): Perennial, 2 feet tall and wide. Light, airy, lavender blooms from midsummer to frost. Space 2 feet apart.

Yarrow (*Achillea* 'Coronation Gold'): Perennial, 2 feet tall. Golden flowering heads in summer to fall. Space 2 feet apart.

Zinnia (*Zinnia* 'Dreamland' hybrids): Annual, 1 foot tall. Dahlia-like flowers in many bright colors in summer. Thin seedlings to 1 foot apart. Deadhead to encourage continued bloom.

NO-FAIL FEATURES

Butterfly Magnets. All of the blooming plants in this bed attract brilliant butterflies that add excitement and extra color to the garden.

Natural Resistance to Disease. The plants presented in the design are all basically tough and trouble-free. This makes things easy for the gardener. It also keeps the garden safe for butterflies, as most insecticides—even organically acceptable types—are toxic to butterflies.

Heat-Loving Plants. All the plants in this garden, except parsley, are heat- and drought-tolerant. The coneflowers and marigolds will bloom profusely through summer's hottest days, when other blooming plants tend to melt in the heat.

A Brilliant Butterfly Garden

Butterflies add movement and magic to a flower garden. Watching butterflies is a fascinating pastime that never loses its appeal. LuAnn Craighton designed this garden to attract butterflies by supplying all the elements that warm a butterfly's heart.

To be specific, it's sunlight that warms butterflies. Like other insects, butterflies are cold-blooded. They rely on the sun's heat to warm them to the temperature at which they can fly. A patch of sun-bathed plants is a favorite butterfly resting place.

Butterflies feed on nectar, and they use color as a cue to find nectar sources. Large splashes of brightly colored flowers that will bloom from spring through fall invite them to call this garden home. The butterflies must land in order to feed, and they like plants that have convenient landing platforms—flat-topped, clustered blossoms—like lantana and purple coneflower.

Butterflies lay eggs on specific host plants, and caterpillars hatch from those eggs. The caterpillars feed on the host plant until they pupate, forming the chrysalis from which a butterfly will emerge. Monarch butterflies use the butterfly weed in this garden as their host plant. Parsley is the host plant for the black swallowtail butterfly. Keep in mind that if butterflies do take up residence in your garden, your parsley and butterfly weed will be chomped on by caterpillars. Be sure to plant plenty.

You can adapt this garden to a smaller space by using one dwarf butterfly bush as the focal point at the back of the bed, surrounded by a trio of tall cosmos. Use the shorter plants as needed to fill in the rest of the garden. For a narrow flower border, position butterfly bushes along the back of the bed, with coneflowers and cosmos between the shrubs. Fill the front of the bed with lantana, marigolds, and verbena.

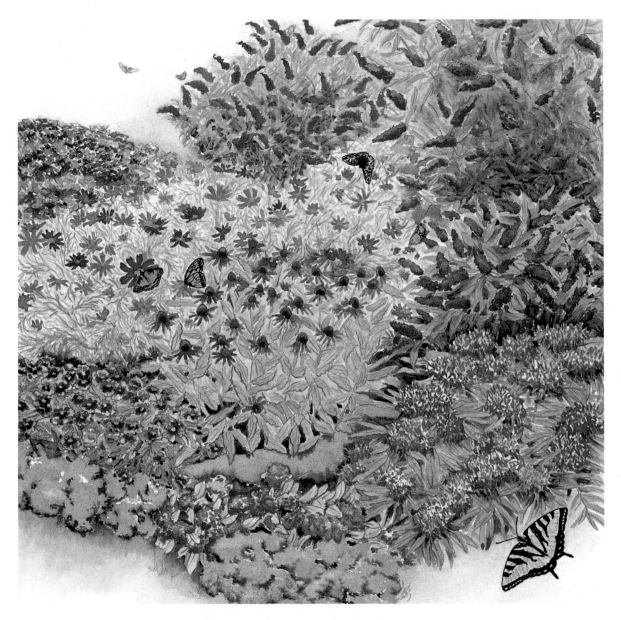

Bold sweeps of lavender, purple, orange, and yellow attract butterflies to feed on nectar from the purple coneflowers, dwarf butterfly bush, cosmos, lantana, butterfly weed, marigolds, and verbena. Parsley provides color and texture contrast, as well as food for the larval stage of the black swallowtail butterfly.

ATTRACTING BUTTERFLIES

Selecting good nectar and host plants for butterflies is the most important requirement for establishing a butterfly garden. Here are some extra things you can do to make your garden a good home for these fascinating insects:

• Include some flat stepping stones. Butterflies often perch on stones to bask in the sun and warm their bodies to flight temperature (80°F).
• Make wet spots or very shallow puddles for butterflies to drink from. Large groups of male butterflies sometimes congregate in wet spots, forming a "puddle club." Sink a shallow saucer filled with pebbles into the ground. Add just enough water to cover the pebbles.
• Don't use pesticides. Even many organically acceptable pesticides, such as pyrethrins and BT, will kill butterflies or caterpillars. Rely on handpicking, predatory insects, and (in emergencies) insecticidal soap sprays to control pest problems.

➺ · ⭠

Creating a Brilliant Butterfly Garden

These disease-resistant plants all thrive in Zones 5 through 8, with the exception of dwarf butterfly bush, which is hardy to Zone 6 with winter protection. Butterfly weed and verbena can handle the heat in Zone 9.

Full sun to partial shade in the afternoon is ideal. The plants in this garden are fairly drought-tolerant and will thrive in a well-drained, average to even slightly poor soil. The one exception is parsley, which prefers richer soil. You can supply this by spot-applying compost each year when you replant the parsley.

For instructions on planting shrubs, like the butterfly bushes, see the illustration on page 275. For instructions on planting perennials, see "Problem-Free Planting" on page 271. After the first year, this garden needs little care during the growing season. Deadhead spent flowers from the butterfly bushes, marigolds, and purple coneflowers all summer to encourage continuous blooms.

Plants for a Brilliant Butterfly Garden

Butterfly weed (*Asclepias tuberosa*): Perennial, 2 to 3 feet tall, 2 feet wide. Bears flat-topped orange flowers atop stiff stems. Space 1 foot apart.

Dwarf butterfly bush (*Buddleia davidii* × *B. fallowiana* 'Lochinch'): Deciduous shrub, 5 to 6 feet tall and 4- to 5-foot spread. Downy-gray foliage with dusty lavender flowers. Space 5 feet apart.

French marigold (*Tagetes patula* 'Disco Golden Yellow' and 'Disco Orange'): Annual, reaches 12 inches tall. Bears numerous 2-inch-wide single blossoms all summer and early fall. Space 8 to 10 inches apart.

Lantana (*Lantana camara* 'New Gold'): Perennial treated as an annual except in the Deep South, grows to 2 feet with 3-foot spread. Abundant yellow blossoms early summer until frost. Space 2 feet apart.

Orange eye butterfly bush (*Buddleia davidii*): Deciduous shrub, reaches 10 feet tall and 6 feet wide. Narrow clusters of purple, fragrant, 4- to 10-inch-long blossoms from mid-spring until frost. Space 12 feet apart. May be killed to the ground in winter in colder areas. Blooms

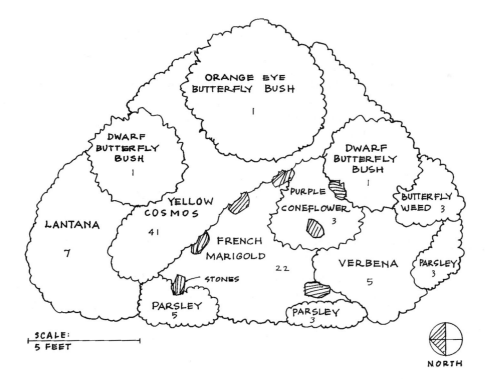

ORANGE EYE
BUTTERFLY BUSH
1

DWARF
BUTTERFLY
BUSH
1

DWARF
BUTTERFLY
BUSH
1

YELLOW
COSMOS
41

PURPLE
CONEFLOWER
3

BUTTERFLY
WEED 3

LANTANA
7

FRENCH
MARIGOLD
22

VERBENA
5

PARSLEY
3

STONES

PARSLEY
5

PARSLEY
3

SCALE:
5 FEET

NORTH

form on new wood; prune growth that is not killed to 12 to 18 inches in early spring.

Parsley (*Petroselinum crispum* 'Paramount'): Biennial treated as an annual, 8 to 12 inches tall. Dark green, finely cut or curled foliage. Start seeds indoors early, or sow in place and thin seedlings to 3 or 4 inches apart.

Purple coneflower (*Echinacea purpurea*): Perennial, 2 to 3 feet tall. From summer to fall, bears flowers with gently curved lavender petals surrounding a spiny, orange cone. Space 2 feet apart.

Verbena (*Verbena canadensis* 'Abbeville'): Perennial, 8 to 12 inches tall, spreads to 3 feet. Dark green foliage and stems; lavender blossoms cloak plant from May until frost. Space 3 feet apart.

Yellow cosmos (*Cosmos sulphureus* 'Bright Lights'): Annual, 3 feet tall. Fine, dark green foliage; yellow, orange, and scarlet blooms. Space 6 inches apart. Will reseed freely if area around the plants is not mulched.

SMALL GARDENS FOR BUTTERFLIES

Even gardeners limited to container gardening on a patio can have a butterfly garden. Most butterfly-attracting plants do well in pots. A container butterfly garden could feature hanging baskets of lantana and verbena, pots of marigolds, window boxes of parsley, and a tub or barrel holding a dwarf butterfly bush. Lantana and verbena could also spill from window boxes or cascade over the edge of a barrel planter.

NO-FAIL FEATURES

Nostalgic Beauty. Many of the plants in this design may bring back memories of Grandmother's garden. Scents have great power to stimulate memories: This garden features the citrus scent of mock orange, the sweetness of tiger lilies, and the musky or violet scent of old garden roses.

Sensational Sun Plants. This collection of plants will grow well near a sunny patio where its mixture of colors and fragrances makes a pleasant backdrop for outdoor gatherings.

Victorian Arbor. A rustic twig arbor supports the climbing clematis and brings its delightfully fragrant flowers right to nose level. With a bench beneath, it's a wonderful retreat for reading, a quiet chat, or just reflecting on the day.

Fragrant Cut Flowers. The lilac provides sweet-smelling cut flowers in spring, and lilies or mock orange can perfume the house in summer.

A Fragrant Heirloom Garden

Everything old can be new again when you create a garden with heirloom shrubs, perennials, and an old-fashioned sapling arbor. Planting these old-fashioned flowers can give you a link to our country's past. The sights and fragrances of these plants may stir memories of gardens you knew and played in as a child.

Heirloom plants date to the eighteenth, nineteenth, and early twentieth centuries, before the whirlwind of modern plant breeding brought a new generation of hybrid and imported plants to home gardens. In an heirloom garden, you'll grow plants used by pioneers and in Victorian times. The early colonists grew many of these plants for practical reasons, such as supplying medicines or providing dyes for clothing. Many of these plants are naturally disease-resistant, favored by early gardeners because they were easy and enjoyable to grow.

You don't have to be a purist about growing heirlooms. There's no rule that says you must plant only venerable cultivars. In some cases, selection has produced improvements over old-fashioned plants. In this design, Marianne Binetti selected a modern rose called a David Austin English rose. These roses have the vigorous, open shrub form and delightful fragrance of classic old shrub roses, but they bloom for a much longer period than heirloom roses do. You can read more about these beautiful shrubs in "English Roses" on page 38.

The focal point of this garden is a stone bench, which is backed by a twig and sapling arbor clothed by fragrant autumn clematis. You'll find directions for making this in "Building an Arbor" on page 188. A stepping stone pathway bordered by fragrant mounds of flowers leads to the bench.

For a smaller version of this garden in a bed or border, eliminate the bench, stepping stones, and fence. Just group the lilac, mock orange, and roses in the background. Fill the middle with foxgloves and lilies, and line the front with the low-growing moss pinks and cranesbills.

Fragrant roses and an informal arbor covered with clematis lend nostalgic fragrance and beauty to an heirloom garden reminiscent of a Victorian front yard. Moss pinks and blood-red cranesbills make a lovely combination to border a stepping stone path.

———————— ➤ · ⬅ ————————

BUILDING AN ARBOR

It's easy to construct a small rustic arbor. Here's how to do it:

1. Cut two pliable saplings about 1 inch in diameter and 8 feet long. Prune off side branches.
2. Sharpen one end of each sapling. Plunge the sharpened ends into the ground 6 feet apart. Pound stakes in beside the saplings for extra support if necessary.
3. Bend the tops together, overlapping them by about 2 feet. Fasten them securely with wire or twine. The arch will be about 5 feet high at its peak.
4. Again using wire or twine, fasten the pruned side branches or other leafless branches to the saplings to form a back wall for the arch.
5. Plant the clematis vine at the center back of the arbor. As it grows, train it over the branches.

You'll need to rebuild this arbor every few years. Prune the clematis back hard before doing so. Burn the worn branches in a bonfire, or chip them to use as mulch.

———————— ➤ · ⬅ ————————

Creating a Fragrant Heirloom Garden

These old-fashioned flowers thrive in Zones 5 through 8 and need only a sunny site with moist but well-drained soil. The plants prefer light afternoon shade in the hot southern states (Zones 7 through 9). The lilacs prefer cooler temperatures, so gardeners in Zones 7 and 8 can use crape myrtle (*Lagerstroemia indica*) as a replacement.

This garden requires good air circulation to help prevent mildew problems on many of the plants. Be sure to situate it at least 15 feet away from fences or buildings. Refer to the illustration on page 275 for instructions on planting shrubs. See also "Problem-Free Planting" on page 271, on planting perennials, and "Planting Bulbs" on page 273. After the first year, this garden needs little seasonal care. Leave the foliage of spring-blooming bulbs to mature naturally after blooming. Pull it out later in summer after it has dried.

Plants for a Fragrant Heirloom Garden

Bearded iris (*Iris* bearded hybrids): Perennial, 2 to 4 feet tall. Straplike blue-green foliage and large, fragrant flowers borne on tall stalks. Blooms in late spring and summer in a wide range of colors. Space 1 foot apart.

Blood-red cranesbill (*Geranium sanguineum*): Perennial, 9 to 12 inches tall. Mounded plant with finely cut leaves and small pink or lavender blooms through summer. Space 2 feet apart.

English rose (*Rosa* 'Gertrude Jekyll'): Deciduous shrub, to 6 feet tall. Bright pink, highly fragrant blossoms all summer. Space 4 feet apart. Cut back lightly after first flush of flowers to encourage reblooming.

Foxglove (*Digitalis purpurea*): Biennial. Broad, slightly furry foliage in tidy clumps first year. In second year, blooms midsummer with bell-shaped florets on 4-foot stalks. Lavender speckled with purple spots, also white. Space 1 foot apart. Prune spent flowerstalks.

Lemon daylily (*Hemerocallis lilioasphodelus*): Perennial. Blooms in June with fragrant, clear yellow, 4-inch flowers borne on 3-foot-tall stalks above straplike 2-foot-long leaves. Space 1 to 2 feet apart.

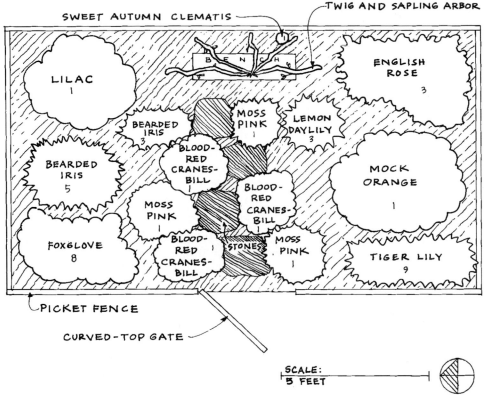

SWEET AUTUMN CLEMATIS

TWIG AND SAPLING ARBOR

LILAC
1

BENCH

ENGLISH ROSE
3

BEARDED IRIS
3

MOSS PINK
1

LEMON DAYLILY
3

BLOOD-RED CRANES-BILL
1

BEARDED IRIS
5

MOSS PINK
1

BLOOD-RED CRANES-BILL
1

MOCK ORANGE
1

FOXGLOVE
8

BLOOD-RED CRANES-BILL

STONES

MOSS PINK
1

TIGER LILY
9

PICKET FENCE

CURVED-TOP GATE

SCALE: 5 FEET

NORTH

Lilac (*Syringa vulgaris* 'Alphonse Lavallée'): Deciduous shrub, to 20 feet tall. Fragrant lavender blooms borne in clusters in mid-spring. Space 5 feet apart.

Mock orange (*Philadelphus coronarius*): Deciduous shrub, to 10 feet tall. Medium green, oval leaves; pristine white, fragrant blossoms in early summer. Space 10 feet apart. Prune after flowering.

Moss pink (*Phlox subulata*): Perennial, 6 inches tall, spreads to 2 feet. Semi-evergreen, needle-like leaves. Pink, white, or lavender blooms in spring. Space 1 foot apart. Shear off one-third of the plant after bloom.

Sweet autumn clematis (*Clematis maximowicziana*): Perennial vine. Dark green, glossy leaves. Masses of 1-inch, fragrant white blossoms in late summer and fall. Plant one plant per support. Cut vine back to 3 feet if it overgrows arbor.

Tiger lily (*Lilium lancifolium*): Bulb, stems grow to 4 feet tall. Deep orange flowers with black spots bloom in summer. Space 1 foot apart.

—→ · ←—

—→ · ←—

A Dooryard Reflecting Pool

For a cool, relaxing touch in the heat of summer, picture a small reflecting pool surrounded by lush plants in the shade of a tree. Adding a small water feature doesn't have to be costly or complicated, and you'll love the way it accents your yard in all seasons.

The basic elements of your small pool are a plastic or fiberglass liner, water, aquatic plants, and fish. With them, you'll create a small, self-sustaining ecosystem. You may find that water gardening becomes as fascinating and satisfying a hobby as gardening on land!

You'll find instructions for digging a pond and installing a liner in "Installing a Pool" on page 192. You may wonder whether you can install the pool, fill it with water, and skip the aquatic plants and fish. Experienced water gardeners would tell you that you won't be happy with the results. Standing water is a breeding ground for mosquitoes. Without fish to eat the mosquito larvae, and plants to use the organic fertilizer produced by the fish, your small pool may produce a big mosquito problem.

Many garden centers and specialized water garden centers can help you decide which plants and fish are best for your garden. You'll find listings of mail-order companies that sell water garden supplies in "Sources" on page 358, and titles of books with complete information on water gardening in "Recommended Reading" on page 359.

If you'd like to plant this shady garden of perennials but you have no inclination to install a water garden, designer Ellen Phillips suggests a waterless adaptation. Just dig a hole the size and shape of a real pool, and fill it with white pebbles, available at large garden centers and landscape supply companies. Or collect smooth, gray stones from around your yard, and arrange the larger rocks around the perimeter of the pool and the smaller ones near the center. Then surround it with the shade-loving perennials that Phillips has selected.

Summer reflections are green, white, and blue in a small pool
surrounded by spotted lamium, Japanese painted ferns, hostas,
rose astilbe, Labrador violets, and Siberian irises. A pair of giant
bubbles at the pool's edge turn out to be two silver gazing balls.

→·←

INSTALLING A POOL

Fiberglass pool forms make adding a water garden an easy project. Here's how to install one:

1. Wash the form with water and liquid detergent to remove residues that may be toxic to fish and plants. Hose it thoroughly with clear water.
2. Slice off the sod at the water garden site, and add it to the compost pile.
3. Place the form upside down on the cleared site. Pour flour or lime around the outside edge to mark the boundary of the pool. Remove the form.
4. Dig inside the boundary to a depth of about 12½ inches, so that the lip of the form will be just above ground level. Check with a builder's level to be sure the bottom of the hole is level.
5. Set the form in the hole right-side up. Fill it with water immediately to keep it in place.
6. Mix some excavated soil with water. Tamp this in around the edge of the pool to form a tight fit. Use the extra soil to build berms or fill in low spots.

→·←

Creating a Reflecting Pool Garden

These hardy plants all thrive in Zones 3 through 8. Almost all the plants need deep, humus-rich, evenly moist soil in partial to full shade. Siberian irises also grow well in full sun. In cooler regions, hostas will also adapt to full sun if kept watered during dry spells. If the Labrador violets are situated to get full sun, you'll notice more purple in their leaves.

For instructions on planting perennials, see "Problem-Free Planting" on page 271. If you opt to install this garden under a tree, be sure it's not a shallow-rooted tree, which could be damaged by digging.

Mulch this garden after planting with an organic mulch like shredded leaves or compost. The pool will lose some water to evaporation, especially if it's very small or located in a hot climate; add fresh water as necessary.

Plants for a Reflecting Pool Garden

Crocus (*Crocus* hybrids mixed): Perennial that emerges each spring from squatty bulbs called corms, 4 to 8 inches tall. Grasslike foliage; cup-shaped blooms in early spring in purple, yellow, white, or lavender, depending on the cultivar. Note: Crocuses are not shown in the design because they are intended to be scattered in clumps throughout the poolside garden. Plant corms in fall, 3 to 4 inches deep. Space 4 inches apart.

Hostas (*Hosta* 'Northern Halo' and 'Francee'): Perennial, to 2 feet tall. Mounded plants; 'Francee' has dark green foliage and narrow, clean white leaf margins; 'Northern Halo' has puckered silver-blue leaves and broad, creamy borders. Space 3 feet apart.

Japanese painted fern (*Athyrium goeringianum* 'Pictum'): Perennial, to 2 feet tall. Graceful weeping habit and silver-splashed green fronds with wine red stems. Space 3 feet apart.

Labrador violet (*Viola labradorica* var. *purpurea*): Perennial, 6 to 8 inches tall. Heart-shaped green and purple leaves; mauve blossoms in spring to summer. Spreads to make a groundcover. Space 1 foot apart.

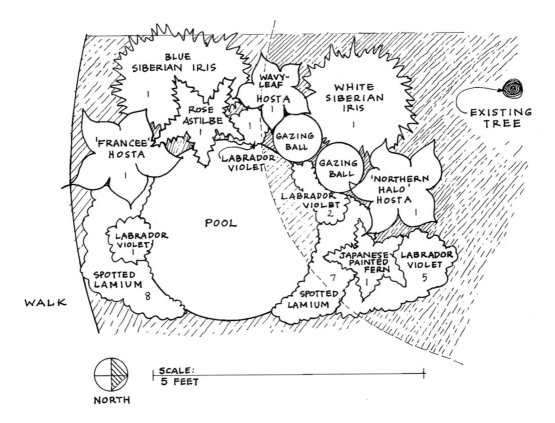

BLUE SIBERIAN IRIS
1

WAVY-LEAF HOSTA
1

ROSE ASTILBE
1

WHITE SIBERIAN IRIS
1

EXISTING TREE

'FRANCEE' HOSTA
1

GAZING BALL

LABRADOR VIOLET

GAZING BALL

'NORTHERN HALO' HOSTA
1

LABRADOR VIOLET
2

POOL

LABRADOR VIOLET
1

SPOTTED LAMIUM
8

WALK

JAPANESE PAINTED FERN
1

LABRADOR VIOLET
5

SPOTTED LAMIUM
7

NORTH

SCALE: 5 FEET

Rose astilbe (*Astilbe* × *rosea* 'Peach Blossom'): Perennial, 2 to 3 feet tall. Fernlike foliage and feathery blooms in summer. Space 2 feet apart.

Siberian iris (*Iris sibirica*): Perennial, 3 feet tall. Grassy leaves with graceful flowers in spring. Choose a blue and a white cultivar. Leave seed heads after bloom for summer interest. Space 2 feet apart.

Spotted lamium (*Lamium maculatum* 'White Nancy'): Perennial, 6 to 12 inches tall. Clusters of small white flowers over heart-shaped silver and white leaves. Blooms spring and summer. Space 8 inches apart.

Wavyleaf hosta (*Hosta undulata* 'Albo-marginata'): Perennial, 1 foot tall, flower spikes to 2 feet. Mounded plant having wavy green leaves with white edges; lavender blooms in summer. Space 3 feet apart.

NO-FAIL FEATURES

Nature's Air-Conditioning. Large shade trees such as the spreading oak in this design are prized by southern gardeners as nature's air-conditioning. This garden makes a pleasant spot for a cooling rest.

Pleasing Symmetry. Formal repetition of colors and plants keeps this design from looking like an untamed mess growing around a tree. The layout of the smaller plants at the outer perimeter of the garden echoes that of the shrubs behind. Soft tones of mauve, pink, and lavender repeat throughout the planting. The tidy stone border adds a finished edge.

A Symphony of Green. Cool green hues help to make this garden a calming retreat when summer is at its worst. Colors range from the soft blue-green of columbine foliage to the chartreuse of the sharply pointed wild cranesbill leaves. Smooth and shiny dark green azalea foliage contrasts with the large and furry dull green of the primroses and multi-lobed oakleaf hydrangea leaves.

A Southern Shade Garden

Shade is a treasure in our yards, but the bare ground or sparse lawn beneath large shade trees can be a gardening trial. This design turns a dark, monotonous area around an oak tree into a colorful collection of shrubs and perennials. Deep-rooted deciduous trees make good candidates for shade gardens since their roots don't interfere with planting. Their bare branches in spring let in plenty of sunlight for blooming flowers and shrubs. Use native stones for a natural-looking border that defines the bed and keeps plants in place. Put benches or lawn chairs in the shade beside this garden for the perfect spot for a restful break on hot summer afternoons.

This garden is easy to care for even in the steamy heat of the southeastern United States, because it includes many plants native to the shady woods of the South. Wild cranesbill, English primrose, wild blue phlox, and wild columbine fill the bed with spring blooms. By early summer, the oakleaf hydrangea, bottlebrush buckeye, and Florida pinxter azalea leaf out fully. Their foliage mixes with the perennials to create a tapestry of green tones and textures.

You may want to adapt this design to a shady area that's not beneath a single tree. For example, you may want a border for a shaded woodland path or a bed on the north side of a house. To do so, designer Barrie Crawford suggests arranging the plants in staggered rows. Place the taller azaleas and hydrangeas at the back of the bed. If you have only a small space to fill, substitute shade-loving perennials such as hostas and astilbes for the shrubs. Keep in mind, however, that these perennials will die back in the fall and not offer a backdrop of colored foliage.

Gardens that aren't beneath a tree will need a yearly boost of organic matter to keep the soil rich enough to satisfy these plants. Use your lawn mower to chop leaves into small pieces, and apply them as a heavy mulch in fall. Oak leaves are especially valuable as a mulch for acid-loving plants such as azaleas.

Drifts of soft pastels from wild cranesbills, Persian epimedium, yellow English primroses, wild columbine, and wild blue phlox make a glorious spring carpet in the deep shade beneath a mature oak tree. Native Florida pinxter azaleas and oakleaf hydrangeas will continue the floral show as the season progresses.

PLANTING UNDER TREES

Not all trees make good garden companions. Many—including poplars, large-leaf maples, and flowering cherries—have shallow roots that would be damaged by digging. Other trees, like firs and cedars, have foliage that doesn't break down easily, and they cast deep shade that many plants can't tolerate.

Don't try making a raised bed garden around the base of a tree. It can suffocate shallow roots or create problems with collar rot. Instead, try carpeting the area beneath shallow-rooted trees with a 1-inch layer of organic mulch or loose gravel. Set large pots on the mulch for container plantings of shade-tolerant plants like begonias, impatiens, hostas, and astilbes.

Another option is a hanging garden. Suspend baskets of fuchsias or other shade lovers from sturdy branches. Doubled loops of strong fishing line over the limbs provide invisible supports.

Creating a Southern Shade Garden

All of these plants thrive in Zones 5 through 9, and all love the shade. They require soil that's high in organic matter, like that formed when leaves accumulate and decompose for many years beneath a large tree. Allow nature's leaf drop to carpet the area each fall, and no other plant food should be necessary.

For instructions on planting shrubs, see the illustration on page 275. See "Problem-Free Planting" on page 271 and the illustration on page 274 for directions on planting perennials. This planting requires little seasonal care after the first year of growth. The shrubs should grow slowly in deep shade, requiring practically no pruning. If planted in light shade, they may require some pruning to keep them in bounds.

The Lenten rose, phlox, and primroses will spread and reseed themselves.

Plants for a Southern Shade Garden

Bottlebrush buckeye (*Aesculus parviflora*): Deciduous shrub, 6 feet tall with 4-foot spread. Pale cream flowers in long panicles in spring. Stout growth form is attractive in winter with large, shiny buds. Space 5 feet apart.

English primrose (*Primula vulgaris*): Perennial, to 8 inches tall. Dense rosettes of leaves; clear yellow blossoms in early spring. Space 18 inches apart.

Florida pinxter azalea (*Rhododendron canescens*): Deciduous shrub, to 10 feet tall with 3-foot spread. White to pink, fragrant blossoms in April. Space 4 feet apart.

Japanese anemone (*Anemone* × *hybrida* 'September Charm'): Perennial, to 2 feet tall. Mauve blossoms in late summer and fall; richly colored yellow fall foliage. Space 1 foot apart.

Lenten rose (*Helleborus orientalis*): Perennial, 18 inches tall and wide. Mostly evergreen, compound leaves with broad, irregular leaflets. Blooms early spring with purplish flowers in clusters. Space 2 feet apart.

Oakleaf hydrangea (*Hydrangea quercifolia*): Deciduous shrub to 5 feet tall, with 3- to 4-foot spread. Large-lobed leaves turn wine color in fall. Cream-colored spring blos-

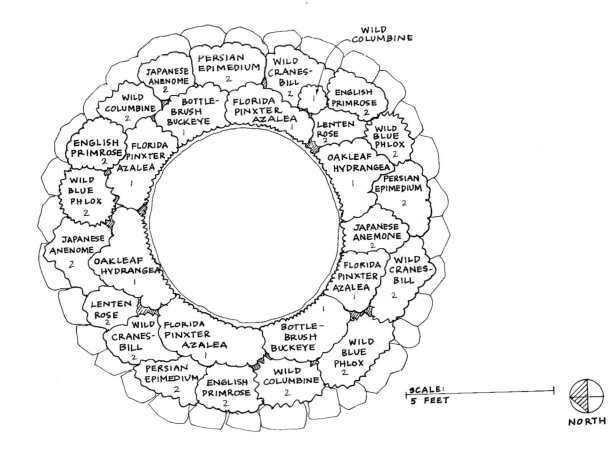

soms retained through summer, turn reddish purple in fall. Space 5 feet apart.

Persian epimedium (*Epimedium × versicolor* 'Sulphureum'): Perennial, 10 to 12 inches tall. Leaves are almost evergreen, turning deep scarlet in fall; pale yellow blossoms in early spring. Space 1 foot apart.

Wild blue phlox (*Phlox divaricata*): Perennial, 9 to 18 inches tall. Gently spreading plants with pale blue blossoms in early spring. Space 1 foot apart.

Wild columbine (*Aquilegia canadensis*): Perennial, to 18 inches tall. In early spring, red and yellow blossoms borne above delicate-lobed foliage. Space 1 foot apart.

Wild cranesbill (*Geranium maculatum*): Perennial, to 1 foot tall with 18-inch spread. Sharply lobed leaves; pale lavender-pink blossoms in spring. Space 1 foot apart.

A Hardy Northern Garden

Winter can bring a dreary mix of rain, sleet, wind, and snow to the upper Midwest and Northeast. Many perennials can't take the combination of cold and wet during northern winters. For this design, Cole Burrell has carefully selected long-lived perennials that can survive these punishing conditions and bloom reliably when warmer weather finally arrives.

This flower border is designed to be viewed from both sides, such as along a walkway or driveway. The center of the bed is planted with peonies, bleeding hearts, Russell lupines, and daylilies, all taller perennials with attractive foliage. They make up the spine or backbone of the bed, around which the low-growing cranesbill and heartleaf bergenia bloom, making curving blocks of color on either side. Moderately tall clumps of Siberian iris to the side of the lupines give this garden depth and a stair-stepping of plants from tallest to lowest. The garden blooms in shades of pink from the bleeding heart and peony, and in lavender and blue from the lupines and irises. Daylilies add bright spots of yellow.

Gardeners who want to start small or save money on buying plants can install this garden in sections over a period of two to four years. To install in phases, just prepare one-fourth or one-half the bed for planting the first year. As the perennials multiply, dig and divide them. Use the divisions to fill in newly dug sections of bed in future years.

Early-spring bulbs and spreading annuals weave the perennials together with splashes of color, and they are easy to add to this cold-resistant flower garden. Set in bulbs of scilla, tulips, and daffodils in the first fall after you plant the garden. They will add spring color, and the perennials will fill in and hide their fading foliage after bloom. In spring, plant annuals like alyssum in gaps between perennials.

NO-FAIL FEATURES

Cold-Hardy Beauty. Winter cold in Zones 3 and 4 is too intense for many perennial plants. And the combination of cold and wet soil can bring on crown and root rots even in hardy species. All the plants in this design are proven survivors of cold, soggy northern winters.

All-Around Views. No matter where you stand, this bed offers an interesting and attractive mix of heights, textures, and color. Tall plants run down the middle of the bed, with low plants bordering on each side and at both ends of the bed. This all-around view makes this a great design for a spot that's open on all sides.

Fabulous Foliage. This bed will teach you to enjoy the design possibilities of leaf textures. There's marvelous contrast between the bold, paddle-shaped foliage of heartleaf bergenia and the finely cut leaves of yarrow and cranesbill. Grassy clumps of tall iris and daylilies punctuate the design.

Tall peonies, bleeding heart, lupines, and daylilies make a colorful center for a long, narrow bed of cold-hardy perennials.
Contrasting leaf shapes and textures add interest. Lacy bleeding
heart leaves mingle with bold peony foliage, spiky daylilies, and
the delicate, notched lupine leaves.

―→·←―

WINTER PROTECTION

Ease perennial plants into the dormant stage by holding back on fertilizer and water as summer comes to an end. Also allow some late-season flowers to go to seed, instead of deadheading them. This helps to lull plants into a protective, dormant state.

After frost kills the plant tops, cut them back to the ground. Remove the trimmings to the compost pile.

When the soil turns cold, cover plants with a layer of loose organic mulch such as straw, pine needles, or shredded leaves. For extra protection from drying winds, top the mulch with evergreen boughs. Don't use a heavy mulch like compost that will retain lots of moisture—it will invite root rot.

Snow cover is wonderful protection for your perennials. Pile it on your beds when you shovel the driveway or walk.

―→·←―

Creating a Hardy Northern Garden

These hardy plants thrive in sun in Zones 3 through 5. Well-drained soil is highly important to avoid problems with root rot; these perennials will grow best in loamy soil that is well drained but retains some water. Partial shade from afternoon heat is acceptable in areas where summers are hot and dry.

For instructions on planting perennials, see "Problem-Free Planting" on page 271. After the first year of growth, maintenance requirements are few for these tough, adaptable plants. Coax the cranesbill, Persian nepeta, and golden marguerite to rebloom by shearing off spent blossoms. Be sure to protect the bed properly during the winter. For directions, see "Winter Protection" on this page.

Plants for a Hardy Northern Garden

Bleeding heart (*Dicentra spectabilis*): Perennial, 2 to 3 feet tall. Delicate fernlike foliage persists all summer in cool, northern areas; strings of 1-inch pink, heart-shaped flowers in spring on tall, arching stems. Space 3 feet apart.

Cranesbill (*Geranium* × 'Johnson's Blue'): Perennial, 1 to 2 feet tall. Mounded growth habit and 2-inch-wide blue flowers that bloom all summer. Space 2 feet apart. Trim plants to ground level after blooming to encourage flush of new leaves in late summer.

Daylilies (*Hemerocallis* spp.): Perennial, usually 2 to 3 feet tall. Lily-shaped flowers borne on tall stems above straplike foliage. Blooms midsummer. Choose gold, yellow, or orange cultivars. Space 2 to 3 feet apart.

Golden marguerite (*Anthemis tinctoria* 'Moonlight'): Perennial, 1 to 2 feet tall. Finely cut, scented foliage; light-yellow daisylike flowers bloom all summer. Long-lasting blooms make excellent cut flowers. Space 2 feet apart.

Heartleaf bergenia (*Bergenia cordifolia*): Perennial, 8 to 12 inches tall. Bold, evergreen foliage turns bronze in fall; bright pink flowers appear on stout stalks in spring. Space 1 foot apart.

Peony (*Paeonia lactiflora*): Perennial, to 4 feet tall and 3 feet wide. Large, 3- to 4-inch-wide, open flowers bloom on

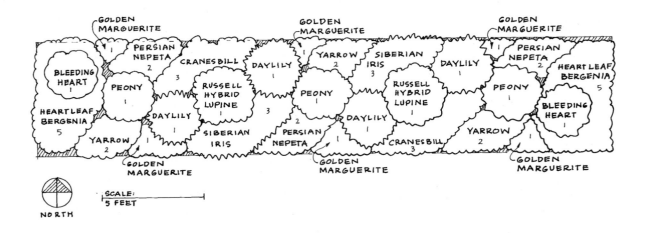

bushy plants in late spring; choose a pink or rose hybrid cultivar; white and red cultivars are also available. Space 3 feet apart. Use cages to support foliage and blooms.

Persian nepeta (*Nepeta mussinii* 'Blue Wonder'): Perennial, 1 to 1½ feet tall, and 1½ to 2 feet wide. Mounded plant with clusters of blue flower spikes in spring to early summer. Space 1 foot apart.

Russell hybrid lupine (*Lupinus* 'Russell' hybrid): Perennial, 2½ to 3½ feet tall. Deeply cut foliage; pea-like flowers on long-stemmed spikes in early summer. Choose a blue or purple cultivar; or for a different color scheme, try pink, red, or maroon cultivars, bicolors, or mixes. Space 3 feet apart. Stake flower spikes before bloom. Cut spent flowers after blooming.

Siberian iris (*Iris sibirica*): Perennial, 3 feet tall. Tidy clumps of grasslike leaves stay attractive all season; graceful 2- to 3-inch-wide flowers in spring. Choose a blue-purple or white cultivar. Space 3 to 4 feet apart since clumps will spread. Leave seed heads after bloom for summer interest.

Yarrow (*Achillea* 'Appleblossom' and 'Hope'): Perennial, 2 to 3 feet tall. Finely cut foliage; flat, multi-floret gold flower heads in late summer. Can be used as a cut flower and is easy to dry. Space 1 to 1½ feet apart.

➡ · ⬅

NO-FAIL FEATURES

Tough Survivors. The perennials in this design can withstand deep freezes in winter and scorching hot summer droughts, and still come through smiling in tones of bright yellow, warm gold, and rust.

Cheerful Cut Flowers. Daffodils make glorious spring bouquets. Use Shasta daisies and torch lilies in long-lasting flower arrangements in summer. Fernleaf yarrow has a long vase life and also is easy to dry and use in fall flower arrangements featuring dried flowers.

Birds and Butterflies. The torch lily is a favorite of hummingbirds, as are the lilies. Butterflies add more movement and color to the garden as they visit the 'Autumn Joy' sedum, Shasta daisies, and melampodium.

➡ · ⬅

A Heat-Tolerant Midwest Garden

Hot summers, fierce winter winds, and alternating thaws and deadly cold make the Midwest a tough climate for many flowering plants. For a no-fail flower garden, designer Sue Bartelette relies on plants that are both heat- and cold-tolerant.

This garden wraps around the corner of a fenced field near the end of a long rural driveway. Its cheerful yellow and gold blossoms could serve as a landmark for visitors trying to find the residence.

This bed is full of color from spring until frost. Yellow daffodils and iris ring in the spring. Summer is a riot of red, orange, and yellow from the blooms of daylilies, lilies, melampodium, and torch lilies. However, the garden's most important feature is drought tolerance. These perennials will need some water after they are first planted, but after they are established they require no additional irrigation. Train your plants to develop deep root systems from the start by offering deep, infrequent waterings—once a week or less. Make every raindrop count by mulching and adding organic matter to your soil. Use organic mulches like wood chips, compost, or partly decomposed leaves around your plants to shade the soil and seal in moisture.

Gardeners who have smaller suburban properties can adapt this design to a traditional rectangular bed. For a small garden, substitute a shorter ornamental grass such as fountain grass (*Pennisetum* spp.) for the zebra grass, or use a garden ornament, such as a piece of sculpture, a birdbath, or a sundial. You can also extend the planting to follow the curve of a horseshoe driveway.

For a traditional border along a fence line or next to a lawn, position the plants so that the tall zebra grass, torch lily, fernleaf yarrow, and lilies are at the back of the bed, and the daylilies, irises, sedum, Shasta daisies, and melampodium are in the middle and front. A bed viewed from all sides should have the tallest plant material in the middle.

A striking clump of zebra grass serves as the anchor for a planting of heat- and drought-tolerant perennials. In mid-summer,
'Enchantment' lilies, melampodium, and torch lilies brighten the
bed with red and yellow. Bring the longlasting blooms of fernleaf
yarrow and Shasta daisies indoors for summer bouquets.

—→·←—

SHELTERING NEW PLANTS

Even tough perennials need special protection from a hot climate when they're first planted. Follow these guidelines for getting young plants off to the best possible start.

• Whenever possible, plant on a cloudy day.
• Water *immediately* after transplanting.
• Form a shallow basin with soil or mulch around the root zone of new plants to help trap every bit of moisture.
• Cover the young plants with newspaper tents weighted with rocks at the corners.
• Check the soil moisture around the plants every few days. Don't let the soil dry out or get too soggy the first week of growth. Keep it evenly moist.
• For the first growing season, check the soil moisture each week. Water deeply whenever necessary, and let the soil dry out between waterings.

—→·←—

Creating a Heat-Tolerant Midwest Garden

All these plants bloom in full sun but will tolerate a few hours of shade a day. These tough plants will grow well in most garden soils in Zones 4 through 8, except for torch lilies, which are hardy only to Zone 5.

For instructions on planting perennials, see "Problem-Free Planting" on page 271. These plants will require 1 inch of water per week during the first summer of growth. Mulching will help conserve moisture.

Allow bulb and lily foliage to ripen naturally after flowering. After frost, pull the faded lily stalks and dead leaves from the iris. Cut back the melampodium and scatter the seedpods to ensure a good show next summer.

Plants for a Heat-Tolerant Midwest Garden

Bearded iris (*Iris* 'Golden Sunshine'): Perennial, 2 feet tall. Straplike foliage; showy yellow-bearded flowers in late spring. Space 6 inches apart.

Melampodium (*Melampodium paludosum* 'Medallion'): Tender perennial, to 1 foot tall. Golden yellow flowers in summer; green foliage. Space 10 inches apart. Short-lived but reseeds easily.

Daffodil (*Narcissus* 'Dutch Master'): Bulb, 1 foot tall. Cheerful yellow trumpet-shaped blooms in early spring. Space 6 inches apart.

Daylily (*Hemerocallis* × *hybrida* 'Stella de Oro'): Perennial, 18 to 24 inches tall. Narrow leaves; bright gold flowers all summer. Space 1 foot apart.

Fernleaf yarrow (*Achillea filipendulina* 'Cloth of Gold'): Perennial, to 4 feet tall. Finely cut foliage and stiff upright form; flat, mustard yellow flower clusters in late summer. Space 18 inches apart.

Lily (*Lilium* 'Enchantment'): Bulb, 3 to 4 feet tall. Huge, fragrant, trumpet-shaped, orange blossoms in summer. Space 6 inches apart.

Sedum (*Sedum* 'Autumn Joy'): Perennial, 2 feet tall. Thick stems and rounded, waxy leaves; pink flowers in late summer turn deep rose and then bronze in late fall. Leave

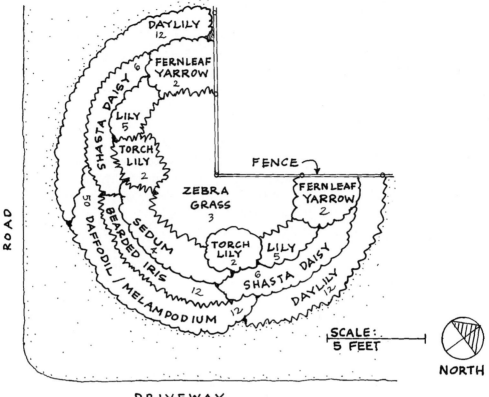

DAYLILY
12

FERNLEAF
YARROW
2

SHASTA DAISY 6

LILY
5

TORCH
LILY
2

FENCE

ZEBRA
GRASS
3

FERNLEAF
YARROW
2

50 DAFFODIL / MELAMPODIUM

BEARDED IRIS

SEDUM
4

TORCH
LILY
2

LILY
5

12

6
SHASTA DAISY

12

DAYLILY
12

ROAD

SCALE:
5 FEET

NORTH

DRIVEWAY

dried seed heads on plants for winter interest.

Shasta daisy (*Chrysanthemum × superbum* 'Starburst'): Perennial, 2 to 3 feet tall. White flowers with bright yellow centers bloom in early summer. Space 10 inches apart.

Torch lily (*Kniphofia uvaria*): Perennial, 3 to 5 feet tall. Long, grasslike leaves; tall flower spikes have tubular yellow flowers at the base and red flowers above in summer. Space 1 foot apart.

Zebra grass (*Miscanthus sinensis* 'Zebrinus'): Perennial, to 7 feet tall. Arching, narrow leaves with yellowish white crosswise stripes; attractive rust-brown seed heads in late summer to fall. Space 2 feet apart.

—→·←—

Tough Shade Plants. The hardy perennials in this garden are shade lovers that will thrive in the cold winters and hot summers of the Midwest.

Spring and Summer Color. By mid-spring, the ajuga and periwinkle display their blue flowers. Bleeding heart and primroses add their pink and jewel-colored blossoms to the scene. Summer color, in shades of blue, pink, and red, comes from great blue lobelia, spiderwort, impatiens, and astilbe.

Built-In Weed Control. Ajuga and periwinkle are vigorous groundcovers that will blanket every inch of available ground surface with their evergreen foliage and spring flowers. These ground-hugging plants can smother all but the most invasive weeds. They also act as a living mulch, shading the soil and keeping things cool for the roots of the neighboring plants.

—→·←—

A Shady Midwest Garden

Shade gardens fill dark spots with a mix of color and texture. They're a pleasant spot to retreat to in the baking heat of a midwestern summer. Scottie Garrett created this garden to lift wilted spirits of gardeners who can't bear another hour in the baking sun. It will thrive in a shady area by a fence or along the north end of a house or garage.

The showy blue-purple flowers of great blue lobelia are the centerpiece of this garden in summer. Spiderwort flowers echo the blue-violet color, and hosta adds rich green foliage edged with white. Astilbe and bleeding heart supply complementary touches of red and pink.

The hardest workers in this summer garden are the aptly nicknamed "Bizzy Lizzy" or impatiens plants. Brightly colored blossoms cover these annuals from early summer until frost. No shade garden seems complete without ferns, and on a hot summer day the tall green fronds of the marginal shield fern wave in the slightest breeze.

Fern leaves also make a fine show in spring as they unfurl against a background of blue periwinkle flowers. Primroses attract attention in mid-spring to early summer with an assortment of yellow, red, pink, white, and purple flowers. Spikes of blue ajuga flowers chime in later during spring or early summer.

For more early color, add spring bulbs that will pop up through the groundcovers, including the minor or smaller bulbs such as snowdrops (*Galanthus* spp.), dwarf daffodils, crocuses, and squills (*Scilla* spp.).

You can create a sitting area in the middle of this bed by putting in stepping stones through the primroses that lead to a bench. Plant the spiderwort at the sides of the seating area, and put in only two plants instead of three.

For a smaller or narrower space, leave out the great blue lobelia and tall ferns, and arrange the hosta, astilbe, and spiderwort in staggered clumps, with the impatiens separating these perennials and the ajuga and vinca groundcovers knitting them together. You'll find another variation on this design on page 210.

Foliage contrasts are an important ingredient in a successful shade garden. The wide, rippling leaves of hosta provide strong contrast to delicate, shiny green fern fronds and the lacy leaves of the bleeding heart. The leaves' many shades of green show off red astilbe as well as blue spiderwort and great blue lobelia flowers.

SETTLING ON A SHAPE

When you plan a garden, remember that flower beds don't have to be shaped like a twin bed! Try one of these variations:

• A serpentine or scalloped edge adds a casual, country look to a bed. Low, spreading plants such as primroses grow well as edging plants for this type of curving border.

• An island planting bed in the middle of the lawn can be viewed from all sides. The island can be shaped like a star, a crescent, or even a daisy. Edge the bed with rocks or bricks.

• A barbell-shaped bed can accent a pair of trees or shrubs.

• A triangular or fan-shaped flower bed will fit nicely in the corner where a driveway and walkway intersect, or at the corner of your property.

• A string of diamond-shaped beds can lend formality to roses, perennials, and annuals.

Creating a Shady Midwest Garden

All of these plants thrive in shade in Zones 3 through 8. Great blue lobelia, hosta, bleeding heart, impatiens, and especially the primroses need soil that is moist but well drained. Add lots of organic matter such as compost or shredded leaves to the soil to help it retain moisture.

For directions on planting perennials, see "Problem-Free Planting" on page 271. After planting, lay a soaker hose on the ground around the plants, and cover it with a bark-chip mulch. The mulch will not only hide the hose, but seal in moisture and cool the soil as well. If you choose not to use a soaker hose, water deeply once a week in hot weather.

Plants for a Shady Midwest Garden

Ajuga (*Ajuga reptans*): Perennial. Evergreen groundcover with deep green, shiny leaves; 6-inch spikes of blue flowers in late spring and early summer. Space 6 inches apart. Cut back foliage that overgrows neighboring plants.

Astilbe (*Astilbe × arendsii* 'Fanal'): Perennial, 2 feet tall. Bronze, fernlike foliage; spikes of dark crimson flowers in early to midsummer. Space 2 feet apart.

Great blue lobelia (*Lobelia siphilitica*): Perennial, to 30 inches tall and 20 inches wide. Showy blue to violet flowers in midsummer to fall. Space 2 feet apart.

Impatiens (*Impatiens wallerana*): Annual, to 1 foot tall. Small, flat blossoms in white, pink, rose, red, orange, lavender, purple, or combinations. Space 6 inches apart.

Marginal shield fern (*Dryopteris marginalis*): Perennial, 2 feet tall. Shiny green fronds. Also called leather wood fern. Space 3 feet apart.

Periwinkle (*Vinca minor*): Perennial, 4-inch evergreen groundcover. Starlike blue flowers in spring. Space 8 inches apart. Cut back foliage that overgrows neighboring plants.

Primrose (*Primula × polyantha* 'Crescendo' hybrids): Perennial, 8 inches tall. Blooms mid-spring in rich jewel-tone colors. Reblooms in fall if kept watered. Space 6 inches apart. Water well during summer to encourage reblooming in fall.

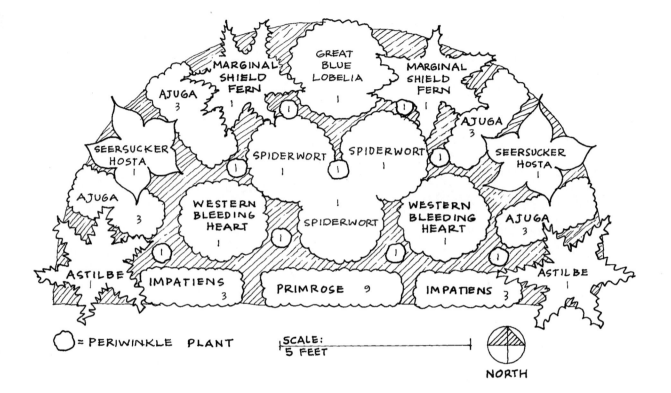

Seersucker hosta (*Hosta sieboldii* 'Snowflakes'): Perennial, to 18 inches tall. Huge, white-edged leaves; skinny stalks of white flowers in midsummer. Space 2 feet apart.

Spiderwort (*Tradescantia* × *andersoniana* 'Zwanenberg Blue'): Perennial, 2 feet tall. Succulent, spreading foliage; blue-violet flowers in early summer. Space 3 feet apart. Cut off old blooms to encourage continued flowering. Plants fade and look bedraggled in hot weather. Cut them back hard and they will respond with new growth and flowers when cooler fall weather arrives.

Western bleeding heart (*Dicentra formosa* 'Bachanal'): Perennial, 15 inches tall. Lacy foliage and pendulant, heart-shaped, rose-red blooms from mid-spring to fall. Space 1 foot apart.

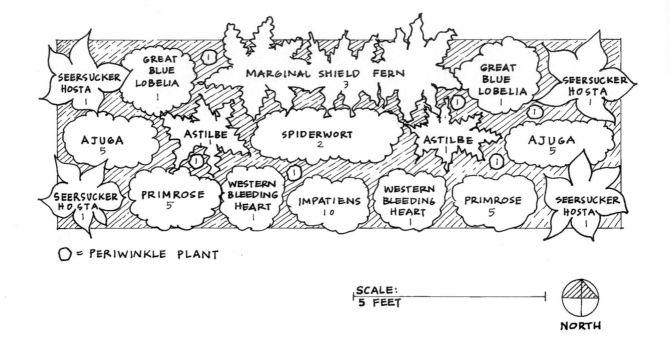

○ = PERIWINKLE PLANT

SCALE:
5 FEET

NORTH

Adapting a Garden Plan

The garden plan above uses the same plants as the plan on page 209. Scottie Garrett transformed the garden from a semicircle to a rectangle to show how easy it is to adapt plans to suit your site.

The basic principle to follow in changing the shape of a design is: tall plants in the back, medium-sized plants in the middle, and low plants in the front. Here, the low primroses and impatiens line the front of both the semicircular and rectangular beds. For a change of pace, Garrett moved bleeding hearts forward in the rectangular bed. Feel free to experiment with plant placement as he did— an occasional tall or medium-sized plant up front can add a delightful visual surprise.

You may increase or decrease the numbers of plants of each species to accommodate the new shape. For example, this rectangular planting has a longer back than the original semicircular planting. So Garrett has used two great blue lobelias instead of one and increased the number of ferns from two to three.

CHAPTER 6

Great Ideas and Finishing Touches

A no-fail garden is more than just healthy plants arranged attractively in a bed. It's the stone bench or lattice arbor, the brass sundial or rock wall, that catches your eye and finishes the picture. These finishing touches are the fun and creative accents that make a garden distinctively yours.

In this chapter, you'll find out where to look for great design ideas and how to adapt them for your home garden. You'll also learn how to incorporate accents and features into your garden plan and how to use finishing touches like edgings and focal points to dress up your plantings.

First, Look Around

Adding finishing touches is an easy way to improve an already successful garden. And you can find ideas right outside your window and just down the street. Notice which details catch your eye as you pass the neighbors' yards, visit the park, or drive to work. If a neighbor has planted a narrow strip in the alley with compact flowering plants, could this work in the narrow planting strip next to your patio?

Pay attention to what looks good in the professionally landscaped businesses where you do your banking or shopping. Do you like the colors in the planting? Does your doctor's office have a large picture window like the one

Flower shows are great idea warehouses for home gardeners! They're often held at the end of winter, when we're dying for flower color and starting to think seriously about our own garden plans. This simple bed of daffodils and polyanthus primroses (*Primula × polyantha*) could have come right off the show floor. Look for similar ideas at your local flower show if you need a colorful solution for a hard-to-mow spot.

you have at home? What kind of plants have the landscapers used to spotlight the doctor's office window?

Ideas found closest to home are usually easiest to imitate, especially when it comes to plants. That's because you can be sure the plants are available in your area and that they'll survive in your climate. The fact that they're already growing in your community is proof of that. Don't let this general rule keep you from branching out, though. You can always find great ideas in garden books and magazines and by visiting display gardens and flower shows. Just check plant hardiness before you duplicate the planting exactly. If the plants used aren't hardy in your area, substitute similar plants that are appropriate.

Branching Out

Once you've sized up the neighborhood plantings, try a few fact-finding tours a bit farther from home. A fun and inexpensive way to pick up great ideas is to visit display gardens, public parks, and any other professionally landscaped areas that appeal to you. Wear comfortable shoes, and bring along a notebook and a camera to record the details of these successful gardens. That way you won't forget all the ideas you want to imitate once you return home to your own turf.

Plants in public gardens are often marked with identification tags. If you're not familiar with a plant but like the way it looks, draw a sketch of its foliage or flowers next to its name in your notebook. Add a brief description to help you remember what it looks like. Don't forget to note down good combinations as well as individual plants. Talk to the horticulturists at the botanical garden about where you can buy plants you admire and whether they'll survive in your area.

Finding Your Garden Accents

Once you've seen an accent you want, look for it in your local garden center, nursery, or specialty garden accent store. If you don't have a garden store where you live, don't despair. You can still buy the best in outdoor accents

EXPERT FLOWER PHOTOS

You can take high-quality photos of good garden ideas if you follow the advice of professional garden photographer Liz Ball. Here are her suggestions for taking better pictures of flowers:

Lens: Purchase an all-purpose 28- to 70-millimeter zoom lens. This gives good shots up close and at a distance.

Film: Use Kodachrome 200 for outdoor shots.

Close-Ups: Use a close-up lens and position yourself about 1 foot away for close-up shots of flowers.

Light: Natural light on a day when the sun is shaded by high clouds is ideal for garden photography.

Professional Tip: You need to use a tripod to get top-quality flower photos. Without one, even the slightest movement of your hand when you snap a picture will blur the photograph. A tripod ensures that the camera will remain motionless for the photo.

Use a notebook or garden diary to record plant combinations at favorite gardens. You'll find it pays to make repeat visits, to find out how plant combinations change through the seasons. The spring combination recorded here, for example, transforms itself into an equally appealing scene in late summer.

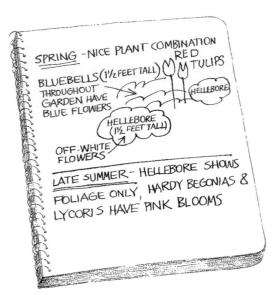

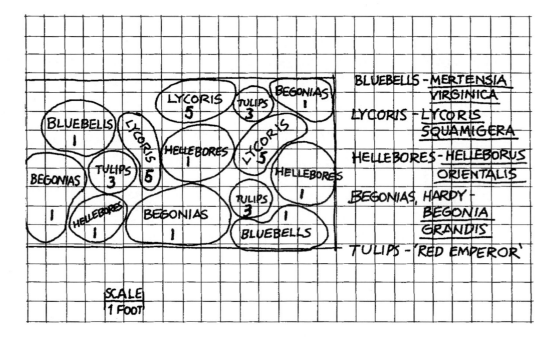

The best way to record the exact design for a plant combination is to make a bubble diagram in your notebook. Pace off the distances between plants, and then draw "bubbles" to record where each plant was located. Be sure to note how many of each type of plant there are. Then you'll be able to reproduce all or part of the planting back home.

from the many mail-order garden catalogs. These colorful catalogs sell everything for the garden, from fine teak benches to small stone frogs. You'll find great ideas for plant supports, garden arches, and even edging materials to keep your garden in line. No matter where you live, fine garden ornaments and accents can be delivered right to your garden gate.

Shortcuts from Garden Shows

Garden and flower shows are held all over the country. Among the biggest are the Philadelphia Flower Show, the New England Flower Show in Boston, and, in Seattle, the Northwest Flower and Garden Show. On a smaller scale, you can find garden shows and fairs held almost every spring weekend throughout the country. To find out about the local shows in your area, call the local garden club or your county extension agent. Both groups are usually associated with local shows.

A garden show is a great place to look for beautiful color combinations and new ways to use familiar plants. Study how garden features, pathways, and arches are used in the show garden designs. Use a notebook and write down or draw what impresses you, in order to recreate the idea back home. This is where a camera can really come in handy, too.

For example, say you saw a flower show garden featuring a river of blue grape hyacinths edged with yellow daffodils that snaked through a very impressively designed garden. Obviously, not many gardeners have the room or the time to plant a river of daffodils and grape hyacinths. But jotting down a note in your garden notebook about such a classic plant combination may be enough to remind you to add a cluster of grape hyacinths to an existing stand of daffodils next fall. When your tiny version of blue and yellow spring color blooms each spring, it will bring back beautiful memories of that full-scale display from the flower show.

You can also use garden show scenes as inspiration for your own designs. For example, at a flower show you may see a beautiful display of irregularly shaped flagstone terraces that's beyond your budget. If you like the look of

TO BUY—OR NOT TO BUY

Garden accents such as benches and artwork may seem expensive when compared to the cost of seeds or bedding plants. But these additions to your garden give you great-looking permanent accents immediately and need very little maintenance.

The stone birdbath you've always wanted may cost you more than a flat of petunias, but it won't need regular feeding, watering, or staking to keep it alive and looking good. And you won't have to buy more every year!

Small garden accents like sundials and gazing balls are easy to move, but heavier items like arbors and stone walls usually have to stay where you put them. Before investing in one of these permanent additions, make sure you know where you want it to go. *Then* buy it. (For tips you can use to visualize a feature in your garden before it's actually there, read "See the Garden Before You Plant" on page 14.)

Before investing in expensive, permanent garden ornaments, like trellises, consider your long-range plans. If you plan on moving in a few years, use this clever shortcut instead: Train quick-growing vines up existing trees for a mature look in short order. Here, 'Madame Julia Correvon' clematis adds glowing color to a blue Atlas cedar (*Cedrus atlantica* 'Glauca').

stones fitting together like a jigsaw puzzle, you can "take it home" in your notebook by drawing a rough sketch of the way the flagstones fit together. Then use chunks of broken concrete or concrete pavers to lay a path in the same casual fashion in your own backyard.

The lesson to be learned here is to always record what appeals to you, using any combination of written notes, photos, and drawings. You can then use these great ideas to create something different, original, and often much more practical than the thing you originally admired. Just because you can't afford a Mona Lisa doesn't mean you stop hanging pictures on the wall.

Tips from a Pro—Mother Nature

Formal, fancy, and professionally landscaped gardens aren't the only sources of inspiration for gardeners looking for great ideas. Every climate and region has its own natural vegetation artistically arranged by Mother Nature. From the majestic rainforests of the West Coast to the rugged rock and cacti landscapes of Arizona, natural landscapes are full of pleasing plant combinations. Imitate them back home, or use them for design inspiration.

Remember that the goal is to take *ideas* from nature, not plants. Leave the plants in the wild where they belong and where others can enjoy them. Many nurseries carry native plants that they have propagated themselves rather than collecting them from the wild. Make sure the native plants you buy are nursery-propagated.

Pay attention to the way plants grow in nature, too. Plants that have similar soil, moisture, and sun requirements often grow together. Moisture lovers like ferns and forget-me-nots are down by the creek, while drought-tolerant cornflowers, oxeye daisies, and yarrows grow well and look great in the gravelly soil next to the roadside and in open fields. Note that there are clumps or clusters of the same plant growing together instead of solitary specimens facing the world alone. You'll see a whole field of Queen Anne's lace or a few miles of mullein along a road. That's why plants look more . . . well . . . natural in groups.

GREAT IDEAS FROM GARDEN SHOWS

You may not want or be able to recreate the grand gardens you see at shows. But great ideas at the show can become great ideas at home if you use fewer plants and some ingenuity. For example:

Mass Plantings. At the show, hundreds of red and yellow tulips make a magnificent display.

Back home: Plant 25 yellow and 25 red tulips, placing the bulbs just 2 inches apart. You'll get solid blocks of color just like the show gardens.

Babbling Brook. Water features like fountains set off flowers. The sound and motion of water draw show visitors like a magnet.

Back home: Create your own small water feature. See "A Dooryard Reflecting Pool" on page 190 for details.

Great Urns of Flowers. Huge clay pots overflowing with blooming plants make a fabulous impression.

Back home: Use a large pot, not a giant one. Give it height by setting it on an overturned pot.

You'll find inspiring ideas for both plant combinations and garden accents at flower shows. This flagstone path accent and the combination of bearded iris, hostas, and lady's-mantle (*Alchemilla mollis*) are two great ideas you might bring home from a show.

Look at other natural elements like fallen logs, streams, and giant boulders. You'll see how to work similar effects into your own garden, working on a backyard scale. Nature has great ideas for mulches, too. Pine needles make a soft mulch on the floor of a pine grove, fallen leaves arrive just in time to mulch the soil and protect woodland plants before winter sets in, and mosses create a velvety evergreen carpet in moist glades. When you use straw as a mulch or for winter protection, you are imitating the way nature provides dead grasses to mulch a field, protecting wildflower seeds from birds and mice and insulating perennial wildflower roots from winter cold.

Taking the Bad with the Good

While noting down the good points of gardens and plants in your neighborhood, look for what you don't like, too. Every weedy shrub, ugly color combination, or mildew-prone flower you don't plant saves you time and money. If you can avoid problems, you've found the key to no-fail flower gardening.

There's no reason to add plants to your garden that are not well adapted to the area. In most cases you can find a related plant that has the features you want without the problems. For example, a quick look at a neighbor's common lilac (*Syringa vulgaris*) will tell you it's a shrub that's susceptible to mildew and several other diseases. Don't spend your time fighting problems; instead, plant a disease-resistant Japanese tree lilac (*Syringa reticulata*) or ask the staff at your local nursery or garden center for disease-resistant common lilac cultivars.

Keep an eye on the pathway materials and garden accents that your neighbors have tried. Is the gravel path in your neighbor's yard always sprouting weeds? Does it look scruffy and unkempt? That should be a signal to you that gravel paths need high maintenance. Does a gardener you know have a cracked or damaged plastic birdbath? Do you remember when a windstorm left it lying forlornly on the ground? That scene should make you consider a more expensive but durable cement or ceramic birdbath.

Bold combinations of flower and leaf colors can light up

NATURE TO THE RESCUE!

You can always use a fallen log, tree stump, or boulder as part of your garden design. But did you know that they're also problem-solving tools?

A fallen log makes a great dividing line between different garden areas. It provides a low screen to serve as a background for the fine texture of ferns and other woodland plants. A log will also visually separate a wooded area or meadow from your landscaped areas.

A tree stump is perfect as a natural pedestal for birdhouses or bird feeders in rustic gardens. If you hollow out the top, it's also a great planter for ivy.

Boulders can fill in those hard-to-handle areas where nothing will grow. Set three or more large boulders into the ground, burying at least the bottom third of each rock. This makes the boulders look like they're part of a natural rock outcropping. You can add smaller stones or loose gravel around the boulders for an even more natural look.

━━━━━━ ⇢ · ⇠ ━━━━━━

IDEAS FROM NATURE

Here's how to take ideas from nature and turn them into something you can use in your garden:

• Wildflowers mix with native grasses on the prairie. Add some ornamental grasses to your perennial bed.

• Azaleas bloom beneath oak trees in southern forests. Plant your azaleas under trees, where they'll be protected from the sun.

• The eastern forests are a mix of evergreen and deciduous trees. This contrast of texture and color is lovely all year, but especially in fall and winter. Add a few evergreen shrubs to your flower garden to give it contrast in the fall and winter months.

• Emerald green West Coast rainforests drip with ferns and mosses. Learn to appreciate and encourage the mosses that grow in the shade of your garden. Plant ferns against dark tree trunks to set off their delicate foliage.

• In the desert, cacti grow near rocks. Use stones around the sedums and hens-and-chickens in your yard.

━━━━━━ ⇢ · ⇠ ━━━━━━

your garden or send you running for your sunglasses. If you move to a new home and discover an overly brilliant mix of colors planted beside the front door, don't despair. You can tone down unusually bright combinations with borders of green. A strip of green groundcover, such as pachysandra, liriope, or English ivy, will rest your eyes and unify the bed. If the combination still offends you, remove one color and replace it with a neutral-colored perennial like 'Silver King' artemisia.

You can learn what you like and what you want to avoid just by noting your first impression of different landscaped areas. Do you find a casual or natural look messy and confusing, or relaxing? Does a formal garden with rows of plants make you feel restricted and confined, or contented? Add your feelings to your list of effects you like or don't like.

Framing Your Flower Garden

What a picture frame does for a work of art, edgings can do for flower gardens. A brick edging defining a rose garden and a fallen log marking a trail through a woodland garden both help to outline and define the space and personality of the garden.

Edgings can be formal and permanent, such as bricks or concrete curbing cemented into the ground. These edgings are low-maintenance because weeds won't grow into them or over them. A less formal and less expensive option is to line your beds with landscape timbers that are sunk into the ground. The problem here is that you can only make a straight edge. The easiest and least expensive edging is to use rocks and stones from your own property to outline your flower beds.

Other options are the strips of flexible plastic and corrugated steel edgings sold at garden centers and home improvement stores. These inexpensive edgings last a long time unless you run over them with the lawn mower and flatten, crack, or chip them. See "Mulch, and Use Edging Strips" on page 58 for tips on installing these products. Stores that sell edging strips will also sell the edging spades

Brick edging and a white picket fence add formal flavor to this garden of 'Johnson's Blue' cranesbills (*Geranium* 'Johnson's Blue'), 'Moonshine' yarrow (*Achillea* 'Moonshine'), Persian cat-mint (*Nepeta mussinii*), lamb's-ears (*Stachys byzantina*), and foxgloves (*Digitalis purpurea*). Notice how both elements serve double duty here: The flat edging makes a great mowing strip, while the fence screens the nearby pool from the garden.

─── ❧ · ❧ ───

FENCING MATCH

By choosing the right fence or edging for your flower bed or border, you can highlight your garden's style. Here's how:

Japanese-Style Garden. Use a bamboo-stake fence or smooth round stones to outline a border.

Cottage Garden. A picket fence is perfect for setting off informal cottage-style gardens. Or try a country fence made of crisscrossed branches.

Colonial Garden. A traditional garden looks best edged with bricks. Place them vertically, horizontally, or with only the corners exposed. You'll need a mowing strip if you set bricks so that their corners show. The corners make an attractive pointed border, but you can't mow over them like bricks laid flat. (See "Mulch, and Use Edging Strips" on page 58 for details.)

Woodland Garden. Show off native plants against a backdrop of fallen logs or a rustic split-rail fence.

─── ❧ · ❧ ───

or rent the sod cutters you'll need to shape the bed's outline and remove lawn grass.

No matter what type of edging material you choose, marking the boundaries of your garden can help you organize your thoughts as well as your flowers. Edgings make a casual garden design look tidier. They can even turn a wild area like a meadow into a garden just by enclosing it.

Screens and Backdrops for Beautiful Gardens

Imagine how much more visible a flower garden would be with a solid fence or house wall in the background, compared to the same garden with a neighbor's carport or open field behind it. It's like trying to read words written with a pen on a piece of white paper compared to reading the same words on a page of newspaper. On the newspaper, all the letters jumble together because the background they are written on is so busy. You can show off your flowers best against a simple background like a fence. Or plant a screen of trees and shrubs for a plain green background. Good choices include Canada hemlocks (*Tsuga canadensis*), pines (*Pinus* spp.), hollies (*Ilex* spp.), bayberries (*Myrica* spp.), and viburnums (*Viburnum* spp.).

A screen or fence will also hide unsightly views like a neighbor's shed or old car. Or you could use a fence to provide support and extra growing space for climbing flowers. Vertical planting is an especially important consideration for small gardens that lack a view in the distance. Train a rose, clematis, or climbing honeysuckle vine up a trellis or fence to give a long, narrow garden bed more height. Adding height draws your eyes up, and that keeps the bed from looking so flat and narrow.

You can also use a trellis and flowering vine to break up a very wide or very deep bed. Imagine a garden arch in the center of a long stretch of lawn with flowering shrubs on each side. Breaking up that open expanse creates a much more intimate space and gives the garden a great focal point even from a distance.

Use Vines to Advantage

Try vertical growing in a naturalistic flower garden by using a stump or tree as a support for a flowering vine. Clematis, trumpet vine (*Campsis radicans*), and honeysuckle will all travel up a tree or stump without a lot of help from you.

A mailbox, a weathervane, and a post with a birdhouse on top are other options for showing off vines. These small structures are best for annual vines such as sweet peas, morning glories, climbing nasturtiums, and scarlet runner beans (*Phaseolus coccineus*).

Think of using a vine and support wherever you don't have room for a tree but still need something tall in the garden. You can also use vines to cover pergolas and other structures, providing shade for sun-sensitive plants and people. Most of all, think of flowering vines when you want an eye-catching garden focal point to build your flower garden around.

Make an Entrance

Creating an impressive entry into your garden by adding a gate or two pillars at the start of the path is a garden design classic. Gates were originally a part of every landscape because they served a very practical purpose of keeping the livestock out but allowing the people in. Different gate designs, from rustic wooden wheels to ornate wrought iron, became fashionable and practical as gardens evolved into beautiful places to grow flowers rather than practical plots to grow food.

Find great gate ideas by looking through garden books and magazines. Pay attention to the entrances of housing developments, business parks, and shopping centers. The brickwork may be a bit pretentious for home gardens, but the way that evergreen plants flank the entryway and the placement of the marigolds or other flowers are things you can try at home.

Most gates match the style of the fence they connect, but

➡️ · ⬅️

FINE FLOWERING VINES

To add that vertical dimension of color, grow these blooming vines where a colorful accent is needed.

Colorful Clematis (*Clematis* spp.). These vines like to have their feet in the shade and tops in the sun and will climb on just about anything without much help. Guide the first shoot up a post or trellis, and the rest of the vine will follow. They prefer loose, rich, moist soil.

Trumpet Honeysuckle (*Lonicera sempervirens*). This well-behaved plant has wonderful two-tone flowers, orange or red outside and yellow inside. Its tendrils will twine away on just about any structure. Honeysuckles look especially good on rustic, unpainted arbors and on split-rail fences.

Climbing Roses. These don't twine or attach themselves with tendrils, so carefully bend the canes through or tie them on a lattice against a wall or archway. Like all roses, the climbers need sun, fertile soil, and lots of water.

➡️ · ⬅️

This moon gate adds an informal Japanese touch to the garden and allows visitors a good view of the colorful azaleas, Japanese maples, tulips, and forget-me-nots (*Myosotis sylvestris*) waiting inside. The round cutout also echoes the shape of the arch at the end of the path. Touches like these can make even a small, simple garden a standout.

there is also a trend toward garden gates that stand alone, without a fence enclosing the rest of the garden. Two posts are all you need to support a gate and latch. Why have a gate without a fence? Because a garden gate can be the most attractive focal point in your yard. A curved gate, a picket gate, even a gate made from an old metal headboard will attract your eye and be a great-looking companion for your flowering plants.

If the thought of building or buying a gate sounds too complex, you can still dress up the entry to your garden. A pair of pillars made from brick or stone, two lampposts, or two boulders marking the start of a path will anchor your garden vista and create a more pleasing composition. Even a simple path of stepping stones can be accented by posts or matching plants on each side at the start of the path.

Picture-Perfect Paths

Another way to create a beautiful and successful flower garden is by making an entryway and path part of your design. Adding a path not only gives you easy access for planting and weeding, it also provides a visual avenue for the eyes to follow.

The width of your walkway depends on where you locate it and how you'll use it. A simple walking path should be at least 24 inches wide for one person and 57 inches wide for two people. Paths that get more traffic, like those at the front of the house, should be wider than those located in the backyard. If your path will be used for maintenance, make sure it's wide enough for you and your wheelbarrow or garden cart: 3 feet wide at least.

Paths can serve many purposes besides being walkways or maintenance alleys. They can draw attention to a particular garden feature or enhance your garden style. Try some of the tips listed below for a pathway with pizzazz.

Accent your garden style with a matching path. A curving path looks casual and works best in a naturalistic or woodland garden. More-formal garden beds look better with straight pathways, especially when the path is bordered by brick or another hard edging to define its lines.

→·←

THROUGH THE GARDEN GATE

An entryway can set the tone of your whole garden. Besides a gate, consider these options:

• Two pillars of brick or stone, or even two fence posts spaced 3 feet apart, are a good choice where space is limited or you want to mark a pathway. You can put a hedge or fence on each side of the posts to enclose the garden.

• An archway or arbor at the entry to your garden is a quick way to add height, a focal point, and a structure for blooming vines. An archway also makes a good transitional structure from the front yard to the backyard or from one garden area to another.

• Two large boulders can mark the entrance to a trail or path in a naturalistic or woodland garden. Boulders draw attention to the start of a path without competing with your plants.

• A pair of matching pots is the traditional way to announce the entrance to a formal rose or herb garden.

→·←

MAKE YOUR PATHS USER-FRIENDLY

Pathways tempt visitors to use them, so design yours with ease of use and safety in mind. Run through the questions below for points to consider.

• Who will use your path? If your visitors include elderly relatives or children, adjust the spacing of stepping stones and steps to accommodate them.

• Are there hanging branches? Walk down your pathway and remove low branches that pose a danger to the eyes.

• Are there wet or slippery areas? Locate your path out of harm's way, or provide stepping stones or stairs to safely guide visitors through hazards.

Even if you garden on a slippery slope, there's no need to turn into a mountain goat. Gravel and landscape timber stairs will help you reach your plants easily. Anchor the timbers securely in place with metal spikes.

Give your path an obvious beginning. Use garden features like a potted plant, gate, or sculpture to mark the beginning of your path. Make it easy for visitors to find the entrance. If you'd like a more subtle look, make the start of the path wider than the rest of the walkway.

Add mystery by hiding your pathway's destination. In an informal garden, you'll pique visitors' curiosity if you use curves to conceal where your path is headed. When you create curves, make sure there's a reason for the path to turn. A path that wanders aimlessly will frustrate visitors more than excite them. Plant a tree or shrub at the path's edge or add a garden feature so there's a reason for the change in direction.

Steps and Stones

Steps make for more secure footing if your garden slopes more than 1 foot in every 10. Make it easy for you (and your

Paths can turn a casual collection of flowers into a lovely formal garden. Here, easy-care perennials like purple coneflowers (*Echinacea purpurea*), lamb's-ears (*Stachys byzantina*), and yarrow have been transformed by a network of pea-gravel paths. The brick edging defines the beds and adds another formal touch, as does the garden art centering the garden.

THEME GARDEN ART

When choosing accents for your garden, consider its theme or style. Add finishing touches that help define this theme. For example:

Heirloom Garden. Use an old plough, wagon wheel, or mill wheel in a garden of heirloom flowers.

Herb Garden. A sundial is a traditional feature for an herb garden. Put the sundial where two paths meet or in the exact center of a bed.

Country Garden. Stone animals and wooden whirligigs look right at home in a cottage or country-style garden. Tuck stone bunnies or cats in a corner of the bed. Use whimsical whirligigs nailed to a fence-post or at the end of a garden path where the wind will move them.

Bird Lover's Garden. Make a unique garden sculpture with a collection of birdhouses nailed to a post. Birdbaths and bird feeders will also attract birds to a garden of fruit-bearing shrubs and other food sources for wildlife.

guests) to get around a sloping property by installing a path of stepping stones. Make your path cross the hillside perpendicular to the slope instead of trying to make a pathway straight up and down. Before placing stones, create a level and stable surface for them—a 2-inch base of sand mixed with crushed rock works well. Set each stone so it fits slightly over the one below, but leave enough exposed surface for your foot to fit comfortably (at least 12 inches).

In a large area, steps formed from stepping stones may not be practical. Another option is to build gravel steps, using rock or pieces of landscape timber as the risers. Cover the tread or step area with gravel or wood chips to keep down weeds and to provide sure footing. Make sure the steps are both wide and deep enough for comfortable walking. Steps that are 5 inches high and 15 inches deep, or 6 inches high and 12 inches deep, work well for most gardens. Try walking up and down steps in other gardens and measure the ones you find easiest to use for a perfect fit. If your slope is gradual enough, a trail with switchbacks is another way to provide easy access to the plants on the hillside.

Adding Garden Art and Focal Points

What do you do with a newly planted flower garden, with lots of empty space and not enough mature plants? A pair of stone geese or several large boulders can help fill the bed while you wait for the plants to get comfortable and spread their leaves.

If your home and garden are more formal, with a symmetrical layout, neatly clipped hedges, and upright plants, choose focal points with a more traditional flare such as brass sundials, urns, or a birdbath on a fluted column. These formal accents look best if you place them in the center of your flower bed.

Cottage or country-style gardens with a mix of flowers and curving beds look better with garden accents that are more casual, such as stone animals and terra-cotta or hollowed stone birdbaths. These gardens can handle touches

of humor, such as wooden whirligigs or wooden tulips stuck in a window box. Casual landscape styles inspire cute or clever garden accents, reminding us to have fun with our garden designing.

Using plants as focal points is another way to punch up a predictable garden plan. In your flower garden, try an evergreen shrub with a dark color and course texture that contrasts with your flowers. Or add a rose trained to a standard or tree form, plants with variegated foliage like some of the striking hosta cultivars, or unusually colored flowers like purple roses or blue hydrangeas as focal points.

A stump can be an eyesore in any garden, and digging one out is an expensive proposition. Here, a sundial turns the stump into statuary and creates a customized touch for this bright garden of annuals, herbs, and perennials.

A mix of blue and variegated hostas brightens the shade under this tree. The hostas create a colorful focus where scruffy grass might have made an eyesore. Turn your "terminator zones" into triumphs with showy but well-suited plants.

Help for Your Terminator Zone

Sometimes a focal point or garden accent is the only solution for an especially challenging area, like the very narrow garden bed sandwiched between the house and the cement path that leads to the front door. Areas like these, which are baked by the sun and by the heat reflected off the wall, are garden "terminator zones." The "soil" in these areas may be partly full of cement chunks left by some builder and full of chemicals or salt used to clean off the nearby pathway.

Terminator zones are torture chambers where no plant should be asked to grow. Instead, try reworking the space by covering it with stones, gravel, or paving and then adding appropriate accents like a few pieces of driftwood, pottery, or a stone pagoda. If you're determined to convert the area into fertile ground, you'll find helpful tips in "Special Considerations and Challenging Situations" on page 133.

Using plants in pots is another solution to difficult growing situations. Potted plants also make colorful, portable, and changeable garden focal points. You can even use pots of flowers to spice up the in-ground plants in your flower garden. Pots can add height, offer better drainage to a touchy plant, or even protect bulbs and other special plants from rodents and insects.

Use a pair of clay pots to mark the entrance to your flower garden, or set them on each side of a garden bench for a touch of color. Set three pots in a row down the middle of a flower bed to give it a formal look, or put a pot of flowers in each corner of a square flower bed or in the center of a circular flower garden.

Think Change—Think Big

A garden is constantly evolving and changing. Don't be afraid to rearrange and improve your garden accents as your plants and experience grow and as your budget allows. For example, if all you can afford for your first patio

---

SPOTLIGHT SHOWY PLANTS

That special plant in your garden needs to be shown off, not tucked in a corner where it can fade into the shrubbery. Try these methods to draw attention to your favorites:

• Surround your prize plant with open space, or plant only groundcovers in the immediate area.

• Grow your best plant on a mound or in a raised bed.

• Use white flowers around the base of a brightly colored plant, such as white petunias with a crimson climbing rose.

• Use a dark mulch around the base of a white- or pastel-flowered plant, such as smooth black river rocks scattered around a clump of pale pink tulips.

• Call attention to an unusual specimen, like a lavender rose or blue poppy, by putting a plant label with the name of the plant at its base.

Don't forget the finishing touches when you're making a garden. This beautiful bench is twice as striking flanked by clay pots of colorful flowers. Notice how the tiny brick terrace under the bench provides dry footing and also acts as a divider, separating the garden areas.

is a backless wooden seat borrowed from an old picnic table and set on a bed of wood chips, that's fine. Perhaps you could upgrade after a few years to an iron and wood-slat park bench sitting on a small patio of gravel. When time and budget allow, you can change the area again to accommodate the courtyard of bricks with roses all around, and the curved stone bench you always dreamed of.

The moral of this story is to dream big, but don't let that stop you from filling in with inexpensive garden accents until you're ready to commit to some serious outdoor art-work. Use a birdbath until you can afford that fancy fountain, or set a clay pot or half-barrel on your porch steps until you can invest in a footed cement urn. And remember, bigger and more expensive isn't always better. An old weathered picnic bench looks right at home in a woodland or cottage garden, where a more elaborate seat might look out of place.

Adding Personality to Your Planting

Planting flower gardens with unusual shapes, such as the sun-shaped garden described in "Plant a Sunny Theme" on page 49, is one way of gardening with a fun-loving attitude. Growing a garden with an unusual theme, such as the pizza herb garden in "Herb Theme Gardens" on page 46, is another. Even if you don't want your whole garden to look distinctive, you can still add whimsical touches by using accents and focal points in unusual ways: Consider a stone turtle peeking out from a clump of peony foliage.

Another way to liven up the garden is to look underfoot. Substitute a customized stepping stone inset with a pattern of rocks or imprints of leaves for one of the plain stepping stones in your garden. You can make your own custom "stones" with ready-mix cement. You can also make them with the handprints of your children or grandchildren. They're not fine works of art, mind you, but they certainly add a personal touch to the garden path.

Make your own garden statement with subtle but colorful customizing. Does your fence look like everyone else's?

WHIMSICAL GARDEN FEATURES

Break out of the bird-bath mold! Choose one of these garden accents to add a personal touch and a sense of fun to your flower garden.

• Use old work boots, rotting stumps, and fallen logs as planters for sedums and other succulents in a sunny informal garden.

• Trim hedges into unusual shapes or topiary animal designs to add a sense of whimsy to a formal garden design or give any garden a touch of fantasy.

• Train ivy to grow around a wire frame shaped like a basket or animal to add drama and a creative touch to a traditional garden.

• Make a tiny path through the flowers leading to a child-sized chair or bench for an enchanting, fairylike quality in a flower garden.

• Hang wind chimes from a branch so you hear music around the bend in a path.

• Make a "pool" in your garden with a round or oval mirror surrounded by flowers.

EASY RECORD KEEPING

The most efficient way to improve your garden is to keep track of how it grows. Make record keeping easy with these practical tips.

Purchase a notebook you'll use. You're more likely to use a notebook if it has features that appeal to you. Pick the one that suits your needs best: a garden calendar, a spiral-bound notebook with pockets, or a three-ring binder.

Keep your notebook handy. Whether you use a calendar or a notepad, place it and a pencil where you'll see it every day and you'll be more apt to use it.

Take your record book to the garden. The best time to jot down notes is when you plant or evaluate your garden. Inspiration fades quickly and you can lose a brilliant idea before you get back to the house.

This garden center has turned a sales area into a showcase by adding a section of fence and a silhouette sculpture to its diamond-shaped "bed." What a great idea for a small home garden!

Dress that fence with half-baskets full of trailing flowers. Mix variegated English ivy or periwinkle with glowing red, blue, or violet trailing lobelias, blue daze (*Evolvulus nuttallianus*), or nasturtiums for a burst of brilliant color. Or create a screen of hanging plants next to your patio or deck. Build freestanding frames (like sturdy hat racks) and suspend hanging baskets full of colorful vines and flowers from them for a distinctive look no visitor will forget!

Many gardeners use garden accents to personalize their flower beds by recycling cast-off items that tell something about themselves. A pharmacist might want to use a mortar and pestle as a focal point in a rock garden. A retired racehorse jockey might use old stirrups as plant hangers. Travel lovers have decorated their gardens with rocks from around the world or pieces of driftwood and shells from every beach

they've visited. What *you* use to personalize your plantings can be as classic or quirky as your own sense of humor.

Keeping a Record

In this chapter you've learned how to capture great garden ideas wherever you are. It's just as important to take notes about and photos of your own garden as it is to record great ideas from elsewhere. Celebrate your ingenious garden efforts in words and photos. Note how your garden grows so you can plan changes and improvements for next year, and record what combinations and features you liked best. When you do, you'll have the memories long after your flowers have faded.

Personalize your garden with whimsical touches that reflect your own tastes. Here, instead of a humdrum birdbath, a frog sculpture greets visitors from his pedestal perch. The frog creates a focus for this cheerful summer garden.

PART 2

NO-FAIL
FLOWER GARDENING
TECHNIQUES

CHAPTER 7

Planting and Propagating No-Fail Flowers

*T*he planning and plotting is done, you've picked the flowers you want to grow, and now it's time to turn your paper garden into reality. As you move from planning to planting, issues of site selection and design give way to other questions. How will you acquire the plants you need? Your options include everything from one-stop shopping at the garden center to growing each and every flower from seed. What equipment will you need? How should you prepare the site you've chosen for your flowers?

In this chapter you'll learn how to fill your garden with healthy plants—even on a budget—and how to grow your own plants from seeds, divisions, and cuttings. In the second half of this chapter (starting on page 259), you'll find out how to prepare your site and plant your flowers so they will grow and look their best. Choose the methods that fit your schedule, budget, and energy level, and use them to grow a flower garden that is successful, enjoyable, and uniquely yours.

Acquiring Plants

Buying plants or seeds, especially in the spring, is almost as easy as buying food or clothes. Nearly every large discount or department store has a garden section that is well stocked for the growing season. Local greenhouses, nurseries, and garden centers are great sources of plants that will do well in your climate. And mail-order companies offer an extensive selection of plants and seeds at a variety of prices.

Consider the amounts of time, money, and energy you have to spend on your carefully planned posy patch. A visit to a well-stocked nursery is a time-efficient, but potentially costly, way to fill a bed with flowers. Fortunately you need not buy every plant in your plan. Many flowers grow readily from seed; friends and neighbors also are often good sources of plants. Here are some guidelines that will help you find the plants you need.

Shop wisely. Visit local garden centers or nurseries to see whether they offer the plants you want. Take your plant list, but also consult knowledgeable employees who can help you make your selections. They may suggest different cultivars of plants you're looking for or other sources of certain plants. If a nursery doesn't have employees who are knowledgeable about the plants, or the plants don't look healthy to you, consider shopping elsewhere. Be flexible as you shop—you may find new plants that fit your plan. But watch out for budget-busting impulse purchases that seem like a good idea but don't suit your plan or your site.

Look for local plant sales. If there's a botanic garden or arboretum in your area, find out whether it holds plant sales or offers classes in gardening or horticulture. Public gardens can be great sources of local growing information. Garden clubs, plant societies, and community colleges also may be good sources of information.

Grow a green tongue. A little communication goes a long way, especially if you're new to gardening or you're gardening in a new place. Start talking to people about gardening: Ask questions, and share your own gardening plans. Plant enthusiasts generally love talking about gardening. They can recommend the best nurseries and garden centers, certain plants or special growing techniques for your area, and other gardeners to meet. If you see a garden you admire, introduce yourself—a wealth of knowledge and friendship can grow right along with the plants!

Organize a seed and plant exchange. To stretch your

SAY HELLO TO GOOD BUYS

The springtime selection of plants that call to you from every nursery, supermarket, and roadside stand can make you wonder where to shop. Use this checklist to help you decide when an inexpensive plant is a good buy and when it's just cheap.

- Do labels clearly identify the plant and its cultural needs?
- Is the plant robust, fresh, and healthy-looking?
- Is the plant free of pest damage or disease symptoms?
- Are the roots healthy-looking and plentiful but not overcrowded, circling, or densely matted?
- Is the sales staff knowledgeable and helpful?
- Is the plant sales area clean and tidy?
- Does the nursery guarantee its plants?

If you can't answer yes to most of these questions, say goodbye and look elsewhere for good buys.

→·←

DIVIDE TO MULTIPLY

When you're shopping for perennials, buying one large pot *may* be a better buy than several small ones. That's because you may be able to buy a large plant in a gallon container and divide it into several smaller ones—and save money in the process.

This trick works well with plants that have fibrous roots or wandering rhizomes, such as asters, bee balm (*Monarda didyma*), coneflowers (*Rudbeckia* spp.), irises, phlox, sedums, and thymes. It also is ideal for clump-forming plants like ornamental grasses, daylilies, and hostas. Plants that are large enough to be divided will have at least two or three separate stems, or growing points. With daylilies and hostas, count the number of "fans," or crowns, which indicate the number of plants you can make.

Don't try to divide tap-rooted or deep-rooted plants, which won't tolerate the disturbance. These include flowers like butterfly weed (*Asclepias tuberosa*), baptisias (*Baptisia* spp.), and gas plant (*Dictamnus* spp.).

→·←
---

budget, ask gardening friends and neighbors to meet and and share or swap extra plants, divisions, cuttings, or seeds. Use this gathering to coordinate group orders of seeds or plants to extend your flower funds even further. Don't forget to trade plants during the growing season, too, as extra seedlings pop up or plants need dividing.

Grow your own. Propagation techniques like starting seeds and growing plants from divisions or cuttings are great ways to fill a garden with flowers. You'll find a complete guide to these techniques in "Starting Flowers from Seed" on the opposite page and "Flowers from Divisions and Cuttings" on page 253.

Ask the experts for advice. Look to local nurseries, botanic gardens and arboreta, your county's Cooperative Extension Service, or your state's land-grant university for additional help. These sources can help you find specific plants, help you with plant identification, and provide information on plant culture

Buy plants by post. Mail-order nurseries and garden supply companies send out a wave of catalogs each winter—infecting gardeners nationwide with a case of spring fever. Selection is one advantage of mail-order shopping— you'll generally be able to choose from many more plants than are offered at your local garden center. (For a list of mail-order suppliers, see "Sources" on page 358.) When you shop by mail, make sure the plants and seeds you order will be as happy in your garden as they are in the catalog photos. Check hardiness before you order, and find out whether the supplier guarantees plants against losses or damage during shipping. Many companies will let you specify a shipping date, to make sure your plants arrive at planting time in your region.

Buying Healthy Plants

In the quest for plants to fill your no-fail flower garden, make healthy plants the basis of your success, and leave any problems you see on the garden center shelf. Don't settle for anything less than the best. An aphid-infested "bargain" plant is no bargain when it leads to a garden full of infested, stressed, and sickly-looking flowers.

Selecting healthy plants is a matter of common sense and practice. Look closely at every plant you buy. Compare it to other plants of the same kind. Does it look weak or strong in comparison, and is it similar in size and shape? Few plants will look picture-perfect, but those you take home should look sturdy, uniform within their population, and generally healthy. If something you see makes you wonder about the plant's health, ask a salesperson for an explanation. If you're not satisfied by what you hear, reconsider your purchase—starting with strong, healthy plants is an important building block in creating your no-fail flower garden.

Shopping for Size

The image of an empty garden drives many plant shoppers past the cell packs to the gallon containers in search of the biggest plants they can buy. Mature plants may provide more visual impact in your garden, but the dent they can put in your budget may send you back to look at their smaller, less costly siblings. One easy, inexpensive trick is to use annuals to fill in between newly planted, more expensive perennials. They'll provide you with quick color while you wait for the smaller perennials to grow and spread. See "Multiplying by Division" on page 254 for another effective way to extend your plant budget.

Starting Flowers from Seed

Starting your own plants from seed isn't just practical, it's fun, too. Lots of flowers are easy to grow from seed, and seed is often the way to go if you're looking for special colors of annuals or unusual perennials that aren't available from local suppliers. With a little bit of time and space and a few supplies, you can grow lots of flowers at minimal cost.

You can start seed indoors before the growing season begins, or direct-sow the seeds in your flower bed after the soil warms up in the spring. Starting seed indoors gives most perennials the time they need to produce blooms by summer. For information on indoor sowing, read on; for details on direct-sowing, see "Outdoor Sowing" on page 251.

BRING 'EM HOME HEALTHY

Before you buy, check plant purchases thoroughly from top to bottom. Look for pests like aphids, especially on the undersides of leaves. Slip the root ball out of its pot to make sure roots look healthy and are not overcrowded.

➜·←

EASY ANNUALS FROM SEED

If you're starting seeds for the first time, bolster your confidence with one or two crops that are almost sure to do well. John Paul Bowles, the executive director of Fernwood Botanic Garden in Niles, Michigan, recommends the following annuals for seed-starting success: cockscomb (*Celosia cristata*), cosmos, flowering tobacco (*Nicotiana alata*), garden forget-me-not (*Myosotis sylvatica*), geranium, globe amaranth (*Gomphrena globosa*), impatiens, love-in-a-mist (*Nigella damascena*), marigold, morning glory, nasturtium, pot marigold (*Calendula officinalis*), rose moss (*Portulaca grandiflora*), salvia (*Salvia* spp.), snapdragon, and zinnia.

➜·←

Indoor Sowing

For successful seed-starting indoors, you'll need containers, growing medium, and seeds. You'll also need a sturdy (and preferably waterproof) flat surface near a good light source—either a south-facing window or a strong source of artificial light. (Newly sown seeds don't need to be under lights or in a window, although they can be. Once the seeds have germinated, a good light source is essential to healthy growth.) A location where you can maintain temperatures of 65° to 75°F will also contribute to good germination and healthy growth. Start out small: You can always add new crops as your technique improves and your confidence grows. Once your seeds are sown, they won't need much attention, but plan to spend some time watering and observing at least once a day.

Seed-Starting Containers

Choose containers that fit your selected growing space and have drainage holes in the bottom. For seed-starting, there are basically two types. Broad, open flats let you sow many seeds in one container; the tiny seedlings are later lifted and transplanted to individual pots. Peat pots, peat pellets, and cell packs are designed for growing individual seedlings, sometimes until they are planted out. (For ideas on recycled containers, see "New Life in Old Containers" on the opposite page.)

Starting seeds in peat pots or pellets simplifies things at transplanting time—just stick both plant and pot in the ground. Your seedlings benefit, too, since their roots are not disturbed during planting.

Growing Mixes for Seed

Sow your seed in any fine-textured, well-drained medium—the pre-mixed ones that are commercially available are excellent and easy to use. A sterile, soilless growing medium is best because it reduces the risk of losing your crop to diseases such as damping-off. (Seedlings don't need a nutrient-rich mix.) A typical seed-starting mix combines equal amounts of peat moss and vermiculite, but you could also use compost, pasteurized potting soil, or perlite, or a combination of these. Essentially any light, porous medium that holds moisture, drains well, and provides physical support will do.

Successful Indoor Sowing

Timing is important when you're growing plants from seed. If you start them too early, you'll have overgrown and leggy seedlings in spring, and if you start them too late, you'd be better off direct-seeding them outdoors. It's easy to avoid both problems by setting a planting schedule and placing your seed order early. Seed catalogs usually arrive in early winter; if you place your order then, you'll get the best selection and possibly a price break. The seed packet should tell you how many weeks the seeds need to reach transplant size, whether they need any pretreatment to sprout, how deep to plant them, and what soil temperature range promotes good germination. Use this information to set a calendar schedule like the one illustrated on page 244. If you stick with your schedule, your seedlings will be the right size when planting time arrives in spring.

Before you open a seed packet or sow a seed, moisten your growing medium thoroughly. You can do this before you fill your containers by filling a bucket with medium and adding water. The medium should be moist and crumbly but not soggy. Fill your containers with moistened growing medium to ¼ inch from the top, and plant your seeds according to package directions. Sow seeds at a depth approximately three times their diameter.

If you're planting in a flat or other open container, use a plant label or pencil to make shallow furrows. Mix very fine seeds with sand and sprinkle them over the surface with a salt shaker. If you're planting in individual containers, plant one to three seeds in each, but be prepared to thin out extras if more than one comes up. Cover seeds lightly with dry growing medium, and mist it gently to moisten the surface. You also have the option of presprouting seeds before you plant and then potting up the sprouted seeds. For directions on this technique, see the illustration on page 246.

NEW LIFE IN OLD CONTAINERS

Since looks are fairly unimportant during seed starting, a collection of recycled containers may suit your needs as well as "store-bought" ones. Any container that holds at least 3½ inches of growing medium—and that you can poke a drainage hole in—can make a serviceable seedling home. Try margarine tubs, milk cartons with the tops cut off, old dishpans, or Styrofoam cups. You can also recycle pots, flats, or cell packs from previous plant purchases.

Keep in mind that uniformly sized containers are easier to handle and to water evenly, so you may want to use all the same kind.

Clean recycled containers thoroughly, and rinse them with a solution of 1 part bleach to 9 parts water. Set them on trays, flats, or old cookie sheets to catch water runoff.

SLICK INDOOR SOWING

For problem-free plant-ing, try these simple seed-sowing ideas.

Sow in rows. Seedlings are easier to transplant from rows than mass plant-ings. And the spaces between rows leave room for watering and provide better air circulation for seedlings.

Plant one cultivar or species per row. It's easy to lose track of plants if you mix different seeds together in a row or pot. Keep them separate for quick identification.

Control seeds with a crease. Small seeds tend to pour out of seed pack-ets all at once. Space them evenly by making a crease along the middle of one side of your seed package. Hold the packet horizontally, and tap the top until the seeds line up and pour out singly.

For foolproof indoor seed sowing, make a calendar schedule. Mark down the frost-free date first; most seedlings can be safely planted outside after that date. Then count back to your seed-starting date using the seed packet information.

Don't count on your memory to tell you what's growing in each container. Label everything at planting time with the plant name and the date. Use waterproof labels and write on them with a permanent marking pen so the infor-mation won't wash off, leaving a mystery crop.

Caring for Planted Seeds

After planting, place a clear plastic bag (or rigid lid) over each container and secure the open end. Place individual pots together on a tray and cover them with a sheet of plastic. This helps hold in the moisture and heat necessary for good germination. If you don't cover your newly plant-ed pots or flats, you'll need to water frequently to keep

them from drying out. Water with a gentle spray or mist to avoid dislodging your seeds.

A source of gentle bottom heat encourages germination. Set your containers on top of your refrigerator, TV, or water heater until the seeds begin to sprout. If you'd rather not adorn your appliances with pots and flats, heating cables and mats are available to keep your future flowers cozy. And most seeds will sprout without bottom heat, as long as the room temperature is appropriate and they're kept moist.

Time from planting to germination varies, but most seeds of herbaceous plants will germinate in one to three weeks. If after waiting patiently you think your seeds will never come up, gently lift one out of the growing mix and check to see whether it is rotten or dry. Seeds that are too wet will rot; dry seeds will never sprout.

Growing Healthy Seedlings

Once your seeds have sprouted, a new phase of care begins. You need to provide good growing conditions to raise strong, healthy seedlings. Here are some guidelines to ensure that your tender new seedlings become vigorous, no-fail plants.

Ensure even moisture. Remove the plastic covering from the seed flats or containers as soon as seedlings appear. Keep the growing medium moist but not wet, preferably by watering from the bottom. To bottom-water, place the container in a larger pan of water and let the water soak up through the drainage holes into the medium. Then set the container aside and let the excess water drain off. Don't let your seedlings sit in water—they'll rot. If bottom watering isn't practical, water your seedlings with a gentle spray or mist, taking care to avoid flattening them or washing them out of the medium.

Provide plenty of light. Light is critical now. Move the seedlings to full sunlight (if they're not in it already), or place them under fluorescent lights for 14 to 16 hours per day. The twin fluorescent tubes found in most shop lights work well. "Plant" or "grow" lights are fine, but they cost more and are unnecessary for successful growth at this

---

FOIL FUNGI WITH HOT WATER

If you plan to start your seeds in a mix that contains soil or compost, here's a way to reduce the risk of damping-off. After you've filled your containers and before you plant, use boiling water to sterilize the soil surface, where damping-off fungi most often attack vulnerable seedlings.

Pour on just enough boiling water to cover the entire surface—½ cup will treat a 4-inch pot. Don't use so much water that it waterlogs your soil. And don't worry about the heat; the soil will cool quickly, so you can get on with your seed sowing.

Presprouting seeds lets you provide good germinating conditions in limited space. To presprout: (1) Spread seeds in the middle of a moistened paper towel; fold the sides over them.
(2) Place the paper towel in a plastic bag with the plant name and the date. Move the bag to a warm place; check daily for germination.
(3) Pot up sprouted seeds and treat them as you would any seedlings.

stage. Don't use incandescent bulbs—they give off too much heat and produce the wrong kind of light for healthy growth. Hang the lights no more than 3 to 6 inches above your seedlings. An inexpensive appliance timer can save you the trouble of remembering to turn the lights on and off every day and helps ensure that your seedlings get the light they need. If your seedlings begin to grow tall and spindly, increase the amount of light they get daily and move them closer to the light source.

Keep track of temperature. Most seedlings grow well under daytime temperatures of 70° to 75°F and night temperatures that range from 60° to 65°F.

Control diseases. Good air circulation is very important at this early stage. The warm, humid conditions seedlings love also encourage damping-off, a common and deadly fungal disease of seedlings. Affected stems turn black at the soil line and collapse. To help prevent this devastating

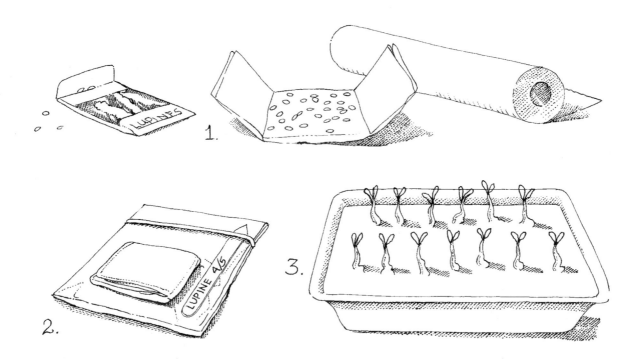

1.

2.

3.

fungus, allow the soil surface to dry slightly between waterings, use a small fan to keep air moving (gently) around your seedlings, and thin out crowded plants. If damping-off does occur, remove and discard the affected seedlings and the medium around them. Improve air circulation and allow the soil to dry somewhat. After the seedlings are several weeks old, their stems toughen and become less susceptible to this fungus.

Feed your seedlings. Fertilize every two weeks once the first set of "true" leaves appears. (The first leaves are "seed leaves" or cotyledons and do not look like the real leaves of the plant. See the illustration on page 248.) Use a liquid fertilizer such as fish emulsion or seaweed, diluted to one-quarter strength of the recommended dose. After two applications, mix the fertilizer at one-half strength if the seedlings seem to be thriving.

Potting On from Flats

If your seedlings are growing in open flats, you'll want to select the strongest, healthiest ones to transfer into individual pots for further growth. Seedlings are ready to pot on after they've developed their first set of true leaves. Fill individual pots with *moistened* potting mix. (Don't plan on just watering afterward; dry potting mix will damage delicate roots.) Then remove each seedling gently, using a Popsicle stick, pencil, fork handle, or similar tool to dig under the roots and lift the plant out. Hold the seedling by a seed leaf, not by its easily crushed stem. With a pencil, make a small hole in the potting mix of the new pot. Lower the roots into the hole and gently firm the medium around them. Carefully water the seedling in.

Newly transplanted seedlings may wilt, but do *not* overwater! Make sure the growing medium is moist, and possibly reduce the amount of light they receive for a day or two. They should perk up in a few days, and you can resume normal light conditions.

If you originally planted two or three seeds in individual pots and all have germinated, transplant the extras to their own pots or thin out and discard the weaker ones.

GROW CULTIVARS FROM SEED

Growing perennial flower cultivars from seed is an inexpensive way to get top-notch plants. But not all cultivars come true from seed; some revert to the characteristics of a parent plant. For sure success, choose the cultivars listed below that do come true from seed:

- Sneezeweed (*Achillea ptarmica* 'The Pearl')
- Hybrid columbines (*Aquilegia × hybrida* 'McKana' strain, 'Biedermeier' hybrids, and 'Nora Barlow')
- Painted daisy (*Chrysanthemum coccineum* 'James Kelway' and 'Robinson's Mix')
- Large-flowered tickseed (*Coreopsis grandiflora* 'Early Sunrise' and 'Sunburst')
- Maiden pinks (*Dianthus deltoides* 'Zing Rose')
- Common foxglove (*Digitalis purpurea* 'Excelsior' mix and 'Foxy')
- Purple coneflower (*Echinacea purpurea* 'Bravado' and 'White Swan')
- Bee balm (*Monarda didyma* 'Panorama Mix')

Transplanting to the Garden

As the last frost date approaches, the time has come to move seedlings to the garden. Hardier annuals and many perennials can be transplanted a week or two before the last frost date; you may need to wait for two or more weeks after that for tender annuals. Use the seed packets or your sowing schedule to plan transplant times for your seedlings.

Your carefully tended seedlings will fare much better in the sometimes cold, windy, sunny, dry, wet, and/or hot outdoor world if you give them a chance to harden off before transplanting. This process of gradually exposing seedlings to the growing conditions they'll face outside gives them time to toughen up and adjust to their new surroundings.

Start hardening off your seedlings two weeks before you

When transplanting seedlings, handle them gently to avoid crushing their fragile stems. Hold each seedling by a seed leaf, or cotyledon, while using a plant marker or similar item to dig under and lift out the roots. Make the planting hole large enough to easily admit the roots, and lower them into their new home.

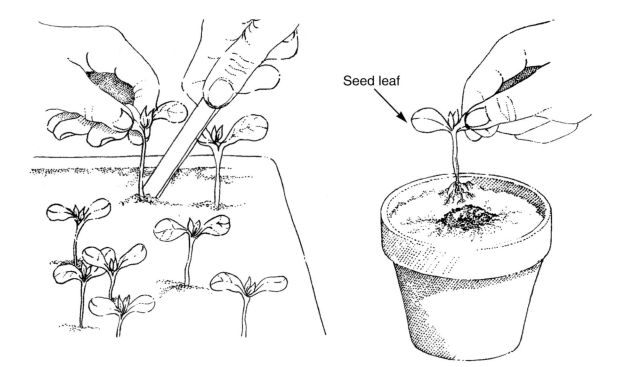

Seed leaf

plan to transplant them to your garden. Stop fertilizing and also reduce the amount of water you give them—but don't let them dry out to the point of wilting. Set the containers in a shaded, sheltered outdoor area during the day. If you have a shaded site on the north side of your house that's protected from wind, use it to harden off your seedlings.

If you're home during the day, or if you start the process on a weekend, leave your plants out for only an hour or so the first day. Gradually increase the amount of time they spend outdoors, taking care to bring your seedlings in at night or if frost threatens. If you must leave your seedlings out all day, make sure the growing medium is moist in the morning—they'll dry out more quickly outdoors.

If you don't have a good site for hardening off your plants, you can build a cold frame shelter. A cold frame is a "box" that has multiple uses. It can be a temporary structure, used just to harden off plants, or a permanent structure used to start seedlings in the spring, to overwinter less-hardy plants, or to extend the growing season.

A temporary cold frame can have walls made of straw or hay bales and a lid made from an old window frame. The back side should face north and be 18 to 24 inches tall, sloping down to a height of 12 to 18 inches in the front. This allows rain to run off and exposes more surface to the sun. Stack bales or pile up partial bales to make the back wall taller than the front. For a permanent structure, use decay-resistant wood. The top can be clear plastic if you're worried about it breaking or don't have an old window to use.

Raise or remove the lid for temperature control. For hardening off plants, you can leave it off or ajar unless frost threatens. For other purposes, a thermometer should be placed inside to help monitor the temperature. A bright, sunny day can raise the temperature inside a cold frame enough to "cook" the plants even if the air temperature outside is very cool. If you use the cold frame to start seedlings, you may want to buy an automatic vent opener. They are available at hardware stores and through seed and supply catalogs and will open and close the cold frame lid as the temperature rises and falls.

PERENNIALS FOR FIRST-SEASON FLOWERS

Starting perennials from seed doesn't mean you can't have a bed full of blooms the first year. For first-season flowers Jim Nau, new variety manager at Ball Seed Company in West Chicago, Illinois, recommends sowing these perennials in January or February: black-eyed Susan (*Rudbeckia hirta* var. *pulcherrima*), butterfly weed (*Asclepias tuberosa*), Carpathian harebell (*Campanula carpatica*), large-flowered tickseed (*Coreopsis grandiflora*), sunflower heliopsis (*Heliopsis helianthoides*), candle larkspur (*Delphinium elatum*), Maltese cross (*Lychnis chalcedonica*), obedient plant (*Physostegia virginiana*), pansy (*Viola × wittrockiana*), violet sage (*Salvia × superba*), purple coneflower (*Echinacea purpurea*), red valerian (*Centranthus ruber*), Shasta daisy (*Chrysanthemum × superbum*), spike speedwell (*Veronica spicata*), sweet violet (*Viola odorata*), yarrow (*Achillea* spp.).

→ · ←

SOWING SEEDS IN OUTDOOR CONTAINERS

If you don't have a garden but you want to direct-sow seeds, prepare outdoor containers just as you would containers for indoor seed starting. Place barrels, hanging baskets, tubs, or window boxes outside where you want them to decorate your house. Use containers with drainage holes, to keep them from becoming waterlogged. Fill them with potting soil instead of soilless seed-starting medium to slow the rate of water loss by evaporation.

Sow your seeds directly in the containers. Protect them with a cheesecloth or wire cover if they are in areas bothered by rodents, pets, strong winds, or small children. Check soil moisture daily; you may need to water twice a day in dry weather.

Thin the seedlings as necessary, and give them the same treatment as seedlings started indoors. But your outdoor seedlings won't need hardening off, since they will have been living outdoors from the beginning.

→ · ←

Transplanting Tips

Use the hints below to make sure your seedlings transplant to the garden as smoothly as possible.

Prepare your soil before you transplant. Make sure your flower beds are ready to receive your transplants. (See "Preparing Your Site" on page 259.) Be sure to water the flower bed before you transplant.

Transplant on the morning of a cool, cloudy day. Cool, cloudy conditions reduce the amount of moisture your seedlings lose to the air and lessen transplant shock. (Transplanting on a drizzly day is ideal.) If sunny days persist, transplant in the late afternoon, after the sun's intensity has diminished, and shade the plants with bushel baskets, floating row covers, or even plastic lawn chairs.

Handle seedlings with care. Thoroughly water your seedlings before transplanting. To minimize disturbance to the root system, remove each seedling gently from its container. Young plants need all the roots they have in order to adjust and grow well in a new location. To remove a seedling from its pot, place your hand over the soil surface with your fingers on both sides of the stem. Turn the pot over and tap on the bottom to release the soil ball into your hand. If you started seeds in peat pots or pellets, you can plant your seedlings pots and all. Tear away any peat pot rim that extends above the growing medium—otherwise it will wick water away from the plant it holds.

Plant at the proper depth. Plant seedlings at the depth they were growing at in the container. Press the soil firmly around the base of each plant and water until the surrounding soil is completely saturated. Once you've planted all your seedlings, use a sprinkler or soaking hose to thoroughly moisten the entire flower bed.

Protect new transplants. Track the weather closely for the first week or two after transplanting. Late spring temperatures can fluctuate dramatically, and even though they're hardened off, transplants will need protection from strong sun, wind, or frost. Check regularly for signs of wilting, sun or wind injury, or damage from insect or animal activity. Use labels or a map of your flower bed to help you keep track of any casualties.

Use bushel baskets, floating row covers, plastic lawn chairs, cloches, leafy branches stuck in the soil, or boards propped up across the bed to shade transplants during the heat of the day. When overnight frost is predicted, protect entire beds with bushel baskets, cloches, or floating row covers. Remove frost protection when the air warms up the next morning.

Outdoor Sowing

If you don't have enough time or space for indoor sowing, don't despair. You can sow many kinds of flowers directly into a prepared seedbed outdoors. Some flowers actually do better started outdoors than inside. Perennials with deep taproots, like butterfly weed (*Asclepias tuberosa*) and poppies, resent transplanting and grow best if you start them where you want them to grow. (You may have to wait two or three years for the seedlings to reach blooming size, but it's the cheapest way to increase your supply of plants.) Certain annual flowers are also good choices for direct-sowing. For those like love-in-a-mist (*Nigella damascena*), which bloom for a short period of time, an early indoor start just means more work, not a longer bloom season. Others, like cosmos and zinnias, are best started outdoors because they'll germinate and grow quickly. There's no need to waste time or take up space growing them indoors.

Flowers with large seeds, like sunflowers, are good choices for direct-sowing, too. They're easy to handle and can be planted in simple-to-tend rows. Small seeds are more difficult to handle and are usually broadcast by hand over the planting area. For best results, mix them with 3 or 4 parts dry sand and use a salt shaker or seasoning jar to scatter them evenly over the seed bed. You'll be less likely to dump a pile of tiny seeds all in one spot.

Seed packets provide instructions for outdoor planting dates, depth, and spacing for species that can be direct-sown outdoors. If you collect your own seeds, you may not know the proper planting instructions, so consult the general gardening books listed in "Recommended Reading" on

SOW AND GROW FLOWERS

At its simplest, no-fail flower gardening involves planting seeds into prepared soil and waiting for plants to appear. Try this casual treatment on the flowers below. Plant annuals in spring; sow biennials and perennials in summer or fall.

Annuals: Alyssum, cornflower (*Centaurea cyanus*), pot marigold (*Calendula officinalis*), California poppy (*Eschscholzia californica*), cleomes (*Cleome hasslerana*), cosmos, flowering tobacco (*Nicotiana alata*), four-o'clocks (*Mirabilis jalapa*), rose moss (*Portulaca grandiflora*), nasturtium, common sunflower (*Helianthus annuus*), zinnia.

Biennials: Common foxglove (*Digitalis purpurea*), hollyhock (*Alcea rosea*), sweet William (*Dianthus barbatus*).

Perennials: Aster, coneflowers (*Rudbeckia* spp.), butterfly weed (*Asclepias tuberosa*), sunflower heliopsis (*Heliopsis helianthoides*), Jacob's ladders (*Polemo-nium* spp.), penstemons (*Penstemon* spp.), blue false indigo (*Baptisia australis*).

→·←

TIPS FOR OUTDOOR SOWING

Sowing seeds directly into your flower garden in spring is an easy and inexpensive way to increase your plant population. Mark off the planting area with a trowel, prepare the seedbed, and then scatter seeds evenly to fill the outlined area.

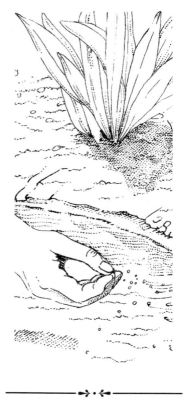

→·←

page 359. As a general rule, plant seeds at a depth of two to three times their width.

Prepare a Proper Seedbed

Before it's time to plant, prepare the soil where you plan to sow your seeds. You can make a planting bed just for starting seedlings—later moving them to more permanent locations—or you can sow them exactly where you want them to grow and flower. In either case, a well-prepared seedbed will help get your seedlings off to a strong start.

Make sure the soil is neither too wet nor too dry before you prepare your seedbed. See "Digging In" on page 270 for a simple test to tell you when the soil is ready to work; it should be slightly moist and crumbly, not wet. To prepare a proper seedbed, turn the soil with a fork, shovel, or rotary tiller, breaking it into fine but not powdery particles. Work the soil to the consistency of very coarse sand or small pebbles.

Successful Outdoor Sowing

Smooth the planting area with a rake and mark the areas for sowing by making a shallow trench or depression where the seeds will go. (Check your seed packets for proper planting depths.) To plant seeds in a natural configuration, make slight depressions in the soil with your fingers or with a dibble (a pointed tool) in a random, scattered pattern. For straight rows, use stakes with a string stretched between them. Sow your seeds at the appropriate depths, and cover them. To avoid giving tiny seeds a hard soil crust to break through, try covering them with a fine layer of potting soil, screened compost, or vermiculite.

After planting, water the seedbed thoroughly but gently, using a spray or mist nozzle on your hose. A hard stream of water can quickly wash away your carefully sown seedbed. Check on your newly planted seeds daily, and keep the soil constantly moist until the seedlings are up and well established. Use a rain gauge to keep track of the amount of moisture your seedlings are getting—most plants need at least 1 inch of water each week. After a rain, stick your finger in the soil to see how deep the rain penetrated. You may be surprised! If the soil is dry beneath the surface, get the hose and water some more. Small seedlings can dry out and wilt quickly on a sunny day. After your plants are 2 to 3 inches tall, start allowing the soil to dry slightly between waterings. Your seedlings will begin to send their roots farther in search of water and will grow stronger.

Caring for Direct-Sown Seedlings

After seedlings develop their first set of true leaves, you can thin them out or transplant them. Treat them much as you would seedlings started indoors, omitting the hardening off step. Hold each seedling by a leaf, supporting the roots from beneath; keep as many roots intact as possible; and try to transplant on a cool, cloudy day or late in the afternoon. Water thoroughly after transplanting, and provide protection from strong sun and wind.

You'll need to protect outdoor seedlings from a few hazards that indoor crops don't face. Keep your seedbed free of moisture- and nutrient-grabbing weeds. And watch out for hungry birds and other animal pests that may go for seeds as well as seedlings. Cover your seedbed with netting or cheesecloth until your plants are big enough to withstand wildlife visits. Use mulch to help preserve moisture, maintain even soil temperature, and prevent weeds from taking over. Check regularly for any signs of disease or insect problems.

Flowers from Divisions and Cuttings

A quick and easy way to increase your plant inventory is to grow new plants from "starts" of another plant via vegetative propagation. Division, stem cuttings, and root cuttings are the most common ways home gardeners propagate plants vegetatively.

Producing new plants in this way offers several advantages. You can propagate a large variety of perennials from divisions or cuttings, and each new plant will have exactly the same characteristics as the original, or parent, plant. And plants grown from divisions are larger and bloom

---

NO-FAIL DIVISION

If you're hesitant about dividing your perennials for fear of harming them in the process, try your technique on the plants listed below. These plants all benefit from division every three to five years and have a high post-division survival rate. They're listed by root type so you'll know what you're getting into when you start digging.

Fibrous roots: Astilbe, bee balms (*Monarda* spp.), boltonia (*Boltonia asteroides*), bellflowers (*Campanula* spp.), Chinese and Japanese anemones (*Anemone hupehensis, A.* × *hybrida,* and *A. tomentosa*), chrysanthemum, coneflowers (*Rudbeckia* spp.), coreopsis (*Coreopsis* spp.), cranesbills (*Geranium* spp.), spotted lamium (*Lamium maculatum*), pinks (*Dianthus* spp.), phlox (border species: *Phlox carolina, P. maculata, P. ovata,* and *P. paniculata*), sedums, speedwells (*Veronica* spp.), and yarrows (*Achillea* spp.).

Fleshy roots: Daylily and hosta.

Rhizomes: Aster, bearded iris, and lily-of-the-valley.

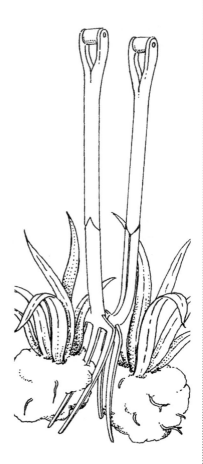

Garden forks take the strain out of dividing densely root- ed perennial flowers like daylilies. First, cut around the plant with a spade. Then loosen the soil with a garden fork and lift the clump from the ground. Place garden forks back-to-back in the center of the clump. Pull the handles together and push them apart until the clump breaks into two pieces.

sooner than those grown from seed. Dividing plants or tak- ing cuttings from them isn't harmful; the parent plant can actually benefit when these practices are done properly.

Multiplying by Division

Easy and reliable, division is the propagation method favored by most gardeners. It involves breaking up one large plant into several smaller plants. You can use the resulting smaller plants—called divisions—to fill your flower beds or to share with other gardeners. Most perenni- als respond well to division, and some actually need to be divided every so often, whether you want more plants or not. Divide invasive plants to keep their rampant growth in bounds. Use division to rejuvenate older plants that are blooming less and looking straggly or for clump-forming plants in which the center dies out.

Times to Divide

Divide perennials when they are growing vegetatively, not when they're in bloom. Use a plant's bloom time to schedule division more specifically: Divide spring- and early-summer-blooming perennials in late summer to early fall, and midsummer- to fall-bloomers in early spring. If you live in USDA Plant Hardiness Zone 5 or farther north, do most of your division in the spring, to give new plants time to get established before cold weather arrives.

Division Techniques

To divide a plant, dig directly around its perimeter with either a trowel, a spade, or a garden fork, and lift it out of the ground. Shake enough soil away to let you see what you're doing; hose soil off if necessary. Some plants, such as coral bells (*Heuchera sanguinea*), are relatively shallow- rooted and lift out easily, while others require more muscle. Large or old clumps of perennial ornamental grasses are very challenging and often require a strong arm to lift them and an ax to cut them apart.

If the exposed roots are thin and fibrous, try tugging and

working them apart into smaller clumps with your fingers. To divide plants such as daylilies or hostas that have dense or thickly intertwined roots, you can use the double-fork method to break a clump into smaller pieces. One at a time, shove two garden forks back-to-back into the center of the clump as close as possible. Push the fork handles together at the top, then pull them apart. As this happens, the forks will break the clump apart into two pieces. Or use an old butcher knife, a sharp spade, or an ax to cut the clump into pieces. Place your cuts so that each new piece has a good amount of roots with it. Cut apart iris rhizomes and other small perennials with a sharp knife.

To rejuvenate a plant whose center has died out, dig the clump and divide it in half. Cut away the woody center and divide the outer ring of healthy growth.

How large or small you make your divisions depends on how you want to use them. If you plan to replant them in your flower bed and want plants that will fill in and bloom immediately, keep the divisions as large as possible. If your goal is to get as many new plants as you can, break each clump into small pieces, but make sure each piece has enough roots to survive. Before you divide a plant, do a little research to see whether it has any quirks about how it is divided. Some plants bounce back easily, while others resent the disturbance and need some extra care to help them get over the shock.

Replanting Divisions

If your divisions are headed for a new flower bed, prepare the soil before you begin dividing plants. Your divisions will fare better if you minimize the amount of time they spend out of the ground. Replant only those divisions that have strong, healthy root systems. If a section of roots appears soft, mushy, or discolored, or shows signs of insect damage, or in any way appears unhealthy compared to the rest of the root system, discard it. It's not likely to get better if you replant it, and you could spread the problem to other plants.

When dividing plants in the spring before they start

DIVIDING PERENNIALS WITH FLESHY ROOTS

When you divide perennial flowers like irises that have thick, fleshy roots, cut away disease or insect problems at the same time. Dig up the clump of plants you want to divide. Shake or wash the soil off so you can see and evaluate the roots. Using a sharp knife, cut off and dispose of any root sections that are diseased or infested with insects. Finally, cut the remaining roots into sections, so each has a clump of foliage and 3 to 4 inches of healthy root.

—→·←—

Use stem cuttings to propagate those perennials that you can't divide or that don't come true from seed. You can also take stem cuttings from divisible plants that are still too small to dig up and divide.

The following perennials propagate readily from stem cuttings: artemisia, balloon flower (*Platycodon grandiflorus*), bee balm (*Monarda didyma*), blue stars (*Amsonia* spp.), butterfly weed (*Asclepias tuberosa*), catmint (*Nepeta* spp.), chrysanthemum, pinks (*Dianthus* spp.), perennial candytuft (*Iberis sempervirens*), sunflower heliopsis (*Heliopsis helianthoides*), garden phlox (*Phlox paniculata*), golden marguerite (*Anthemis tinctoria*), goldenrods (*Solidago* spp.), lavender, gooseneck and yellow loosestrife (*Lysimachia clethroides* and *L. punctata*), obedient plant (*Physostegia virginiana*), violet sage (*Salvia × superba*), sedum, and speedwells (*Veronica* spp.).

—→·←—

putting out new growth, simply replant the divisions immediately. If you're dividing plants that have produced full stems and leaves, remove one-half to two-thirds of the foliage before you replant. The reduced root system is unable to replace the amount of water lost through substantially larger top growth. Don't worry; new sprouts will emerge as soon as the roots get reestablished.

As soon as possible after dividing a plant, replant the divisions at a depth slightly higher than that of the original plant to allow for settling. Firm the soil around them and water them well.

If you can't replant new divisions immediately, keep them moist, cool, and shaded. Place them in a flat, and cover them loosely with damp soil, peat moss, or burlap. If they seem dry when you're ready to plant, soak them in a bucket of shallow water for an hour before replanting.

After replanting new divisions, keep them moist and protect them from hot sun and drying winds. Check soil moisture daily and provide partial shade during the hottest part of the day.

New Plants from Cuttings

You can propagate some plants by cutting pieces of the stem or root and forcing them to grow into new plants. The first part—taking the cutting—is easy; convincing the cutting to grow can be somewhat trickier. But cuttings grow into flowering plants more quickly than plants grown from seed, and taking stem cuttings is tidier than digging and dividing portions of your flower bed. Starting new plants from cuttings is a good way to propagate plants that don't come true from seed or that have taproots and can't be divided. You can also take cuttings from plants that can be divided but aren't yet large enough.

Successful Stem Cuttings

Stem cuttings are also called tip or shoot cuttings, and sometimes "slips." The best time to take stem cuttings is in late spring or early summer, before the new stems harden and mature. See "Surefire Stem Cuttings" on the opposite page for a list of flowers that are easy to grow from cuttings.

Collect cuttings in the morning if possible, when they're full of moisture. Cutting size depends on the type of plant you're collecting from. Smaller cuttings tend to root better and faster, but you may need to take longer cuttings from plants with large leaves and lots of stem space between them.

Fill pots or flats with at least 3 inches of a sterile, loose growing medium. Sand, vermiculite, perlite, and peat moss all work well and may be used alone or in combinations. Moisten the mix thoroughly before you begin planting, and let the excess water drain off.

Cut off any flowers or flower buds from the tip of the cutting; they will interfere with new root formation. Cut off leaves from the bottom leaf nodes so that you have a bare stem to stick into the soil. To keep your cuttings from wilting, especially during warm weather, you may need to remove a few more leaves. Don't cut off more than half the foliage; leave some leaves for photosynthesis. Dipping the bottom end of the cutting in a rooting hormone can help stimulate root formation but is not necessary. If you shop for rooting hormones, check the ingredients to avoid buying hormone-fungicide combinations. Tap off any excess rooting hormone before planting; too much can be detrimental.

Plant your cuttings with about 1 inch of stem and at least one node below the surface of the planting medium. Separate different species or cultivars into their own pots or rows within a flat, and label them clearly with plant name and the date you took the cuttings. Firm the medium around your cuttings and water them in well. Cover each container with clear plastic to hold in moisture—cuttings need close to 100 percent humidity.

Give your cuttings bright, indirect light. Direct sunlight will cause heat to build up under the plastic, killing the cuttings. Check moisture daily and keep the medium moist without overwatering. Most cuttings will root in two to four weeks; start checking for rooting after two weeks.

Once your cuttings are well rooted, you can transplant them to individual pots or to an outdoor nursery bed—

TAKING CUTTINGS

To take cuttings, snip 1½- to 4-inch portions from the stem tips. Make the cut about ¼ inch below a leaf node, where a leaf or set of leaves attaches to the stem. Place your cuttings in a plastic bag so they won't dry out. Plant them in a flat or pot as soon as possible and cover with clear plastic to maintain high humidity.

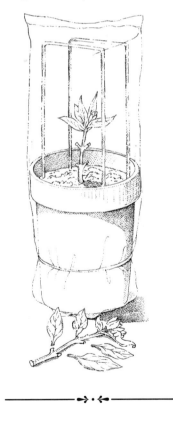

⇢·⇠

much like the seedbed described in "Prepare a Proper Seedbed" on page 252—until the new plants are large enough to go into your flower bed.

Growing Flowers from Root Cuttings

Gardeners who've pulled up thistles, only to have several thistle "babies" appear later in the same area, have unwittingly propagated their foes via root cuttings. Fortunately you can use this technique to propagate more-desirable perennials, too. Here's how:

Collecting root cuttings. Collect root cuttings when plants are dormant—in fall, winter, or early spring. Actively growing plants transfer most of their energy from the roots to the shoots. Root cuttings taken during late spring or summer generally don't succeed, because their natural energy supply has been diminished.

Taking healthy roots. Dig and lift the plant you wish to take root cuttings from. Hose excess soil away to expose fleshy, mature roots, which are usually tan colored. Remove up to one-third of the strongest, healthiest roots with a sharp knife. Cut off the thin ends of the roots and take cuttings from the middle section. Keep track of which end of the root was closest to the plant—and which end was growing away from the plant. Cuttings from roots growing more or less vertically in the soil will not grow if you plant them upside down. As you make your root cuttings, cut the upper ends horizontally and the lower ends diagonally, so you'll know which is which.

Preparing the cuttings. Make each root cutting about 1½ to 2 inches long. You can take more than one cutting from each root. If you can't plant your root cuttings right away, keep them cool and moist in a plastic bag or other container in the refrigerator until you are ready. Make a label for each type of cutting.

Planting root cuttings. Fill flats or shallow wooden boxes with moistened loose, sterile medium, such as sand, vermiculite, perlite, peat moss, or potting soil, or some combination of these. Place root cuttings at a 45-degree angle in the medium, about an inch apart, with the top end

---

TIPS FOR TOP CUTTINGS

Try these tricks to produce top cutting crops.

• Turn an empty soda bottle into a humid home for cuttings. Cut off the bottom and fill it with potting mix, stick in the cuttings, water it, and reattach the top with tape. Leave the bottle cap off for ventilation.

• In cool weather, supply bottom heat to keep the rooting medium between 60° and 75°F. Use your TV, water heater, or refrigerator as a heat source, or place containers on heating cables or mats.

• Water with unsoftened water or rainwater; salts in soft water are harmful to plants.

• To check for root growth, grasp the base of a cutting and tug gently. If it resists, roots have formed.

• Once roots begin to grow, open or remove the cover and gradually increase light levels.

⇢·⇠

up. Do not use a rooting hormone on root cuttings. Leave about ⅛ inch of each cutting's upper end exposed to promote top growth. Lay thin cuttings horizontally on the growing medium; cover them to a depth of one to two times their thickness. Label each container or row.

Caring for root cuttings. If you take your root cuttings in early spring, late summer, or early fall, cover the containers with plastic and place them in a warm (70° to 75°F) location, out of direct sun. Root cuttings may take from three weeks to two months to sprout new stems. Keep the medium barely moist to avoid problems with rotting. Check occasionally for dryness, and water only as needed.

Once the cuttings begin to sprout, open the plastic to allow air circulation. After several days, remove the plastic and place plants where they'll get more light. Care for them as you would young seedlings; see "Growing Healthy Seedlings" on page 245. When they are 2 to 3 inches tall, prepare them for transplanting (see "Transplanting to the Garden" on page 248).

If you took your root cuttings in late summer or fall, overwinter them in a cold frame in their dormant state until spring. Then transplant the new plants to pots or a nursery bed for the upcoming growing season.

Preparing Your Site

Good site preparation is the foundation of a successful flower garden. By preparing the site carefully—removing lawn grass, weeds, or other vegetation and improving the soil before you plant—you provide your flowers with the best possible foundation for a long, healthy, and attractive life. And you save yourself a lot of work spent trying to fix problems down the road.

It's best to prepare your beds well before planting time: Preparing them in the fall for spring planting or in summer for fall planting is best. This schedule leaves plenty of time for removing unwanted vegetation, getting a soil test, and working and amending the soil.

GIVE ROOT CUTTINGS A TRY

If you want to try your hand at taking root cuttings, start with the perennials listed below. Each propagates readily from root cuttings.

Bleeding hearts (*Dicentra* spp.), garden phlox (*Phlox paniculata*), oriental poppy (*Papaver orientale*), plume poppy (*Macleaya cordata*), Siberian bugloss (*Brunnera macrophylla*), spiny bear's-breech (*Acanthus spinosus*).

With root cuttings taken in late winter or early spring, you'll have new plants to move to the garden that summer. If you take root cuttings in fall, you'll need to overwinter the plants in a greenhouse or cold frame until spring.

----------→·←----------

DON'T TILL WEEDS

Tilling plant material into the soil adds organic matter and nutrients; covercropping is a time-honored soil-improvement method. But tilling under sod or weeds to make a flower bed can do more harm than good when perennial weeds and grasses cover the area.

Think twice about tilling covering plants into your flower bed when you see perennial weeds present. Chopping up these tough customers effectively propagates them by cuttings— each piece can sprout into a new weed! Tilling also brings weed seeds to the soil surface, exposing them to the light that they need to germinate.

Listed below are weeds you don't want to till under—it will only encourage them! See "Weeds" on page 289 for control information.

Bermuda grass (*Cynodon dactylon*), Canada thistle (*Cirsium arvense*), dandelion (*Taraxacum officinale*), Johnsongrass (*Sorghum halepense*), quackgrass (*Agropyron repens*).

----------→·←----------

Clearing Your Site

If the site you've chosen for your flower bed is a patch of lawn or weeds—or an existing bed filled with plants you no longer want—you first need to remove all the weeds, lawn grass, and other undesirable vegetation growing there. If you don't, these established plants will compete with your newly planted flowers, and they'll very likely win. Use the guidelines below to eliminate existing vegetation effectively and efficiently.

Outline your bed. Before you dig, use string and stakes or a sprinkled line of flour to outline your bed. If you haven't tried to visualize its size already, take a moment to step back to make sure the size, shape, and placement work for you.

Slice away lawn grass. To remove lawn grass, use a spade to cut around rectangular strips and then to slice under the roots to create strips of sod. Roll the strips up as you go, and set them aside. You can use them to patch bare spots in your lawn, or add them to your compost pile. If you're clearing a large area, a rented sod cutter can save you a great deal of time and effort. For another way to eliminate lawn grass, see "Mulch Away Lawn" below.

Mulch away perennial weeds and brush. These tough customers present a greater challenge than lawn grass, but you can conquer them with some effort and some advance planning. Starting in spring or summer, pull out as much of the unwanted vegetation as possible, making sure to dig out all the roots you can. Mow the weeds close to the ground. Cover the area with a layer of newspaper, 1 inch or several sections thick. Top the newspaper with a thick layer of compost. (You can also use straw or hay, but compost will look more attractive while you wait.) Leave this thick mulch in place until the following spring. Then pull back the mulch and amend and turn the soil, or install your plants directly into the mulched area. See "A Mulch-and-Grow Garden" on page 152 for a garden design that can be planted directly over a weedy site.

Mulch away lawn. A layer of newspaper topped by

compost will also kill lawn grass over a period of two to three months. If you'd rather not skim off the sod, you can turn it under to add organic matter to the soil. You can also use a newspaper-and-compost mulch over soil where you've removed sod to help kill any surviving grass roots. It's particularly useful if you've removed an especially weedy patch of lawn.

Improving Your Soil

If you do only one thing to prepare your soil for planting, add organic matter. Spreading an inch or two of compost over your cleared site and planting directly into it will give your flowers an adequate start. Even better, spread the compost, and dig it into the surface of the soil with a shovel or fork.

That said, keep in mind that the more you do to improve your soil before planting, the better off your flowers will be. Annuals can usually survive the season with only minor

Use a thick mulch to improve poor soil and to smother unwanted vegetation. In spring or early summer, mow the area closely and cover it with an inch of newspaper, topped by 3 to 4 inches of compost. Plant in the mulch the following spring.

SOIL HEALTH MAKES GOOD SCENTS

The nutrients in your soil play a part in determining the color, color intensity, and aroma of the flowers growing in it. Sulfur and micronutrients, especially iron, are critical in the biochemical processes that create the delicate hues and scents of our favorite flowers.

Different soil characteristics affect plant color and fragrance in different ways. When they are present in the soil, the metallic elements that make paint colors vivid have the same effect on flower colors. When it's applied as a fertilizer, seaweed's balanced micronutrients intensify flower colors. Soil acidity or alkalinity affects the colors of some flowers as well: Bigleaf hydrangea (*Hydrangea macrophylla*) has blue blossoms when grown in acid soils and pink ones when grown in more alkaline soils.

In general, for the brightest, most beautiful flowers, make sure your soil is healthy, biologically active, and well amended with compost and other organic fertilizers.

---

soil preparation, but they are absolutely glorious in a well-prepared site. Perennials are a long-term investment, and the more time and effort you take to improve the soil they're planted in, the better. And once perennials are planted, full-scale soil preparation and amendment becomes much more difficult. For complete instructions on preparing your soil, see "Digging In" on page 270.

Ideally, you want soil that has good drainage, ample organic matter, near-neutral pH, and plenty of available nutrients. The site you've chosen for your flower bed should contribute to these conditions. See "Sizing Up Your Soil" on page 21 if you haven't evaluated your soil yet. If you suspect you have problem soil, you'll want to take extra time and effort to improve it before you plant. You'll find instructions for caring for problem soils in "Fertilizing Plans" on page 287. You also may want to have a soil test done; see "Soil Testing Options" on page 268 and "Taking Soil Samples" on page 269 for directions.

Making and Using Compost

Compost is the number one soil amendment for organic gardeners. It's gardener's gold. Finished compost is a dark, crumbly-textured, nutrient-rich substance that makes a great soil amendment, fertilizer, or topdressing for your garden. Adding it to a clay soil helps to increase pore space, thus improving drainage and making more room for soil air, which is essential to healthy root growth. In sandy soil, adding compost promotes greater moisture-holding capacity. Compost adds nutrients that plants need in forms they can use. Your flower garden will thrive on a steady diet of compost, because compost releases its nutrients slowly, encouraging steady, sturdy growth.

Compost also encourages a healthy population of soil microorganisms. These microscopic workhorses feed on organic matter and release nutrients your plants can use. Earthworms love compost, too, and their activity helps aerate the soil, making a happy home for your plants' roots. And earthworm castings are among the finest fertilizers available.

Another benefit of compost is that it's made by decomposing organic materials that you have to dispose of any way, such as leaves, yard wastes, and kitchen scraps. You can make compost slowly, with little effort, or quickly, but with much more work. A tidy compost bin may suit your neighbors' aesthetic tastes better than a loose pile of yard waste, but organic matter will decompose in either system. If you haven't composted before, you may want to start by following the directions in "Making Compost the Easy Way" on this page. Use the techniques that follow to fine-tune the process—to speed it up and to control the quality and quantity of the finished compost. Start your compost pile today; your flowers will thank you.

Choose the Right Location

A compost pile relies on microorganisms to carry out the decomposition process. Many of these busy decomposers need oxygen to do their jobs, so a well-drained site is very important. When oxygen is lacking, other microorganisms take over, and decay proceeds anaerobically. When this happens, the compost pile develops unpleasant odors. Adding air to the pile by turning it can help correct the situation, as can aerating by adding hollow poles or stalks to the pile.

Locate your compost pile where it is accessible to your garden and a water source—moisture is also important to the minidecomposers. It doesn't matter whether it's in the sun or the shade. If you are concerned about your compost pile's looks, contain it in any one of several commercially available or homemade compost bins. Or hide it behind a planting of tall flowers, shrubs, or vines.

Get the Size Right

Approximately 3 cubic feet of materials are needed to provide a good home for the organisms that carry out decomposition. The pile's height contributes to the presence or absence of oxygen for its microorganisms. If it is over 3 to 4 feet high, the weight of the materials on top will compress the pile, reducing the available oxygen; under 3 feet, the pile will not heat up sufficiently and decomposi-

—◆·◆—

MAKING COMPOST THE EASY WAY

To build a basic, slow but relatively labor-free compost pile, you need a space of roughly 3 cubic feet in a well-drained area, a collection of materials to compost, and some soil. Pile leaves, grass clippings, and other yard wastes together as they become available, adding a couple shovelfuls of soil every now and then. Form the pile so that the top is concave, to collect moisture from rain. Stop adding to your pile when it reaches 3 to 4 feet tall—start another one if you need to. After 12 to 18 months, you'll have a supply of dark, earthy-smelling compost.

—◆·◆—

———— ⇢·⇠ ————

COMPOST MYTHS

Compost is such a valuable soil amendment that people think it must be difficult to make, but it's not! Read over the compost myths below and the facts that follow them for the true story.

•**You must have a compost bin.** False. You do not need a compost bin to make good compost. You can make great compost in a pile or heap 3 to 5 feet tall and wide.

•**You must turn your compost pile often.** False. Turning the pile will speed up the decomposition process, but it's not necessary. A pile that's never turned will produce compost in one to two years.

•**You must use special bioactivators or inoculants.** False. The bacteria needed to break materials down into compost are present in ordinary garden soil or finished compost. Mix a shovelful of either into new compost now and then and you'll have plenty of activators—free!

———— ⇢·⇠ ————

tion will occur more slowly. A width and length of 3 to 5 feet will keep the pile within comfortable reach for turning or adding materials.

Do You Need Equipment?

Compost happens, whether you own all the equipment shown in garden catalogs or not. Compost bins, aeration tools, bioactivators, and thermometers are all useful but not necessary to the process.

Turning forks, shovels, and aeration tools are used to mix the pile's contents and to incorporate oxygen, speeding the composting process. Bioactivators add the microorganisms necessary for decomposition, but so does a shovelful of healthy garden soil or finished compost. A compost thermometer measures the heat that builds up as your pile breaks down; when the temperature peaks and then falls, it's time to turn your pile again.

Use the Right Ingredients

Your pile needs sources of both carbon and nitrogen to feed the decomposers; both are readily available in your yard or neighborhood. If you chop or shred the materials you add to your compost pile, you expose more surfaces for the microorganisms to feed on, speeding the process. Whole ingredients tend to decompose very slowly. Use the guidelines below to decide what to add to your pile.

Nitrogen Sources. Nitrogen-rich plant materials are green and/or moist; examples include fresh grass clippings, weeds (seed-free), leafy hedge trimmings, vegetable and fruit trimmings, and coffee grounds. Animal byproducts are also sources of nitrogen; these include barnyard manures, hair, and bloodmeal.

Carbon Sources. These tend to be brown, dry, and bulky. They include dried grass clippings, fallen leaves, shredded newspapers (not whole), sawdust, cornstalks, and straw. Woody twigs and stems contain carbon but break down slowly if not shredded.

Other Nutrients. Other materials can enhance the compost's mineral content. These include rock powders, wood

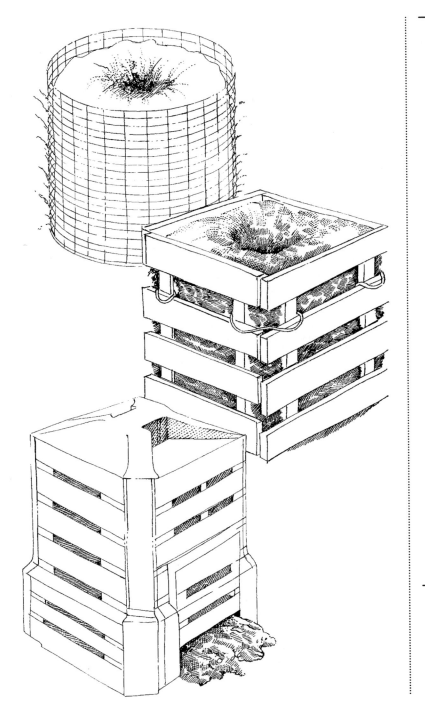

➔ · ◀

COMPOST BIN STYLES

You can build a compost bin from any number of readily available materials—wood, wire, bricks, concrete blocks, or just about anything you have on hand.

The bin shown here on the upper left is made from an 11-foot section of 3- to 4-foot-wide dog-pen fencing. The ends were tied together with twine or wire to form a circular enclosure.

The bin shown in the middle is made from four wooden pallets. They are usually available for free from businesses that ship or receive large amounts of goods. Simply tie the pallets together to form an enclosure.

The bin shown on the bottom is made from recycled plastic. Many commercial composters are made of this durable material, but shop around, since prices vary widely.

➔ · ◀

→ · ←

TROUBLE-FREE COMPOSTING

Composting need not be a difficult, time-consuming, or complicated process, reports "Compost King" Joe Keyser, director of programs at the American Horticultural Society in Alexandria, Virginia. Keyser recommends a passive composting system, using the schedule below to produce 20 to 30 cubic feet of fresh compost annually after the second year.

YEAR 1: Spring: Begin pile #1; add to it all year.

Late Fall: Finish pile #1; leave it alone.

YEAR 2: Spring: Begin pile #2; add to it all year.

Late Fall: Finish pile #2; leave it alone.

YEAR 3: Spring: Use well-done compost from pile #1 as mulch, soil amendment, or fertilizer.

Begin pile #3; add to it all year.

Late Fall: Finish pile #3; leave it alone.

YEAR 4: Spring: Use well-done compost from pile #2. Begin pile #4.

To accelerate this process, turn the pile once a month (except when it's frozen in winter) and increase additions of nitrogenous ingredients.

→ · ←

ash, seaweed, greensand, and hoof and horn meal. Many gardeners add lime to their compost, but it can react with nitrogen sources to form ammonia, reducing the nitrogen content of your finished compost.

Materials to Avoid. Do not put these materials in your compost pile: dog, cat, or bird manure, or human feces. All of these can carry disease microorganisms that are infectious to humans. Do not add dairy products, meat, grease, fat, or bones, which will attract foraging rodents and pets.

Also avoid diseased plant matter and plants or grass clippings that are contaminated with pesticides or other dangerous chemicals. And do not compost noxious or invasive grasses or weeds, or their roots or seeds: You don't want to spread problems along with your compost. Use care when composting wet materials like grass clippings or leaves; break them up and mix with drier materials.

Keep Your Compost Moist

Moisture lets your pile's microorganisms move around. Keep your compost about as moist as a damp sponge at all times. If it becomes dry, turn the pile, moistening it thoroughly as you go. An overly wet pile may smell bad and turn slimy. Turn the pile and incorporate some dry, carbon-rich materials; if necessary, cover it loosely to keep rainwater out.

Speeding Up the Process

Air, moisture, amounts of carbon and nitrogen, particle size, and weather all contribute to the amount of time your pile of ingredients needs to become compost. If all you do is assemble a pile according to the information above, your compost may take anywhere from a few months to one to two years to "cook." By chopping materials finely, keeping the pile moist, and turning it at least once a week, you can speed up the process and have a finished product in a few weeks or a few months.

How can you tell when your compost is "done?" Finished compost is crumbly, dark brown to black, with a good, earthy smell. If it doesn't look or smell quite right, keep it turned and moist a little longer.

Other Soil Amendments and Fertilizers

Although compost is the most important soil amendment, there are others you can use. See "Soil Amendments" on this page for a quick-reference guide to these all-important materials.

The quickest and surest way to find out how fertile your soil is—and whether you need to add fertilizer before you plant—is to have a soil test done. A soil test will tell you the soil's pH, its organic matter content, and the availability of macronutrients and micronutrients. Without a soil test, you may add the wrong nutrient or the wrong amount of the right one. By tinkering blindly with your soil, you risk wasting time and money without getting the results you want, or creating a mineral toxicity problem. For more on soil testing, see "Soil Testing Options" on page 268 and "Taking Soil Samples" on page 269.

Understanding Nutrient Availability

There are several factors that affect how easily your flowers can take up the minerals in your soil. Soil pH is one of them. Availability also depends on how well the soil holds nutrients. Most plants thrive in a slightly acidic soil, with a pH between 6.5 and 6.8. When the pH is lower than 6 or higher than 7.5, minerals in the soil bind together in forms unavailable to plants. For example, in very acidic soils, potassium, calcium, and magnesium are in short supply. Alkaline soils limit the iron needed to make leaves green— for that reason, plants in alkaline soils often have yellow leaves with green veins. Phosphorus and boron are less available at both extremes. Your best bet in dealing with pH is to grow flowers that will thrive in the existing pH. If you have alkaline soil (pH above 7), for example, stay away from rhododendrons and azaleas (*Rhododendron* spp.). Instead, look for plants that thrive in the existing conditions in your area.

In addition to the pH, the soil texture—the amounts of clay, sand, and silt—affects nutrient availability. Plants take up nutrients that are dissolved in the water held in the pores between soil particles. The large pores in sandy soils

---

SOIL AMENDMENTS

Choose the amendments most readily available to you, and use them to add humus, improve soil structure and water retention, and neutralize pH. Some amendments also add nutrients to the soil.

• Commercially prepared or homemade, compost is an ideal, balanced soil amendment that also supplies nutrients.

• Plentiful and free (for most gardeners), green grass clippings decompose quickly, adding little bulk to the soil.

• Dry, brown materials, such as hay, straw, autumn leaves, and sawdust, add bulk to the soil. To speed breakdown, add blood meal or another nitrogen source with any of these.

• The manure from most farm animals improves the soil and is a balanced nutrient source. Let fresh manure dry before adding it to the soil, or use a commercial dried-manure product.

• Earthworm manure, called castings, is a good soil conditioner. Healthy soil brings earthworms (and castings) to your garden. You also can buy castings.

—>·<—

SOIL TESTING OPTIONS

You can test your soil yourself. Or send a sample to your state's land-grant university or a private testing lab.

Commercial Home Test Kits. Results from home test kits are less accurate than those from a soil lab, because labs factor in differences in soil samples, such as moisture content. The more sophisticated home test kits give fairly accurate results, but if they indicate imbalances, you may want to confirm them with a professional test.

Cooperative Extension Soil Tests. Extension soil tests are generally inexpensive (or free). Test kits are available from your local Cooperative Extension Service office. Their analysis may be less complete than that offered by private testing labs.

Private Laboratory Soil Tests. Private soil test labs usually charge $30 or more for their analyses, but they often provide a more complete test and final report. It may also be easier to find a soil lab familiar with making organic recommendations.

—>·<—

let water drain away before the plants can absorb it. In clay soils, the pores can be so small that roots can't penetrate them to get to the nutrients.

The amount of organic matter also influences how available nutrients are. Organic matter particles absorb nutrients on their surfaces, then release them into the soil water. (This is another reason that adding organic matter is so beneficial.) And because organic matter helps sandy soils hold water and makes clay soils looser, it makes it easier for plants to absorb the nutrients in these soils.

Organic Fertilizers

Fertilizers can supply a single nutrient or a combination of nutrients. A single-nutrient fertilizer may contain only one mineral, or a high percentage of one plus a small amount of one or more others. They are often used to correct a deficiency. A balanced fertilizer supplies nitrogen, phosphorus, and potassium in nearly equal percentages. Examples of balanced fertilizers include compost, rotted manure, seaweed, and blends of single-nutrient fertilizers. They are used to replaced the nutrients that plants remove from the soil.

If you're shopping for commercial organic fertilizers, read the label to determine which kind you're getting. If it supplies nitrogen, phosphorus, or potassium, the label will have three numbers separated by hyphens. The first number is the percentage of nitrogen (N), the second is the percentage of phosphorus (P), and the third is the percentage of potassium (K). If it doesn't have any of these, the label will tell what nutrient it does contain and the percentage in the product.

Plant Nutrient Guide

Use the results of your soil test along with the list below to determine the best way to amend your soil before planting. You'll find the nutrients that plants need, organic fertilizers and soil amendments that supply them, and what they do for plants.

Nitrogen. Alfalfa meal, fresh bat guano, blood meal, fish emulsion, and fish meal all provide nitrogen. Nitrogen encourages stems and leaves to grow and gives plants a deep green color. Because its result are so dramatic, gardeners often overdo it; when they do, they get lush green growth but no flowers. Unlike most other nutrients, nitrogen isn't held in the soil. That's one of the most important reasons for continually adding organic matter to the soil. Organic fertilizers release nitrogen slowly, making it available steadily in small amounts.

Phosphorus. Aged bat guano, colloidal phosphate, rock phosphate, and steamed bonemeal all provide phosphorus. Rock phosphate is a good choice for acidic soils, because its phosphorus is more available when the pH is less than 6.2. Steamed bonemeal is also a good source of calcium. Phosphorus promotes root growth, flowering, fruiting, and disease resistance. Because phosphorus doesn't move down through the soil, you need to put it near your plants' roots. Work it in to a depth of about 6 inches for annuals or 12 inches for perennials.

Potassium. Also called potash, potassium is in granite meal, greensand, kelp meal, and langbeinite. Langbeinite also contains magnesium, so don't use it in soils already containing enough magnesium. Although wood ashes also provide potassium, they are so alkaline that they can damage roots. Potassium is important for strong roots, disease resistance, and general plant vigor.

Calcium. Calcium is found in gypsum, lime, and finely ground clam and oyster shells. (Gypsum is a soil conditioner that loosens clay soils; lime is used to raise pH.) Calcium helps build strong cells.

Sulfur. Sulfur is sold in pure form, and it is also found in magnesium sulfate, iron sulfate, and other compounds. It is a building block in proteins.

Magnesium. Sources of magnesium include magnesium sulfate, dolomitic limestone, and liquid seaweed. Magnesium sulfate is also used to lower pH. Magnesium is part of chlorophyll, the stuff that makes plants green. Excess magnesium in soil can cause potassium deficiency.

TAKING SOIL SAMPLES

Follow these steps to prepare a sample that accurately reflects the content of your soil.

1. Scrape away any surface litter or plant growth from a small area of soil. Dig a hole with a stainless steel trowel or other tool, and collect a slice of soil from the side of the hole. For cultivated areas, collect a core or slice to a depth of 6 inches.
2. Repeat the sampling procedure at 10 to 15 different spots in each flower bed.
3. Mix the samples in a clean plastic or stainless steel container.
4. Place some of the mixed sample in a plastic container or bag, and put it in the bag supplied by the testing laboratory.

Don't touch the sample with soft steel, brass, or galvanized tools, or with your skin. All can alter soil test results for some minerals.

Send your sample to the testing laboratory by mail. Note on the accompanying information form that you want recommendations for organic soil amendments.

—→·←—

SHOPPING FOR ORGANIC FERTILIZERS

Bill Wolf, founder and owner of Necessary Trading Company, a supplier of organic gardening materials, offers these pointers for buying organic fertilizers.

• Although more garden centers carry organic products now than a few years ago, the selection is still limited compared to what's available. Mail-order catalogs have a larger selection, but their products and claims are less regulated.

• Read the label. Look for the word "natural," more than the word "organic," which has a looser definition.

• If you can't tell from the label what it's made from or how much to apply, don't buy it.

• If the label says the product will solve problems or it promises specific results, be sure they include the problem you have or the results you want. If the claims seem fantastic, be cautious. Fertilizers are tools, not cure-alls.

—→·←—

Micronutrients. Iron, boron, manganese, zinc, copper, cobalt, molybdenum, chlorine, and nickel are all called micronutrients. Plants need these trace elements in such minute amounts—ounces per acre in some cases—that you should apply them only if a soil test shows they're deficient. Deficiencies are most common in very sandy or extremely alkaline soils. Applying too much can throw off the balance of other nutrients or be toxic to plants. You can safely replace the micronutrients removed in one growing season by mulching or by fertilizing with liquid seaweed.

Digging In

Digging—the process of breaking and turning and amending the soil—may not be the most appealing step on the road to a no-fail flower garden, but it's surely one of the most important. It turns a potentially hard, crusty, airless environment into a soft, fluffy, friable one that welcomes and nurtures your new plants.

Focus your attention on the top 12 inches of the soil. That's where most of your flowers will want to spread their roots. If your soil is heavy with clay, consider the onerous but worthwhile task of double digging to improve drainage and aeration. Otherwise, turning and amending the upper 12 inches is sufficient.

Make sure the soil is neither too wet nor too dry when you dig and amend. To tell when soil moisture is right for digging, squeeze a handful of soil from your seedbed. If it sticks together in a clump, the soil is too wet to work—wait two or three days, then check the moisture again. If the soil is so dry that it doesn't stick together at all, wet the area thoroughly and let it drain overnight. When the soil is slightly moist and crumbly, you are ready to begin.

Begin by turning the soil to the depth of your spade or fork. Or use a rotary tiller to turn it to a similar depth. Top the turned area with compost or other organic matter and any amendments you wish to add. Then work the area over again with your spade, fork, or tiller to incorporate these additions and to break up any clods. Water the soil when finished to help settle the bed. If you're preparing your bed well in advance of planting time, cover it with a layer of organic mulch to keep weeds out and to further improve the soil. If you have poorly drained soil or just want to go to the extra effort of preparing an ideal home for your flowers, see "Double Digging" on this page.

Problem-Free Planting

It's finally time to install your new flower garden. The design is ready, the bed is prepared, the plants are waiting. Try to time your planting for a dull or overcast day to avoid the additional stress of intense sunlight on your newly transplanted flowers. Before you actually plant them, set potted plants in the bed according to your design; substitute markers or empty pots for bareroot plants or seedlings. Step back and see how you like it. Of course it will look a little sparse at this stage; but with a strong start and continuing care, your plants will fill in quickly. Don't be tempted to squeeze in more plants; your flowers need room to grow. If the bed looks too empty, fill in with annuals and mulch. Fine-tune your design, if necessary, then grab your trowel, spade, and garden gloves and get planting.

Preparation and Planting

Water your plants thoroughly before planting. To help your plants survive the rigors of transplanting, don't let them dry out enough to wilt before or after planting. If you're putting in bareroot plants, take them out of their packaging and soak their roots in water or compost tea for an hour or two before planting.

Make each planting hole large enough to accommodate a plant's entire root system without crowding. But don't make the holes too deep; each plant needs to grow at the same level in your garden as it was in its container. Use the soil line on the stem as a guideline, if necessary. If the soil in your flower garden is newly turned and fluffed up, set each plant about ½ inch higher than it grew in its pot. It will settle lower as the soil settles around it.

DOUBLE DIGGING

This method of bed preparation works the soil to twice the usual depth. The hard work it involves turns off many gardeners, but its advantages in heavy soils are well proven.

Start by digging a trench 1 foot wide and deep across one end of your bed. Set the soil aside, preferably in a cart or wheelbarrow. Use a garden fork to work up the soil at the bottom of the trench.

Repeat this process on the next foot of bed, moving the soil from the second trench into the first. Continue digging trenches, moving the soil into the previous trench, and forking up the bottom of each. When you reach the other end of the bed, fill the last trench with the soil from the first one.

Spread organic matter and amendments over the top of the newly dug bed, and work them into the upper 4 to 6 inches of the soil. The finished bed will be fluffy because of the added organic matter and air.

—→ · ←—

GIVE YOUR GARDEN A RAISE

The time and effort needed to turn very poor soil, such as heavy clay, into rich, loose soil can make you feel as if you'll never have a flower garden. But a raised garden bed, built over the top of a difficult site, lets you get on with the planting.

While you can start a raised bed by double digging, you may choose simply to cover the bed with enough good soil to plant in. Here are a few things to consider when planning a raised bed.

• If the bed is very large or very deep, it will take a lot of topsoil and organic matter to fill it.

• If your bed is deeper than 6 to 8 inches, you'll probably need to frame it with landscape timbers, stones, bricks, or other material to hold the soil.

• The bed's frame should be sturdy, long-lasting, attractive, and suited to your landscape.

• In poorly drained sites, start your bed with a layer of gravel, then top it with the soil you'll plant in.

—→ · ←—

Removing Plants from Containers

To remove a plant from its container, place your fingers over the soil on either side of the plant, turn the pot upside down, and tap the bottom until plant and soil ball slide out into your hand. If needed, slide a table knife between the pot and the soil to loosen things up. If roots are growing out of the pot's drainage holes, they may have to be cut off to free the root ball from the pot. If you still can't get the plant to slide out of its container, or if the plant and pot are too heavy to easily tip into one hand, cut the pot with a knife and pull it away from the roots in sections.

Pop small plants out of thin cell packs by pushing up on the bottom of each cell. This will crinkle the cell but preserves the majority of roots. If roots are growing out the drainage holes, cut them off.

Settling Plants in the Soil

When you're planting container-grown annual or perennial flowers, take a minute to inspect each plant's root system, and cut off any broken, diseased, or dead roots. If the roots circle at the bottom of the container, gently pull them apart and spread them open before planting. If they are extremely dense and circled, make a perpendicular cut across the bottom of the soil ball to split it in half. Turn it and make another cut through the soil ball to cut it into quarters. Before planting, pull each "quarter" up and away from the center of the soil ball to prevent the roots from growing together and choking each other. Dig a hole that's wide enough to accommodate the plant's roots without bending or breaking them. Set the root ball in the hole so the soil level is the same as it was when the plant was growing in the pot. If the soil is newly prepared, plant slightly higher. The soil will settle when you water and the plant will sink to a lower level. See the illustration on page 274 for details. (Perennial and annual bulbs aren't sold in containers, so they require different planting procedures. For instructions, see "Planting Bulbs" on the opposite page.)

Small trees and shrubs can be purchased as container-grown plants, too. Larger specimens are balled-and-burlapped to save a larger part of the root system than would fit in a container. Plant container-grown trees and shrubs just as you would an annual or perennial flower in a pot. For information on purchasing and planting balled-and-burlapped plants, see "Buying Large Trees" and the illustration on page 275.

Perennial plants, trees, and shrubs can also be ordered bareroot, which means you will receive a dormant plant with roots that are washed clean of any soil. Bareroot plants cost less to ship and are cheaper than container-grown ones. They won't look like much when they first arrive, but once planted, they'll adapt and grow quickly.

Place bareroot plants at the same depth as they were grown originally. Use old stems or soil-line marks to guide you in setting them at the proper depth, and read any directions that come with them. See page 274 for an illustration of how to plant a bareroot perennial plant.

There's no need to add fertilizer to the hole at planting time—you've already amended your soil when you prepared the bed. Place each plant in its hole and hold it upright while filling around its roots with soil. Firm the soil around the roots to hold the plant in place and eliminate large air pockets.

Labels will help you track the progress of your new flower garden and will keep you from accidentally pulling or cultivating late-emerging plants. They need not be prominent or obtrusive; a discreet plant tag tucked beneath the leaves is all you'll need. If you prefer to keep your planting label-free, make sure your design reflects the location of every plant you install. Don't rely on your memory—add labels or notes to your design as you plant.

Aftercare

Although the techniques you've used to start and select the plants for your no-fail flower garden are designed to reduce maintenance, your plants still need some care after planting. And your flower garden will truly flourish if you tend it regularly, even for brief periods of time.

Once they're transplanted from their seedbeds, seedling

PLANTING BULBS

Plan a fall planting session to add hardy spring-flowering bulbs to your new flower bed. You can plant late-summer-bloomers such as Japanese anemones (*Anemone* × *hybrida* and *A. tomentosa*) in spring along with your perennials. Use spring-flowering bulbs to fill spaces that annuals or slow-emerging perennials will occupy later in the season or to brighten expanses of groundcover.

Space bulbs according to flower stalk height. For greatest impact, plant in clusters of ten or more rather than singly in rows. Plant large bulbs 5 to 6 inches apart and small bulbs 1 to 3 inches apart. Plant each bulb at a depth three to four times the bulb's height to protect it from frost, animals, and damage from soil cultivation. Don't add fertilizer to the planting holes; instead, cover the bulbs with soil, and top-dress with balanced organic fertilizer or compost. Top-dress again in spring, when the foliage is just beginning to emerge.

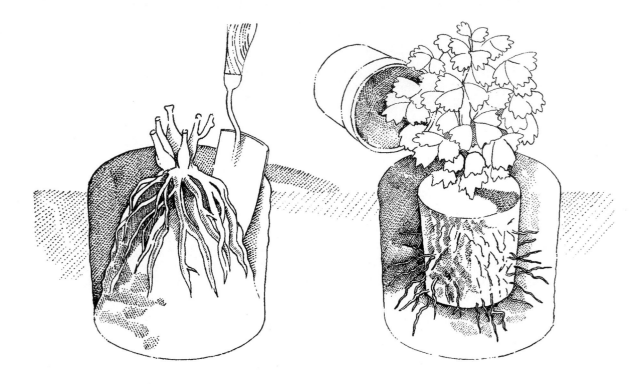

Plant container-grown plants (*right*) at the same depth as they were in their pots. Mound soil in the bottom of a planting hole for a bareroot plant (*left*). Keeping the crown at the depth at which it grew in the nursery, set the plant atop the mound, so the roots drape over the sides, and fill around them with soil.

containers, or nursery pots, your plants continue to need your help. Moisture, nutrients, and protection from injury are the major requirements of newly transplanted flowers. In the first few days and weeks after planting, your vigilance in attending to these requirements can make the difference between survival and death for your plants.

Water your newly installed plants well. Use a soft spray, a soaker hose, or a sprinkler to apply enough water to gently soak the plants in and settle the soil around them. Do not fertilize until the plants have adjusted and show distinct signs of growth, and then only as needed.

Use mulch to give your newly planted flower bed a professional, "finished" look. In addition to its aesthetic contributions, mulching provides many benefits important to the health of your plants. See "Mulching" on page 279 for a description of the advantages of mulching and a list of mulch materials.

Be a protective parent to your plants. Check them regu-

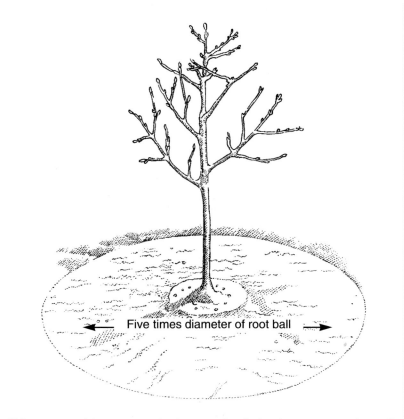

When you add a tree or shrub to a mixed planting, prepare the soil by tilling or spading up an area that's five times the diameter of the root ball. This loosens the soil so the roots can spread freely.

Dig a saucer-shaped hole for your tree or shrub that's two to three times the width of the root ball. Make the hole deep enough to place the plant at the same depth it grew at the nursery.

BUYING LARGE TREES

If you want to add a large tree to your garden, visit a nursery or garden center and look over their balled-and-burlapped plants. Choose one that looks healthy and has no scrapes or wounds on the bark. Look carefully at the root ball. If it's loose and falling away from the trunk, do not buy it. Pick a solid root ball that's held together by healthy roots.

Handle the tree by the root ball, not the trunk. Wrap cloth or burlap around the trunk to protect it while you move it, and place the root ball in a sling made from a piece of burlap to help you maneuver it. If you have the plant delivered to your home, make sure it isn't injured in the process. Do not accept a tree that has scraped or gouged bark.

For the best results, follow the planting instructions illustrated on this page.

➝ · ⬅

AN AFTERCARE CHECKLIST

If there's to be life after planting, there needs to be care. Use the following checklist to help your flowers through the first season after planting.

IN THE FIRST WEEKS:
• Check soil moisture regularly; water thoroughly when beds become dry. Never let transplants wilt.
• Monitor plants for signs of pests and diseases. Transplanting stresses plants and makes them more susceptible to problems.
• Remove weeds as soon as they appear.

AFTER ONE MONTH:
• Fertilize with fish emulsion or liquid seaweed after new growth appears.
• Continue to monitor and control pests, diseases, and weeds.

THROUGH THE SEASON:
• Pinch leggy plants to promote compact growth.
• Renew mulch as needed.
• Evaluate design and plant combinations.

➝ · ⬅

larly for pest and disease symptoms, and take action quickly when such problems arise. Watch, too, for damage caused by harsh sun, strong winds, or pounding rain; young plants may need shelter from the elements until they get established. And guard your garden from feeding and incidental damage caused by animals (including the human kind); take steps to exclude intentional and unintentional animal activity from your flower beds.

Don't despair that your flower garden will never be independent enough to survive without constant care. A little support through the weeks following planting will translate into a long, healthy, low-maintenance lifetime for your no-fail flower garden.

CHAPTER 8

Taking Care of Your Garden

Now that your flowers are planted, you can start enjoying them as they grow and mature into a beautiful garden.

If you've done a good job of planning and preparing and planting, your garden will give you little trouble. From now on, simple maintenance—mulching, watering, fertilizing, weeding, pruning, and staking—will prevent many of the problems that you can't eliminate beforehand.

The most important thing you can do to make sure your garden stays healthy is to visit it often—every day if you can. Gardening is more intuitive than analytical. Through regular observation, you'll gain the experience that's known as a green thumb. You'll know when to add more mulch, get a feel for how often to water and fertilize, keep ahead of weeds, know which plants need pruning or staking, and see pests before they get out of hand.

As you read this chapter, it may seem that keeping up a flower garden requires a lot of know-how and time. Keep in mind that this chapter presents many options for carrying out the basic maintenance tasks. Once you choose the best options for you, maintaining your garden involves a half-dozen or so simple routines.

True, caring for your flower garden isn't effortless. But it's the most enjoyable part of gardening, the part where you can see rewards for your efforts. And your diligence

277

PLANT CARE BASICS

Caring for a flower garden involves a few simple but important routines:

• Mulch to a depth of 3 to 4 inches to control weeds and to hold moisture in the soil. Organic mulches also improve the soil's drainage and fertility.

• Water deeply when plants start to wilt slightly in the heat of the day. Water as the day is warming up, so plants dry quickly—wet leaves encourage disease. Or use a soaker hose to water the soil.

• Fertilize to give plants a boost or, if necessary, to correct a nutrient deficiency.

• Weed by pulling or hoeing when weeds are small, to keep them from setting seed or storing the food they'll need to come back next year.

• Prune off faded flowers to promote continued flowering and growth rather than seed production.

• Stake weak-stemmed, tall, or climbing plants to give them support.

• Monitor plants for signs of insect, disease, or animal pest problems.

will be rewarded—if you tend your garden well from the start, with time you'll find that you tend it less and enjoy it more.

Maintaining Appearances

What makes for a good-looking garden? Partly, it's the things you considered when designing your flower beds, such as color scheme, balance of plant heights, and pleasing texture combinations. But there's more to it.

Take a walk through your neighborhood, and analyze the difference between gardens that please your eye and those that don't. Attractive gardens look healthy. They're clean, because mulch keeps soil from splashing onto the plants. They're well watered and perky. They're vigorous and flowering, because the plants are well fed. The weeds are under control, and faded flowers and browning seedheads have been removed. Tall plants are standing upright because they're staked, and no disease or insect problems are evident.

By keeping up with the maintenance routines in this chapter, you can have an attractive garden. But don't expect it to always be perfect. Flower gardens, like all living communities, go through cycles: They have good years and bad years. If a few plants don't work out, neither you nor your flower garden is a failure. And by using sound gardening practices, you'll have more good years than bad, and the bad years won't be devastating.

Gardening Techniques

Now that you've acknowledged that flower gardening won't always be a bed of roses, learn to use the techniques that increase your chances for success.

As you've no doubt noticed, there are right ways and wrong ways to do just about everything. By using right ways to keep up your garden, you'll prevent problems. For example, by watering deeply you'll encourage deep roots that will help your plants withstand dry spells. By giving plants the right kind of fertilizer, you'll encourage healthy blooms. The sections that follow cover different ways to water, mulch, fertilize, weed, prune, and stake your plants. Use them to help you choose the right ways that suit you and your plants best.

Mulching

If you do nothing else to your garden—if you never water, weed, or fertilize, never pick off a diseased leaf or a voracious Japanese beetle—you still should mulch it. Because even if you neglect all other tasks, mulching will give your garden a fighting chance to limp along. And if you're a conscientious gardener who tends to all these tasks, mulching will help you do them a lot less often.

A mulch is simply a material that covers the soil. In doing so, it performs several labor-saving functions. Mulch suppresses weeds, so you hoe and pull less. It reduces water evaporation from the soil and also lessens stress on the plants by moderating soil moisture and temperature. And mulch keeps soil from splashing up onto the leaves, so they stay cleaner. That not only makes for a prettier garden, it keeps disease-causing soil fungi and bacteria from reaching the leaves. Mulches fit into two broad categories: organic mulches, such as wood chips and grass clippings; and nonorganic mulches, such as landscape fabrics and stones.

Organic Mulches

In addition to the benefits all mulches provide, organic mulches add organic matter to the soil, improving its fertility and drainage. You can use dozens of materials as organic mulches. Some, like newspapers and grass clippings, you may have around the house. Others, such as corn cobs or cocoa bean shells, are industry by-products that are more common in some areas than others. And some, like bark, are available anywhere. Commercially available mulches are sold in bags or in bulk at garden centers and other businesses that supply landscape materials.

Apply the organic mulch of your choice in a 3- to 4-inch-deep layer around your plants. A 3-cubic-foot bag of mulch

---

A QUICK CARE CHECKLIST

Use this checklist to keep track of the tasks that keep flowers in top shape.

AT LEAST ONCE A WEEK:
• Check leaves and stems for signs of disease and insect or animal damage.
• Pull or hoe young weeds before they get established.
• Water plants when they show they need it—wilting slightly in the heat of the day but recovering when it cools off.
• Remove fading flowers.

A COUPLE OF TIMES DURING THE SEASON:
• Fertilize as needed to give plants a boost.
• Replenish organic mulches to maintain a 3- to 4-inch depth.
• Pinch off the growing tips of leggy annuals to encourage fullness.

ONCE EACH SEASON:
• Stake tall, weak-stemmed, or climbing perennials.
• Prune roses and shrubs, if they need it.

➜ · ⬅

SIZING UP BARK MULCHES

Texas A & M University Researchers Jayne Zajicek and Lorraine Billeaud tested four bark mulches to see which controlled weeds best. They compared fine pine bark mulch (½ to ¾ inch long), large pine bark nuggets (3 to 4 inches long), shredded oak mulch (½ to 3 inches long), and shredded cypress mulch (½ to 3 inches long). They evaluated 2-, 3-, and 6-inch layers of each bark.

The pair found that pine bark nuggets did the best job of controlling weeds. Weeds were able to root in the fine-textured and shredded mulches.

While a 6-inch layer of mulch let the fewest weeds through, it also inhibited landscape plants grown in the study. Zajicek and Billeaud recommend 4 inches of mulch for the best weed control without damage to your plants.

➜ · ⬅

will cover 6 square feet to about 4 inches deep. If mulched too deeply, annuals and perennials can smother.

If you're mulching perennials, apply the mulch when the new growth peeks out of the soil. If you're growing plants from seed, wait to mulch until the seedlings are several inches high and have firm stems. Transplants are usually large enough to mulch right after planting. To prevent rot and eliminate hiding places for cutworms, keep mulch 1 to 2 inches away from stems.

Here are some materials commonly used as mulches:

Bark. Bark is readily available during the growing season. It generally costs a few dollars for 3 cubic feet. The bark pieces may be large nuggets, small chips, or shredded strands. The larger the pieces, the slower they break down—good if you want a long-lasting decorative mulch, bad if you want to turn it into the soil as organic matter.

Compost. Compost is a good fertilizer as well as a mulch. To make sure it has enough bulk to suppress weeds, apply it before it breaks down completely—you should still be able to identify some of its components.

If you don't have a compost pile, check with your city or town's parks or public works department. They may compost grass, leaves, and other yard waste and make it available to residents for free or for a small fee. You can buy bagged compost, but it's relatively expensive. Expect to pay $7 to $10 for 3 cubic feet.

Grass Clippings. Many people let their grass clippings fall to the ground as they mow, which returns nutrients to the soil. If you bag your clippings, you can use them as a nitrogen-rich mulch that breaks down quickly. Clippings heat up as they decompose, so keep them away from the stems of seedlings and young transplants.

If you have weeds that have gone to seed in your lawn, compost the clippings before you mulch with them; turn the compost pile every couple of weeks so the center is hot enough to kill the weed seeds.

Before you collect grass clippings from your neighbors, make sure they haven't used pesticides or synthetic fertilizers on their lawns.

Manure. Manure, like compost, is a fertilizer as well as a good source of organic matter. It's a good idea to compost manure first, both to kill weed seeds and because manure may hold enough nitrogen to burn plants.

If you or your friends don't have barnyard animals, you can buy bagged manure, for under $5 for 3 cubic feet.

Leaves. Shred leaves before using them as mulch, because whole leaves can mat and become soggy, encouraging stem and crown rots. Few shredding machines handle leaves well; a better approach is to shred them with your mower, catching the leaves in the mower bag. Either mow a leaf-laden yard as you usually would, or rake the leaves into low rows and mow the piles.

Cocoa Bean Shells. In some areas, you can buy cocoa bean shells as a mulch. They are clean and weed-free; however, they're so light they can blow around if the wind is strong. Fresh shells have a chocolate odor that fades with time.

Ground Corn Cobs. Garden centers in corn-producing states often sell ground corn cobs. They break down slowly and stay put in all but the heaviest downpour.

Pecan Shells. You may find pecan shells sold as a mulch if there's a pecan grove in the area. The hard shells break down more slowly than bark. They can attract mice, cockroaches, and squirrels.

Newspaper. Because it's dense, newspaper makes a great mulch. Anchor it with a thin layer of grass clippings, bark chips, compost, or another mulch. By summer's end, a layer about 7 sheets thick breaks down enough for you to incorporate it into the soil. Don't use heavily colored sections, because the dyes may contain toxic metals that can build up in the soil.

Sawdust. If you have access to a wood shop, you can collect sawdust for a mulch. Sawdust is reputed to repel fleas and ticks. Some woods contain chemicals that can harm tender plants, so let the sawdust age outdoors, or compost it, before you use it. Do not use sawdust from pressure-treated lumber.

Straw. Straw is a lightweight mulch that breaks down slowly. It attracts spiders that control insect pests. But it can also be a fire hazard. You can pick up a 3-cubic-foot bale for a few dollars.

PROTECT PERENNIALS WITH WINTER MULCH

Gardeners in the know apply mulch in the winter, too, not to protect plants from the cold but to keep them safely in the ground. Unmulched soil expands and contracts as it thaws and refreezes. That shifting earth can push a plant out of the soil, where it will die.

Applied after the ground has frozen, a thick layer of mulch insulates the soil from temperature fluctuations, keeping it frozen. Leave summer mulch in place when winter arrives. Once the ground freezes, cover the bed with a layer of light, loose mulch, such as shredded leaves or straw. Avoid mulches that might mat down and smother plant crowns. If you live in an area that has snow cover through most of the winter, you're in luck—a blanket of snow is the perfect winter mulch.

Once spring arrives, rake back the mulch so the soil warms faster and your plants start growing sooner. Replace it when they start growing.

—→•←—

HIDDEN MULCH HAZARDS

The good things organic mulches do for your garden are so good that you may not notice their drawbacks. But there are a few things you need to know before you begin piling on the mulch.

Organic mulches make good hiding places for slugs. See "Trouble-shooting" on page 313 for solutions.

If an organic mulch closely surrounds a plant's stem, excess moisture can encourage stem rot—this is especially likely if you use unshredded leaves.

Finally, some mulches are so high in carbon that soil microorganisms have to take nitrogen from the soil to digest them. These high-carbon or "brown" mulches include bark, straw, paper, and other materials that feel more woody than moist. Nitrogen-rich "green" mulches are easier for microorganisms to digest—examples include grass clippings, pulled weeds, and kitchen scraps.

If you use a brown mulch, add nitrogen to the soil to compensate for the nitrogen the soil organisms remove. Green mulches don't require extra nitrogen.

—→•←—

Peat Moss. In spite of the benefits that acidic peat moss offers azaleas and rhododendrons, it makes a poor mulch. Peat is difficult to wet thoroughly, and when it dries out, it becomes crusty and sheds water.

Pine Needles. Pine needles, also called pine straw, are used widely in the southern United States. Collect them from your yard or your neighbors'; they make an excellent mulch. Don't gather them from the forest; leave that organic matter to fertilize the trees.

Nonorganic Mulches

Nonorganic mulches include landscape fabric, stones of various sizes, indoor/outdoor carpeting, aluminum foil, plastic, and just about anything else you can think of that holds down weeds, keeps moisture in the soil, and isn't derived from a plant.

Most nonorganic mulches last longer than most organic ones. Their biggest disadvantage is that they don't add organic matter to the soil. You can solve that problem by applying compost, manure, or another organic material to the soil surface before you put down the mulch.

Another drawback of many nonorganic mulches is that they suppress the offshoots many perennials send out, which makes them a bad choice if you want those plants to fill in bare areas. And if the mulch forms a dense barrier on the soil surface, as landscape fabric does, you have to fertilize with a liquid fertilizer, since solid ones can't penetrate the mulch to reach the soil.

Here are a few common nonorganic mulches:

Landscape Fabrics. These porous fabrics of spun or pressed plastic, also called weed barriers or geotextiles, let water and air reach the soil but don't let anything grow up through them (unless you cut a hole in them, which you do for each plant you set into the soil). You can cover the fabric with decorative mulch and forget about it until it disintegrates in a few years.

The downside of landscape fabric is that plants' roots can grow up into it, making removal of the fabric downright difficult when it needs to be replaced. See "Landscape Fabric Limits" on the opposite page.

Stones. As a mulch, stones last forever. They come in different sizes, from tiny pea gravel to fist-sized river rocks. They are especially appropriate in Xeriscape gardens in the West and Southwest, but they look out of place in woodland gardens and are difficult to remove.

Stones keep soil from splashing onto plants but aren't very effective for controlling weeds. To keep weeds in check, cover the soil with newspaper before spreading the stones.

Other Materials. Some gardeners use indoor/outdoor carpeting to suppress weeds and make a walkway between plants. You can probably think of other materials that would work. The idea is to let water through, keep plants clean, and keep weeds from emerging. Of course, if your flower garden is part of your landscape and not just a source of cut flowers, you'll want to avoid funky-looking mulches.

Watering

Water is one of a plant's most basic needs. Plants can eke out a neglected season in infertile soil, besieged by insects and diseases. But without water, they perish quickly.

Plants use some of the water they absorb through their roots to make sugars during photosynthesis—the process that turns light energy into plant food. They use some water in the chemical reactions that create new cells. And they use some to keep themselves turgid—that is, firm and upright, rather than droopy.

Most of the water that plants absorb, however, goes in one end and out the other. Leaves have tens of thousands of microscopic pores, called stomates, on both the upper and lower surfaces. The stomates open so the plant can take in the carbon dioxide it uses in photosynthesis. But when those pores are open, water evaporates from nearby cells in a process called transpiration. Up to 98 percent of the water that roots absorb can be lost through transpiration.

When and How to Water

You may have heard that plants need an inch of water per week. But when you consider that transpiration is a form of evaporation, it's easy to see how a plant's thirsti-

---

→ · ←

LANDSCAPE FABRIC LIMITS

When you're planting a mixed border of flowers and woody plants, landscape fabric might seem like a perfect barrier against weeds. But before you spend money and time on these air- and water-permeable sheets of plastic, make sure their benefits outweigh their disadvantages.

Although they're made of plastic, landscape fabrics break down over time (most need replacing every five to seven years). Plant roots may grow up into the fabric, making removal difficult; a layer of rock mulch over the fabric further complicates replacement. Weeds that sprout in mulch over landscape fabric often root through the fabric, making them hard to pull. And removing such weeds leaves holes to admit other weeds.

Landscape fabric limits perennials' spread, keeping them from filling your garden's empty spaces. And the soil-improving qualities of organic mulch that's spread over landscape fabric are lost, since the organic matter can't work its way into the soil below.

→ · ←

—→ · ←—

WATERING WITHOUT WASTE

Robert Peek, an information specialist with the St. John's River Water Management District in Palatka, Florida, says little changes can make a big difference in saving water in the garden. He offers these suggestions:

• Put plants where they belong. Don't put shade- and moisture-loving plants in a sunny, dry spot.

• Group plants with similar water needs. If you plant marigolds with roses, you end up underwatering the roses or overwatering the marigolds.

• Water slowly, deeply, and not until plants show need by wilting slightly.

• Use a watering system that puts water at the base of the plant, not on the leaves or on bare soil.

• Check your watering system for leaks, and repair any you find—drips add up.

• If you use a sprinkler system, water in the morning when evaporation is low. If the system is automatic, install a switch to shut it off when it rains.

• Mulch bare soil between plants and in walkways to keep moisture in the soil.

ness varies with the weather; plants lose more water through transpiration on sunny, windy, warm, or dry days than on cloudy, cool, still, or humid days. Plants near sidewalks and buildings that reflect light and heat lose more water than plants near a cool lawn.

The type of soil also influences how often plants need watering. Water drains quickly from a sandy soil with little organic matter—often too quickly for plants to absorb it. Sandy soils may need to be watered daily. Conversely, a tight clay soil with little organic matter traps water in its tiny pores and may become waterlogged if watered more than every five to seven days.

While there's no hard-and-fast rule about how often to water, there are solid guidelines about how to water. First, water deeply. Roots grow where the water is, and if you soak only the top inch or so, you'll encourage shallow roots. The top 2 inches of soil heat up and dry out faster than the soil 5 or 6 inches down; shallow roots will heat up and dry out, too.

Second, soak the soil slowly. Water moves only so fast through the little spaces between the soil particles. If you apply too much too fast, the water will puddle on the surface and run off before it reaches the roots. Your soil type will determine how quickly water penetrates the soil— water penetrates sandy soils faster than clay soils, because sandy soils have larger spaces between their particles than clay soils do.

Finally, let the soil dry out between waterings. Roots need oxygen as well as water. Waterlogged soils encourage roots and crowns to rot.

To get a feel for how much water your garden needs, use a spade to take a vertical slice from the soil after you've watered and the water has sunk in. If the top 6 inches of soil is moist, you've put on enough. If just the surface inch or so is moist, keep watering.

You can use the same soil-slice method to check how quickly the soil dries out. Water your soil well, then take a slice every day until it's time to water again. If the top 6 inches dries out in a day or two, your soil drains too quickly.

—→ · ←—

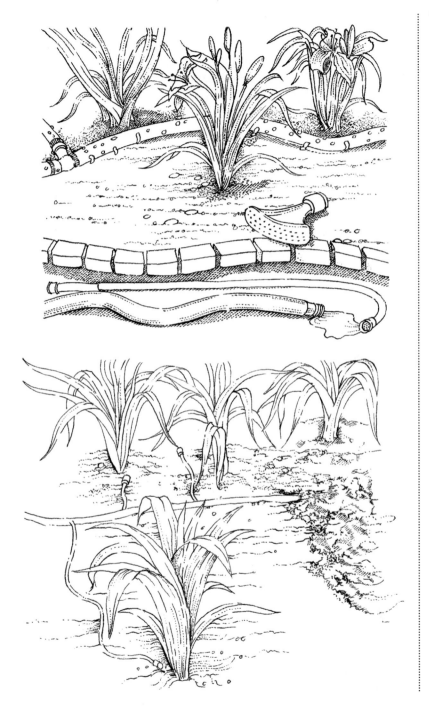

WHO'S THIRSTY?

In addition to environmental conditions, a plant's origins also affect how much water it requires. Some species have characteristics that help them adapt to dry conditions. Most desert plants, for example, have small, thick leaves covered by a waxy coating called a cuticle. Small leaves expose less surface area to the air, so there's less transpiration. And the waxy cuticle is a barrier that slows water loss. By comparison, the thin, broad leaves of woodland plants make them water hogs.

Soaker hoses (*top*) and drip irrigation systems (*bottom*) both release water slowly, so it soaks into the soil instead of running off. Mulch hides the tubing from sight and reduces moisture loss to the air. Spray nozzles and watering wands (*top*) slow the flow of water from your hose, so you can soak the soil without washing plants away.

—→·←—

KNOW WHEN TO WATER

Rather than watering by the calendar, learn to recognize when it's time to water. Plants that need water wilt slightly during the heat of the day but perk up when it cools off; their leaves may look duller than normal. The leaves of succulent plants, like sedums, shrivel slightly and feel softer than usual when thirsty. The key word here is "slightly"; you don't want leaves to droop or to roll in from the sides. When that happens, the plant is severely stressed.

Wilting can be a sign of too much water, too, so look at your plants carefully before irrigating. Plants that stay wilted may have waterlogged or rotten roots. Check the soil before watering, and if it's saturated, do not add more water. Give the plant roots time to dry out and recover.

—→·←—

If it takes more than five days, your soil is prone to waterlogging. You can improve both situations by adding organic matter to the soil, as discussed in "Mulching" on page 279 and "Fertilizing" on the opposite page.

Watering Tools

There are many tools available for watering flower gardens. One of the most common and worst is the lawn sprinkler, either the type you attach to the hose or a built-in sprinkler system.

Sprinklers have two big drawbacks. First, sprinkling wets the foliage, which encourages some fungal leaf diseases. Second, since the water flies through the air before it reaches the garden, much is lost to evaporation.

If you choose to use a sprinkler, timing is critical. To make sure leaves dry off as quickly as possible, water when temperatures are rising. Early morning is ideal: Not only will the leaves dry as the day grows warmer, but morning's calm wind and relatively cool temperatures ensure that less water is lost to the air and more reaches the garden. Don't worry that the sun will strike the moist leaves; contrary to the old wive's tale, water droplets on leaves will not act as a magnifying glass and burn them.

Watering devices that put water on the soil instead of on the plant are preferable to sprinklers, because they don't encourage leaf diseases and they conserve water. And they let you water slowly, giving the soil time to soak up the water so it doesn't run off onto the sidewalk or street.

Two good devices for watering the soil are soaker hoses and drip irrigation pipes. One type of soaker hose is a broad, flat plastic tube with holes along the upper surface. Lay the hose with the holes down, and you soak the soil. Lay it with the holes up, and you have a lawn sprinkler. Another type of soaker hose, sometimes called a leaky pipe, is a rubbery black tube covered with tiny pores that make its surface rough. Water seeps out the entire length of the hose, so leaky pipes are good for gardens planted in beds. You can get solid, poreless sections to cross areas where there are no plants.

Drip irrigation systems are made with plastic tubes. You can punch a hole in the main tube near every plant, or you can attach small tubes to the main tube then run a small tube to each plant. Drip irrigation lets you place the water close to the plants, instead of in the empty space between them. Drip irrigation is good where plants are widely spaced, as in rose beds.

You can buy soaker hoses, leaky pipes, or drip irrigation tubes at garden centers or hardware stores. You can also get all sorts of widgets and gizmos that let you join the hose pieces at angles, so you can design a watering network that meanders all over the garden. You can even get a timer so you don't have to turn the system on and off, and devices that let you add liquid fertilizers when you water.

Fertilizing

There are probably as many schools of thought on fertilizing a flower garden as there are on raising children. And if you're a hardcore rosarian or raise prize-winning dahlias, it's probably worth your while to learn about all of them.

However, if you want an approach that's simple, you just need to learn a few things about fertility in general and your soil's fertility specifically, then pick a fertilizing plan that suits it. "Improving Your Soil" on page 261 discusses soil improvement methods and the various plant nutrients, their sources, and how to use them.

If you don't have your soil tested—and many gardeners don't—you can get an idea of how fertile your soil is by observing it for a few seasons. If your flowers grow and bloom well and aren't bothered by many insects or diseases, your soil is giving them the nutrients they need. But if they're stunted or pale, or if they bloom poorly, you need to improve the soil's fertility.

Fertilizing Plans

Healthy Soil. If you have a healthy soil—one that lets your flowers grow the way they're supposed to—you just need to replace the nutrients that the plants remove. The

---

MIX-AND-MATCH FERTILIZER

You can mix your own general-purpose organic fertilizer by combining individual amendments in the amounts shown here. Pick one ingredient from each of the three groups below. Because these amendments may vary in the amount of the nutrients they contain, this method won't result in a fertilizer with a precise NPK ratio. Its ratio will be approximately between 1-2-1 and 4-6-3, with additional insoluble phosphorus and potash. The blend will provide a balanced supply of nutrients that will be steadily available to plants and that will encourage soil microorganisms to thrive.

Nitrogen (N): 2 parts blood meal or 3 parts fish meal.

Phosphorus (P): 3 parts bonemeal or 6 parts rock phosphate or colloidal phosphate.

Potassium (K): 1 part kelp meal or 6 parts greensand.

---·---

GET RESULTS WITH LIQUID FERTILIZERS

Fertilizing the soil is the best long-term solution to nutrient deficiencies. But if your plants need immediate help, give them a boost with the liquid fertilizers listed below. Apply these sprays directly to leaves in early morning or evening.

Compost Tea. Put a shovelful of compost in a burlap bag and tie it shut. Sink the bag in a 5-gallon bucket of water and let the "tea" steep for one to seven days. Strain the solution through cheese-cloth and spray directly on plant leaves.

Fish Emulsion. Mix with water according to package directions. One application lasts six to eight months. Smells fishy.

Seaweed Extract or Kelp. These products are good sources of trace minerals. Mix with water according to package directions. One application lasts 6 to 12 months.

---·---

You can supplement your soil-improvement efforts by foliar feeding your plants. Spray a liquid fertilizer, like compost tea or seaweed extract, directly onto leaves.

easiest way is to add fine-textured organic matter, one that breaks down during the season. Grass clippings, compost, and rotted manure are good choices. In beds of annual flowers, you can apply it to the soil surface as a mulch, then turn it into the soil in the fall. In perennial beds that you don't want to disturb, just spread it over the soil surface or scratch it in lightly.

To give your flowers an optional boost, you can feed with a balanced fertilizer—the three numbers on the label will be the same or close to it—in either liquid or dry form. Apply it to annuals when you transplant them and to perennials when they send out new green growth. For annuals, apply it again in midsummer. Follow the directions on the label for how much to apply and how to apply it.

Clayey or Sandy Soil. You can improve both of these problem soils by adding organic matter each year, as described above for the healthy soil.

Supplemental feeding is essential for clayey and sandy soils for the three to five years it takes the organic matter to change them from problem soils to healthy soils. To side-step the too-fast drainage in sands and the too-tight pores in clays, spray a liquid fertilizer directly on your plants' leaves two or three times each season. Liquid seaweed, or liquid seaweed mixed with fish emulsion, is a good choice. Before you spray, add a few drops of liquid dish soap to the fertilizer solution so that it will stick to the leaves long enough to be absorbed.

Something's-Wrong Soil. If your garden doesn't grow well year after year, despite your efforts, it may either be low in one or more of the essential minerals or have a pH that limits nutrient availability.

In either case, it's worth investing the $25 or so for a professional soil test. See "Soil Testing Options" on page 268 and "Taking Soil Samples" on page 269 for more information about having your soil tested.

In most cases, it takes a few annual applications of lime (to raise the pH), sulfur (to lower the pH), or a single-nutrient fertilizer to correct a soil problem. To encourage healthy growth and blooms in the meantime, add organic matter and use a liquid fertilizer, as described above for clayey or sandy soils.

Weeds

Weeds are plants that are better at surviving than anything you want to grow. If you can evaluate them impartially, you'll be impressed with the many ways they've evolved for competing with your flowers for light, water, and nutrients. However, few people who've spent months planning and planting a flower garden are in the mood to admire weeds; they'd rather just get rid of them. A weed is categorized by its life cycle, which influences how you control it. Annuals germinate, mature, and set seed in one season (winter annuals germinate in the fall and complete their cycle in the spring). Biennials germinate and grow ground-hugging clusters of leaves, called rosettes, the first season; the next year they send up

---

REASONS TO HATE WEEDS

In the midst of doing battle to reclaim your flower beds from the weeds that would invade them, you may ask yourself, "Why?" After all, what harm can a few weeds do?

Grab a cold drink, take a seat in the shade, and review the following anti-weed facts.

For one thing, a mass of weeds will reduce air circulation near plants, which encourages fungal diseases. And many weeds have an allelopathic effect, producing substances in their roots that are toxic to, and inhibit growth of, nearby plants.

Weeds also give insects and diseases a place to hide. For example, common lamb's quarters (*Chenopodium album*), red-root pigweed (*Amaranthus retroflexus*), shepherd's purse (*Capsella bursa-pastoris*), field bindweed (*Convolvulus arvensis*), and other weeds get tomato spotted wilt virus, which insects carry to your flowers.

To their credit, weeds reduce erosion on soils that otherwise would be bare. But mulch can do the same thing, and it won't take over your garden.

Large crabgrass
Digitaria sanguinalis
(grows prostrate or
upright to 16")

Redroot pigweed
Amaranthus retroflexus
(grows to 10' tall)

flowerstalks, set seed, and die. Perennials set seed each year and live for several years.

Both annuals and biennials increase their numbers only by producing seeds. Perennials set seed, but they also produce new plants by sending out rhizomes or stolons, or both, from the main plant. Rhizomes are underground stems; new plants arise from nodes on the stem. Stolons, or runners, grow above ground. Not only do perennials have two means of reproducing, but they also are able to store food in rhizomes or tubers to give them energy to draw on when they begin growing in the spring.

If you don't mulch, be prepared to do battle with all three types of weeds. If you mulch, annuals and biennials are little problem, because their seedlings can't fight their way up through the mulch. Perennials are a problem in either case, but less so if you mulch.

The best thing you can do to control weeds, besides mulching, is to visit your garden regularly and pull up anything that doesn't belong there. Dig out the entire root of each perennial weed and take care not to accidentally chop it up—plants grow from those little pieces.

Hoeing is also an effective weed control. It wipes out annuals and drains the energy from perennials. When you hoe, skim the blade along the soil surface. If you dig the blade into the soil, you expose weed seeds to sunlight, which may break their dormancy. You also run the risk of damaging the roots of plants you like.

Whether you pull weeds or hoe them, you'll find both methods easier when the soil is moist. If you're unable to weed or hoe each week, a few well-timed attacks will reduce the number of weeds you see next year. Remove annuals before they set seed, and you'll be able to keep them under control. For perennials, cut them off at the ground after a period of rapid growth that depletes their underground food reserves; for example, after they emerge or flower. Trying to grow back will make them even weaker. Also, as the season ends, perennials store food for winter, so if you're going to be diligent only for part of the season, make it the last part. As with annuals, make sure perennials don't set seed.

Eight of the most common and troublesome weeds are illustrated on pages 290–292. Large crabgrass, common purslane, shepherd's-purse, prostrate spurge, and redroot pigweed all are annuals, shown on this page and the opposite page. In addition to these, you are also likely to encounter the annual weeds common lamb's quarters and hairy galinsoga. Common lamb's quarters has triangular leaves and grows 2 to 6 feet tall. Hairy galinsoga grows 18 inches tall and has a hairy, branching stem, pointy and toothed leaves, and flowers that resemble tiny daisies. The perennials Canada thistle, Johnsongrass, and quackgrass appear on page 292. Bermuda grass, a perennial, and yellow nutsedge, an annual, are two other grasslike garden invaders. Bermuda grass is a wiry plant, about 18 inches tall, with scaly stolons that creep along the ground. It's used as a

You can keep weeds under control if you pull or hoe them as soon as they come up. Make sure you remove the annual weeds shown below and on the opposite page before they set seed.

Prostrate spurge
Euphorbia supina
(grows prostrate)

Shepherd's-purse
Capsella bursa-pastoris
(grows to 12" tall)

Common purslane
Portulaca oleracea
(grows prostrate)

To control perennial weeds, cut them off at ground level after a growth period, such as emergence or flowering, to deplete their food reserves. Or go after them late in the growing season, when they're storing carbohydrates for winter. Don't let perennial weeds set seed.

turfgrass in the extreme South; its range as a weed extends into New York. Yellow nutsedge, also called nutgrass, has long, waxy, yellowish green, narrow leaf blades, arranged in a triangle. Two to four weeks after yellow nutsedge emerges from the soil, small round tubers form at the end of its rhizomes; the plants are at their weakest at this time.

Pruning

When you prune, you remove a part of the plant that is unhealthy or that interferes with the plant's appearance. This broad definition includes pinching and deadheading as well as branch removal.

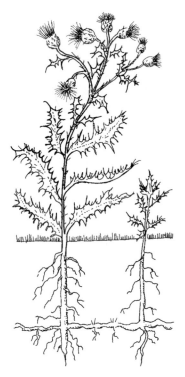

Canada thistle
Cirsium arvense
(grows to 36" tall)

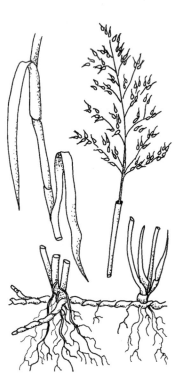

Johnsongrass
Sorghum halepense
(grows to 60" tall)

Quackgrass
Agropyron repens
(grows to 36" tall)

Be kind to your back when you tackle weeding chores. Crouch or kneel, rather than bending over, and take frequent breaks, gently stretching backward from the waist.

———— ❖·❖ ————

GIVE YOUR BACK A BREAK

You know how it starts. You're in the garden and notice a few weeds. Before you know it, you end up stooped over for an hour and sore for three days.

Rebecca Robinson, a licensed physical therapist with the Austin (Texas) Diagnostic Clinic, gives this advice for weeding without throwing your back out of whack.

• Stretch lightly before you begin, to warm up your muscles.
• Crouch, kneel, or sit while pulling; don't just stand and bend over.
• Change position often.
• Don't overreach when pulling or hoeing. Your torso shouldn't move forward when you reach for a weed.
• Take frequent breaks.
• Straighten up occasionally and bend gently backward at the waist.
• Be realistic about how much you can do at a time.

———— ❖·❖ ————

If your flower garden includes flowering shrubs and trees such as roses, hydrangeas, lilacs, and crab apples, you'll need to include pruning in your plan for upkeep. The purpose of pruning is to improve the shape of the plant and to remove wood that's injured, diseased, or dead.

Pruning Flowering Shrubs and Trees

Pruning is not the horrible practice of hacking off the top 1 or 2 feet of a tree or shrub, straight across the top. In addition to ruining the natural form of the plant, this uniform hacking encourages branching near the top, which reduces air circulation, promotes disease, and shades out the lower branches, which lose their leaves.

Pruning Shrubs into Shape. The trick to improving the shape of a shrub is to cut back branches about ¼ inch above a bud that faces the direction you want the branch to grow in. If you want the shrub to have a more compact,

—⇒·⇐—

SANE, SELECTIVE PRUNING FOR "CANE GROWERS"

Cass Turnbull, founder of the pruning-education group PlantAmnesty, offers these tips for rational shrub pruning.

It's hard to hurt what Turnbull calls "cane growers"—shrubs, such as red-osier dogwood (*Cornus sericea*), forsythia, and hydrangea, that send up new branches from the base of the plant. First, remove all dead branches, cutting them off at the base. Then remove about a fourth of the biggest branches, which don't flower well. Finally, cut out branches that cross from one side of the plant to the other.

Turnbull's tips for pruning mounding shrubs and treelike shrubs appear in "Pruning Flowering Shrubs and Trees" on page 293.

For a copy of their pruning guide, write to PlantAmnesty, 906 Northwest 87th Street, Seattle, WA 98117.

—⇒·⇐—

upright form, cut the branch off just above a bud on the inside of the branch. Make the cut over a bud on the outside of the branch to encourage an open, spreading form. Make your cuts at a slant rather than straight across. The cut should angle across the stem from a point just above the bud to a point opposite the base of the bud.

Some shrubs form a mound, have supple branches, and are usually planted in masses—such as spireas (*Spiraea* spp.), boxwoods (*Buxus* spp.), and hollies (*Ilex* spp.). To prune these, follow the longest unruly branch into the heart of the shrub, and clip it off, preferably just above a side branch or bud. Repeat with the remaining long branches until the plant looks tidy.

Pruning Treelike Shrubs. Treelike shrubs with stiff branches, such as camellias, lilacs, rhododendrons, and common viburnums, usually only need dead wood removed. If necessary, remove the skinny suckers that sometimes grow from the base and branches, and cut out branches growing across the bush or perpendicular to another branch. Don't remove more than an eighth of the leaf tissue in any one year. If the plant is in bad shape, spread its reformation over three years. When you remove damaged or diseased branches, prune to a bud in healthy wood, several inches past the damaged or diseased wood, to ensure that you've removed disease-causing pathogens that may have traveled beyond the area that's visibly wounded or infected. It's a good idea to disinfect your pruning tool after every cut, but it's essential if you know the branch is diseased. Disinfect with denatured rubbing alcohol, not a bleach solution, because bleach can corrode the metal.

If the branch is dead, prune it back to its origination point—the main truck or branch, or the crown. Make the cut just beyond the branch side of the collar, which is the slightly swollen circle of tissue where the side branch meets the trunk, main branch, or crown. Cambium, the living tissue just below the bark, can grow from the collar to seal off the cut. Don't cut into the collar, or you'll leave an opening for pathogens. Don't leave a stub, or cambium won't grow over the cut. It's not necessary to paint the cut with wound dressing.

Pruning to Renew or Rejuvenate Shrubs. With some shrubs, such as honeysuckles, hydrangeas, lilacs, mock oranges (*Philadelphus* spp.), and spireas (*Spiraea* spp.), you can remove branches that no longer flower well. This renewal pruning channels more energy into young wood, making it produce more flowers. Remove about a fourth of the old, woody branches, cutting them off near the ground.

Some types of flowering shrubs will also respond to severe or rejuvenative pruning with improved vigor. In late winter or early spring, before growth starts, cut off all the branches about a foot from the ground. While this method will make your neighbors doubt your sanity, it gives a real boost to shrubs that bloom on new wood, like buddleias (*Buddleia* spp.), crape myrtle (*Lagerstroemia indica*), and bluebeard (*Caryopteris* × *clandonensis*). You can try rejuvenative pruning on overgrown forsythias, honeysuckles, and lilacs, too, but don't count on a good floral show until the following year.

Whichever type of pruning you have planned, make sure your pruning tool is sharp. Dull tools make ragged or crushed cuts, and the damaged tissue invites disease.

Prune Shrubs When the Time Is Right. If you're pruning to remove diseased, dead, or damaged branches, you can prune anytime. If you're removing healthy branches to improve the form, time the pruning so it doesn't interfere with flowering. If the shrub blooms in late spring or summer, prune in the late winter or early spring, before new buds set. This group include hibiscus (*Hibiscus* spp.), hydrangeas, honeysuckles, and spireas.

If the shrub blooms in early spring from buds set the previous year, prune shortly after flowering ends. This rule applies to azaleas (*Rhododendron* spp.), lilacs, magnolias, and deutzias (*Deutzia* spp.).

Pruning Roses. The goal of rose pruning is to maintain the plant's height and form, as well as to remove dead, diseased, or injured canes. In early spring, just as the buds begin to swell, remove dead canes at the base and cut back

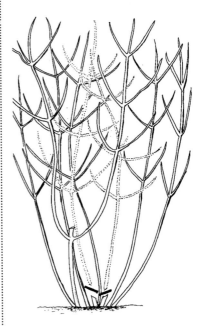

Renewal pruning removes branches that no longer flower well. Remove about a fourth of the old, woody branches, cutting them off near the ground.

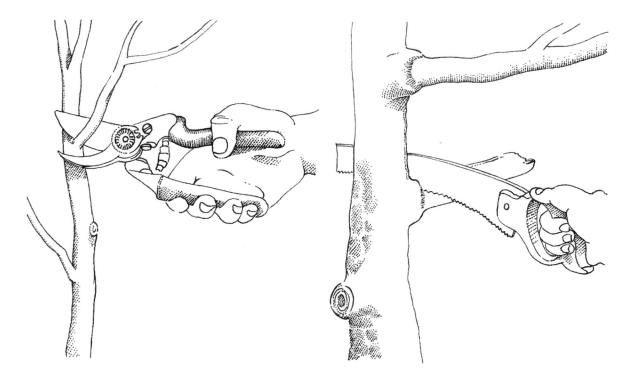

Use bypass pruners (*left*) to cut small branches flush to a main branch or trunk of a tree. Remove larger branches (*right*) with a pruning saw. Cut just to the swollen area of the branch collar. Use sharp tools to make a clean cut without ragged edges.

diseased or injured canes below the damaged portion. Cut winter dieback off to sound, green wood.

Additional pruning, to shape plants, depends on the type of rose you have. Cut the canes of hybrid tea roses back to 12 to 18 inches tall as part of their spring pruning. Also remove any weak, crowded, or crooked canes. Shape the plants as you prune in spring, and when you remove dead flowers in summer, prune by cutting to a bud that's pointed in the direction you want the branch to grow. In most cases you'll prune to buds that are pointed out, away from the center of the plant. This opens the rose up and gives it more light and better air circulation. Prune to a bud that faces in, toward the plant's center, only if you need to fill a hole. Shrub roses don't need as much pruning or maintenance as hybrid teas. Just remove one-third of the growth from their new long canes in spring if the plants have grown too tall. Prune climbing and rambling roses immediately after they finish flowering by removing the oldest and weakest canes.

Pruning Trees. Tree pruning is similar to shrub pruning. You can remove dead, diseased, or broken branches any time of year. If you want to improve the shape of a deciduous tree, wait until it is dormant and the leaves have fallen off so you can see its shape clearly. Use bypass pruners to cut small, pencil-sized branches, and loppers for branches that are up to ¾ inch thick. For larger branches, use a sharp pruning saw. Cut the limb back to the branch collar as illustrated on the opposite page. Remove large branches with three pruning-saw cuts. First, undercut the branch a few inches out from the branch collar; when you can't cut upward anymore, use a second, downward cut to the outside of the first cut to remove the branch. Make a third cut to remove the stub next to the branch collar. If the branches you need to remove are very high on a tree, use a pole saw or call an arborist. Whenever you prune trees, be careful not to touch utility wires.

Pinching off the stem tips (*left*) promotes branch formation and growth, making plants bushier and more compact. Deadheading (*right*) improves plants' looks by removing browning flowers and also encourages continued flowering by preventing seed formation.

Carefully store the seeds you want to save. Put them in labeled plastic bags, seal the bags in a glass jar, and place in a cool, dark place like a refrigerator.

---------→·←---------

SAVING SEEDS

If you want to save money (or preserve heirloom plants) by saving seeds, know what you're getting before you start. Hybrids, cultivars, and open-pollinated species may not produce plants that resemble their parents; the first two types may not produce viable seeds at all.

Gather seeds as soon as they ripen; look for seeds that are dry, have changed color, or have started splitting out of seed-bearing structures. Remove any husks, pods, or chaff, and put each kind of seed you collect into its own bag. Label immediately.

Spread your seeds on newspapers or fine screens to dry for one to two weeks. Label dry seeds, then store in the refrigerator in labeled, clean, dry glass jars with lids. Let them warm gradually to room temperature before sowing.

---------→·←---------

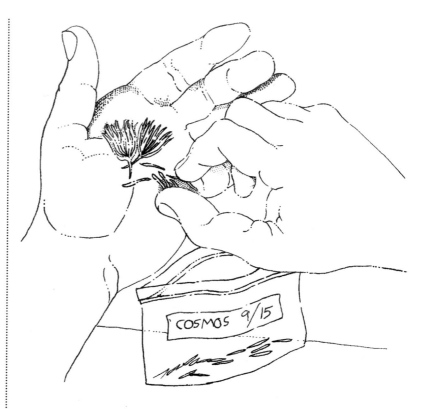

Pinching and Deadheading

For most annual and perennial flowers, pruning means pinching and deadheading. Pinching removes the stem tip, which contains the apical dome, a cluster of cells that produces a growth hormone that inhibits branching. The apical dome is quite tiny, so you don't need to remove much plant tissue. For most plants, simply removing the very tip of the stem is enough, although you may want to pinch off the uppermost pair of leaves to make sure you've removed the stem tip. If your flowers have grown overly tall and leggy, you can pinch off a few inches of stem tip, effectively combining pinching and pruning. Ageratum, coleus, chrysanthemum, dahlia, dusty miller, Madagascar periwinkle (*Catharanthus roseus*), petunia, and zinnia all benefit from pinching.

Deadheading involves cutting or breaking off spent flowers. Many plants stop blooming once they set seed. By deadheading, you keep them from setting seed, thereby prolonging flowering. Deadheading also keeps the garden more attractive because you remove the flowers just as they start to brown. Don't deadhead plants that have ornamental seeds, since they'll give your garden an added attraction. And leave flowers on plants that you want to set seed for the following year. If you aren't sure whether your plant has nice seeds, leave a few flowers and watch what happens. You may discover that your shrub rose has showy rose hips, or that the seed heads on your sedum plants look attractive even when they're brown and dried.

Staking

Staking provides support for flowers that have weak stems, are tall and top-heavy, or climb. Some plants have

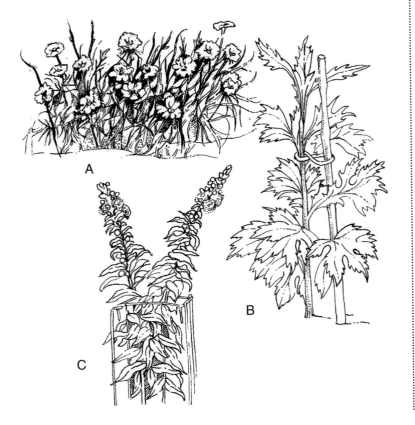

LET PLANTS LEND SUPPORT

Staking plants is a time-consuming process that's easy to avoid. Instead of using sticks and string, surround your tall, flopping plants with supportive neighbors. Rows of sturdy daylilies on either side of a planting of peonies will hold drooping leaves in place and will hide them if they become unsightly. Use a clump of *Artemisia ludoviciana* 'Silver King' to support lazy daisies. Or, keep a patch of goldenrod (*Solidago* spp.) from falling down by bordering it with a mounded planting of rue (*Ruta graveolens*).

Choose stakes that support your flowers without spoiling their looks. (A) Let floppy, clump-forming flowers like coreopsis (*Coreopsis* spp.) lean on twiggy branches. (B) Bamboo stakes and green garden twine provide inconspicuous support for tall plants like delphinium. (C) Linking stakes can encircle top-heavy plants like snapdragons or form a serpentine support through a bed.

—→·←—

LOW-FLOP PEONIES

The big, beautiful, heavy blooms on peonies make their stems prone to falling over, especially after a rain. You can buy circular cages to support them, but the stems still flop over the top of the cage. Another staking method uses three or four stakes around each plant, with supporting strings running around and through the plant from the stakes.

Another choice is to grow peonies that are less inclined to recline. William Radler, director of the Boerner Botanical Gardens near Milwaukee, keeps an eye on how the gardens' peonies perform. Radler suggests the following cultivars:

Double: 'Aviateur Lindberg', 'Guidon', 'Kansas'.

Japanese: 'John Gardener', 'Walter Mains', 'White Cap', 'White Gold'.

Single: 'Burma Ruby', 'Dawn Pink', 'E. St. Hill', 'Kickapoo', 'Mischief', 'Nellie', 'Salmon Glow', 'Your Majesty'.

Semidouble: 'Coral Charm', 'Dandy Dan', 'Firebells', 'Helen', 'Minnie Shaylor'.

—→·←—

weak stems that flop over and give the plants a scraggly demeanor. A few scragglers are baby's-breath, large-flowered tickseed (*Coreopsis grandiflora*), balloon flower (*Platycodon grandiflorus*), farewell-to-spring (*Clarkia amoena*), and some speedwells (*Veronica* spp.) To support these floppy clumps, stick twiggy branches into the ground behind them. As the plant grows, it leans on and hides the supporting branches. Cherry and birch branches work well, although anything twiggy will do. Make sure the twigs are shorter than the plant at maturity.

Peonies have a similar problem but are too heavy for small branches to brace. For peonies, you can buy wire cages that encircle the base of the plant. Or support them in a triangle of twine tied between three stakes.

Tall plants—cosmos, some dahlias, delphiniums, tall foxgloves (*Digitalis* spp.), hollyhocks (*Alcea rosea*), some sunflowers (*Helianthus* spp.), and tall zinnias—need sturdy stakes to brace them against wind and rain.

For tall plants that need support, use plastic, wire, or wooden stakes. Each type of stake has advantages: Redwood and cedar resist rotting; wire and bamboo are flexible; green stakes are less conspicuous. You can even get stakes that have an arm at the top that hooks across to the stake beside it in a daisy-chain arrangement. Choose stakes that are strong enough to support your plants in stormy weather and that are a few inches shorter than each plant's ultimate height.

For a new plant, sink the stake about 8 inches into the ground at planting so you won't disturb the roots later. Stake established plants as they begin growing in the spring, taking care not to gouge crowns or roots.

To tie a plant to its stake, use thin strips of fabric, commercially available green garden string, wire twist ties, or any inconspicuous material. Tie them in a loose figure eight to avoid girdling the stem.

When you remove stakes at the end of the season, dip plastic or wire ones in a 10 percent chlorine bleach solution (1 part bleach to 9 parts water) to kill any bacteria or fungi they might carry from the soil. Store stakes in a dry place for the winter.

To provide the desired effect, climbing plants need supports to twine around. Keeping them upright also improves circulation and prevents disease. You can build or buy trellises, or create a supporting backdrop of strings or netting. Climbing plants include some roses and many vines, such as black-eyed Susan vine (*Thunbergia alata*), bougainvillea (*Bougainvillea* spp.), clematis, honeysuckle, jasmine, and sweet peas (*Lathyrus* spp.).

Pest Prevention and Control

It can be alarming to go out to your garden and find a marigold plant nibbled to the ground, or black spots on your roses, or big holes chewed in your hostas. Your initial reaction might be dismay or panic, especially if you're new to gardening.

Be calm. As you will learn, few garden pests do enough damage to warrant panic; in fact, many don't do enough to warrant action. Plants have all sorts of natural defenses to help them survive attack. Unless so much leaf tissue is gone that a plant can't photosynthesize, it can usually recover from whatever ails it.

However, this is not to recommend complacency. While pest problems usually aren't devastating, there's no point in encouraging them. You can take steps to minimize the likelihood that pests will visit your garden and to limit the damage if pests do arrive.

First, when you buy plants, make sure you aren't buying trouble. See "Acquiring Plants" on page 238 for helpful plant-shopping hints. Choose cultivars that resist or tolerate pests better than others.

Second, keep your plants vigorous. Mulch them. Water them. Fertilize and weed them. Stress weakens plants' natural defenses against pests and diseases.

And finally, develop an easygoing attitude. Gardening, like living, has balances and cycles. You may have some aphids, but you also have predators that eat them. You may have rainy years when fungal diseases are rampant, but you'll also have dry years when you can forget about diseases and concentrate on keeping your zinnias from wilting.

Ground beetle
and larvae

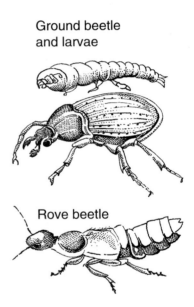

Rove beetle

Soil-dwelling ground beetles and rove beetles are general predators that thrive in the same conditions that slugs love: shade, humidity, and organic matter. Ground beetles prey on slugs, snails, and cutworms. Rove beetles attack mites, aphids, springtails, nematodes, and flies. Both control cabbage maggots.

━━━━ ➡️·⬅️ ━━━━

HOMETOWN PESTS

While many pest species occur over broad areas of the country, the amount of damage they do varies by location. Entomologists in five states cite aphids, spider mites, and the following pests as the prime suspects when flower damage occurs in their states:

Connecticut: Several beetle species' grubs eat flower roots. Black vine weevils attack *Rhododendron* species. Voles pull plants into their tunnels.

Nebraska: Nebraskans face honeysuckle aphids, lace bugs, borers in lilacs and irises, thrips, and slugs.

Nevada: Strawberry root weevils infest some perennials and shrubs. Cabbage loopers pester petunias.

North Carolina: Japanese beetles, slugs, various caterpillars, and disease-carrying thrips feed on flowers. Voles are a problem, too.

Texas: Whitefly problems are increasing in the Lone Star State, where slugs also roam.

━━━━ ➡️·⬅️ ━━━━

A beneficial creature like this black and yellow garden spider (*Argiope aurantia*) will provide free pest control if you leave her web intact.

Insects and Other Pests

In the post–World War II glory days of pesticides, controlling insects and similar pests, such as spider mites and slugs, meant eradicating them. Only more recently has the idea caught on that control means managing pest populations, not eradicating them.

Managing pest populations necessitates an awareness that not all bugs are bad. Not every insect that sits on a flower is there for a meal. By observing your garden often and well, you'll learn to recognize which insects do damage, which are good guys that eat the bad guys, and which ones are just passing through.

Pest management also requires the acceptance that some damage is okay. A few chewed leaves won't kill an otherwise healthy plant.

When you suspect pests are at work in your flower beds, the first step is to identify the assailant. Sometimes you can catch the pest in the act, but often you'll have to figure it out based on the type of damage. Compare your plant's symptoms to the symptoms listed in bold under "Troubleshooting" on page 313, to help you find the perpetrator.

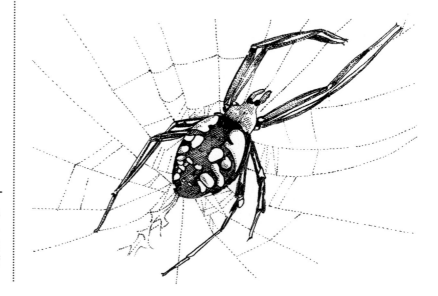

Pest Control Techniques

Techniques for managing insects include prevention, handpicking, spraying with water, trapping, encouraging predators and parasites, and—as a last resort—spraying or dusting with an organic pesticide.

Prevention. To reduce the damage insects do, follow practices that encourage healthy plants, such as watering and fertilizing properly. Foliar sprays of kelp, liquid seaweed, and micronutrients are believed to improve plants' pest resistance by promoting overall health. Pull weeds or remove plant parts that harbor insects. Clean up leaf litter to get rid of eggs.

Handpicking. Some insects are big enough to pick off. These include caterpillars, large beetles, and slugs. Squash them, or drop them into a bucket of soapy water. The soap reduces the surface tension of the water, so the pests sink rather than swim. In the morning, when insects are too cold to move, you can shake pests off your plants onto a sheet, which you then empty into the soapy water. To flush out hidden pests, try spraying plants with a fine mist of water.

Spraying with Water. Blasting spider mites and soft-bodied insects like aphids with a strong stream of water from your hose can knock them from the plant or kill them outright. Be sure to get the undersides of the leaves, too.

Trapping. Trapping works for small populations. Don't use it for heavy infestations, or you'll attract more pests to your yard. Buy commercially available traps that are coated on the inside with sex hormones and floral fragrances that attract specific insects.

Because many insects are attracted to yellow, you can make indoor pest traps by painting cardboard bright yellow and coating it with commercially available insect trap glue or a mixture of petroleum jelly and liquid dish soap.

Encouraging Beneficial Insects and Animals

Beneficial insects include predators, which eat insects, and parasites, which lay their eggs in the insect's body so their developing young have a fresh food supply. Predators kill many insects during their lives, while parasites kill just one.

Some beneficials are better adapted to gardeners' purposes than others. Lady beetles (or ladybugs) (*above*), for example, are notorious for flying off, because their instinct is to disperse. Lacewings (*below*) are more likely to stick around.

---------→·←---------

IT'S A BUG'S LIFE
Many control methods are most effective when applied at a specific stage in an insect's life cycle. So it's useful to understand the stages that insects pass through between hatching and maturity.

Moths, butterflies, flies, and beetles have three distinct stages of growth. The larval stage begins once eggs hatch and wormlike creatures emerge. Larvae are called caterpillars if they'll become moths or butterflies as adults, maggots if they'll become flies, or grubs if they'll become beetles. During the next stage, the larvae pupate—they become pupae and encase themselves in hard shells while they develop into adults. The adults emerge, mate, and lay eggs, and the cycle repeats.

---------→·←---------

An overturned clay pot with a doorway chipped into its rim makes an inviting home for insect-eating toads. One toad will eat 10,000 to 20,000 insects a year! Toads need moist conditions to survive; provide a shallow saucer of water, too.

Lady beetles, also known as ladybugs, are perhaps the best known beneficial insect; there are thousands of species of lady beetles, and their young feed on everything from aphids to scale. Lacewings are also well known, as are praying mantids and spiders. Many species of wasp are parasitic. Less well known beneficials include some midges, which are tiny flies, and mites.

Unless you tamper with the balance by using pesticides, including the organic ones described in "Soaps, Oils, and Other Pesticides" on page 306, the ratio of carnivorous beneficial insects to the more numerous herbivorous insects that eat your flowers should be stable. Encourage aboveground beneficials by making sure they have food and shelter. For food, grow small-flowered plants in the mint, daisy, and carrot families, which are good sources of pollen and nectar— examples include yarrow, sweet alyssum (*Lobularia maritima*), cosmos, and coreopsis (*Coreopsis* spp.). The more diverse the plants, the more diverse the beneficials you'll attract. For shelter, include a clump of herbs or some shrubs in your garden. Some gardeners leave a small weed patch, although there's always the possibility that the patch will harbor harmful as well as beneficial insects.

Several types of predaceous insects often touted as beneficials are really general feeders. They'll eat both the bad

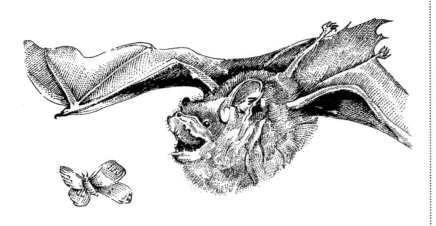

Smart gardeners count birds and bats among the beneficials they encourage in and around their gardens. Both of these active insect eaters prefer pesticide-free environments.

━━━━━━━━━━ ⇢ · ⇠ ━━━━━━━━━━

COPPER SLUGS IT OUT WITH BEER

A favorite method of slug control is to set out a pan of stale beer in the garden. But extension entomologist Phil Nixon of the University of Illinois no longer recommends this method. Over the years, he's found that although many slugs do drown in the beer, their demise doesn't decrease the slug population significantly. Plenty are left to continue causing damage.

A more effective method for thwarting slugs, Nixon says, is to encircle valuable plants or bedding areas with copper strips buried 2 inches into the soil and extending 2 inches above the soil. Although researchers aren't sure why this technique works, they hypothesize that a slight current running through the copper gives the slimy slugs a jolt, encouraging them to turn around and head elsewhere. You can buy copper strips under the trade name Snail-Barr.

━━━━━━━━━━ ⇢ · ⇠ ━━━━━━━━━━

and the good. Examples include soil-dwelling ground beetles, rove beetles, and soldier beetles.

Some gardeners try to tip the balance in favor of the beneficials by buying some to release into the garden. Depending on the insect, this approach can work if there are enough pests for the beneficial insects to feed on.

As a side note, some insects are worth protecting not because they're predators but because they are useful or beautiful. Bees, for instance, pollinate flowers. And although the celery worm or parsley worm may annoy you by eating a little of your dill or fennel, it pays you back by becoming the beautiful black swallowtail butterfly.

Earthworms are not insects, but they are great soil improvers that deserve your appreciation. They drag organic matter from the surface into the soil and digest it. Their tunnels aerate the soil and make spaces for roots, and their manure—called castings—adds nutrients. The calcium carbonate that they secrete helps neutralize soil pH.

Birds, bats, spiders, and toads are other beneficial creatures that help keep insect populations under control. Encourage them to patrol your garden by providing food, shelter, and water. Nesting boxes can attract insect-eating birds like purple martins and bluebirds. Keep them supplied with clean, fresh water in a shallow birdbath, and

Do you think the only good bug is a dead bug, or that organic insecticides are safe for beneficial insects? Expand your pest control knowledge with the following facts.

• When it comes to insects and similar creatures, it's usually better to tolerate than control them. Few pests do enough damage to kill a plant, although they may make it look a bit ratty. The best approach is to keep plants healthy.

• In spite of their plant origins, some "organic" insecticides, including rotenone, nicotine, and sabadilla, are more toxic than some synthetic insecticides. And relatively nontoxic insecticidal soap kills most insects, good and bad, under ¼ inch long. Use any of these as a last resort.

• Mulch can increase some pest problems. Slugs, earwigs, cutworms, and other soil dwellers like the cover that organic mulches provide. If you have a heavy infestation, consider removing the mulch until the problem is under control.

plant fruiting shrubs and trees for extra shelter and food. Bats eat tremendous numbers of insects and ask little in return. Place a bat box in a tree or on a shed near your garden to encourage them to live nearby. There's no need to be frightened of them or of spiders, which can help you control pest insects if you leave their webs intact. Like other beneficials, toads have few needs but give great pest control results. Attract these insect eaters to your garden with a saucer of water and a flowerpot home like the one illustrated on page 304.

Soaps, Oils, and Other Pesticides

Pesticides, even organic ones, disturb the balance between beneficial and harmful insects. And in the long run, they usually disturb it in favor of the harmful ones. Because populations of beneficials grow more slowly than those of harmful insects, you should only use pesticides as a last resort.

Last resort means that the plant's ability to photosynthesize has been reduced to a level that can kill the plant. That level varies from species to species. As a rule of thumb, it's about 30 percent of the plant tissue. You have to decide how much damage you can tolerate. If you plan to enter your roses in flower show contests, for example, you might put up with less damage than someone who wants a few cut flowers for the table.

Two relatively benign sprays are insecticidal soaps and horticultural oils, also known as summer oils and ultra-fine oils (UFOs). Both are contact insecticides; they kill only the insects they touch and have no residual effect. They work especially well on small insects—those ¼ inch long or less. They are generally harmless to lady beetles, lacewings, and predatory wasps. However, they can kill tiny beneficial mites and midges and may harm butterfly caterpillars.

If you use an insecticidal soap, buy one that's available commercially, rather than mixing up your own with dish detergent or whatever. Commercially available soaps are derived from organic sources and don't burn leaf tissue. Neither can be said of do-it-yourself soaps.

More-toxic treatments include pyrethrins, neem, and

diatomaceous earth. Pyrethrins and neem are derived from plants, while diatomaceous earth is made from ground-up fossils of shells. These pesticides kill larger insects, both pests and beneficials, than do soaps or oil sprays. Pyrethrins, neem, and diatomaceous earth have low toxicity for humans, but because they kill beneficials, use them as a last resort. Follow label instructions exactly when applying any of these controls.

A popular product for controlling leaf-eating caterpillars is *Bacillus thuringiensis* (Bt). Bt is a bacterium that paralyzes the alkaline intestines of caterpillars but is harmless to humans and other beasts with acidic guts. Three varieties are available: *kurstaki* kills the larvae of most moths and butterflies; *san diego* is specific to larvae of the black vine weevil, boll weevil, colorado potato beetle, and elm leaf beetle; and *israelensis* is for black fly, fungus gnat, and mosquito larvae.

Diseases

When it comes to diseases in the flower garden, prevention and tolerance are the watchwords. Prevention is important because once plants are infected, there's little you can do to treat them. Tolerance comes into play because, although their symptoms are unsightly, few common diseases are devastating. Fungi, bacteria, viruses, and mycoplasmas all infect plants and cause disease symptoms. Environmental and cultural problems, such as air pollution and overwatering, also are considered diseases, since they disrupt plants' normal functions.

Fungi cause leaf spots, mildews, rusts, blights (large dead areas), wilts, and rots. Simple garden practices reduce the number and severity of fungal diseases. When you plant, space plants correctly. Air and sunlight have trouble penetrating crowded plants; the resulting dark, humid conditions are perfect for leaf spot, blight, and powdery mildew. And when you water, soak the soil, not the leaves, so fungi in the soil don't splash onto the leaves. Because soggy soils can cause root rots, water more deeply and less often, and add organic matter to the soil to improve drainage.

FIGHTING FUNGI

Leaf spots and mildews are symptoms of fungal diseases that infect a broad range of plants.

Humidity and poor air circulation foster fungi. To prevent rust (shown below) and other fungal diseases, space plants correctly and prune crowded branches to improve air circulation and sunlight penetration. Rake up and destroy affected leaves. Wet leaves promote most fungi—water as the day warms up so that leaves dry quickly, and put water on the soil around plants, not on the plants.

Fungal diseases are hard to prevent in cloudy, rainy years. Use baking soda spray to help control fungi after symptoms appear. (See "Diseases" on this page.)

Rust

BACTERIA AND VIRUSES

Plant diseases caused by bacteria and viruses are less common than those caused by fungi but may be more serious.

Bacterial diseases can cause rots in stems, crowns, and roots or make plants wilt. They may also produce a foul odor.

Sanitation helps keep bacteria in check. Clean up plant debris. Pull up and destroy infected flowers when they first show symptoms. If a shrub shows signs of blight, prune the affected area as described in "Pruning" on page 292.

Viruses cause bizarre symptoms—stunted or off-color plants, mosaic or mottled patterns on the leaves, or distorted growth. Sucking insects, such as aphids and thrips, often spread viruses. You can carry viruses on your hands or tools, or by smoking near plants, which spreads tobacco mosaic virus.

The best way to prevent viruses is to buy certified disease-free plants. If a virus shows up, pull and destroy the infected plant.

To keep existing fungal infections in check, collect diseased leaves that fall from your plants. If just a few leaves on any plant are diseased, pluck those off; if the infected area is substantial, focus on curing the plant or destroying it to prevent the disease's spread.

If you have a large flower garden, work in healthy areas first and diseased areas last, so you don't carry fungus to healthy areas on your clothes. Wash your gardening togs before you garden again, and scrape the mud off your shoes.

You can control two common fungal diseases—leaf spot and powdery mildew—with a homemade baking soda spray. Combine 1 teaspoon of baking soda with 1 quart of water and 2 teaspoons of SunSpray Ultrafine Oil (available from garden centers). Apply every five to seven days.

Like fungi, bacterial diseases can cause leaf spots, blighted stems and leaves, and rots. Unlike fungi, bacterial infections usually smell bad, too.

Sanitation and rotation are the best tools for preventing bacterial infections. As with fungal diseases, work in diseased areas last and wash your clothes and tools afterward. Because bacteria overwinter in plant debris, clean up all litter after your plants finish flowering. Don't plant annuals and tender bulbs in the same place every season—rotate them on a three-year cycle; bacteria can't survive without a host for more than two years. If a flowering shrub is diseased, prune and destroy all affected branches.

Viruses cause spots and streaks on leaves, and abnormal growth, such as twisted leaves. Insects often transmit viruses. To prevent viruses, buy resistant plants. If a plant is infected, remove and destroy it. Don't compost it; while a hot compost pile can kill fungi and bacteria, it won't damage viruses.

Mycoplasmas are microscopic organisms that share characteristics of both bacteria and viruses. Mycoplasmas cause plant diseases, such as aster yellows, that are similar to those caused by viral infections. Like viruses, they're often transmitted by insects. But like bacteria, mycoplasmas respond to treatment with antibiotics.

Mammals

A whole mythology has sprung up around controlling mammals, because mammals are tricky to control. You can't pick them off and dunk them in soapy water. Improving air circulation doesn't make them go away. They're big, they're bright, and they want your garden.

Deer

Of all the garden-munching mammals, deer probably inspire the most creative control methods. Some techniques work better than others but none of them is guaranteed. The best approach is to try one method until the deer get wise to it, then switch to another.

As your first attempt, try a strongly scented deodorant soap. Place slices of it near the garden on spikes, fence posts, rocks, or other supports. Make sure it's far enough from the garden that it won't drop—or, when it rains, drip—on any valuable plants.

FENCING OUT DEER

A fence is an effective but potentially costly way to keep deer off your property. Here are a few fencing options.

• A wire fence must be about 8 feet tall, so that deer can't jump over it, and low to the ground, so deer can't squeeze under it.

• Deer won't go where they can't see. A wooden privacy fence that's about 6 feet tall will block their view and keep them away.

• Deer don't like to jump long distances, so increase the width of your fence by installing it at a 45-degree angle. Slant it away from your property.

• Lay a band of wire fencing flat on the ground. Deer dislike walking or jumping across it.

• Try an electric fence in a straight, slanted, or double-fencing arrangement.

Deer are a beautiful nuisance in areas where they feed on garden and landscape plants. Under population pressure or harsh winter conditions, deer will eat nearly any plant they can reach, and they often kill or damage young shrubs and trees.

...ES

...ng to
... your
...arks,
footprints, and other animal calling cards to identify your visitors.

Deer graze on flowers and bite off tree and shrub branches, leaves, and shoots. Look for jagged cuts, droppings, and cloven hoof prints.

Gophers leave a mound of soil at their tunnel openings. They chew plant roots from below ground and may pull whole plants down into their tunnels.

Mice, rats, and voles eat roots from below-ground tunnels and gnaw bark off young trees.

Moles eat insects, but their tunnels can damage plant roots. Look for tunnels along fences or other protected areas.

Rabbits bite off plants with slanted, clean cuts, nibble tender plants to the ground, and chew the bark off young trees in winter.

———— ➜•◄— ————

Chipmunks dig up and nibble plants, especially recently planted ones. Bulbs are a common target.

Another repellent, reputed to be quite effective, is human urine. While it's possible to go on at length about the amusing methods for applying this substance, suffice it to say that you need to reapply it after each rain. Human hair sometimes offends deer; check with a salon to see whether you can collect their clippings. Tie handfuls of hair in cloth bags and hang them near the garden.

Blood meal is another popular repellent. However, don't sprinkle it in the garden, or you run the risk of adding too much nitrogen to the soil and inhibiting flowering. Instead, suspend the meal in cloth bags near the garden. You'll need to replace the bags once rains dissolves their contents.

Or you can try liquid blood from a butcher or meat processing plant. Mix 1 teaspoon of blood with 2 gallons of water and spray it around—not on—the garden. It should last until the next rain. Be warned that either form of blood can attract dogs.

Dogs, however, are pretty good at scaring off deer and

other unwanted mammals. So are cats—especially well-fed cats, because they have enough pep for the chase.

Other methods include placing radios or blinking lights in the garden to frighten the deer. You need to keep moving the devices, however, or the deer will quickly become accustomed to them.

Fencing is the surest protection. Cover your tender shrubs with a mesh cage until they are woody enough to be unappetizing.

Rabbits

Rabbits are notorious for damaging flower gardens; they frequently nibble flowers to the ground. They favor ageratums, marigolds, snapdragons, zinnias, and other flowers with soft foliage.

Controls include dusting plants with talcum powder or spraying them with a solution of hot sauce and water. Blood meal also works, but it can alter the nitrogen balance of the soil. All three need to be reapplied after a rain.

Other Animal Pests

Unlike deer and rabbits, other mammals that we think of as pests aren't out to get your flowers. Your garden just happens to be in the path of their tunnels. These include moles, voles, pocket gophers, chipmunks, and 13-lined ground squirrels, which are sometimes called gophers.

Chipmunks. Territorial and curious, chipmunks will dig up newly installed bulbs, seeds, and plants to investigate these additions to their domain. Protect new plantings for a few days to allow your scent on them—and chipmunks' interest in them—to fade.

Moles and Voles. For moles and voles, try soaking their active tunnels with a mixture of castor oil, detergent, and water, as described on page 312. The animals find the smell offensive and will abandon your yard.

To find an active tunnel, look for a straight, not meandering, ridge just below the soil surface. Mash down part of the ridge with your foot and flag it. If the tunnel is rebuilt in a day or two, you know it's active.

FENCING OUT BUNNIES

You can fence your flower beds to keep out rabbits, if you don't mind putting a wall of ugly metal around a bed of beautiful flowers.

Phil Nixon, extension entomologist with the University of Illinois, says that since rabbits can jump about 18 inches, your fence needs to be at least 2 feet tall. He suggests using 24- to 36-inch-wide wire fencing. Bend the bottom 6 inches outward at a 30- to 45-degree angle, then bury the bottom inch or so under the soil. That way, when the rabbit tries to dig under the fence, it will be standing on it.

BUNNY BATTLES

Elizabeth Winston, the founder and director of The Peaceable Kingdom School, an organic gardening research and education institution in Washington, Texas, suggests this bunny-exclusion method. Winston fortifies a fence with a band of roof flashing. She buries one edge of the flashing 2 feet into the soil and lets the other edge extend 2 feet above, against the inside of the fence. Small animals can't climb through the flashing, and burrowing animals such as gophers can't dig under it. The flashing also keeps out creeping grasses, like Bermuda grass, and prevents climbing weeds from using the fence for support. To disguise the flashing, plant verbena (*Verbena* spp.) or sweet alyssum against it.

Insect-eating moles (*top*) won't dine on your flowers, but they may disturb them with their tunnels. Mouselike voles (*bottom*) feed on plant roots and may use moles' tunnels to get to their meals.

You can buy a commercial castor oil preparation or concoct your own by mixing 1 tablespoon of castor oil with 2 tablespoons of liquid detergent. Whisk or mix with a blender until it's foamy, then add it to a gallon of warm water. Sprinkle or spray the solution over active tunnels after you water the yard or after a rain.

Pocket Gophers. Effective controls for pocket gophers include lethal choker traps and equally lethal carbon dioxide cartridges that, when placed in a burrow that is then sealed with soil, displace all the oxygen. You can also try

flushing the tunnel with water to force the gopher out.

Cats. One other mammalian pest, depending on your feelings about felines, might be the cat that uses your flower bed as a litter box. Because cats like loose garden soil, the solution is to give them something looser: sand. Create a sandy area in between the garden and the cat's usual starting point—your back door, the hole under the fence, wherever. And be sure to cover the kids' sandbox.

Troubleshooting

The key to keeping on top of plant problems is to visit your garden often—daily is best, a few times a week is fine. Take along a hand lens to check leaves for the fuzzy threads that characterize fungus. Take a small notebook and a pen to jot down your observations. If you think you'll be tempted to prune, take along sharp shears. Maybe even take a bucket of soapy water for drowning any harmful insects you encounter.

Check leaves—both sides—for speckles, off-color spots, or streaks. If there are holes in the leaves, note their size and whether they're on the edge or in the middle. If you find a curled leaf, see what's inside.

Check stems for dark or soft areas and for swellings. Flick a few fingerfuls of soil away from the base of a stem or two to check for soil insects or rot. If some plants have

Pocket gophers spend most of their lives tunneling and feeding on bulbs, roots, seeds, and any plants they can pull down into their tunnels.

———————➡·⬅———————

CHEAP TRICKS

If fences aren't for you, try a few of these less expensive control methods:

• If chipmunks are eating your bulbs, plant them inside a wire mesh cage. The foliage will grow through the wire, but varmints can't get in.

• If you have a cat, use its litter to scent the yard. When you change the litter, dump some of the used stuff into burrow openings to disgust moles, voles, and mice. Scatter the rest outside the garden to ward off rabbits.

• Use blood meal or ZooDoo (manure from zoo animals) when you fertilize; the smell repels some animal pests.

• Create annoying vibrations in gopher, vole, and mole burrows by inserting the stem of a whirligig or a child's pinwheel into the tunnel.

• Fake snakes will scare rabbits. Be sure to move them every few days.

• Treat gopher burrows with a commercial ferret scent to repel them.

———————➡·⬅———————

Aster yellows

Flea beetles

big bites out of them, have been pulled up, or have disappeared, look for animal tracks. If you notice an unfamiliar insect on a leaf, take a closer look: Is it chewing on the leaf, or is it just passing through?

If you notice a plant with a problem and you're not sure of the cause, watch it to see whether it holds its own or gets worse. See whether the problem spreads to plants of the same species or to any nearby plant.

Diagnosing plant problems is tricky. Diverse diseases, insects, animals, and nutrient deficiencies may cause similar symptoms in your garden. This section lists symptoms (in boldface), and some of their potential causes, that are common to a wide range of ornamental plants.

Leaves or Plants Yellowed. Aster yellows affects asters, chrysanthemums, marigolds, and other plants. Affected plants are yellowed, stunted, and distorted, especially at growth points. Remove and destroy affected plants. Control leafhoppers, which spread the disease, with a spray of insecticidal soap and rubbing alcohol. Use 1 tablespoon of alcohol per pint of insecticidal soap solution. Apply it once every three to five days, making three applications.

Spider mite infestations can also turn leaves yellow. See "Leaves Speckled" on page 317.

Overwatering, ozone pollution, and nitrogen deficiency also cause yellowing.

Leaves and/or Flowers with Holes. Blister beetles feed on many plants. The larvae of these ½-inch-long, dark, metallic beetles eat grasshoppers in the early summer. But by midsummer, large populations may drive adults to feed on flowers. Wear gloves if you handpick blister beetles. Apply pyrethrins if damage is severe.

Earwigs, when their populations are high, eat the leaves and flowers of ageratums, daylilies, marigolds, roses, zinnias, and other plants. These nocturnal insects are ½ inch long and have pincers at their tail end. Earwigs hide in tight, dark places during the day; trap them by creating hiding places of rolled newspaper, then tap out the paper into a bucket of soapy water.

Flea beetles are tiny (⅒-inch) black insects, named for

their habit of jumping when disturbed, which eat tiny holes in the leaves of a broad range of plants. Because the holes are so small, flea beetles seldom warrant control. If you must control them, use pyrethrins or neem.

Grasshoppers are large green leapers that feed on the leaf edges of lilies, marigolds, zinnias, and many other flowers. You can pick them off by hand, or use pyrethrins for plagues. Their natural enemies include blister beetle larvae and birds.

Japanese beetles are inch-long metallic green beetles that skeletonize foliage as they feed. A heavy infestation can defoliate roses and other favored plants. They begin feeding in early July and are active for about two months. To prevent damage, cover roses in fine netting. Handpick and drop the beetles into soapy water. Where infestations are light (fewer than 50 or so per rose bush), use commercial Japanese beetle traps. Keep traps at least 50 feet away from your garden, and don't use them for heavy infestations; beetles will fill the trap and eat your roses. You can also use a hand-held vacuum to vacuum beetles off the leaves.

Slugs are elongated, fat, legless, slimy, grayish or yellowish blobs ranging from less than an inch to several inches long. They eat big, ragged holes in foliage, especially of shade-loving plants, and leave slime trails. To prevent slugs, space plants to improve air circulation and reduce humidity, and improve soil aeration. Because slugs hide under organic matter, consider removing organic mulch from the area until you get a severe infestation under control.

Other options for controlling slugs include using traps and repellents and encouraging predators. Make your own traps by setting flowerpots or boards in your garden near plants with slug damage. Slugs are active at night but need shaded, moist places to rest during the heat of the day. Pots and boards provide slugs with perfect hiding places and provide you with an easy trap. Check underneath the pots or boards every few days and destroy the slugs you find there. Slugs are also attracted to pieces of food, like raw potatoes or cabbage leaves. Check the food and collect and dispose of slugs every morning.

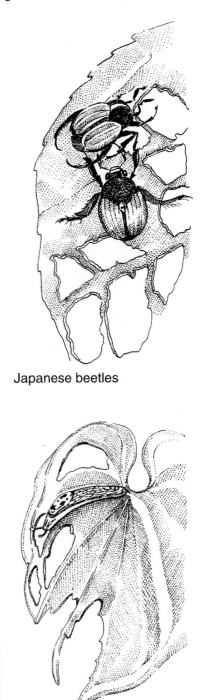

Japanese beetles

Slug

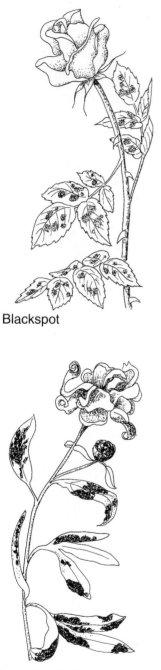

Blackspot

Botrytis blight

Copper strips make effective slug repellents and are described in detail under "Copper Slugs It Out with Beer" on page 305. You can also try placing 2-inch-wide bands of cinders, wood ashes, or diatomaceous earth around tender seedlings to protect them. Reapply these materials frequently, especially after rain.

Another way to control slugs is to encourage predatory beetles and toads to take up residence in your garden. Make permanent walkways of clover, sod, or stone mulch to give beetles shelter. And provide toads with homes like the one illustrated on page 304.

Leaves or Petals with Spots or Streaks. Leaf spot fungi cause dark or colored spots on leaves. Many plants, including bellflowers (*Campanula* spp.), chrysanthemums, impatiens, marigolds, peonies, and phlox, get leaf spot. A common leaf spot of roses is called blackspot because of the circular, black spots that appear on infected leaves. Humidity promotes leaf spot; to prevent it, improve air circulation and avoid wetting leaves. Clean up fallen leaves to reduce sources of fungal spores. If control is necessary, apply baking soda spray (see "Diseases" on page 307).

Botrytis blight affects peonies, petunias, and other plants, especially during cool, wet weather. Look for stems that wilt suddenly and fall over, black or brown rotted stems, irregular brown leaf spots, gray mold, and withered blooms. Cut infected peonies off at the ground in the fall, and dispose of affected parts. Avoid overwatering. Provide good air circulation and soil drainage. If plants are shaded, move them to a sunnier spot.

On tulips, Botrytis blight, also called tulip fire, causes small, sunken, water-soaked spots that make the leaves look speckled. As the disease advances, the spots enlarge and turn grayish. Plants look stunted and pale, and flowers do not open. Bulbs develop dark, round spots. Remove and dispose of infected leaves and flowers as soon as you see them. Place diseased plant parts in a plastic bag to avoid spreading spores. Dig and dispose of infected bulbs and the soil around them. Do not add infected materials to compost. Don't replant tulips in the same spot for two years. Avoid blight by cleaning up and destroying fallen petals, brown leaves, and old stems after blooming.

Tomato spotted wilt virus causes varying symptoms, depending on the plant. It may appear as leaf spots in a ring or bull's eye pattern, brown leaf spots, or reddish brown to purple streaks on stems, leaves, or petals. Tomato spotted wilt virus affects more than 400 plant species, including begonias, chrysanthemums, columbines (*Aquilegia* spp.), cyclamen (*Cyclamen* spp.), geraniums, gladiolus, petunias, snapdragons, and zinnias. Destroy infected young plants, but leave mature annuals—they'll keep flowering. Control thrips, which spread the virus.

Thrips are tiny yellow or black flying insects that suck plant sap, often spreading viral diseases in the process. Infested leaves have silvery streaks or speckles and should be removed and dropped into soapy water. Trap thrips with yellow sticky traps, or use predaceous mites that feed on thrips—either *Amblyseius cucumeris* or *Amblyseius barkeri.* The minute pirate bug, a black and white pinhead-sized insect, also eats thrips. Attract this beneficial bug by planting daisies, goldenrod, and yarrow, which are good sources of pollen and nectar. As a last resort, use insecticidal soap, horticultural oil, or neem, or dust the undersides of the leaves with diatomaceous earth.

Leaves Speckled. Tiny spider mites infest a wide array of ornamentals as well as many food crops. Look for reddish speckles on the undersides of yellowing leaves. You might also see fine webbing on leaves and stems. Infested foliage may turn bronze; heavy infestations cause pale blotches on leaves, distortion, leaf browning, and defoliation. Mites usually aren't a problem if you don't use pesticides—even insecticidal soap can increase their populations by killing off mite predators. Spider mites thrive in hot, dry conditions; knock them off plants with a stream of water and increase watering of plants. Consider spraying with insecticidal soap or horticultural oil only if 20 percent of the foliage shows severe damage, or if webbing covers 20 to 30 percent of the growing tips.

Lace bugs are small flying insects (up to ¼ inch long)

Tomato spotted wilt virus

Spider mite

Spider mite damage

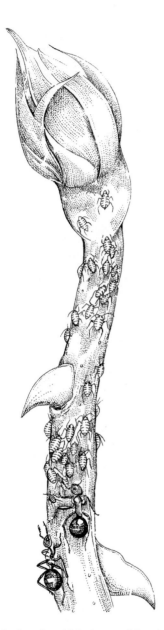

Ants herd aphids toward food sources then feed on aphid secretions.

with transparent wings. Their feeding causes white or gray speckles on leaf surfaces, accompanied by dark spots of excrement. Lace bugs are common on azaleas and rhododendrons, as well as other plants. To control, use insecticidal soap, horticultural oil, or pyrethrins.

A deficiency of the micronutrient manganese can cause yellow speckles on leaves.

Leaves or Stems Discolored. Nutrient deficiencies and environmental problems are the most common causes of discoloration. Deficiencies of nitrogen, iron, or magnesium cause chlorosis, a yellowing due to lack of chlorophyll. When iron or magnesium is lacking, the veins stay green but the rest of the leaf turns pale. Lowering the pH usually remedies the problem. Overwatering and ozone pollution also cause general yellowing. A lack of phosphorus makes stems purple, while a lack of copper makes them blackish. Frost damage can also turn plant tissue black.

Leaves or New Growth Distorted or Twisted. Aphids are tiny, soft-bodied, pear-shaped insects that distort leaves by sucking sap from them. White, brown, red, or light green, aphids favor tender young growth. As they feed, aphids secrete sugary honeydew, which often coats the leaves below infested areas, attracting ants and bees. Aphids have several natural predators, including lady beetles, lacewings, parasitic wasps, syrphid fly larvae, and some midges. You can wash aphids off your plants with a strong stream of water. Use insecticidal soap, horticultural oil, or pyrethrins as a last resort.

Tarnished plant bugs are quick-moving, green or brown, ¼-inch insects with yellow, black, or red splotches. Adults and nymphs suck plant sap, stunting and distorting growth and causing bud drop. To discourage them, control weeds all season, starting early in the spring. You may get an onslaught if a nearby field is mowed halfway through the summer; bugs that had been feeding there have to find a new home. Use pyrethrins or summer oil as a last resort. Spider mite infestations also may cause distortion. See "Leaves Speckled" on page 317.

Herbicide spray drift or runoff also causes distorted

leaves. To help plants outgrow an herbicide hit, drench the root zone with a balanced liquid fertilizer.

Leaves with Sticky Sap or Gray-Black Mold. Aphids secrete sugary honeydew on which gray-black sooty mold grows. See "Leaves or New Growth Distorted or Twisted" on the opposite page.

Scale insects attack roses and other shrubs. Like aphids, scales excrete sugary honeydew that becomes covered with a gray mold. The scale life cycle has two stages. After hatching, tiny crawlers move around the stem until they settle down to molt, lose their legs, and cover themselves with a scale-like casing. Both crawlers and scales suck sap from the plant. To control, encourage lady beetles. Cut off heavily infested branches. Spray off crawlers with a hard stream of water. Scales are not easily controlled with pesticides, once they're beneath their covers. Spray dormant oil in the winter or horticultural oil in the summer to smother scale eggs.

Whiteflies are tiny white flying insects that fly up like a cloud of dust when disturbed. Whiteflies suck sap from plants and excrete honeydew, which grows sooty mold. They are common greenhouse pests that often infest bedding plants, especially in humid regions. Check bedding plants carefully before buying to avoid bringing them home. Yellow sticky traps catch lots of whiteflies. Encourage parasitic wasps and predatory beetles for additional control. Use insecticidal soap, horticultural oil, or pyrethrins for heavy infestations.

Leaves with White Powder. Powdery mildew coats the leaves of many annuals, perennials, shrubs, and trees. Lilacs, phlox, roses, and zinnias are particularly susceptible. Hot weather with cool nights promotes this fungus, which may distort new growth. Good air circulation helps prevent powdery mildew, so make sure plants are spaced properly; sprays of sulfur or lime sulfur help reduce its spread. Spray with baking soda solution (see "Diseases" on page 307) to help control the disease.

Leaves with Orange or Red Fuzzy Patches. Rust fungi affect many plants; rust diseases are common on holly-

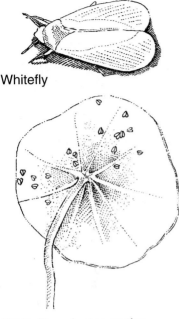

Whitefly

Whiteflies cluster on the undersides of leaves.

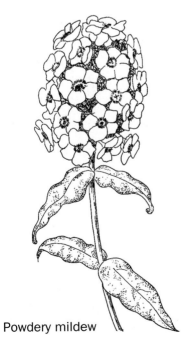

Powdery mildew

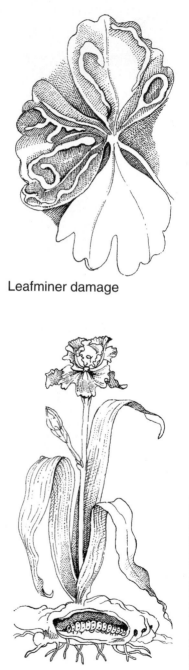

Leafminer damage

Iris borer

hocks (*Alcea rosea*), crab apples, and hawthorns (*Crataegus* spp.). Cultural practices—improving air circulation and avoiding wetting leaves—prevent rust infections, as do applications of sulfur dust starting early in the growing season.

Leaves Rolled. Leafroller and leaftier are names given to several different ½- to 1½-inch-long, drab-colored caterpillars. Leafrollers and leaftiers web leaf edges together and feed on the enclosed leaves and buds. Control light infestations by opening the webbing and picking off the caterpillars; spray leaves with Bt if you're severely outnumbered.

Leaves, Stems, or Rhizomes with Tunnels. Leafminers are tiny fly larvae that tunnel beneath the leaf surface on columbines (*Aquilegia* spp.) and other plants, leaving unsightly, meandering streaks and blotches. Once the maggots are protected between leaf surfaces, no spray will disturb them. Pick off and destroy the mined leaves when you first see damage.

Iris borers are 2-inch larvae that attack the foliage in the spring just as the spears elongate. They mine down the leaves and into the rhizome to feed. Infested rhizomes become mushy when bacterial soft rot infects the damaged tissue. Borers most often affect tall bearded iris. Patrol iris foliage in spring and early summer, and crush any borers you see before they reach the rhizomes. Dig up severely infested plants and destroy them. In small plantings, you can dig up rhizomes, sift the soil to remove larvae, then replant the healthy rhizomes. After the first hard frost, remove and destroy iris leaves, stems, and debris, which can harbor eggs.

European corn borer larvae tunnel into the stems of glads, dahlias, asters, and other plants. Look for inch-long pinkish caterpillars with brown spots. Sprays of Bt control borers if you get to them before they start tunneling—usually sometime in July.

Stems or Stalks Cut Off or Broken. Damping-off is a disease that rots young seedlings at the soil line. To prevent it, let soil dry out slightly between waterings and don't fertilize until seedlings develop true leaves. Use a sterile, soilless growth medium for starting seeds.

Cutworms eat through the stems of tender seedlings and transplants in the spring. Nocturnal, 1- to 2-inch-long, gray or brown caterpillars curl around stems and chew them off at the soil line. To prevent damage, place collars, such as open-ended cans or cardboard rings, around the base of young plants. Press each collar into the soil so that at least half of it is below ground.

Sowbugs, also called pillbugs, rarely do any damage to established plants, but they may feed on seedlings when their populations are high. Gardeners often see these ½-inch crustaceans, since they feed on decaying organic material. If sowbugs pose a problem, sprinkle diatomaceous earth in areas where they gather.

Rabbits and other wildlife feed on plants. See "Mammals" on page 309 for more information about animal pests.

Plants Wilt. If watering doesn't make a wilting plant perk up, it might have root damage from root-feeding insects such as grubs, from a burrowing animal, or from a hoe or other cultivating tool.

Verticillium wilt and Fusarium wilt are fungi that live in the soil and affect hundreds of plants. Wilting often starts with the bottom or outer leaves and may affect one side of the plant more than the other. Pull up and destroy affected plants. To prevent these diseases, choose resistant cultivars.

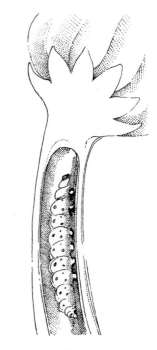

European corn borer

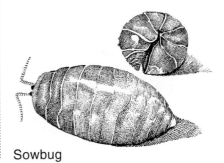

Sowbug

CHAPTER 9

Keeping Your Garden's Good Looks

Plants grow! Living, blooming plants change constantly, and this is what makes gardening both interesting and challenging. Vines and trees grow bigger and cast more shade. Aggressive plants fill in and squeeze out less assertive neighbors. Plants self-sow, and they may produce different-colored flowers in the second or third generation. As plants grow and change, the successful gardener learns to help the garden age gracefully.

In this chapter you'll find simple solutions, timely tips, and ingenious ideas for coping with change in your garden. Whether you need to clear out an overgrown bed, fill in a new plot, add shade or let in light, or change your garden's style, there's help at hand in the pages that follow.

Renewing Existing Gardens

Most of us buy houses with existing landscapes—gardens designed by someone else, or yards that just evolved in a random manner. Working with an existing flower garden or improving the landscape you already have can be a challenge. If your existing garden has major problems, then prepare for major surgery. Consider using a chainsaw to cut down trees and shrubs that must go, or cut back overgrown plants that must stay. (Make sure you identify plants before you hack them down, in case you have a secret treasure hidden in your yard.) Pull out the desperate-looking survivors that deserve death with a little dignity. Remember there are no plant police that will arrest a home gardener for digging up and throwing away a living plant!

Once you have cleared out the jungle or disposed of the seriously ill plants, consider the type of garden you would like, the shape of the bed, and the amount of time and money you have to spend, just as you would with a new garden. Take another look at the existing plants. Old gardens may have mature flowering shrubs or trees that you can use as a starting point for redesigning the bed into your preferred garden style.

Don't be afraid to move plants to better sites. Digging up and moving perennials and small shrubs around in an existing garden is not much more difficult than rearranging the furniture in the living room. Choose a cloudy day, preferably in early spring or fall. Don't move plants that are in full bloom or in bud. Instead, always try to perform the transplant while the plant is under the natural anesthetic of dormancy.

The addition of a birdbath, sundial, or other focal point is a quick shortcut to giving any garden space a feeling of direction and focus. In formal garden beds, the focal point should be centered, but in casual gardens the focal point can be off to the side of the bed.

Don't forget that the quickest shortcut you can use to fill in a flower garden is to find out what grows best in your site and plant more of it. If irises always crowd out the peonies, add more irises. If your shrub roses spread out over a struggling herb garden, let them grow.

Lollipops and Polka Dots

When you're considering changes in your landscape, look for lollipops and polka dots. Home gardeners—and even professionals—often create these hard-to-maintain globes and circles in their gardens. Here's how to avoid them:

Lollipops: Are your shrubs overpruned into cubes and balls? If a formal planting reminds you of a group of lol

---

FAST AND SLOW GROWERS

As your flower garden matures, you'll notice that some plants will grow more quickly than others. Use their different growth rates to your advantage. If you need to fill in bare spots, choose quick spreaders.

Flowers that fill a bed in quickly include spring-blooming forget-me-nots (*Myosotis sylvestris*), which are biennial but self-sow prolifically, bluebells (*Hyacinthoides* spp.), which are perennial bulbs, daylilies, and lily-of-the-valley (*Convallaria majalis*), a groundcover that spreads by rhizomes.

Use slow growers if you want well-behaved plants that stay in bounds. Choose perennials like balloon flower (*Platycodon grandiflorus*), peonies, and sea lavender (*Limonium latifolium*), which take their time growing and seldom need division.

Before. If you've bought a house with an overgrown landscape, or have let your own get out of hand, don't despair. Even a landscape like this—where perennial flowers and a vine are overwhelming a shrub (and the adjacent fence), watersprouts and suckers are ruining a beautiful tree, and a groundcover has escaped into the lawn—can be saved with a good cleanup.

After. A beautiful garden emerges now that the tree is pruned and mulched, the vine trimmed back, the perennials divided, and the shrubs judiciously shaped and sized.

lipops, create a more natural design for your yard. Let the shrubs grow out, or replace them with shrubs like euonymus and boxwood that need little pruning.

Polka Dots: Does your landscaping seem scattered, with different kinds of plants spotted over the grounds like polka dots? For a more organized look, use plants more than once in the planting, and group them together. Train yourself to buy three or more of the same plant instead of just one. Plantings with just one of each kind of plant can be confusing, since your eyes skip from plant to plant, trying to take it all in. Repetition lets your eyes rest, since there's a pattern to follow.

Reshaping Your Flower Bed

An existing flower bed that has healthy plants but just lacks pizzazz, or a flower garden that is too small for the enthusiastic plants it was meant to contain, is a garden that needs reshaping or enlarging. If you need to change the size or shape of your flower bed, try using a rope or hose to outline the future shape.

This outline will give you an idea of how bends and curves will look, and you'll see exactly how much widening or lengthening the bed will change it. Once you have the shape the way you want it, use a shovel or mattock to cut away the sod and make the changes permanent. For more on how to change the look of your beds, see "Changing Your Garden Style" on page 337.

Help for a Young Garden

What do you do if you buy a new house—a really new house, just built on a bare, bulldozed lot? When a homeowner is faced with an empty lot and a desire to fill it with plants immediately, there is no such thing as a plant that grows too fast. This is when annual flowers and quick-growing groundcovers seem like a godsend.

This is also the time when a few garden accents, such as a birdbath in the middle of a perennial garden or a collec-

---

⇢ • ⇠

SHORT- AND LONG-LIVED PLANTS

Some perennials die out over the years and need to be replaced. Balance these in your garden with long-lived plants that grow more beautiful as they mature.

Try these perennials that only improve with age:

• Peonies don't need to be divided; their large flowers increase with age.
• Asiatic lilies (*Lilium* hybrids) live for many years in well-drained soil; their flowers increase over time.
• Hostas are shade-loving foliage plants that grow into magnificent clumps.

Grow the following short-lived plants as annuals, divide them regularly, or just enjoy them for a few seasons:

• Tulips live longest with well-drained soil. But even with good growing conditions, they may last only a few years. Treat them as annuals for best results.
• Delphiniums are prone to mildew and die out after several years.
• Snow-in-summer (*Cerastium tomentosum*) is a low-growing, white-blooming groundcover that dies out in the center after a few years.

⇢ • ⇠

FILLING IN GARDEN GAPS

You can make a newly planted garden look more mature by filling in the space between the plants:

• Set boulders and logs randomly in a woodland or shade garden.

• Add an interesting or whimsical piece of garden art in a casual garden.

• Use stepping stones as a path in a more formal flower bed.

• Spread an attractive mulch such as bark chips to cover bare soil.

• Fill gaps with colorful potted plants.

• Use fast-growing, spreading annuals like petunias and impatiens to fill in around perennials.

• Plant a temporary, easy-to-remove groundcover such as Irish moss (*Sagina subulata*) or the chartreuse-leaved Scotch moss (*S. subulata* 'Aurea') between the plants.

tion of boulders filling up the space between the flowering shrubs, are most appreciated. Getting a lawn and shade trees in place is usually a top priority in a new landscape, and not much thought goes into the flowering plants in the beginning.

As Your Garden Grows

Soon, the new landscape becomes established, and usually, an interest in flowers grows along with the gardener's skill. Perennials, roses, and flowering vines and groundcovers begin to replace the easy-to-grow annuals. This is when that sparsely planted garden begins to fill in. This is also when the fast-spreading English ivy groundcover becomes a nuisance and the bed of pink petunias looks a bit boring.

The next stage in the education of a gardener could be called the experimental stage. Many budding gardeners begin to try unusual plants or different types of weed-blocking mulches, or begin to move existing plants around to satisfy cultural requirements or new color schemes.

Maintenance of any flower garden often moves beyond the routine tasks of watering, weeding, and feeding to a deeper level that involves improving the existing landscape. The benefits of actually improving—not just maintaining—a landscape are one of the real joys of gardening. Maintaining a garden's good looks involves not only the art of adding, subtracting, and dividing, but also evaluating the changing conditions of the garden site and how they affect the plants.

Filling In the Blanks

While you wait for your new garden to mature, you can take advantage of some plants' aggressive tendencies to help fill empty garden spaces. Some plants spread or self-sow vigorously, filling the garden with volunteers. Volunteer plants are those brave (and sometimes unwelcome) green things that pop up in the flower bed but were never planted there.

You'll find perennials like yarrows and columbines, biennials like common foxgloves (*Digitalis purpurea*) and dame's rocket (*Hesperis matronalis*), ornamental grasses, and lots of groundcovers like sweet woodruff (*Galium odoratum*) and bugleweed (*Ajuga reptans*) appearing far from their garden homes. Experience will teach you to recognize these invaders when they are just sweet young things. But just because you recognize them for what they are, don't be in a rush to pull them up.

It makes sense that any plant that can grow without your planting it must be hardy and adaptable to your region. It also must find your soil, weather, and light conditions to its liking. This is a plant that already likes your garden and won't demand much from you. And most volunteers are easy to transplant if they pop up in the middle of a pathway or other inconvenient location.

Volunteer plants may be easy to grow, but they also can be spoilers when it comes to maintaining your garden's good looks. There comes a point where enough is enough. The artemisia and lily-of-the-valley may grow too enthusiastically in your garden. They're so happy to be given the chance to grow and bloom that they may take advantage of your good nature, and every few years you'll be forced to get tough and rip them out by their roots. If you're tender-hearted, do it in the fall when the flowers have faded and you won't feel so guilty. The ex-volunteers can go into the compost pile.

Keeping Your Garden in Shape

An important law of nature is that as your flowering plants grow, they will become larger. This is usually a good thing. Bigger plants tend to have more flowers. But sometimes a plant grows too large for its space. When that happens, you may have to move the plant or make room around it. Another possibility is shaping the plant to fit with a little pinching or shearing.

It is far better for the health of your plants and the maintenance demands on your time to transplant flowers that

---

PLANT VOLUNTEERS

Many great gardens have more plants than their owners ever planted. That's because some flowering plants self-sow or spread readily without human assistance. They tend to take over the part of a garden that provides the growing conditions they need.

Shady Volunteers. Biennial forget-me-not (*Myosotis sylvestris*) and perennial hostas, coral bells (*Heuchera* spp.), primroses, lily-of-the-valley, common bleeding heart (*Dicentra spectabilis*), and ferns will all multiply in a moist, partially shaded part of the garden.

Sunny Volunteers. In a sunny, well-drained site, these flowers will self-sow: annual California poppies (*Eschscholzia californica*), biennial Johnny-jump-ups (*Viola tricolor*), and perennial feverfew (*Chrysanthemum parthenium*), New England aster (*Aster novae-angliae*), and blood-red cranesbill (*Geranium sanguineum*).

A new garden can look bare unless you dress it up with a few finishing touches. Here, the gardeners have laid the foundation for their garden with railroad ties, a small flowering tree and shrub, perennials, and groundcovers. To add interest while the plants mature, they've put in a birdbath and filled in the blanks with colorful annuals. Mulch adds the finishing touch.

are growing too large for their space rather than to keep cutting them back. If your lilac is growing taller than the window it is planted under, move the shrub to a spot where it can reach for the sky. If your perennials become overcrowded and compete for food and water, dig out several plants from the grouping, even if you have no more room in your yard and have to give them away. Better to live with fewer, healthier plants than to struggle with a crowded flower garden where nothing can grow to perfection.

Flowering perennials often grow taller or wider than you expected, and they may block the blooming plants behind them from view. Some tall perennials such as irises, lilies, and peonies do not take kindly to shearing, pruning, or

A garden over time: first year

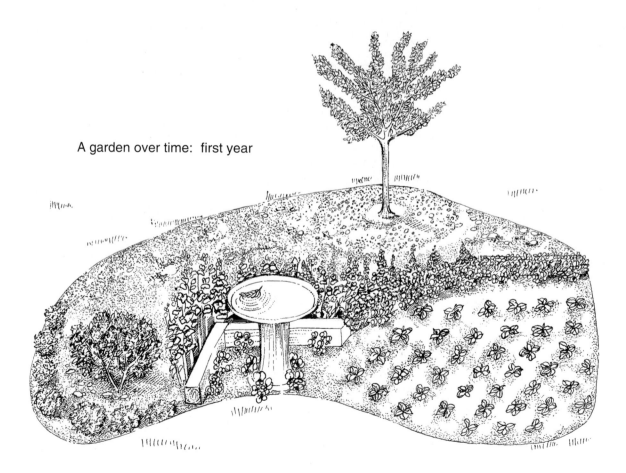

A garden over time: third year

pinching. Whenever possible, move shorter plants to the front of the bed rather than pruning to try to control the height of taller perennials.

Pinching and Shearing

Both shearing and pinching remove just a small amount of the new growth to encourage branching and a more bushy plant. Pinching means using your fingers to pinch out or remove the new tip growth from an herbaceous plant,

The tree is already big enough to cast some shade and the shrub is blooming by the third year. The groundcover has spread to fill most bare areas. As their budget allowed, the gardeners have extended the garden around the tree and added perennials. However, they still plant annuals for nonstop summer color.

A garden over time: tenth year

In its maturity, the once-sunny site has become a shade garden. The shrub and perennials have matured, the tree is nearly as tall as a house, and groundcovers luxuriantly blanket the ground. This lovely bit of woodland will attract birds to nest and enjoy the birdbath.

such as a chrysanthemum. Many annual flowers such as petunias and geraniums also respond with shorter, bushier growth habits and more blooms when you pinch out new growth tips in the beginning of the growing season.

You can shear many perennials right after they bloom to remove dead flowers. Use the same scissor pruners you'd use on a hedge. Not only does this tidy up the garden, it saves the plant's energy reserves, since it no longer has to work on setting seeds. Once the dead flowers are gone, so are the seed-making supplies.

A word of warning to flower gardeners who find them-selves spending a lot of time pruning back plants: You may be stuck doing maintenance pruning for the life of your plant. Giving the plant more room, not making the plant smaller, is the way to rid your garden of routine mainte-nance pruning. The best way to avoid maintenance pruning is to plant things in appropriate spaces, allowing enough room for the size of the plant at maturity.

Dealing with Rampant Growers

Some gardeners are reluctant to prune back any plant growth because they are so proud of the fact that their gar-den is growing. An example is a couple who underplanted their shade garden with the blooming groundcover com-mon periwinkle or vinca (*Vinca minor*). Most plants grow rather slowly in the shade, and this lovely flower garden was designed with bleeding hearts (*Dicentra* spp.), hostas, azaleas, and astilbes. The vinca groundcover was added to help cover the bare ground while the couple waited for the other perennials to grow larger and fill the space.

Several years passed, and the vinca began to swallow up the bleeding hearts, mow down the astilbes, and choke out the hostas. This groundcover had gone beyond the call of duty and turned into a plant blanket. It was suf-focating all the plants it was supposed to complement. The couple eventually pulled out every strand of vinca and added a bark-chip mulch as a groundcover in its place. Their other plants were shaken up by this near-death experience but survived and went on to become vigorous growers themselves.

The whole nasty episode could have been avoided had the vinca been cut back heavily each spring after it had bloomed. Another option would have been to plant this groundcover under a tree where it could spread out as nature intended without bothering other plants. The moral of this story isn't to avoid vinca as the secret strangler of flowering shade plants, but rather to realize that over time, more-vigorous plants will take over their less aggres-sive neighbors.

TAME THE MAINTENANCE MONSTER

If the maintenance on an existing flower garden is holding you hostage, free up some time by using these tips:

• Replace high mainte-nance roses and perenni-als with disease-resistant cultivars.

• Straighten sharply curved borders and gently curve the tight corners of flower beds that are diffi-cult to mow around.

• Add stepping stones to wide or steep gardens for easier access.

• Replace flowers that need staking with shorter flowers.

• Place a soaker hose or drip irrigation system in your flower bed for easy deep watering.

• Mulch your flower bed to seal in moisture and seal out weed seeds.

• Install 1-foot-wide strips of mulch around flower beds so you can mow around them without trimming. If you want a more formal look, use brick or flat stones.

DOES YOUR GARDEN NEED MAJOR SURGERY?

Are weeds taking over your garden? Do your flowers look anemic? Are they covered with spots? Take a close look at the patients. If the entire garden looks ready to give up the ghost, major surgery may be the answer. Here's what to do:

Invasive Weeds: Get weeds under control by repeated hand-pulling. (For taprooted weeds like dandelions, use a weed puller.) Don't let weeds set seed in your garden. Suppress weeds by laying down newspaper or cardboard under a very heavy mulch.

Weak, Yellowed Plants: Work compost or manure around the plants and keep them mulched. Sprinkling chicken manure, watering with manure tea, and spraying with liquid seaweed are other ways to give a tonic to weak, yellowing plants.

Diseased Plants: Rip out, prune back, and thin overgrown plants. Good air circulation cuts down on disease. Consider pruning overhead branches or thinning background trees and shrubs to let in more air.

➡ · ⬅

When Perennials Get Too Big

Flower gardens planted in island mounds or in borders alongside the lawn also grow larger over time. Many homeowners find themselves cutting back perennials and pruning off the branches of flowering shrubs because they get in the way of the lawnmower. Often the easiest solution is to remove a wide strip of grass around the bed to enlarge it. This is especially effective for a flower garden with many tall plants but no room for low border plants in front. Make the bed bigger, and add low-growing plants where the lawn was removed.

You can tame overgrown perennials that grow into bigger and bigger clumps by dividing them. One perennial that benefits from regular division is bearded iris. After a few years, a clump of iris may triple in size, invading the space of a neighboring plant or pushing out the boundaries of the bed.

Dig and divide a large iris clump after it blooms, and replant only a few healthy fans (sections) of fresh growth from the side of the clump. Give away the other plants or move them to another section of the garden. Your new small clump of iris will bloom better and take up less space in the crowded bed. (For more information on dividing plants, refer to "Multiplying by Division" on page 254.)

Let There Be Light—and Shade

Over time, the light conditions in your garden will probably change. They can change very quickly, such as when the sudden removal of a large tree lets extra sunlight pour in, or more gradually, as trees and shrubs mature and begin to shade the area surrounding them. This section will show you how to help your plants adapt to changes in your site's light.

A Shady Situation

Shade can creep up on a garden slowly. Here's one typical scenario: A family moves to the suburbs and is in love with all the trees on their lot. They tell the builder to save all the trees, and they add a lawn and shrubs to this sun-dappled landscape. A few years go by and the trees fill out. They cast more shade, and a few more homes go in around the house. Bigger trees, houses next door, and even the trees growing across the street affect the amount of sunshine that comes into the yard. Flowers that bloomed when the shade was light start to decline as more sun is blocked by maturing trees and shrubs.

There are several options for solving this common problem. Cutting down all the trees on your lot isn't the only answer! Selective thinning of branches not only allows more light to reach your plants but can also open up and improve the branch structure of the tree. Thin deciduous trees by removing all dead wood, branches that cross or are diseased, and the lowest overhanging branches. Evergreen trees are more difficult to prune because it's not as easy to see their branch structure. But if you remove the lowest branches, the spread of the evergreen tree won't be as wide and more sunlight will be able to reach the plants below.

Picking Plants for Shade

Pruning trees is a big job that often requires professional help. A less drastic way to deal with increased shade is to gradually introduce shade-loving plants to your garden as the sun lovers begin to grow leggy and have fewer blooms. Move the irises and coreopsis (*Coreopsis* spp.) to another area when you notice leaf blights, mildew, and fewer flowers. Replace sun lovers with shade-tolerant hostas, astilbes, bleeding hearts (*Dicentra* spp.), and foxgloves (*Digitalis* spp.).

In your annual bed, don't get stuck in a rut planting only geraniums and marigolds in an area that used to be in full sun. Instead, try shade-tolerant plants such as begonias and impatiens as the bed becomes partially shaded or when you notice that the geraniums are getting leggy every summer and the marigolds have moldy buds. Replace flowering shrubs like lilacs that develop mildew in the shade with

---

THE CHANGING DEMANDS OF PLANT PARENTHOOD

The responsibilities of plant parenthood change as your plants mature. There are four stages of seasonal growth, with different demands at each stage.

Infancy: For seedlings or newly set out bedding plants, protection from cold, insects, and even rainstorms is important.

Adolescence: During this period of rapid growth and preparation for flowering, fertilizing is most important. Pinch plants such as petunias and fuchsias to encourage bushiness. Provide a support system for tall or top-heavy plants such as peonies and delphiniums now before they flower.

Parenthood: Provide plenty of water, protection from wind, and good nutrition while plants are setting buds and blooming.

Retirement: Deadhead spent flowers to prevent early retirement, and pull off dead leaves to keep older plants looking their best. Food and water needs will diminish as plants finish flowering.

GRABBING MORE SUNSHINE

As a landscape matures, growing trees and shrubs cast more shade on the plants below. Thinning the dead wood from trees and shrubs is sometimes all you need to do to let in light. Many plants will bloom in filtered shade, but few plants flower well in deep shade.

Tall trees that are too big to thin out can be limbed up. This involves removing just the lowest branches that spread out the farthest. Another option, to be chosen only after careful consideration, is to remove sun-blocking trees or problem shrubs. (First make sure they are on your property!)

If you or your neighbors remove a tree or shrub so more light comes into the garden, your plants may sunburn. Signs include light, washed-out leaf color, dry brown spots on leaves, and wilting.

Protect plants by applying a heavy mulch to shade and cool the soil. Provide shade with a cardboard or bamboo screen from 11 A.M. to 3 P.M. until your plants adjust.

more shade-tolerant shrubs such as viburnums or rhododendrons.

Less light reflects from the flowers in shady gardens, and you may notice that your darker-colored flowers don't stand out as well. Brighten shady beds with lots of white flowers, which reflect light, and with plants that have variegated green-and-white or green-and-yellow foliage. A hosta with a white stripe down the middle of the leaf stands out more in the shade than a blue-green hosta cultivar. White impatiens brighten up a shady corner more than those with deep red or violet flowers.

Using white, gray, or beige rocks and stepping stones or light-colored garden accents will also help combat the increasing shade and darkness. White arches, benches, and fences stand out impressively in a shady bed.

Coping with More Sun

Sometimes, the problem is not creeping shade but sudden sun. For example, a storm might blow down almost every tree in your front yard. You might not mourn the loss of your trees as much as what the increased sunshine has done to your flower garden. Large camellias and rhododendrons planted 20 years ago might suddenly be blighted with leaf spots and faded foliage. Flower buds on your astilbes might dry up and primrose foliage might curl. The plants in your formerly shaded front yard could not handle the instant change in light intensity.

The good news is that many plants will adapt to more sunshine once they develop a "tan" or thicker epidermis. Your large flowering shrubs may recover from the shock of direct sun exposure. New foliage that's more adapted to the heat will cover the sun-damaged plants. And you can always replace the plants that didn't make it. It may take several years, but you can eventually add more sun-loving flowers such as moss pink (*Phlox subulata*) and low-growing thymes to your now sunny front yard to replace the yellowing pachysandra and violets that used to serve as groundcovers.

The Best of Both Worlds

While some plants must have full sun or partial shade in order to thrive, many are capable of adapting, over time, to a wide range of light conditions. Your responsibility as gardener is to ease plants through such changes. Use cardboard tents or even umbrellas during the hottest part of the day to protect plants exposed to more sunlight. In a week or two, the plants will adapt to the extra light if they're ever going to. Perennial columbines (*Aquilegia* spp.), veronicas (*Veronica* spp.), and bleeding hearts (*Dicentra* spp.), biennial foxgloves (*Digitalis* spp.), and annual impatiens will thrive in sun or shade as long as they have adequate water, good soil, and a mulch over their roots to keep them cool.

Caring for a Maturing Garden

There is another change that gardeners must adapt to, and this is the aging and changing needs of their plants. Newly planted gardens have different requirements than established plantings do. When a flower garden is young, winter protection is more important, fertilizing is more important, and watering, pinching, and staking are considerations. As plants mature, they develop root systems that can more easily adapt to cold and drought.

Fertilizing needs also change as a garden matures. This is a change for the better if the garden has been mulched and the soil improved over the years. Over time, adding a light mulch of compost to roses, perennials, and annuals will create a soil that is so soft and fertile that for most plants, no additional fertilizers will be necessary.

The disadvantage to this annual mulching practice is that after many years, the level of the soil will have been built up to such a depth that some plants will find themselves planted too deep. One of the most-asked gardening questions is how to get old peony plants to bloom again. Often, just pulling back the soil so that the roots of the peony are nearer to the surface is all that is needed to get them budding. Irises and many other fleshy-rooted plants also suffer

---

PRUNING FOR MORE PLANTS

Sometimes a mature shrub's branches trail all the way to the ground, and this robs your garden of planting space. You can prune many shrubs, including viburnums, photinias (*Photinia* spp.), and rhododendrons, so that there is space beneath their branches for low plants that are shade-tolerant. Here's how:

1. Start at the bottom of the shrub and remove the lowest branches where they meet the main trunk.
2. Stop pruning when the new length of the trunk is about one-third of the total height of the shrub.
3. Remove all dead wood and crossing or diseased branches from the upper part of the shrub. You should now have a thinned-out, lightly pruned shrub with a treelike shape.
4. Improve the soil around the newly pruned shrub by adding organic matter before putting in flowering plants. Remember that a garden under a large shrub will need extra water and fertilizer to help the smaller plants compete.

—❖·❖—

—❖·❖—

when mulch builds up over time and the roots become buried in too much soil.

What do you do when your plants are buried under this new soil? First of all, don't panic. The change is so gradual that the plants don't even notice the extra soil for the first four or five years. By then, most of the perennials need to be dug, divided, and replanted anyway.

Here's how to rejuvenate a tired perennial bed: Renew the bed on a cloudy day in the spring. Dig your plants, divide them, and reset them clump by clump so the roots don't dry out. Cut out the old, weak centers of the clumps and reset the perennials at the proper depth in soil that has been refreshed by working a 2-inch layer of compost or other organic material into the top 8 inches of soil.

Roses don't respond as well to being dug and reset into improved soil. As your rose garden ages, just continue to improve the soil with a mulch each fall. Scrape away the protective mulch mound from around the base of the plants when new growth starts in the spring.

Living with Lawn Art

Like plants, garden accents can be moved or transplanted to different parts of the garden when you change your mind about your garden's design. You can rotate birdbaths, sundials, and other portable garden accents to different flower beds so that your garden's look is constantly changing. You can even take your favorites along with you if you move.

Don't forget that garden accents need TLC to survive outdoors. Some need more winter protection than others. Terra-cotta pots and wooden benches can be damaged if left outdoors in severe weather. Take them into the garage or basement until spring.

Birdbaths also need winter protection if you live where water freezes. To keep the bowl from cracking, either drain and store it in winter or use a special heater (sold in mail-order catalogs) to keep the water from freezing.

Changing Your Garden Style

Garden designers know that the mood of a garden changes as the plants mature. Over the years, a formal flower garden may fill in until it becomes as natural and casual-looking as a woodland garden. Annual gardens change very quickly as summer progresses, and they are a good example of how a flower garden can change in a short time. The bedding plants you space evenly apart in neat rows in June will flow smoothly together in colorful clumps by August. The same thing happens to perennial flower gardens, but it may take several seasons for the plants to fill in their space.

Flower garden styles also change as vigorous plants or energetic groundcovers are removed from overgrown gardens. A casual flower border may appear suddenly more formal when the groundcover is replaced with a dark wood-chip mulch and the plants stand out against the contrasting background. The addition of a brick border or concrete pathway will also introduce a more formal feeling to a casual garden design.

Many gardeners go from a more formal flower garden style to a more casual look as their plants fill in, but there are others who have casual gardens and want to make them look more formal. Neatness counts more in formal gardens than in casual designs. Before attempting to formalize your flower garden, be sure that you can handle the extra maintenance it will need. Lining up your roses in a row of evenly spaced plants means that when one dies, you will need to replace it immediately or be constantly confronted by the obvious thinning of the ranks.

We have all seen the wonders that a fresh edging, thorough weeding, and new blanket of mulch can do for the appearance of a flower garden. Any garden will look more formal after a few hours spent on routine maintenance. Tying up or staking the tall blooming plants that always seem to be leaning over, and throwing out the unruly specimens that can't keep their branches to themselves, are other ways to make a casual bed more formal.

LIVING WITH CHANGE

As your garden evolves and changes, your appreciation of certain plants and the amount of time you're willing to devote to them may also change. Here are some tips to help you adjust to the changes your garden will go through.

- Remove less-desirable plants that are crowding out your favorites. You don't have to keep every plant in your garden for as long as you live. Donate extra plants to a plant sale or share them with new gardeners.
- Get rid of the problem plants that have always demanded more attention than you care to give them. This could include plants that need staking or pruning, or plants that are plagued by insects and diseases.
- Give yourself a deadline to make changes, then stick to it. If adding a rose garden or removing an oversized tree are changes you'd like to see, write down a date, then announce the deadline to as many people as possible. This will encourage you to make the change.

➜ · ⬅

SWITCHING STYLES

If you want to make a formal garden more casual, or a casual garden more formal, here are simple but effective techniques that will do the trick.

Formal to Casual: As the garden matures and plants fill out, widen or curve the borders.

When one plant dies in a formal row, replace it with something different.

As high-maintenance specimen plants die, replace them with easy-care informal plants.

Give your sheared hedge a more relaxed look. Stop shearing, and prune selectively to shape.

Casual to Formal: Edge your beds with straight lines of brick or landscape timbers.

Trade in folksy or country-style garden accents for more-formal focal points like brass sundials.

Resurface informal gravel or wood-chip pathways with brick or stone.

Choose just one or two colors of annual flowers instead of mixed colors.

➜ · ⬅

A Gardener's Choices Never End

Choosing the flower garden that is right for you is not a one-time deal. As gardeners evolve and change, so do their gardens. A young couple with a growing family may choose a garden of ornamental edibles to help out with the grocery bills, then decide to stop growing lettuce and get into perennials as the children leave home and there's more time for hobbies. Large flower gardens may need to be made smaller as interests or the time available to garden shrinks.

As time goes by, your taste in landscaping may also change. This transformation is especially common when gardeners discover a particular plant or group of plants that they are most interested in growing. A mixed perennial garden may be transformed into a rock garden or even a desert-style garden featuring colorful rocks and sand as a backdrop to succulents and hardy cacti.

The most likely change occurs after several springs, when the budding beginner turns into a full-blown gardener who decides to grow something new and exciting. This is when theme gardens pop up where petunias once grew, and collections of heritage iris or rose cultivars bloom where only a strip of lawn and a hedge once took up space. Experienced gardeners know that a garden is never done. Plants constantly grow, and so do gardeners.

A Plant-by-Plant Guide to No-Fail Flowers

ANNUALS FOR FULL SUN

Annual flowers are great for brightening up a planting with inexpensive color. Use them to fill in bare spots between perennials or to create a temporary screen. The annuals listed below thrive in full sun and many are tolerant of high heat, humidity, and dry soil. Some of these plants are actually tender perennials, but all are grown as annuals.

PLANT NAME	DESCRIPTION	COMMENTS
Ageratum houstonianum **Ageratum**	Puffy clusters of blue, white, or pink flowers; heart-shaped leaves. **Height:** 6"–18". **Spacing:** 8"–12".	Plant in light shade in hot climates.
Amaranthus tricolor **Joseph's-coat**	Upright foliage plant with red, yellow, bronze, and green leaves. **Height:** 2'–4'. **Spacing:** 1½'–2'.	Drought-tolerant.
Brachycome iberidifolia **Swan River daisy**	Small, fragrant, blue, pink, or white daisy flowers; feathery foliage. **Height:** 8"–18". **Spacing:** 6".	Prefers cool temperatures and moist but well-drained soil.
Canna x *generalis* **Canna**	Showy red, yellow, pink, or orange blooms; large tropical-looking green or bronze leaves. **Height:** 1½'–6', depending on the cultivar. **Spacing:** 1½'–2'.	Prefers rich, well-drained soil. Dig and store clumps after frost. Plants may be left in the ground in Zones 8–10.
Catharanthus roseus **Madagascar periwinkle**	Large, pink or white flowers, often with a red eye; upright or sprawling plants with glossy green foliage. **Height:** 1'–2'. **Spacing:** 1'.	Heat- and drought-tolerant. Blooms profusely, and self-cleaning flowers never need deadheading.
Celosia cristata **Cockscomb**	Dramatic yellow, orange, pink, or red feathery-plume or velvety-crested flowers. **Height:** 1'–3'. **Spacing:** 1'–1½'.	Tolerates heat and poor, dry soil. Excellent for cut flowers or drying.
Cleome hasslerana **Cleome, spider flower**	Airy white, pink, or purple flowers; compound leaves on bushy plants; beanlike seed pods. **Height:** 3'–5'. **Spacing:** 1'–3'.	Heat- and drought-tolerant. Plants self-sow. Strongly scented foliage.

ANNUALS FOR FULL SUN—CONTINUED

PLANT NAME	DESCRIPTION	COMMENTS
Coreopsis tinctoria **Calliopsis**	Single, broad-petaled daisies in yellow, gold, red, brown, or combinations. **Height:** 1'–2'. **Spacing:** 8".	Self-sows. Needs good drainage but tolerates poor soil.
Cosmos bipinnatus **Cosmos**	Daisylike pink, red, lavender, or white flowers with yellow centers. Yellow cosmos (*C. sulphureus*) has orange, yellow, and red flowers that attract butterflies. **Height:** 2'–6'. **Spacing:** 1'–2'.	Choose shorter cultivars to avoid staking. Tolerates heat and poor, dry soils.
Euphorbia marginata **Snow-on-the-mountain**	Showy white bracts over bright green leaves with white edges. **Height:** 2'. **Spacing:** 8"–12".	Tolerates poor soil, heat, drought, and light shade. Milky sap may irritate skin.
Gaillardia × *grandiflora* **Blanket flower**	Large red blooms with yellow edges; rounded plants. **Height:** 1'–2'. **Spacing:** 1'.	Drought-tolerant; needs good drainage. Deadhead to encourage repeat blooming.
Gazania rigens **Gazania, treasure flower**	Large orange, pink, red, or yellow daisy-like flowers on long stalks. **Height:** 8"–12". **Spacing:** 6"–8".	Prefers well-drained soil. Heat- and drought-tolerant. Flowers close at night.
Gomphrena globosa **Globe amaranth**	White, pink, magenta, orange, red, or lavender, cloverlike flowers. **Height:** 8"–24". **Spacing:** 10"–12".	Tolerant of heat and humidity. Flowers are excellent for drying.
Helianthus annuus **Common sunflower**	Cream, yellow, orange, or red-brown single or double daisy flowers. **Height:** 2'–10'. **Spacing:** 2'–4'.	Heat- and drought-tolerant.
Lobularia maritima **Sweet alyssum**	Clusters of tiny white, pink, or purple flowers cover this mounded plant. **Height:** 6". **Spacing:** 6".	Shear off faded flowers to encourage rebloom. Excellent border plant.
Matthiola incana **Stock**	Spikes of fragrant white, pink, red, or lavender flowers. **Height:** 12"–30". **Spacing:** 10"–15".	Biennial. Tolerates light shade and cold, but not heat.

ANNUALS FOR FULL SUN—CONTINUED

PLANT NAME	DESCRIPTION	COMMENTS
Melampodium paludosum 'Medallion' **'Medallion' melampodium**	Golden yellow, daisylike flowers on bushy plants. **Height:** 12". **Spacing:** 10".	Reseeds readily. Extremely heat-tolerant.
Mirabilis jalapa **Four-o'clock**	Fragrant, red, pink, white, yellow or bicolored trumpet-shaped flowers. **Height:** 1'–3'. **Spacing:** 14".	Tolerates heat, humidity, and light shade.
Ocimum basilicum 'Dark Opal' and 'Purple Ruffles' **Purple-leaved basil**	Dark purple leaves; small white to purple flowers. **Height:** 2'. **Spacing:** 1'.	Leaves are edible as well as ornamental.
Papaver rhoeas **Corn poppy**	Silky-petaled flowers of pink, red, or white with dark centers in early summer; 'Shirley' selections have light centers. **Height:** 2'. **Spacing:** 1'–2'.	Flowering season is short, so interplant with longer-lasting flowers. Provide well-drained soil.
Petunia × *hybrida* **Common garden petunia**	White, pink, red, yellow, blue, or purple single or double trumpet-shaped flowers. **Height:** 10"–18". **Spacing:** 12".	Shear back plants to promote bushy growth and repeat bloom.
Portulaca grandiflora **Rose moss**	White, pink, red, yellow, orange, or magenta single or double roselike flowers; spreading plants with needle-like, succulent leaves. **Height:** 4"–8". **Spacing:** 12".	Thrives on very hot, dry sites and poor soils.
Rudbeckia hirta 'Gloriosa Daisy' **Gloriosa daisy**	Yellow, gold, orange, and mahogany daisy flowers with dark, cone-shaped centers. **Height:** 2'–3'. **Spacing:** 1'.	Plants self-sow and are drought-tolerant. Excellent cut flowers.
Salvia splendens **Scarlet sage**	Spikes of white, pink, purple, or brilliant red tubular flowers. **Height:** 8"–36". **Spacing:** 12".	Plant light-colored flowers in partial shade for best color.

ANNUALS FOR FULL SUN—CONTINUED

PLANT NAME	DESCRIPTION	COMMENTS
Sanvitalia procumbens **Creeping zinnia**	Small, yellow, daisylike flowers with dark centers; creeping plant. **Height:** 6". **Spacing:** 12".	Heat-and drought-tolerant. Plant as an edging or in rock gardens.
Tagetes erecta **African marigold**	Large, pom-pom-shaped semidouble or double flowers of orange, gold, yellow, cream, or white. **Height:** 14"–36". **Spacing:** 18"–30", depending on the size of the cultivar.	Strongly scented foliage. Plant shorter cultivars to avoid staking against rain and winds.
Tagetes patula **French marigold**	Orange, yellow, gold, or maroon solid or bicolored flowers in a variety of forms including single, double, and crested. **Height:** 6"–14". **Spacing:** 6"–12".	Strongly scented foliage. More compact than African marigolds. Deadhead for continuous bloom.
Tithonia rotundifolia **Mexican sunflower**	Reddish orange, daisylike flowers with yellow centers. **Height:** 3'–6'. **Spacing:** 2'.	Heat- and drought-tolerant.
Tropaeolum majus **Garden nasturtium**	Edible flowers in yellow, orange, or red; rounded leaves. **Height:** Climbing types can reach 8'; dwarf types reach 1'. **Spacing:** 2'–3' for vines; 1' for dwarfs.	Prefers average soil; rich soil results in many leaves and few flowers. Grow climbers up a trellis or as a groundcover.
Verbena x *hybrida* **Garden verbena**	Dense clusters of white, yellow, pink, red, or violet flowers, some with white centers; upright and trailing forms. **Height:** 8"–12". **Spacing:** 10"–12".	Plant in well-drained soil.
Zinnia angustifolia (also sold as *Z. linearis*) **Narrowleaf zinnia**	Single, golden orange, daisylike flowers; white-flowered cultivars are available. **Height:** 1'. **Spacing:** 1'.	Extremely tolerant of heat and humidity; mildew-resistant.

ANNUALS FOR SHADE

Few annuals thrive in shade; most need lots of sunlight to complete their breakneck life cycles in a summer's time. But a select group of annuals—many actually tender perennials—will brighten shady spots without complaint. Several of the plants listed below will also grow in sunny conditions, if they have shade to protect them from the hot midday sun.

PLANT NAME	DESCRIPTION	COMMENTS
Anchusa capensis **Summer forget-me-not**	Clusters of ¼" blue, pink, or white flowers; somewhat coarse, hairy foliage. **Height:** 16". **Spacing:** 12".	Tolerates poor soil; needs good drainage. Will flower again if cut back after first bloom.
Begonia Semperflorens-Cultorum hybrid **Wax begonia**	Flowers and seedpods in shades of white, pink, and red; succulent, waxy, bright green, bronze, maroon, or white-variegated foliage. **Height:** To 15". **Spacing:** 6"–10".	Full or partial shade; rich, evenly moist soil. Tolerant of sun in cool-summer climates.
Browallia speciosa **Browallia**	Showy, funnel-shaped flowers in white and shades of blue; mintlike foliage. **Height:** 8"–14". **Spacing:** 6"–10".	Moist soil; excess fertility results in many leaves and few flowers.
Caladium x *hortulanum* **Caladium**	Heart-shaped leaves marked with various combinations of pink, white, red, and green. **Height:** 12"–24". **Spacing:** 8".	Dig up tubers after the first frost and save to replant next spring.
Coleus x *hybridus* **Coleus**	Brightly colored, sometimes ruffled, foliage in various mixtures of red, yellow, pink, chartreuse, purple, and white; spikes of small, lavender-white flowers. **Height:** 8"–18". **Spacing:** 6"–10".	Moist soil; tolerates full shade. Pinch off flowers as they emerge for best appearance. Tolerates sun, but foliage may fade.
Impatiens New Guinea hybrids **New Guinea impatiens**	Flat, brightly colored flowers of white, pink, red, orange, or purple; leaves elongated (to 8") and often variegated with yellow, white, and/or red. **Height:** 1'–2'. **Spacing:** 1'–2'.	More sun-tolerant than *I. wallerana,* but only in cool regions and with moist soil.

ANNUALS FOR SHADE—CONTINUED

PLANT NAME	DESCRIPTION	COMMENTS
Impatiens wallerana **Impatiens**	Flat, single or double pink, red, orange, lavender, or white flowers; succulent stems and glossy foliage. **Height:** 6"–24". **Spacing:** 12".	Performs best in moist, richly organic soil; tolerates full shade.
Lobelia erinus **Edging lobelia**	Blue, white, or red irregular flowers on low, trailing plants. **Height:** 6". **Spacing:** 6".	Tolerates sun in cooler regions. Cut plants back in midsummer to promote continued bloom.
Myosotis sylvatica **Garden forget-me-not**	Tiny blue, pink, or white flowers appear to float over low, oval foliage. **Height:** 10". **Spacing:** 6".	Prefers moist sites; tolerates wet soil. Biennial; reseeds readily.
Nemophila menziesii **Baby-blue-eyes**	Bright blue flowers with white centers; bright green, lobed leaves. **Height:** 6"–10". **Spacing:** 6".	Well-drained soil. Sun-tolerant with even moisture and cool temperatures. Self-sows.
Nicotiana alata **Flowering tobacco**	Fragrant, star-shaped flowers in white, yellow, green, or shades of red; low rosettes of large leaves. **Height:** 12"–36". **Spacing:** 9"–12".	Rich, moist soil; tolerates heat and humidity. Self-sows.
Nierembergia hippomanica var. *violacea* **Blue cupflower**	Cup-shaped violet-blue flowers with yellow centers; fine-textured foliage. **Height:** 6". **Spacing:** 6".	Tolerates full sun, but needs shade in hot-summer climates.
Torenia fournieri **Wishbone flower**	Snapdragon-like flowers combine white, yellow, and shades of purple; glossy foliage. **Height:** 12". **Spacing:** 6"–8".	Tolerates full shade; prefers moist conditions.
Viola x *wittrockiana* **Pansy**	Showy, flat blooms in solid colors or with markings that look like faces, in white or shades of yellow, blue, purple, red, and orange. **Height:** 6"–12". **Spacing:** 6".	Cold-resistant. Performs best in cool weather in rich, moist, well-drained soil.

PERENNIALS FOR FULL SUN

Look up the cultural requirements for most perennials and you'll see "Thrives in full sun and evenly moist soil." But what can a gardener plant in spots where the sun beats down on *unevenly* moist soil or, worse yet, dry soil?

Choose durable plants from the list below. Most will grow in full sun and dry soil with minimal watering once they're established. Exceptions are noted.

PLANT NAME	DESCRIPTION	COMMENTS
Achillea 'Moonshine' **'Moonshine' yarrow**	Flat heads of pale yellow flowers in summer; ferny blue-gray foliage. **Height:** 1'–2'. **Spacing:** 1'–2'.	This compact yarrow seldom needs staking. **Zones 3–8.**
Allium spp. **Alliums**	Rounded or flat-topped clusters of pink, purple, or white flowers in spring, summer, or fall, depending on the species; fleshy, straplike leaves. **Height:** ½'–5'. **Spacing:** 1'–2', depending on the species.	Well-drained to almost-dry soil. Plant alliums where other plants will hide their fading foliage. **Zones 4–8.**
Anemone tomentosa 'Robustissima' **Japanese anemone**	Single pink flowers in fall; divided, dark green, grapelike foliage. **Height:** 2'–3'. **Spacing:** 2'.	Rich, evenly moist soil. Tolerates light shade. **Zones 3–8.**
Armeria maritima **Common thrift**	Dense, 1" heads of rose-pink flowers on long stems in late spring and summer over gray-green grassy foliage. **Height:** 10"–14". **Spacing:** 10".	Tolerant of salt and poor soil; dislikes high heat and humidity. **Zones 3–8.**
Artemisia 'Powis Castle' **'Powis Castle' artemisia**	Deeply cut, aromatic, silvery white foliage; compact form. **Height:** 2'–3'. **Spacing:** 2'–3'.	Drought-tolerant once established; may need winter protection. **Zones 5–8.**
Asclepias tuberosa **Butterfly weed**	Flat clusters of orange, red, or yellow flowers in summer; lance-shaped leaves. **Height:** 1'–3'. **Spacing:** 1'.	Tolerates light shade. Resents transplanting. **Zones 3–9.**
Aster novae-angliae **New England aster**	Showy purple daisies with yellow centers in late summer; leafy stems. Cultivars with pink, red, or blue flowers are available. **Height:** 3'–6'. **Spacing:** 2'–4'.	Evenly moist soil. Tartarian aster (*A. tataricus*) is more drought-tolerant. **Zones 3–8.**

PERENNIALS FOR FULL SUN—CONTINUED

PLANT NAME	DESCRIPTION	COMMENTS
Baptisia australis **Blue false indigo**	Spikes of pealike blue or white flowers in early summer; plants reach shrublike proportions. **Height:** 2'–4'. **Spacing:** 1'–3'.	Gray-black seedpods add interest through the winter. **Zones 3–9.**
Bergenia cordifolia **Heart-leaved bergenia**	Rosettes of rounded, leathery, evergreen leaves; nodding clusters of fleshy pink or white flowers in early spring. **Height:** 12"–14". **Spacing:** 18".	Tolerates partial shade. Foliage turns bronze to purple in cold weather. **Zones 3–9.**
Boltonia asteroides **Boltonia**	Single, white or pink daisylike flowers in late summer and fall; blue-green willowlike foliage. **Height:** 4'–6'. **Spacing:** 3'.	Drought-tolerant once established. May need staking in rich soil. **Zones 3–9.**
Chrysanthemum pacificum **Gold-and-silver chrysanthemum**	Attractive gray-green foliage edged with white; yellow button flowers in fall. **Height:** 12"–18". **Spacing:** 12".	Well-drained soil; tolerates drought and partial shade. Mulch for winter protection in northern areas. **Zones 5–9.**
Chrysanthemum ×superbum **Shasta daisy**	White daisies with bright yellow centers in late summer and fall; deep green foliage. Cultivars offer double flowers, compact growth. **Height:** 1'–3'. **Spacing:** 1½'–2'.	Tolerates dry, sandy soils; good drainage is a must. Hardiness varies by cultivar; generally **Zones 4–8.**
Coreopsis verticillata **Threadleaf coreopsis**	Numerous daisylike yellow flowers in summer; fine-textured foliage. 'Moonbeam' bears pale yellow flowers on 1'–2' plants. **Height:** 1'–3'. **Spacing:** 2'.	Drought-tolerant once established. Blooms for 2–3 months. **Zones 3–9.**
Echinacea purpurea **Purple coneflower**	Single, daisylike rose-pink or creamy white flowers with cone-shaped brown centers in summer; coarse, lance-shaped leaves. **Height:** 2'–4'. **Spacing:** 2'.	Drought-tolerant. Seed heads provide winter interest; may self-sow. **Zones 3-8.**
Eupatorium purpureum **Joe-Pye weed**	Mounded clusters of pale rose or purple, sweetly scented flowers in late summer to fall; whorled, lance-shaped foliage. **Height:** 3'–6'. **Spacing:** 2'–4'.	Best in moist sites; tolerates light shade. **Zones 3–8.**

PERENNIALS FOR FULL SUN—CONTINUED

PLANT NAME	DESCRIPTION	COMMENTS
Filipendula rubra **Queen-of-the-prairie**	Large, fluffy clusters of pink or rose flowers in summer; bold, pinnately divided foliage. **Height:** 4'–6'. **Spacing:** 2'.	Thrives in moist sites; tolerates partial shade. **Zones 3–9.**
Gaillardia aristata **Blanket flower**	Yellow-petaled daisies (often with brown bands) with purple-brown centers; lobed, hairy foliage. **Height:** 2'–2½'. **Spacing:** 1'–1½'.	Tolerates drought, heat, and salt; may flop in rich soil. **Zones 2–10.**
Gaura lindheimeri **White gaura**	Spikes of white flowers from summer to frost; shrubby, deep green foliage. **Height:** 3'–4'. **Spacing:** 1'–2'.	Drought-tolerant once established, but best with evenly moist soil. **Zones 5–9.**
Geranium sanguineum **Blood-red cranesbill**	Flat, pink flowers in summer above mounds of rounded, finely cut leaves. **Height:** 9"–12". **Spacing:** 2'.	Moist, well-drained soil. Tolerates light shade and drought. **Zones 3–8.**
Hemerocallis hybrids **Modern daylily cultivars**	Showy, trumpet-shaped summer flowers in every color but blue; strap-shaped to grassy foliage. Some selections have fragrant flowers. **Height:** 2'–3'. **Spacing:** 2'–3'.	Tolerates light to partial shade. Divide clumps every few years for propagation or to control spread. **Zones 2–9.**
Iris sibirica **Siberian iris**	Purple, blue, white, or yellow flowers in late spring; narrow, sword-shaped foliage. Many excellent cultivars are available. **Height:** To 3'. **Spacing:** 3'.	Moist, well-drained soil. Foliage is attractive all season. **Zones 2–9.**
Liatris spicata **Spike gayfeather**	Spikes of densely packed red- to blue-violet or white flowers in summer; long, grasslike leaves cover stems. **Height:** 2'–3'. **Spacing:** 1'.	Average, well-drained soil. Plants grow tall in rich soil and need staking. **Zones 3–9.**
Lilium lancifolium **Tiger lily**	Clusters of wide, nodding, trumpet-shaped orange flowers with black spots; grasslike leaves cover stems. **Height:** 4'–6'. **Spacing:** 2'.	Needs well-drained soil. May self-sow from bulbils, or small bulbs, produced in leaf axils. **Zones 3–9.**

PERENNIALS FOR FULL SUN—CONTINUED

PLANT NAME	DESCRIPTION	COMMENTS
Monarda didyma **Bee balm**	Red, pink, creamy white, or purplish flower heads borne on square stems above aromatic mintlike foliage. **Height:** 2'–4'. **Spacing:** 1½'.	Good for moist sites in sun or partial shade; needs good air circulation. **Zones 4–8.**
Nepeta × *faassenii* **Catmint**	Spiky clusters of deep violet flowers in early summer; soft, gray-green leaves cover stems. **Height:** 1½'–2'. **Spacing:** 1½'.	Cut back by one-half to two-thirds after flowering to promote compact growth and possible rebloom. **Zones 3–8.**
Oenothera fruticosa **Sundrops**	Bright yellow, saucer-shaped flowers in spring and summer; lance-shaped foliage. **Height:** 1½'–2'. **Spacing:** 1'.	Tolerates drought and light shade. Spreads to form dense clumps. **Zones 4–8.**
Patrinia scabiosifolia **Patrinia**	Profuse clusters of tiny yellow flowers in late summer and fall. **Height:** 3'–6'. **Spacing:** 1'.	Tolerates dry conditions and light shade. Self-sows. **Zones 4–9.**
Phlox paniculata **Garden phlox**	Clusters of magenta, pink, or white flowers in summer to early fall; stiff upright stems clothed in dull green, lance-shaped leaves. Many cultivars offer other flower colors and mildew resistance. **Height:** 3'–3½'. **Spacing:** 2'.	Best in cool-summer regions and well-drained soil. Thin stems to promote good air circulation. Long blooming period. **Zones 3–8.**
Platycodon grandiflorus **Balloon flower**	Balloon-shaped buds open to single or double flowers of blue, white, or pink in summer; triangular leaves on clump-forming plants. **Height:** 2'–3'. **Spacing:** 1'.	Tolerates partial shade. Remove spent flowers to prolong bloom. Slow to emerge in spring. **Zones 3–8.**
Rudbeckia fulgida **Orange coneflower**	Showy orange-yellow daisies with deep brown centers in mid- to late summer; coarse, broadly lance-shaped leaves. *R. fulgida* var. *sullivantii* 'Goldsturm' is a compact, long-blooming cultivar. **Height:** 1½'–3'. **Spacing:** 1½'.	Tolerates average soil, heat, and humidity. Flowering may continue for over a month. **Zones 3–9.**

PERENNIALS FOR FULL SUN—CONTINUED

PLANT NAME	DESCRIPTION	COMMENTS
Salvia × *superba* **Violet sage**	Stiff spikes of violet-blue flowers in early to midsummer; bright green, triangular leaves. 'East Friesland' is compact with deep purple blooms. **Height:** 1½'–3½'. **Spacing:** 1½'–2½'.	Tough and extremely drought-tolerant; takes light shade. Deadhead to encourage rebloom. **Zones 4–7.**
Sedum spp. **Sedums and stonecrops**	Thick, succulent, waxy foliage in many colors, tints, and variegations; domed or flat flower clusters of white, pink, red, or yellow in spring or summer. Mostly grown for foliage, but hybrids such as 'Autumn Joy' offer showy flowers, too. **Height:** Low trailing forms and upright plants to 2'. **Spacing:** 1'–2', depending on species.	Very tolerant of drought and heat; low-growing species tolerate partial shade. **Zones 4–8.**
Solidago spp. **Goldenrods**	Spikelike, flat-topped, or plumelike clusters of lemon-yellow or golden flowers in summer to fall; lance-shaped to oval foliage. *S. canadensis* spreads invasively. **Height:** 1'–5'. **Spacing:** 1'.	Tolerates drought, poor soil, and light shade. May grow rampant and floppy in rich soil. **Zones 4–8.**
Veronica spp. **Speedwells**	Spikes or clusters of tubular, flat-faced flowers of white, pink, purple, or blue in spring or summer; narrow, lance-shaped to oblong leaves. **Height:** Creeping or upright forms to 4'. **Spacing:** 1'–1½'.	Tolerates heat, drought, and light shade. **Zones 4–8.**

PERENNIALS FOR SHADE

Your garden's shady spots deserve flowers, too. Dress up the areas beneath trees and around buildings with the shade-tolerant and shade-loving perennials listed below. In addition to these plants, try spring-flowering bulbs. They need full sun, but they thrive beneath deciduous trees since they bloom before the trees leaf out.

PLANT NAME	DESCRIPTION	COMMENTS
Aquilegia canadensis **Wild columbine**	Nodding red-and-yellow flowers in spring and early summer; mounds of compound, blue-green leaves. **Height:** 1'–3'. **Spacing:** 1'.	Plants may be short-lived but self-sow readily. **Zones 3–8.**
Aruncus dioicus **Goat's beard**	Upright plumes of creamy white flowers in late spring and early summer; mounds of shiny, deep green, compound leaves. **Height:** 3'–6'. **Spacing:** 3'–4'.	Best in partial shade; tolerant of sun in cool areas with constantly moist soil. **Zones 3–7.**
Astilbe x *arendsii* **Astilbe**	Upright plumes of white, pink, purple, or red flowers in summer; glossy divided foliage. **Height:** 2'–4'. **Spacing:** 1½'–2½'.	Needs consistently moist soil. Deer-resistant. **Zones 3–9.**
Begonia grandis **Hardy begonia**	Nodding clusters of pink flowers, followed by pink seedpods, appear over large, pointed leaves in late summer. **Height:** 1'–2'. **Spacing:** 1'.	Best in moist shade; tolerates more sun in cooler climates. **Zones 6–10.**
Brunnera macrophylla **Siberian bugloss**	Blue flowers, similar to forget-me-nots, in early spring. Heart-shaped leaves expand to 6"–8" and are attractive all season. **Height:** 1'–1½'. **Spacing:** 1'.	At its best in moist soil. Tolerates drier sites but produces smaller leaves. **Zones 3–8.**
Chelone lyonii **Pink turtlehead**	Spikes of inflated rose-pink flowers in late summer; lush, broadly oval leaves. *C. glabra* has pink-flushed white flowers. **Height:** 1'–3'. **Spacing:** 1'–2'.	Partial shade to full sun, with constantly moist soil; good plants for wet areas. **Zones 3–8.**
Chrysogonum virginianum **Green and gold**	Yellow daisies in spring; hairy, nearly evergreen, tidy foliage. **Height:** To 1'. **Spacing:** 1'.	Partial shade and well-drained soil. May bloom into fall. **Zones 6–9.**

PERENNIALS FOR SHADE—CONTINUED

PLANT NAME	DESCRIPTION	COMMENTS
Cimicifuga racemosa **Black snakeroot**	Tall branching spikes of white flowers in early summer; large, compound leaves. **Height:** 4'–7'. **Spacing:** 2'.	Plants take several years to reach mature size. **Zones 3–8.**
Convallaria majalis **Lily-of-the-valley**	Fragrant, bell-shaped, white flowers in spring; broad, pointed leaves. 'Rosea' has pink flowers. **Height:** 6"–8". **Spacing:** 12".	Tolerates partial to full shade. Forms a dense groundcover. **Zones 2–8.**
Dicentra eximia **Fringed bleeding heart**	Clusters of pink or white heart-shaped flowers in late spring to early fall; ferny blue-green foliage. **Height:** 10"–18". **Spacing:** 12"–18".	Tolerates more sun in cool climates with moist soil. Flowers over a long period of time. **Zones 3–9.**
Digitalis grandiflora **Yellow foxglove**	Spikes of soft, yellow, tubular flowers in summer; dense rosettes of broad green leaves. **Height:** 2'–3'. **Spacing:** 1'–1½'.	Sow seeds outdoors in late summer; may not bloom until second year. Deer-resistant. **Zones 3–8.**
Epimedium spp. **Epimediums**	Sprays of white, yellow, bronze, red, or pink flowers in spring; groundcovering semi-evergreen, heart-shaped leaves. **Height:** 6"–15". **Spacing:** 12"–18".	Tolerates dry shade once established. Deer-resistant. **Zones 4–8.**
Geranium maculatum **Wild cranesbill**	Loose clusters of pink or white flowers in late spring; open clumps of starry, rounded leaves **Height:** 1'–2'. **Spacing:**1'.	Tolerates more sun in cool regions and moist, well-drained soil. **Zones 4–8.**
Helleborus orientalis **Lenten rose**	Clusters of nodding white, pink, rose, or purple flowers in early spring; mostly evergreen, compound leaves. **Height:** 1½'. **Spacing:** 2'.	Tolerates deep summer shade if given sun in spring before trees leaf out. May self-sow. **Zones 4–9.**
Hosta spp. **Hostas**	Spikes of sometimes-fragrant, narrowly funnel-shaped, white to lavender flowers in summer and fall; green, yellow, or blue leaves, in single colors or variegated forms, with rough or smooth textures. **Height:** 10"–3'. **Spacing:** 1'–4', depending on species.	Best in evenly moist soil. Flowers not showy in many selections. Many hostas grow slowly and take 2–4 years to reach full size. **Zones 3–8.**

PERENNIALS FOR SHADE—CONTINUED

PLANT NAME	DESCRIPTION	COMMENTS
Iris cristata **Crested iris**	Sky-blue spring flowers with a yellow-and-white blaze over fans of short, broad leaves. *I. cristata* var. *alba* has white flowers. **Height:** 4"–8". **Spacing:** 12".	Moist soil and partial shade. Plants spread via creeping rhizomes. **Zones 3–9.**
Lobelia siphilitica **Great blue lobelia**	Dense spikes of deep to light blue or violet-blue flowers from midsummer into fall on leafy stems; clumps of medium green, oblong leaves. **Height:** 2'–3'. **Spacing:** 1.'	Needs constantly moist soil; tolerates full sun in cool-summer regions. **Zones 4–8.**
Mertensia virginica **Virginia bluebells**	Pink buds open to nodding clusters of sky-blue, bell-shaped flowers in spring; low, broad, green leaves. **Height:** 1'–2'. **Spacing:** 1½'.	Plants go dormant after flowering. Self-sows readily. **Zones 3–9.**
Phlox divaricata **Wild blue phlox**	Open clusters of fragrant blue or white flowers in early spring; broadly lance-shaped leaves. **Height:** 9"–18". **Spacing:** 12".	Light to full shade. Forms dense clumps of evergreen leaves. **Zones 3–9.**
Phlox stolonifera **Creeping phlox**	Open clusters of magenta to pink, blue, or white flowers in spring; dense clumps of oval evergreen leaves. **Height:** 6"–8". **Spacing:** 12".	Light to full shade. A creeping groundcover with attractive foliage. **Zones 2–8.**
Polemonium reptans **Creeping polemonium, creeping Jacob's ladder**	Clusters of cup-shaped blue flowers in late spring; mounds of fernlike foliage. **Height:** 8"–16". **Spacing:** 12".	Tolerates full sun, but prefers partial shade in warm regions. **Zones 2–8.**
Polygonatum odoratum **Fragrant Solomon's seal**	Long, fragrant, white flowers hang in pairs from arching stems in late spring; oval green leaves. 'Variegatum' grows to 3' and has white-edged leaves. **Height:** 1½'–2½'. **Spacing:** 1'.	Prefers humus-rich, moist soil but will tolerate drought. **Zones 3–9.**
Primula vulgaris **English primrose**	Clear yellow blossoms in early spring above dense rosettes of leaves. **Height:** To 8". **Spacing:** 10".	Enjoys moist to very moist soil. **Zones 4–8.**

PERENNIALS FOR SHADE—CONTINUED

PLANT NAME	DESCRIPTION	COMMENTS
Pulmonaria saccharata **Bethlehem sage**	Clusters of pink buds and blue, pink, or white flowers in early spring; heart-shaped green leaves spotted with silver. **Height:** 9"–18". **Spacing:** 2'.	Moderately drought-tolerant once established; tolerates full shade. **Zones 3–8.**
Saxifraga stolonifera **Strawberry geranium, Mother-of-thousands**	Airy spikes of tiny white flowers in summer; rounded green leaves with silver veins and red undersides. **Height:** 4"–9". **Spacing:** 6"–12".	Tolerates dry shade. Often sold as a houseplant. **Zones 6–8.**
Smilacina racemosa **False Solomon's plume**	Plumes of fuzzy white flowers in late spring; oval green leaves cover arching stems. **Height:** 2'–4'. **Spacing:** 1'–1½'.	Tolerates light to full shade. Red-and-white speckled berries. **Zones 3–8.**
Tiarella cordifolia **Allegheny foamflower**	Spikes of fuzzy white to pale pink flowers in spring; rosettes of heart-shaped to triangular leaves. **Height:** 6"–10". **Spacing:** 18".	Tolerates partial to full shade in moist soil. Spreads to form an attractive groundcover. **Zones 3–8.**
Tricyrtis hirta **Common toad lily**	White or yellow, purple-spotted flowers cluster in leaf axils and atop stems in late summer and fall. Broadly lance-shaped foliage. **Height:** 2'–3'. **Spacing:** 1½'.	Best in light to partial shade. Plants may self-sow if seeds have time to ripen. **Zones 4–9.**
Trollius chinensis **Chinese globeflower**	Waxy, bowl-shaped, single or double yellow flowers in spring; finely divided palmate foliage. **Height:** 2'-3'. **Spacing:** 1'.	Moist to wet, rich soil in partial shade. Dislikes hot summer temperatures. **Zones 3–6.**
Viola spp. **Violets**	Irregularly shaped purple, blue, white, red, or bicolored flowers in spring amid rounded, heart- or kidney-shaped basal leaves. **Height:** 1"-12". **Spacing:** 6"-12".	Spreads by creeping stems and seedlings; may become invasive. Canada violet (*V. canadensis*) and woolly blue violet (*V. sororia*) are hardy to Zone 3. **Zones 6-9.**

GROUNDCOVERS

Groundcovers offer a quick way to hide your garden's bare spots, and they serve as a living mulch against weeds and moisture loss. Choose sun-loving groundcovers for banks and rock gardens. Use shade lo[...] and shrubs. Most of the gr[...] thrive in average to rich soil.

PLANT NAME	DESCRIPTION	COMMENTS
Aegopodium podagraria **Goutweed, bishop's weed**	Light-green, divided leaves. 'Variegatum' has creamy-white-edged leaves and is less invasive than the species. **Height:** 1'–1½'. **Spacing:** 1'.	Full or partial shade. Thrives in the dry shade under trees. Can be invasive. **Zones 4–9.**
Ajuga reptans **Ajuga**	Green or bronze leaves; blue flower spikes in late spring and early summer. 'Burgundy Glow' has white, pink, and green leaves. 'Pink Beauty' has pink flowers and green foliage. **Height:** 4"–10". **Spacing:** 8".	Well-drained soil; sun or shade; tolerates dry shade. **Zones 3–9.**
Asarum europaeum **European wild ginger**	Glossy, evergreen, heart-shaped leaves, delicately veined with white; small, brown, jug-shaped flowers are hidden by the foliage. **Height:** 6"–8". **Spacing:** 12".	Moist, humus-rich soil; shade. Plant under shrubs or along walks. **Zones 4–8.**
Ceratostigma plumbaginoides **Leadwort, plumbago**	Deep-blue flowers in midsummer and fall; neat, diamond-shaped foliage turns deep red in autumn. **Height:** 6"–12". **Spacing:** 12".	Moist, well-drained soil; full sun or light shade. Shear plants back if leggy. **Zones 5–8.**
Fragaria spp. **Strawberries**	White flowers and edible red fruits from spring through late summer. Alpine strawberries (*F. vesca*) produce few or no runners. 'Pink Panther', a garden strawberry hybrid, has pink flowers and produces runners. **Height:** 8"–10". **Spacing:** 8".	Humus-rich soil; full sun or partial shade. Strawberries without runners make neat border plants. **Zones 3–9.**
Galium odoratum **Sweet woodruff**	Whorls of green, lance-shaped leaves; dainty white flowers in spring. **Height:** 4"–10". **Spacing:** 12".	Moist soil; partial shade. Dried foliage smells spicy. **Zones 4–8.**

GROUNDCOVERS—CONTINUED

PLANT NAME	DESCRIPTION	COMMENTS
Gypsophila repens **Creeping baby's-breath**	Clusters of airy flowers; blue-green foliage; spreads to form a low mat. 'Alba' has white flowers. 'Rosea' has pale-pink flowers. **Height:** 4"–8". **Spacing:** 1'.	Moist, neutral to slightly alkaline, well-drained soil; full sun or light shade. **Zones 3–8.**
Hedera helix **English ivy**	Glossy, evergreen, 3–5 lobed leaves on long, trailing stems. 'Bulgaria' is very cold-hardy. **Height:** 6"–8". **Spacing:** 2'.	Moist, well-drained soil; full to partial shade. **Zones 4–9.**
Hypericum calycinum **St.-John's-wort**	Bright, puffy, yellow flowers in summer and fall; dark green foliage turns reddish purple in autumn. **Height:** 1'–1½'. **Spacing:** 1½'.	Thrives in sandy soil; full sun or light shade. Does not flower well in rich soil. **Zones 5–8.**
Lamiastrum galeobdolon **Yellow archangel**	Whorls of yellow flowers in spring; silver-variegated leaves. 'Herman's Pride' is less aggressive than the species. **Height:** 8"–14". **Spacing:** 2'.	Well-drained soil; full or partial shade. Plants spread rapidly and may be invasive. **Zones 4–9.**
Lamium maculatum **Spotted lamium**	Pink flowers in spring; silver-variegated leaves. 'Beacon Silver' has rose-pink flowers. 'White Nancy' has white flowers. **Height:** 6"–12". **Spacing:** 12".	Humus-rich, moist but well-drained soil; full or partial shade. Shear leggy plants back. **Zones 3–8.**
Liriope muscari **Big blue lilyturf**	Grasslike, evergreen leaves; violet or white flowers in late summer. 'John Burch' has yellow-variegated leaves and lilac flowers. **Height:** 1½'. **Spacing:** 1'.	Well-drained soil; full sun to full shade. Plant under trees or use as an edging. **Zones 6–9.**
Matteuccia struthiopteris **Ostrich fern**	Tall, feathery, light green leaves. **Height:** 2–4'. **Spacing:** 1½'–2'.	Rich, moist soil; full or partial shade. **Zones 2–9.**
Miscanthus sinensis **Japanese silver grass**	Clumps of narrow, arching, green leaves; variegated forms are available; feathery flowers on tall stalks in summer, may turn reddish, silvery, or brown in fall. **Height:** Varies from 3'–8', depending on the cultivar. **Spacing:** 2' or more.	Rich, moist soil; full sun. Use these grasses to cover large, open areas. Their tall size gives them a bold look. Both foliage and flowers are attractive. **Zones 5–9.**

GROUNDCOVERS—CONTINUED

PLANT NAME	DESCRIPTION	COMMENTS
Origanum vulgare **Wild marjoram**	Fragrant, hairy leaves; white to purple flowers in summer. 'Aureum' has yellow leaves. **Height:** 1½'–2½'. **Spacing:** 1'.	Average, well-drained soil; full sun. Avoid rich soil. **Zones 3–10.**
Pachysandra terminalis **Japanese pachysandra**	Glossy, evergreen leaves; white flowers in spring. Allegheny pachysandra (*P. procumbens*) is not as vigorous but has attractive purple mottled leaves. **Height:** 6"–12". **Spacing:** 18".	Full to partial shade. Use under trees for a low-maintenance carpet. **Zones 5–9.**
Phlox subulata **Moss pink**	Bright pink, blue, or white flowers in early spring; low, mounded plants with bright green, needle-like foliage. **Height:** 4"–8". **Spacing:** 10"–12".	Well-drained soil; full sun. **Zones 2–9.**
Sedum spurium **Two-row sedum**	Mat-forming plants covered with small, succulent leaves; pink or red flowers. 'Dragon's Blood' has reddish bronze leaves. **Height:** 2"–6". **Spacing:** 1½'.	Well-drained soil; full sun. Drought-tolerant and excellent for rock gardens. **Zones 3–8.**
Sempervivum tectorum **Hens-and-chickens**	Thick, succulent, evergreen leaves arranged in tight rosettes; reddish purple flowers. **Height:** 8"–12". **Spacing:** 10".	Well-drained soil; full sun. New plants form around the base of the mother plant. **Zones 3-8.**
Thymus serpyllum **Mother-of-thyme**	Tiny, fragrant, evergreen leaves on low, mat-forming plants; purple flowers in summer. 'Albus' has white flowers. 'Coccineus' has red flowers. **Height:** 4". **Spacing:** 10".	Well-drained soil; full sun; light shade in the South. **Zones 3–9.**
Vinca minor **Common periwinkle**	Small, evergreen leaves on trailing stems; lavender flowers in spring. 'Alba' has white flowers. 'Bowles' Variety' has blue flowers. **Height:** 4"–6". **Spacing:** 2'.	Moist but well-drained soil; full or partial shade. **Zones 4–9.**
Waldensteinia ternata **Barren strawberry**	Small yellow flowers in spring; mats of evergreen, strawberry-like leaves. **Height:** 8"–12". **Spacing:** 12".	Well-drained soil; full sun or light shade. Does best in cool climates. **Zones 4–7.**

Sources

The following mail-order companies are listed according to the types of plants or garden supplies they offer. For best results, buy plants that were grown in the region of the country where you live.

Annuals, Bulbs, and Perennials

Bluestone Perennials
7211 Middle Ridge Road
Madison, OH 44057

W. Atlee Burpee and Co.
300 Park Avenue
Warminster, PA 18974

Carroll Gardens
P.O. Box 310
444 East Main Street
Westminster, MD 21158

Hastings Seeds
P.O. Box 115535
1036 White Street SW
Atlanta, GA 30310-8535

Holbrook Farm & Nursery
115 Lance Road
P.O. Box 368
Fletcher, NC 28732

McClure & Zimmerman
P.O. Box 368
108 West Winnebago Street
Friesland, WI 53935

Milaeger's Gardens
4838 Douglas Avenue
Racine, WI 53402

Park Seed Co.
P.O. Box 31
Cokesbury Road
Greenwood, SC 29647

Thompson & Morgan, Inc.
P.O. Box 1308
Jackson, NJ 08527

White Flower Farm
Litchfield, CT 06759

Herbs

Companion Plants
7247 North Coolville Ridge
   Road
Athens, OH 45701

Nichols Garden Nursery
1190 North Pacific Highway
Albany, OR 97321

Sandy Mush Herb Nursery
316 Surrett Cove Road
Leicester, NC 28748

Water Gardens

Lilypons Water Gardens
P.O. Box 10
6800 Lilypons Road
Buckeystown, MD 21717

William Tricker, Inc.
7125 Tanglewood Drive
Independence, OH 44131

Wildflowers and Native Plants

Forestfarm
990 Tetherow Road
Williams, OR 97544

Niche Gardens
1111 Dawson Road
Chapel Hill, NC 27516

Plants of the Southwest
Route 6, Box 11-A
Santa Fe, NM 87501

Prairie Nursery
P.O. Box 306
Westfield, WI 53964

Wildseed Farms, Inc.
P.O. Box 308
Eagle Lake, TX 77434

Tools, Supplies, and Garden Accessories

Gardener's Supply Co.
128 Intervale Road
Burlington, VT 05401

Gardens Alive!
5100 Schenley Place
Lawrenceburg, IN 47025

The Kinsman Co.
River Road
Point Pleasant, PA 18950

Peaceful Valley Farm Supply
P.O. Box 2209
Grass Valley, CA 95945

Recommended Reading

General Gardening

Ball, Jeff and Liz Ball. *Rodale's Flower Garden Problem Solver*. Emmaus, Pa.: Rodale Press, 1990.

Bradley, Fern Marshall, and Barbara W. Ellis, eds. *Rodale's All-New Encyclopedia of Organic Gardening*. Emmaus, Pa.: Rodale Press, 1992.

Bubel, Nancy. *The New Seed-Starters Handbook*. Emmaus, Pa.: Rodale Press, 1988.

Bush-Brown, James, and Louise Bush-Brown. *America's Garden Book*. rev. ed. New York: Charles Scribner's Sons, 1980.

Ellis, Barbara W., ed. *Rodale's Illustrated Encyclopedia of Gardening and Landscaping Techniques*. Emmaus, Pa.: Rodale Press, 1990.

Ellis, Barbara W., and Fern Marshall Bradley, eds. *The Organic Gardener's Handbook of Natural Insect and Disease Control*. Emmaus, Pa.: Rodale Press, 1992.

Wyman, Donald. *Wyman's Gardening Encyclopedia*. 2d ed. New York: Macmillan Publishing Co., 1986.

Perennials

Harper, Pamela, and Frederick McGourty. *Perennials: How to Select, Grow, and Enjoy*. Los Angeles: Price Stern Sloan, Inc., 1985.

McClure, Susan, and C. Colston Burrell. *Rodale's Successful Organic Gardening: Perennials*. Emmaus, Pa.: Rodale Press, 1993.

Phillips, Ellen, and C. Colston Burrell. *Rodale's Illustrated Encyclopedia of Perennials*. Emmaus, Pa.: Rodale Press, 1993.

Taylor, Norman. *Taylor's Guide to Perennials*. rev. ed. Boston: Houghton Mifflin Co., 1986.

Special Gardens

Appleton, Bonnie Lee, and Alfred F. Scheider. *Rodale's Successful Organic Gardening: Trees, Shrubs, and Vines*. Emmaus, Pa.: Rodale Press, 1993.

Bales, Suzanne F. *Burpee Container Gardening*. New York: Prentice Hall General Reference and Travel, 1993.

Gardner, Jo Ann. *The Heirloom Garden: Selecting & Growing Over 300 Old-Fashioned Ornamentals*. Pownal, Vt.: Storey Communications, 1992.

Greenlee, John. *The Encyclopedia of Ornamental Grasses*. Emmaus, Pa.: Rodale Press, 1992.

Johnson, Lady Bird, and Carlton B. Lees. *Wildflowers across America*. New York: Abbeville Press, 1988.

Michalak, Patricia S. *Rodale's Successful Organic Gardening: Herbs*. Emmaus, Pa.: Rodale Press, 1993.

Proctor, Rob. *Country Flowers*. New York: HarperCollins Publishers, 1991.

Schenk, George. *The Complete Shade Gardener*. Boston: Houghton Mifflin Co., 1991.

Schneck, Marcus. *Your Backyard Wildlife Garden*. Emmaus, Pa.: Rodale Press, 1992.

Squire, David. *The Complete Guide to Using Color in Your Garden*. Emmaus, Pa.: Rodale Press, 1991.

Stadelmann, Peter. *Water Gardens*. Hauppauge, NY: Barron's Educational Series, 1992.

Taylor, Norman. *Taylor's Guide to Annuals*. rev. ed. Boston: Houghton Mifflin Co., 1986.

———. *Taylor's Guide to Bulbs*. rev. ed. Boston: Houghton Mifflin Co., 1986.

———. *Taylor's Guide to Water-Saving Gardening*. Boston: Houghton Mifflin Co., 1990.

Taylor's Guide Staff. *Taylor's Guide to Ground Covers, Vines, and Grasses*. Boston: Houghton Mifflin Co., 1987.

359

USDA PLANT HARDINESS ZONE MAP

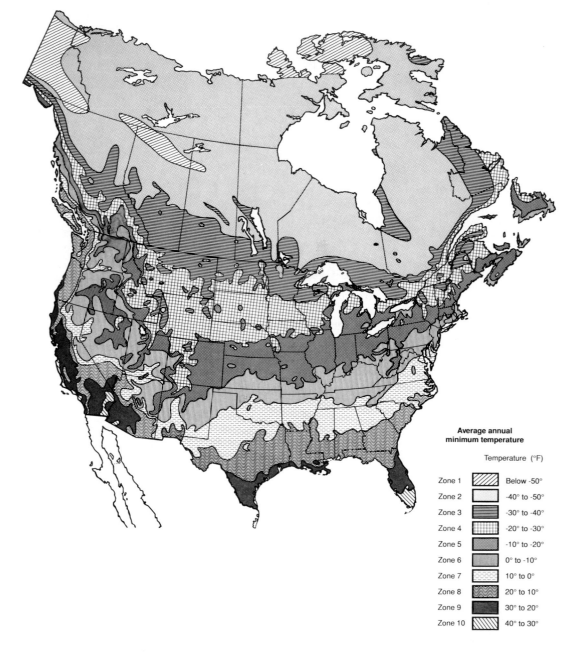

Average annual minimum temperature

Temperature (°F)

Zone 1		Below -50°
Zone 2		-40° to -50°
Zone 3		-30° to -40°
Zone 4		-20° to -30°
Zone 5		-10° to -20°
Zone 6		0° to -10°
Zone 7		10° to 0°
Zone 8		20° to 10°
Zone 9		30° to 20°
Zone 10		40° to 30°

Index

Note: Page references in *italic* indicate photographs or illustrations.
Boldface references indicate tables.

A

Acanthus, 70, 120
Accents, 213, 215, 233. *See also* Art,
    lawn and garden
Achillea. See Yarrow
Achillea filipendulina, 130, 202–5
Achillea ptarmica, 33
Acidic soils, 267
Acquiring plants. *See* Buying *entries;*
    Selecting *entries*
Adam's needle, 148–51
Adiantum pedatum, 68, 69
Aegopodium podagraria, **355**
Aesculus parviflora, 196
Aftercare, 273–76
Ageratum, **340**
Ageratum houstonianum, **340**
Agropyron repens. See Quackgrass
Air circulation for seedlings, 246–47
Ajuga
    description, **355**
    in rock garden, 44
    in shady Midwest garden, 206–10
Alcea rosea, 300
Alchemilla mollis, 218
Alkaline soils, 267
Allenstein, Pam, 170
Allium
    with barberry, 113
    in combination for color, 70, *71*
    description, **346**
Allium cernuum, 164–65
Allium schoenoprasum
    in cool-colored garden, 100, *101*
    in herb garden, *45,* 174–77

Allspice, Carolina, *138*
Alyssum
    sweet, 312, **341**
    in theme garden, 50
Amaranth, globe, 127
    description, **341**
    in mulch-and-grow garden,
        152–55
Amaranthus retroflexus, 290
Amaranthus tricolor, **340**
Ambler, Wayne, 125, 132, 134
Amelanchier, 136
Amelanchier arborea, 119
Amsonia tabernaemontana, 144–51
Analysis. *See* Evaluation *entries*
Anchusa capensis, **344**
Anemone, Japanese
    in color theme garden, 144–47
    description, **346**
    planted in spring, 273
    in southern shade garden, 196
Anemone blanda, 123
Anemone × *hybrida. See* Anemone,
    Japanese
Anemone tomentosa, 273, 346
Animals, controlling, 309–13
Annuals, 27, 28
    for cottage gardens, 32
    easy-care, choosing, 127
    for full sun, **340–43**
    no-fail gardening, 251
    from seed, 242
    for shade, 141–42, *142,*
        344–45
    sources, 358
    weeds, 289, 290, *290, 291*

Anthemis tinctoria
    in colorful and bountiful border,
        90, *91*
    in hardy northern garden,
        198–201
Aphids, 318, *318,* 319
    bargain plants and, 240–41
Apple, crab, 170–73
Aquilegia. See Columbine
Aquilegia canadensis. See Columbine,
    wild
Aquilegia vulgaris, 148–51
Arabis caucasica, 42, 117
Arbors
    building, 188
    at garden entry, 225
    Victorian, 186
Archangel, yellow, **356**
Arctostaphylos uva-ursi, 156–59
Argiope aurantia, 302
Armeria maritima
    in cool-colored garden, 100, *101*
    description, **346**
Art, lawn and garden, 228–29, 336. *See*
    also Accents
Artemisia
    in cool-colored garden, 100, *101*
    in cottage garden, *33*
    description, **346**
    in mulch-and-grow garden,
        152–55
Artemisia canascens, 135
Artemisia ludoviciana. See Artemisia;
    Sage, white
Aruncus dioicus, 34, **351**
Asarum europaeum, **355**

Asclepias incarnata, 166–69
Asclepias tuberosa. See Butterfly weed
Aster
    azure, 160–65
    combinations with, 92, 130
    heath, 160–63
    lavender, *121*
    New England
        description, **346**
        in moist meadow wild-
           flower garden, 166–69
        scale and, *111*
        in spring and fall garden,
           148–51
Aster azureus, 160–65
Aster ericoides, 160–63
Aster novae-angliae. See Aster, New
    England
Aster yellows, 314, *314*
Astilbe
    description, **351**
    as foundation planting, 7
    rose, 190–93
    in shade, 206–10, 333
    in spring combination, 64, *65*
Astilbe × arendsii. See Astilbe
Astilbe × rosea, 190–93
Athyrium goeringianum, 190–93
Aubrieta deltoidia, 42
Aurinia, 42
Aurinia saxatilis, 72, *73*
Autumn, shrubs for, 136
Autumn and spring garden, 148–51,
    149, 151
Avens, 72, *73*
Azalea, 136
    Florida pinxter, 196
    pruning, 295
    in shade, *17,* 196
    under shrubs and trees, 135, 220
    in sunny-shady garden combina-
        tion, 72, *73*
    in water garden, 47

B

Baby blue eyes, **345**
Baby's-breath
    creeping, **356**
    site, *11*
    staking, 300
Bacillus thuringiensis, 307
Backdrops, 222–23
Bacteria, 308
Balance, 111, *112,* 113
Ball, Liz, 213

Balloon flower
    in color theme garden, 144–47
    as slow grower, 323
    staking, 300
Baptisia, buying, 240
Baptisia australis. See Indigo, blue
    false
Baptisia leucantha, 166–69
Barberry, 113
Bareroot plants, 273, *274*
Bargain plants, 60, 240–41
Bark mulches, 280
Bartelette, Sue, 202
Basil, purpleleaf, 174–77
Basket-of-gold
    in raised bed, *42*
    in sunny-shady garden combina-
        tion, 72, *73*
Bats, as beneficials, *305,* 306
Bean, runner, 170–73
Bearberry, 156–59
Beardtongue, large-flowered, 160–63
Bear's-breeches, 70, 120
Beds. *See* Flower gardens; Island beds;
    Raised beds
Bee balm
    in color combination, 114
    color contrast with, 114
    in colorful and bountiful border,
        90, *91*
    description, **349**
    performance, 129
    pest and disease avoidance, 130
    in romantic combination, 88, *89*
Beetles
    blister, 314
    flea, 314–15, *314*
    ground, *301*
    Japanese, 315, *315*
    lady, *303,* 304
    rove, *301*
Begonia
    hardy, **351**
    in shade, 333
    wax, **344**
Begonia grandis, **351**
Bellflower
    clustered, *59*
    as foundation planting, 7
    in rock garden, *43*
    site, *11*
Bellis perennis, 54
Benches, *232*
Beneficial insects and animals, *302,*
    303–6, *303*
Benjamin, Joan, 152

Berberis thunbergii var. *atropurpurea,*
    113
Bergamot, wild, 90
Bergenia
    heartleaf
        in color theme garden,
           144–47
        description, **347**
        in hardy northern garden,
           198–201
    texture, 120
Bermuda grass, 260, 291–92
Biennials, 28
    no-fail gardening, 251
    weeds, 289–90
Billeaud, Lorraine, 280
Bindweed, field, 22
Binetti, Marianne, 156, 186
Biological controls, beneficials, 303–6
Birdbaths, 336
Bird lover's garden, accents for, 228
Birds
    attracting, 122
    as beneficials, 305–6, *305*
    in heat-tolerant Midwest garden,
        202
    in native prairie garden, 160, 162
Bishop's weed, **355**
Black-eyed Susan, *113*
    butterflies and, *49*
    combinations with, 130
    for late-summer color, 86, *87*
    in prairie garden, 160–65
Black-eyed Susan vine, staking, 301
Blackspot, 316, *316*
Blanket flower
    in cottage garden, *33*
    description, **341, 348**
    in mixed garden, 178–81
Bleeding heart
    fringed
        in color theme garden,
           144–47
        description, **352**
        in shade, 34
    in hardy northern garden,
        113
    light conditions and, 335
    in shade, *17,* 333
    western, in shady Midwest gar-
        den, 206–10
Blight, 316–17, *316*
Blister beetles, 314
Bluebeard, 295
Bluebell, 323, **353**
Blue daze, 234

Blue star, willow
    in color theme garden, 144–47
    in spring and fall garden, 148–51
Bluestem, little, 160–65
Boltonia, 144–47, **347**
Borders, 8, *59*
    colorful and bountiful, 90, *91*
    fences and, *9, 12*
    foliage for front of, 80, *81*
    lawn width and, 111
    mixed, for all-season interest, 78,
        79
    walkways and, *105*
Botrytis blight, 316–17, *316*
Bougainvillea, 301
Boulders, 219, 225
Bouteloua curtipendula, 160–63
Bowles, John Paul, 242
Boxwood, *31, 294*
Brachycome iberidifolia, **340**
Breezes, 18
Brick edgings, 220, *221, 227*
Brilliant butterfly garden, 182–85
Browallia, **344**
Bruckenthalia spiculifolia, 43
Brunnera macrophylla, **351**
Bt (*Bacillus thuringiensis*), 307
Buckeye, bottlebrush, 196
Buddleia, pruning, 295
Buddleia davidii, 135, 182–85
Buddleia davidii × *B. fallowiana,*
        182–85
Budget, 58, 60, 62
Bugloss, Siberian, **351**
Bulbs, 28
    for extra-early color, 30
    maintenance, *54*
    planting, 273
    sources, 358
Burrell, Cole, 198
Butterflies
    attracting, 184
    in heat-tolerant Midwest garden,
        202
    in native prairie garden, 160, 162
    small gardens for, 185
Butterfly bush
    dwarf, 182–85
    orange eye, 135, 182–85
Butterfly garden, 46, 49, *49*
    design idea, 182–85, *183, 185*
Butterfly weed
    in butterfly garden, 182–85
    buying, 240
    in color combination, 114
    color contrast with, 114

    in combination for hot and dry
        site, 96, *97*
    description, **346**
    outdoor sowing, 251
    in prairie garden, 160–65
Buxus, 31, 294
Buying large trees, 275
Buying organic fertilizers, 270
Buying plants, 58, 238–41
Bypass pruners, *296,* 297

C

Cabbage, flowering, 122
Caladium, **344**
Calamagrostis arundinacea var.
    brachytricha, 111
Calcalia atriplicifolia, 166–69
Calcium, 269
Calcycanthus floridus, 138
Calliopsis, **341**
Cambium, 294–95
Campanula. See Bellflower
Campanula glomerata, 59
Campsis radicans, 223
Candytuft
    fences and, *9*
    perennial, *52*
    in sunny slope garden, 156–59
Cane growers, pruning, 294
Canna, **340**
Capsella bursa-pastoris, 291
Carbon, 264, 282
Care of garden. *See* Maintenance
Carpet garden, 48
Caryopteris × *clandonensis,* 295
Castings, earthworm, 262, 267
Catharanthus roseus, **340**
Catmint
    description, **349**
    height contrasts and, 117
    shearing, 129
Cats, 313
Cedar, blue Atlas, *216*
Cedrus atlantica, 216
Celosia cristata, **340**
Centranthus ruber, 82, *83*
Cerastium tomentosum
    in late-spring color combination,
        92, *93*
    life span, 325
Ceratostigma plumbaginoides, **355**
Cercis canadensis, 178–81
Chamaemelum nobile, 174–77
Chamomile, 174–77
Changes in garden, 322–38, *328–30*

Cheiranthus, 78, 79
Chelone lyonii, **351**
Chemical controls, 306–7
Chionanthus virginicus, 138
Chipmunks, *310,* 311, 313
Chives
    in cool-colored garden, 100, *101*
    in herb garden, *45,* 174–77
Choosing plants. *See* Buying *entries*;
    Selecting *entries*
Chrysanthemum
    combinations with, 130
    gold-and-silver, 152–55, **347**
    seasons and, 122
Chrysanthemum leucanthemum, 148–51
Chrysanthemum pacificum, 152–55, **347**
Chrysanthemum parthenium, 25
Chrysanthemum × *superbum. See* Daisy,
    Shasta
Chrysogonum virginianum, **351**
Cilantro, 174–77
Cimicifuga racemosa, **352**
Cinquefoil, silvery, 22
Cirsium arvense, 22, *292*
    tilling and, 260
Citrus limon, 174–77
Clarkia amoena, 300
Clary, *56*
Clayey soil, 22–23, 24, 26
    fertilizing, 288–89
Clematis, *216,* 223
    purple, fence protection, *18*
    staking, 301
    sweet autumn, in fragrant heirloom
        garden, 186–89
Clematis maximowicziana, 186–89
Cleome, 28
    in island beds, 8
    in mulch-and-grow garden, 152–55
    scale and, *110*
Clethra alnifolia, 136
Climate, 14, 16. *See also* Temperature
Clover, purple prairie, 160–63
Cockscomb, **340**
Cocoa bean shells, 281
Colchicum speciosum, 135
Cold frames, 249
Coleus, *142,* **344**
Colonial garden, fencing for, 222
Color
    bulbs for, 30
    combinations for
        bountiful borders, 90, *91*
        compatibility, 82, *83*
        contrasts, 94, *95*
        perennials, 70, *71*

Color *(continued)*
 design and, 114, 117
 in late fall and early winter, *121*
 soil nutrients and, 262
 toning down, 219–20
Color theme garden, 144–47, *145, 147*
Coltsfoot, 22
Columbine
 light conditions and, 335
 in spring and fall garden, 148–51
 wild
  description, **351**
  in prairie garden, 164–65
  in southern shade garden,
   196
Combinations, 63–103, 129–31
 mixed garden, 178–81, *179, 181*
 recording, *214*
Comfrey, 98, *99*
Compost
 gardening costs and, 58
 making and using, 262–66
 as mulch, 280
Compost bin styles, 265, *265*
Compost tea, 288, *288*
Coneflower
 orange, **349**
 pale, 160–65
 purple
  in butterfly garden, 182–85
  in contrasting-textures combination, 84, *85*
  description, **347**
  height contrasts and, 117
  paths and, *227*
  in prairie garden, 164–65
  with purple-leaved perilla,
   113
 shining, 152–55
 sweet, 166–69
Conifers, dwarf, 48
Connecticut, pests in, 302
Consolida ambigua, 76, 77
Container-grown plants, planting, *274*
Containers
 outdoor, sowing seeds in, 250
 recycling, 243
 removing plants from, 272
 for starting seed, 242
Contrast, *115–16*
Convallaria majalis, 323, **352**
Convolvulus arvensis, 22
Cool-colored garden, 100, *101*
Cooperative Extension Service soil
 tests, 268
Coral bells, 34, 254

Coreopsis, *5*
 in colorful and bountiful border,
  90
 disease and, 333
 staking, 299
 stiff, in prairie garden, 160–63
 threadleaf, *52*
  combinations with, 130
  description, **347**
  with lamb's-ears, 114
Coreopsis grandiflora, 300
Coreopsis palmata, 160–63
Coreopsis tinctoria, **341**
Coreopsis verticillata. See Coreopsis,
 threadleaf
Coriander, 32
Coriandrum sativum, 174–77
Corn cobs, ground, 281
Corner beds, *107*
Corner herb garden, 174–77
Corn poppy, 94, *95*
Cornus controversa, 114
Cornus sericea, 294
Cosmos
 in mulch-and-grow garden,
  152–55
 outdoor sowing, 251
 scale and, *110*
 staking, 300
 yellow, in butterfly garden,
  182–85
Cosmos bipinnatus. See Cosmos
Cosmos sulphureus, 182–85
Cost considerations, 58, 60, 62
Cotinus coggygria. See Smoke tree,
 purple
Cottage garden, 32, *33,* 34
 annuals for, 32
 art for, 228–29
 combination for, 76, *77*
 fencing for, 222
Country garden, accents and art for,
 228–29
Crab apple, 170–73
Crabgrass, large, *290*
Craighton, LuAnn, 182
Cranesbill
 American, 78, *79*
 blood-red
  combinations with, 130
  description, **348**
  in fragrant heirloom garden,
   186–89
 in color theme garden, 144–47
 in combinations
  color, 82, *82*

 late spring, 92
 season-long interest, 74
 in hardy northern garden,
  198–201
 height contrasts and, 117
 in island beds, 8
 lilac, *116*
 shearing, 129
 wild, 196, **352**
Crape myrtle, 188, 295
Crawford, Barrie, 194
Cress, rock, *42,* 117
Crocus, 30
 fall, 123
 in reflecting pool garden, 190–93
 in rock garden, 44
 showy autumn, *135*
 in sunny slope garden, 156–59
Cultivars, growing from seed, 247
Culver's root, 166–69
Cupflower, blue, **345**
Cutouts, designing with, 132
Cuttings, 256–59, *257*
Cutworms, 321
Cynodon dactylon, 260

D

Daffodil, 30, *212*
 dwarf, in rock garden, 44
 in heat-tolerant Midwest garden,
  202–5
 in mixed garden, 178–81
 in mulch-and-grow garden,
  152–55
Dahlia, *25,* 300
Daisy
 English, *54*
 gloriosa, **342**
 oxeye, 148–51
 Shasta, *128*
  description, **347**
  in heat-tolerant Midwest
   garden, 202–5
 Swan River, **340**
Damping-off, 245, 320–21
Dandelion, 22, *23,* 260
Daphne, Burkwood, 74, *75*
Daylily, *15*
 buying, 240
 in combination for color, 70, *71*
 in cottage garden, *33*
 as fast grower, 323
 fence protection, *18*
 in hardy northern garden,
  198–201

in heat-tolerant Midwest garden, 202 5
lemon, in fragrant heirloom garden, 186–89
in mixed garden, 178–81
modern, cultivars, description, **348**
in romantic combination, 88, *89*
tawny, in sunny slope garden, 156–59
Deadheading, *297,* 298–99
Decision making, garden design and, 124–33
Deer, 309–11, *309*
Delphinium
life span, 325
in mixed garden, 178–81
winds and staking, 18, 56, 300
Design of garden, 104–42
drawing, 108–9, 131, *131, 133*
ideas and finishing touches, 211–35
mixed plantings, 180
specific garden ideas, 143–210
Design patterns, 124–25, *126*
Design styles, maintenance and, 53, 55
Deutzia, 295
Dianthus. See Pinks
Diatomaceous earth, 306–7
Diboll, Neil, 160, 166
Dicentra. See Bleeding heart
Dicentra eximia. See Bleeding heart, fringed
Dicentra formosa, 206–10
Dicentra spectabilis, 198–201
Dictamnus, 240
Digging, 270–71
Digitalis. See Foxglove
Digitalis grandiflora, **352**
Digitaria sanguinalis, 290
Dill, 32
Disease, 219, 307–8, 332
plant selection and, 130, 240–41, *241*
seedlings and, 246–47
Diversity, *112, 123*
Division, 253–56
garden forks for, *254*
of perennials with fleshy roots, *255*
root type and, 253, 254–55
Docks, 22
Dogwood, *114,* 294
Dooryard reflecting pool, 190–93
Double digging, 270, 271
Drainage problems, 132

Drawing garden design, 108–9, 131, *131, 133*
Drip irrigation systems, 87, *285*
Driveways, borders and, *105*
Dropseed, prairie, 164–65
Dryopteris marginalis, 206–10
Dry soil
perennials for, 55
prairie garden for, 160–63, *161, 163*
wildflower combination for, 96, 97

E

Earthworm manure, 267
Earthworms, 262, 305
Earwigs, 314
Echinacea pallida, 160–65
Echinacea purpurea. See Coneflower, purple
Eddleman, Edith, 148
Edgings, 220, *221,* 222, *227*
Edging strips, 58
Edible garden, 170–73, *171, 173*
Edibles in landscape, suggestions, 172
Elymus, 84, *85*
Entrances, 223, *224,* 225
Epimedium
description, **352**
Persian, 196
in shade, 34, 196
Epimedium × *versicolor,* 196
Eupatorium, 111
Eupatorium maculatum, 166–69
Eupatorium purpureum, **347**
Euphorbia, 37, 78, 79
Euphorbia epithymoides, 148–51
Euphorbia marginata, **341**
Euphorbia supina, 291
European corn borers, 320, *321*
Evaluation of existing gardens, 109
Evaluation of garden purpose, 6
Evaluation of plants, 127–29
Evergreens
for privacy, 138
in rock garden, 44
shrubs in flower garden, 220
Evolvulus nuttallianus, 234
Exposure. *See* Winds, protection from

F

Fall, shrubs for, 136
Fall and spring garden, 148–51, *149, 151*

Farewell-to-spring, 300
Feely, Joan, 122
Fences, *221, 222, 234*
for deer control, 309, 311
flower baskets on, 233–34
for flower protection, *18*
for rabbit control, 311, *311, 312*
Fennel, bronze, *45*
Fern, 220
with hostas, 119
Japanese painted, 190–93
maidenhair, 68, *69*
ostrich
description, **356**
in shade, 55, *140*
sensitive, 66, *67*
shield, *47,* 206–10
Fertilizer, 267–70. *See also* Soil amendments
liquid, 288, *288,* 289
for maturing garden, 335–36
organic, 268
mixing, 287
shopping for, 270
for roses, 38
for seedlings, 247
Fertilizing, 287–89
Feverfew, *25*
Filipendula rubra, 166–69, **348**
Financial considerations, 58, 60, 62
Fish emulsion, 288
Flea beetles, 314–15, *314*
Flower beds. *See* Flower gardens; Island beds; Raised beds
Flower gardens
divided, design tips, *131, 137*
divided for easy planting, 62
no-fail, definition, viii
options, 6–9, 27–62
as outdoor living areas, 26
Flower pots, 217. *See also* Containers
as accents, 231, 232
at garden entry, 225
space and, 136
Flowers
calculating number needed, 132–33, *133*
uses, 4, *5*
Flower shows, 215, 217, *218*
Foamflower, Allegheny, **354**
Focal points, 229, *230,* 231
Foeniculum vulgare var. *purpureum, 45*
Foliage. *See also* Leaves
color, 113

Foliage (continued)
    combinations
        front of border, 80, *81*
        season-long interest, 74, *75*
        shady site, 68, *69*
    in hardy northern garden, 198
    shape, *116*
    texture, 120
Foliar feeding, *288*
Forget-me-not
    as fast grower, 323
    garden, 35, **345**
    with lilac, *54*
    in shade, *17, 35*
    summer, **344**
    in water garden, *47*
Forks, garden, *254*
Form, 117
Forsythia, 294
Foundation flowers, 7, *7, 15*
    between house and sidewalk, *107*
    soil and, *25*
Fountain grass, *120, 121*
    in heat-tolerant Midwest garden,
        202
    in low-maintenance combination,
        102, *103*
Four-o'clock, **342**
Foxglove
    in herb garden, *30*
    in island beds, 8
    light conditions and, 335
    in shade, 333
    staking, 300
    yellow, **352**
Fragaria, **355**
Fragrance of flowers, soil nutrients
    and, 262
Fragrant heirloom garden, 186–89,
    187, 189
Framing, 220, *221,* 222
Fringe tree, white, *138*
Frost protection for seedlings, 250
Fruits for birds, 122
Function of garden, 2, 4, 6
Fungi, 307–8
    damping-off, 245
Fusarium wilt, 321

G

Gaillardia, 33
Gaillardia aristata, **348**
Gaillardia × *grandiflora,* 178–81, **341**
Galanthus, 30
Galinsoga, hairy, 291

Galium odoratum, **355**
Garden accessories, sources, 358
Garden art, 228–29, 336
Garden for a sunny slope, 156–59
Garden forks, *254*
Garden for spring and fall, 148–51
Gardens. *See* Flower gardens
Garden shows, 215, 217, *218*
Garrett, Scottie, 178, 206, 210
Gas plant, buying, 240
Gates, 223, *224,* 225
Gaura, white
    description, **348**
    location, 119
    in raised beds, *56*
Gaura lindheimeri. See Gaura, white
Gayfeather
    button, 160–63
    Kansas, 164–69
    purple, *15*
    spike, **348**
Gazania, **341**
Geranium
    shade and, 333
    strawberry, **354**
    in theme garden, 48
Geranium. See Cranesbill
Geranium himalayense, 116
Geranium maculatum, 196, **352**
Geranium psilostemon, 78, *79*
Geranium sanguineum. See Cranesbill,
    blood-red
Germander, 174–77
Geum, 72, *73*
Ginger, European wild, **355**
Ginger mint, golden, 94, *95*
Glattstein, Judy, 120
Gleditsia triacanthos var. *inermis,* 119
Globeflower, Chinese, **354**
Goat's beard, 34, **351**
Goldenrod
    Canada, 53
    description, **350**
    dwarf, in spring and fall garden,
        148–51
    in prairie garden, 160–65
    scale and, *111*
    showy, 53, 160–63
    stiff, 53, 164–65
Gomphrena globosa. See Amaranth,
    globe
Gophers, 310, 311, 312–13, *313*
Goutweed, **355**
Gramma grass, side oats, 160–63
Grass, lawn, removing, 260–61
Grass clippings, 267, 280

Grasses, ornamental, 134, 220
Grasshoppers, 315
Gravel paths, 219
Green and gold, **351**
Ground beetles, *301*
Groundcovers, *55,* **355–57**
Growing mixes for seed, 242–43
Growth stages of plants, 333
Gypsophila repens, **356**

H

Habit, 117
Hamamelis, 136
Hanging garden, 196
Hardening off seedlings, 248–49
Hardiness zones, 16
    USDA plant hardiness zone map,
        360
Hardy northern garden, 198–201, *199,*
    201
Heat, cuttings and, 258
Heat protection for seedlings, 250
Heat-tolerant Midwest garden, 202–5
Hedera helix, 92, *93,* **356**
Hedges, 233
Height, 117, *118,* 119
Heirloom garden, 186–89, *187, 189*
    accents for, 228
Helenium autumnale, 94
Helianthus. See Sunflower
Helianthus annuus, 127, **341**
Helianthus occidentalis, 160–63
Helichrysum petiolare, 135
Helictotrichon sempervirens, 56
Heliopsis, *18, 25*
Hellebore, 34
Helleborus, 34
Helleborus niger, 123
Helleborus orientalis, 196, **352**
Hemerocallis. See Daylily
Hemerocallis fulva, 156–59
Hemerocallis × *hybrida,* 202–5
Hemerocallis lilioasphodelus, 186–89
Hens-and-chickens, *50,* **357**
Herb garden, *31,* 45–46, *59*
    accents, 228
    color, *45*
    design idea, 174–77, *175, 177*
    flowers, 45
    themes, 46
Herbs
    in cottage garden, 32
    mixed with flower beds and bor-
        ders, 98, *99*
    sources, 358

Heuchera × *brizoides, 34*
Heuchera sanguinea, 254
Hibiscus, 90, *91,* 295
Hibiscus syriacus, 51
Hoeing, 290
Holly, 136, 294
Hollyhock, 300
Honesty, *35,* 76, *77*
Honey locust, 119
Honeysuckle
    birds and, 57
    boxleaf, 78, *79*
    pruning, 295
    staking, 301
    trumpet, 223
Horticultural oils, 306
Hoses, soaker, *285,* 286, *287*
Hosta, *114*
    in color theme garden, 144–47
    in combinations
        color, 70, *71*
        late spring, 92
        beside paths, *218*
        shady site, 68, *69*
        spring, 64, *65*
        sunny-shady garden, 72, *73*
    curled leaf, *37*
    description, **352**
    with ferns, 119
    as focal point, *230*
    life span, 325
    in reflecting pool garden, 190–93
    seersucker, 206–10
    in shade, 34, 206–10, 333, 334
    wavyleaf, 190–93
Hosta crispula, 37
Hosta sieboldii, 206–10
Hosta undulata, 190–93
Hot and dry sites, wildflower combination for, 96, *97*
House, fitting flowers to, 106, *107*–8
Hyacinth, grape, 64, *65*
Hyacinthoides, 323
Hydrangea
    bigleaf, 262
    oakleaf, 136, 196
    pruning, 294, 295
Hydrangea macrophylla, 262
Hydrangea quercifolia, 136, 196
Hypericum, 138
Hypericum calycinum, **356**

I

Iberis sempervirens, 52, 156–59
Iberis umbellata, 9

Idea sources, 211, 213, 215
    nature, 217, 219, 220
    shows, 215, 217
Ilex, 294
Ilex verticillata, 136
Impatiens
    description, **345**
    light conditions and, 335
    New Guinea, **344**
    in shade, 333, 334
    in shady Midwest garden, 206–10
    in theme garden, 50
Impatiens wallerana, 206–10, **345**
Incredible edible garden, 170–73
Indigo
    blue false, *52*
    combinations with, 130
    description, **347**
    prairie wild, 166–69
Indoor sowing, 242–45, *244*
Insecticidal soaps, 306
Insecticides, toxicity, 306
Insects
    life cycles, 304
    management, 302, 306
        beneficials, *302,* 303–6, *303*
        control techniques, *301,*
            303
Inula, swordleaf, *43*
Inula ensifolia, 43
Iris
    bearded
        in fragrant heirloom garden,
            186–89
        in heat-tolerant Midwest
            garden, 202–5
        in late-spring color combi-
            nation, 92, *93*
        in path combination, *218*
        in sunny-shady garden
            combination, 72, *73*
    blue flag, 57
    crested, **353**
    disease and, 333
    division, *255*
    height and, 117, 119
    reticulated, 30
    shade and, 139, 141
    Siberian
        description, **348**
        in hardy northern garden,
            198–201
        with phlox, 117
        in reflecting pool garden,
            190–93
        shape and, *115*

    in spring and fall garden,
        148–51
    texture, 120
    sweet, 114
    wild, 166–69
Iris borers, 320, *320*
Iris cristata, **353**
Iris pallida, 114
Iris pseudacorus, 118
Iris reticulata, 30
Iris shrevei, 166–69
Iris sibirica. See Iris, Siberian
Iris versicolor, 57
Ironweed, western, 166–69
Island beds, 7–8, *107,* 208
    site selection, *12*
Italian herb garden, 46
Itea virginica, 136
Ivy, 233
    English
        description, **356**
        on fence, 234
        in late-spring color combi-
            nation, 92, *93*

J

Jacob's ladder, creeping, **353**
Japanese beetles, 315, *315*
Japanese-style garden, fencing for, 222
Jasmine, 301
Joe-Pye weed
    description, **347**
    scale and, *111*
    spotted, in moist meadow wild-
        flower garden, 166–69
Johnsongrass, 260, *292*
Joseph's coat, **340**
Juniper, Sargent, 102, *103*
Juniperus chinensis var. *sargentii,* 102,
    103

K

Kelp, 288
Keyser, Joe, 266
Kieft, Janis, 130
Kniphofia uvaria, 202–5

L

Lace bugs, 317–18
Lacewings, *303*
Lady beetles, *303,* 304
Ladybugs, *303,* 304
Lady's-mantle, *218*

Lagerstroemia indica, 188, 295
Lamb's-ears
   in color combination, 114
   combinations with, 130
   in cool-colored garden, 100, *101*
   for foliage in front of border, 80,
     81
   in mixed border, 78, *79*
   paths and, *227*
   with threadleaf coreopsis, 114
Lamb's quarters, common, 291
Lamiastrum galeobdolon, **356**
Lamium, spotted
   in color theme garden, 144–47
   description, **356**
   in reflecting pool garden, 190–93
Lamium maculatum. See Lamium,
  spotted
Landscape, overgrown, *324*
Landscape fabrics, 282, 283
Lantana, 182–85
Large sites, 136, *137,* 138, *138*
   developed in phases, 138–39,
     142
Larkspur, rocket, 76, 77
Larvae, 304
Lathyrus, 301
Lavender, *5*
   sea, 178–81
Lavender cotton, *5, 31*
Lawn art, 228–29, 336
Lawn grass, removing, 260–61
Lawn width, flower borders and, 111
Leadwort, **355**
Leafhoppers, 314
Leafminers, 320
   damage from, *320*
Leafrollers, 320
Leaf spot, 307, 308, 316
Leaftiers, 320
Leaves. *See also* Foliage
   as mulch, 281
   trouble symptoms, 313, 314–20
   water needs and, 285
Leek, 170–73
Lemon, 174–77
Lemon trees, potted, 176
Lettuce, 170–73
Liatris, 15
Liatris aspera, 160–63
Liatris pycnostachya, 164–69
Liatris spicata, **348**
Licorice plant, *135*
Light
   plant adaptability to, 335
   for seedlings, 245–46

Lilac, *54*
   common, 219
   in fragrant heirloom garden,
     186–89
   Japanese tree, 219
   littleleaf, 98, *99*
   Persian, 178–81
   pruning, 295
   shade and, 333
Lilium. See also Lily
   in combination for color, 70, *71*
   in heat-tolerant Midwest garden,
     202–5
   life span of hybrids, 325
Lilium lancifolium. See Lily, tiger
Lily
   Asiatic, 325
   in combination for color, 70, *71*
   common toad, **354**
   in heat-tolerant Midwest garden,
     202–5
   in late-spring combination, 92
   tiger
     description, **348**
     in fragrant heirloom garden,
       186–89
     soil and, *25*
   torch, 202–5
Lily-of-the-valley
   description, **352**
   as fast grower, 323
   in shade, *17*
Lilyturf, big blue, **356**
Limonium latifolium, 178–81, 323
Liriope muscari, **356**
Lobelia
   decorating a fence, 234
   edging, 36, **345**
   great blue
     description, **353**
     in moist meadow wild-
       flower garden, 166–69
     in shady Midwest garden,
       206–10
   in theme garden, 48
Lobelia erinus, 36, **345**
Lobelia siphilitica. See Lobelia, great
  blue
Lobularia maritima, **341**
Location of garden. *See* Site for garden
Locust, honey, 119
Logs, 219
Lollipops, plants shaped like, 323, 325
Lonicera nitida, 78, *79*
Lonicera sempervirens, 223
Love-in-a-mist, 251

Lunaria annua, 35, 76, 77
Lungwort, 92
Lupine, Russell hybrid, 198–201
Lupinus, 198–201
Lychnis coronaria, 128, 156–59

M

Magnesium, 269
Magnolia, 295
Mail-order plant shopping, 240
Maintenance, 277–78
   adjusting to changes, 337
   appearances, 278
   low, 51–59
     combination for, 102, *103*
   pest prevention and control,
     301–21
   reducing, 331
   routines, 278, *279*
   techniques, 278–301
Malus, 170–73
Mammals, controlling, 309–13
Manure, 267, 280–81
Maps for sun and shade analysis,
   20–21, *21*
Marguerite, golden
   in colorful and bountiful border,
     90, *91*
   in hardy northern garden,
     198–201
Marigold
   African, **343**
   French
     in butterfly garden, 182–85
     description, **343**
     in design pattern, *126*
   shade and, 333
   in theme garden, 49
Marjoram, sweet, 174–77
Marvelous mixed garden, 178–81
Mass plantings, 217
Matteuccia struthiopteris
   description, **356**
   in shade, *55, 140*
Matthiola incana, **341**
Maturing garden
   caring for, 335–36
   different growth rates of plants,
     323
Meadow
   management, 168
   moist meadow wildflower gar-
     den, 166–69, *167, 169*
Melampodium, 202–5, **342**
Melampodium paludosum, **342**

Mertensia virginica, **353**
Mice, 310, 313
Microclimate, 16
Micronutrients, 270
Microorganisms in soil, mulch and, 28
Midwest garden
    heat-tolerant, 202–5, *203, 205*
    shady, 206–10, *207, 209, 210*
Mildew, 307
    powdery, 130, 308, *319*
Milkweed, swamp, 166–69
Mint, golden ginger, 94, *95*
Mirabilis jalapa, **342**
Miscanthus sinensis. See Silver grass,
    Japanese
Mixed garden, 36, *37*
    balanced, 36
    design idea, 178–81, *179, 181*
    designing, 180
Mock orange
    in fragrant heirloom garden,
        186–89
    pruning, 135, 295
Moist meadow wildflower garden,
    166–69, *167, 169*
Moist soil, combination for, 66, *67*
Moisture. *See also* Watering
    for compost, 266
    for seedlings, 245
Moles, 310, 311–12, *312,* 313
Monarda didyma. See Bee balm
Monarda fistulosa, 90
Morning glory, 50
Moss, 220
    Irish and Scotch, for filling gaps,
        326
    rose, **342**
    soil and, 22
Moss pink
    description, **357**
    in fragrant heirloom garden,
        186–89
    in mixed garden, 178–81
    sunlight and, 334
    in sunny slope garden, 156–59
Mother-of-thousands, **354**
Mother-of-thyme, **357**
Mulch, 58
    bark, 280
    hazards, 282
    for lower maintenance, 331
    for maturing garden, 335–36
    natural, 219
    for newly planted flower bed,
        274
    nonorganic, 282–83

organic, 279–82
pests and, 306
for roses, 38
for site clearing, 260–61
for soil improvement, *261*
winter, perennials protected with,
    281
Mulch-and-grow garden, 152–55, *153,*
    155
Mulching, 279–83
Mullein, olympic, *33*
Muscari armeniacum, 64, *65*
Mycoplasmas, 308
Myosotis. See Forget-me-not
Myrtle, crape, 188, 295

N

Narcissus. See Daffodil
Nasturtium
    eating, 173
    in edible garden, 170–73
    on fence, 234
    garden, description, **343**
Native plants
    for low maintenance, 53
    sources, 358
    working with, 134
Nature, ideas from, 217, 219, 220
Nau, Jim, 249
Nebraska, pests in, 302
Neem, 306–7
Nemophila menziesii, **345**
Nepeta
    height contrasts and, 117, 129
    Persian, 198–201
    shearing, 129
Nepeta × *faassenii,* **349**
Nepeta mussinii, 198–201
Nevada, pests in, 302
Newspaper, as mulch, 281
Nicotiana alata, **345**
Nierembergia hippomanica var. *vio-*
    lacea, **345**
Nigella damascena, 251
Nitrogen, 269
    in compost, 264
    in mulch, 282
    in organic fertilizers, 268,
        287
Normandy, Phil, 142
North Carolina, pests in, 302
Northern garden, hardy, 198–201, *199,*
    201
NPK ratio, 287
Nursery bed, building, 139

Nutgrass, 292
Nutsedge, yellow, 292

O

Oat grass, *56*
Obedient plant, 166–69
Ocimum basilicum, 174–77
Oenothera fruticosa, **349**
Oenothera missouriensis, 152–55
Oils, horticultural, 306
Ondra, Nancy, 144
Onion, nodding wild, 164–65
Onoclea sensibilis, 66, *67*
Opuntia humifusa, 96, *97*
Orange, mock. *See* Mock orange
Origanum majorana, 174–77
Origanum vulgare, **357**
Outdoor sowing, 251–53
Overgrown landscape, *324*
Overhaul of garden, 332
Oxydendrum arboreum, 144–47

P

Pachysandra, Japanese, 64, *65,* **357**
Pachysandra terminalis, 64, *65,* **357**
Paeonia. See Peony
Pansy, *114*
    description, **345**
    in theme garden, 50
Papaver nudicaule, 112
Papaver rhoeas, 94, *95,* **342**
Parsley
    in butterfly garden, 182–85
    curly
        in edible garden, 170–73
        for foliage in front of bor-
            der, 80, *81*
    Italian, in herb garden, 174–77
Pastels, in romantic combination, 88,
    89
Paths, *3,* 233
    borders and, *105*
    design, 225–28
    gravel, 219
    in large sites, 136, *137*
    plant combination for, *218*
Patrinia, **349**
Patriotic garden, 48
Patterns, design and, 124–25, *124, 126*
Peat moss, 282
Pecan shells, 281
Peek, Robert, 284
Pennisetum, 102, *103,* 202
Pennisetum alopecuroides, 120, *121*

Penstemon, foxglove, 164–65
Penstemon digitalis, 164–65
Penstemon grandiflorus, 160–63
Peony, *52*
    for color, *59*
    in contrasting-textures combina-
        tion, 84, *85,* 116
    as foundation planting, 7
    in hardy northern garden,
        198–201
    less-floppy cultivars, 300
    life span, 325
    old plants, 335
    selection, 129
    as slow grower, 323
    staking, 300
    texture, 120
Perennials, 28
    buying, 240
    changes over time, 328–29
    in combination for color, 70, *71*
    for cost savings, 60, *61*
    division, roots and, 253, *255*
    for dry spots, 55
    for full sun, **346–50**
    growing cultivars from seed, 247
    life span, 325
    low-maintenance, *52*
    no-fail gardening, 251
    overgrown, 332
    rejuvenating, 335–36
    from root cuttings, 259
    for shade, 34, **351–54**
    shearing, 330
    soil and, 262
    sources, 358
    starting from seed, first-season
        flowers, 249
    from stem cuttings, 256
    summer-blooming, in shade gar-
        den, 141
    tough, 132
    weeds, 289–90, *292*
    winter protection, 200, 281
Performance of plants, 128–29
Perilla, purple-leaved, 113
Periwinkle
    common, 36
        description, **357**
        overgrown, 331
        in shady Midwest garden,
            206–10
    on fence, 234
    Madagascar, **340**
Personal touches, 233–35
Perspective, *113,* 119

Pesticides, 306–7
    butterflies and, 184
    meadows and, 168
Pests, 301–21
    disease, 307–8
    insects, 301–7
    mammals, 309–13
    outdoor seedlings and, 253
    plant selection and, 130
    troubleshooting, 313–21
Petalostemon purpureum, 160–63
Petroselinum crispum, 182–85
Petroselinum crispum var. *crispum,* 80,
    81
Petroselinum crispum var. *neapoli-*
    tanum, 174–77
Petunia, 48, 50
    common garden, **342**
Petunia × *hybrida,* **342**
Philadelphus coronarius. See Mock
    orange
Phillips, Ellen, 190
Phlomis, 148–51
Phlox
    creeping, **353**
    garden
        description, **349**
        fungal disease and, 19
        in late-spring combination,
            92
        pest and disease avoidance,
            130
        with Siberian iris, 117
    Iceland poppy and, *112*
    soil and, *25*
    wild blue, 196, **353**
Phlox divaricata, 196, **353**
Phlox paniculata. See Phlox, garden
Phlox stolonifera, **353**
Phlox subulata. See Moss pink
pH of soil, nutrients and, 267
Phosphorus, 269
    in organic fertilizers, 268, 287
Photinia, 335
Photography, 213
Physical controls, 303
Physostegia virginiana, 166–69
Pigweed, redroot, *290*
Pillars at garden entry, 225
Pillbugs (sowbugs), 321, *321*
Pinching, *297, 298,* 329–31
Pine needles, 282
Pinks
    in herb garden, *30*
    moss (*see* Moss pink)
    site, *11, 43*

Places for flowers, 8
Planning, 124–33
Plantago, 22, *23*
Plantain, 22, *23*
    pale Indian, in moist meadow
        wildflower garden, 166–69
PlantAmnesty, 294
Planting and propagation, 238–76
Planting pockets on steep slope, 158,
    158
Platycodon grandiflorus. See Balloon
    flower
Plumbago, **355**
Polemonium, creeping, **353**
Polemonium reptans, **353**
Polka dots, plants spaced like, 325
Polygonatum, 68, 69
Polygonatum odoratum, **353**
Polygonatum odoratum var. *thun-*
    bergii, 68
Polystichum, 47
Pool garden, reflecting, 190–93, *191,*
    193
Pools, installing, 192
Poppy, *9*
    Celandine, *55*
    corn, 94, *95,* **342**
    Iceland, *112*
    outdoor sowing, 251
Portulaca grandiflora, **342**
Portulaca oleracea, 291
Potassium, 269
    in organic fertilizers, 268, 287
Potentilla argentea, 22
Potted plants. *See* Containers; Flower
    pots
Powdery mildew, 130, 308, *319*
Prairie gardens, native
    for average soil, 164–65, *165*
    for dry soil, 160–63, *161, 163*
Presprouting seeds, 246
Price, Sarah, 117, 129
Prickly pear, 96, 97
Primrose
    English, 196, **353**
    Japanese
        in combination for moist
            soil, 66, *67*
        height contrast with, *118*
        in shade, *140*
    Missouri, 152–55
    polyanthus, *212*
    in shady Midwest garden,
        206–10
Primula japonica. See Primrose,
    Japanese

Primula × *polyantha*, 206–10, *212*
Primula vulgaris, 196, **353**
Propagation, 238–76
   for cost savings, 60
Proportion, 109, *110*, 111, *111*
Pruning, 141, 292–99
   for more plants, 335
   pinching and deadheading,
     298–99
   renewal, *295*
   roses, 295–96
   routine maintenance, 331
   shrubs, 293–95
   tools, *296*
   trees, 297
Pruning saw, *296*, 297
Pulmonaria, 92
Pulmonaria saccharata, 34, **354**
Pupae, 304
Purpose of garden, 2, 4, 6
Purslane, common, 291
Pyrethrins, 306–7

Q
Quackgrass, *292*
   soil problems and, 22
   tilling and, 260
Queen-of-the prairie, 166–69, **348**

R
Rabbits, 310, 311, *311,* 312, 313
Radler, William, 300
Rainfall, 16, 18
   regional information, 20
Raised-bed rock gardens, 42, *43*
Raised beds, 272
   maintenance and, 55–56, *56*
Rats, 310
Record keeping, 217, 235
   bubble diagram, *214*
   indoor sowing, *244*
   notebook, *214,* 234
Redbud, eastern, 178–81
Reed grass, *111*
Renewing existing gardens, 322–25
Repetition, 113–14, 136
Rhizomes, 290, 320
Rhododendron, *37,* 335
Rhododendron. See Azalea
Rhododendron canescens, 196
Rhubarb, 119, 170–73
Robinson, Rebecca, 293
Rock cress, 42, 117
Rock gardens, 42, *42–43,* 44

arrangement of rocks, *44*
   raised-bed, 42, *43*
   with water, *48*
Rock outcroppings, 159
Root cuttings, 258–59
Roots, division and, 253, 254–55
Rosa. See Rose
Rosa arkansana, 51
Rosa carolina, 51
Rosa palustris, 51
Rosa rugosa. See Rose, rugosa
Rose, *31*
   Arkansas, 51
   Christmas, 123
   climbing, 223
   in combination for all-season
     interest, 78, *79*
   in cottage garden, 76, *77*
   disease-resistant, 40–41
   English/David Austin, 38, 41,
     186–89
   in fragrant heirloom garden,
     186–89
   fungal disease and, 19
   hybrid tea, *39,* 40–41
   Lenten, 196, **352**
   Meidiland shrub, 38
   old plants, 336
   options, 51
   pasture, 51
   pruning, 295–96
   rugosa, 38, *40*
     in edible garden,
       170–73
     in sunny slope garden,
       156–59
   selecting, 38, *39,* 40–41
   shrub, 32, 38, *39,* 41
   swamp, 51
Rose astilbe, 190–93
Rose campion, *128,* 156–59
Rose gardens, 38–41, 122
Rose moss, 342
Rose-of-Sharon, 51
Rove beetles, *301*
Rudbeckia fulgida, **349**
Rudbeckia fulgida var. *sullivantii*, 86,
   87
Rudbeckia hirta, **342.** *See also* Black-
   eyed Susan
Rudbeckia nitida, 152–55
Rudbeckia subtomentosa, 166–69
Rue, purple meadow, 166–69
Rumex, 22
Runner bean, 170–73
Rust, *307,* 319–20

Ryania, 307
Rye, wild, 84, *85*

S
Sage
   Bethlehem, 34, **354**
   in herb garden, 174–77
   mealy-cup, *126*
   purple, *45,* 98, *99*
   scarlet, **342**
   violet, *52*
     in cool-colored garden, 100,
      101
     description, **350**
     in mulch-and-grow garden,
      152–55
     shearing, 129
   white, 114, 117
Sagina subulata, 326
St.-John's-wort, *138,* **356**
Salty sites, 135
Salvia farinacea, 126
Salvia officinalis, 45
   in herb garden, 174–77
   mixed with flower beds and bor-
     ders, 98, *99*
Salvia sclarea var. *turkesta-niana,* 56
Salvia splendens, **342**
Salvia × *superba. See* Sage, purple
Sandy soil, 22–23, 24
   fertilizing, 288–89
Santolina, 5, 31
Sanvitalia procumbens, 126, **343**
Satureja montana, 174–77
Savory, winter, 174–77
Sawdust, 281
Saxifraga stolonifera, **354**
Scale (proportion), 109, *110,*
   111, *111*
Scales, 319
Schizachyrium scoparium, 160–65
Scilla, 30
Screens, 222–23
Sculpture, *235*
Sea lavender, 178–81, 323
Seasonal planting, cost considerations,
   62
Seasons
   four-season flowers, 120–23
   shrubs for, 136
Seaweed extract, 288, *288*
Sedum
   in combinations, 130
     contrasting textures, 84
     late spring, 92

Sedum (continued)
  description, **350**
  for foliage in front of border, 80,
    81
  for late-season color, 120, 121
  site, 11
  in spring and fall garden, 148–51
  in theme garden, 48
  two-row, **357**
Sedum spectabile, 86, 87
Sedum spurium, **357**
Seed
  growing cultivars from, 247
  growing plants from, for cost sav-
    ings, 60
  presprouting, 246
  saving, 298, 298
  sowing in outdoor containers,
    250
  starting flowers from, 241–53
Seedlings
  growing healthy, 245–47
  transplanting, 248–51, 248
Selecting flower gardens, 27–62
Selecting flowers, 125, 127–33
Sempervivum, 50
Sempervivum tectorum, **357**
Serviceberry, 119, 136
Settling plants in soil, 272–73
Shade, 34, 35
  annuals for, **344–45**
  combinations for
    bountiful blooms, 72, 73
    foliage, 68, 69
  groundcovers for, 55
  increasing, 332–33
  mapping, 19–21, 21
  perennials for, 34, 141, **351–54**
  plants for, 56
    selection, 333–34
  working with, 139, 140, 141–42
Shade garden, southern, 194–97, 195,
  197
Shady Midwest garden, 206–10, 207,
  209, 210
Shady volunteers, 327
Shape of garden, 55, 106–8, 208
  drawing, 108–9
Shapes of plants, 128
Shaping garden, 327–31
Shearing, 329–31
Shepherd's-purse, 291
Shoot cuttings, 256–58
Shows, 215, 217, 218
Showy stonecrop, 86, 87
Shrub roses, 32, 38, 39, 41

Shrubs
  for all seasons, 136
  in cottage garden, 32, 34
  for large sites, 137, 138, 138
  in mixed beds, 36, 37
  overgrown, 141
  planting, 275
  pruning, 293–95
  sunlight and, 334
Side oats gramma grass, 160–63
Sidewalks, borders and, 105
Silt soil, 22–23
Silver foliage, in herb garden, 46
Silver garden, 100, 101
Silver grass, Japanese
  description, **356**
  in heat-tolerant Midwest garden,
    202–5
  in island beds, 8
  in season-long foliage combina-
    tion, 74, 75
Site for garden, 10, 11, 12, 13
  choosing, 13–14
  climate and microclimate, 14, 16,
    18
  exposure, 18–19
  large, 136, 137, 138
    developed in phases,
      138–39, 142
  matching plants to, 56, 57, 58
  options, 8
  preparation, 259–61
  rainfall, 16, 18, 20
  salty, 135
  small, 134–36, 135
  soil assessment, 21–24, 23
  special considerations and chal-
    lenging situations, 133–42
  sun and shade mapping, 19–21
  temperature, 16
  topography and soil moisture, 24,
    26
  traffic flow and circulation, 12–13
  visualizing, 14
Size of garden, 106, 108
Skarphol, Brenda, 127, 136
Skunk cabbage, 66, 67
Slips, 256–58
Slope, sunny, garden for, 156–59, 157,
  158, 159
Slugs, 305, 315–16, 315
Small sites, 134–36, 135
Smilacina racemosa, **354**
Smoke tree, purple
  in contrasting-textures combina-
    tion, 84, 85

  in herb and shrub border, 98
  in sunny slope garden, 156–59
Snakeroot, 141, **352**
Sneezeweed, 94
Sneezewort, 33
Snowdrops, 30
Snow-in-summer, 92, 93, 325
Snow-on-the-mountain, **341**
Soaker hoses, 285, 286, 287
Soaps, insecticidal, 306
Soil
  clayey, 22–23, 24, 26
    fertilizing, 288–89
  composition, 22
  drainage, watering test, 24
  dry (see Dry soil)
  fertilizing plans and, 287–89
  foundation plantings and, 25
  improving, 261–70
  moisture, 24, 26
  pH, nutrients and, 267
  for roses, 38
  sampling, 269
  sandy, 22–23, 24
    fertilizing, 288–89
  settling plants in, 272–73
  silt, 22–23
  structure, 23–24
  texture, 22–23, 23, 24
    nutrients and, 267–68
Soil amendments, 132, 267–70. See also
  Fertilizer
  compost, 262–66
  options, 267
Soil analysis, 21–22
  testing options, 268
  texture test, 22
  weeds and, 22
Soil nutrients
  availability, 267–68
  in compost, 262, 264, 266
  flower characteristics and, 262
  guidelines, 268–70
  from organic fertilizers, 268
  pH and, 267
Solidago. See Goldenrod
Solidago canadensis, 53
Solidago rigida, 53, 164–65
Solidago speciosa, 53, 160–63
Solidago sphacelata, 148–51
Solomon's plume, false, **354**
Solomon's seal, 68, 69, **353**
Sonchus oleraceus, 22
Sorghum halepense, 260, 292
Sources, 358–59
Sourwood, 144–47

Southern shade garden, 194–97, *195, 197*
Sowbugs, 321, *321*
Sowing
    indoor, 242–45, *244*
    outdoor, 251–53, *252*
Space between plants, filling in, 326
Spacing of plants, 130
Specialty gardens, 46–50, *47–48*
Speedwell
    description, **350**
    height contrasts and, 117
    staking, 300
Spider flower. *See* Cleome
Spider mites, 317, *317*
Spiders, black and yellow garden, *302*
Spiderwort
    Ohio, in prairie garden, 160–65
    in shady Midwest garden, 206–10
Spiraea, 294, 295
Spirea, 294, 295
Sporobolus heterolepis, 164–65
Spring
    combinations, 64, *65*
        late spring, 92, *93*
    shrubs for, 136
Spring and fall garden, 148–51, *149, 151*
Sprinklers, 286
Spurge
    cushion, in spring and fall garden, 148–51
    in mixed bed, *37*
    in mixed border, 78, *79*
    prostate, 291
Squills, 30
Stachys byzantia. See Lamb's-ears
Staking, 299–301, *299*
Stem cuttings, 256–58
Stem rot, 282
Stems, trouble symptoms, 313–14, 318, 320–21
Stepping stones, 226, 228, 233
Steps, 226, *226,* 228
Stock, **341**
Stolons, 290
Stonecrop, 86, *87,* **350**
Stones
    as mulch, 283
    stepping, 226, 228, 233
Straw, 281
Strawberry, **353, 357**
Stumps, *229,* 336
Style changes, 337–38
Stylophorum diphyllum, 55
Sulfur, 269

Summer
    late-summer combination, 86, *87*
    shrubs for, 136
Summer oils, 306
Summersweet, 136
Sundials, 228, *229*
Sundrops, **349**
Sunflower, 127
    in color combination, 94
    common, **341**
    in island beds, 8
    Mexican, 127, **343**
    outdoor sowing, 251
    staking, 300
    western, 160–63
Sunlight
    adding, 334
    annuals for full sun, **340–43**
    increased, 334
    mapping, 19–21, *21*
    perennials for full sun, **346–50**
Sunny slope, garden for, 156–59, *157, 158, 159*
Sunny theme garden, 49
Sunny volunteers, 327
Supply sources, 358
Sweet pea, 301
Sweetspire, 136
Symmetry, 111, *112,* 113
Symphytum officinale, 98, *99*
Symplocarpus foetidus, 66, *67*
Syringa microphylla, 98, *99*
Syringa × persica, 178–81
Syringa reticulata, 219
Syringa vulgaris, 186–89, 219

T

Tagetes erecta, **343**
Tagetes patula. See Marigold, French
Taraxacum officinale, 22, 260
Tarnished plant bugs, 318
Techniques for maintaining garden, 278–301
Temperature, 14, 16
    for seedlings, 246
    testing, 18
Tender perennials, 28
Terminator zones, *230,* 231
Teucrium chamaedrys, 174–77
Texas, pests in, 302
Texture, 119–20
    contrasts in combination, 84, *85*
Thalictrum dasycarpum, 166–69
Theme gardens, 48, 49–50
    art for, 228

    color, 144–47, *145, 147*
Thistle
    annual sow, 22
    Canada, 22, *292*
        tilling and, 260
Thrift, common, 100, *101,* **346**
Thrips, 317
Thunbergia alata, 301
Thyme
    in herb garden, 174–77
    sunlight and, 334
    in theme garden, 48
Thymus serpyllum, **357**
Thymus vulgaris, 174–77
Tiarella cordifolia, **354**
Tickseed, large-flowered, 300
Tiger lily
    description, **349**
    in fragrant heirloom garden, 186–89
    soil and, *25*
Tilling, weeds and, 260
Tip cuttings, 256–58
Tithonia rotundifolia, 127, **343**
Toad lily, common, **354**
Toads, as beneficials, *304,* 306
Tobacco, flowering, **345**
Tomato, in edible garden, 170–73
Tomato spotted wilt virus, 289, 317, *317*
Tools
    for pruning, *296*
    sources, 358
    for watering, 286–87
Topography, soil moisture and, 24, 26
Torenia fournieri, **345**
Trace elements, 270
Tradescantia × andersoniana, 206–10
Tradescantia ohiensis, 160–65
Traffic flow and circulation, 12–13
Transplanting to garden, 248–51, *248*
Treasure flower, **341**
Trees
    buying large, 275
    in cottage garden, 32, 34
    for large sites, 136, *137, 138*
    in mixed beds, 36, *37*
    overgrown, 141
    planting, 275
    planting under, 196
    pruning, 297
    sunlight and, 334
Tree stumps, 219, *229,* 336
Tricyrtis hirta, **354**
Trollius chinensis, **354**

Tropaeolum majus, **343**
Troubleshooting symptoms of plants, 313–21
Trumpet vine, 223
Tulip
    extended color and, 30, *54*
    Kaufmanniana, 44, 156–59
    life span, 325
    in spring combination, 64, *65*
Tulipa. See Tulip
Tulipa kaufmanniana, 44, 156–59
Tulip fire (Botrytis blight), 316–17, *316*
Turnbull, Cass, 294
Turtlehead, pink, **351**
Tussilago farfara, 22
Two native prairie gardens, 160–65

U

Ultra-fine oils (UFOs), 306
USDA plant hardiness zone map, *360*
USDA plant hardiness zones, 16

V

Valerian, red, 82, *83*
Variety, *112, 123*
Verbascum olympicum, 33
Verbena
    in butterfly garden, 182–85
    fencing and, 312
    garden, **343**
Verbena bonariensis, 56, 119
Verbena canadensis, 182–85
Verbena × hybrida, **343**
Vernonia fasciculata, 166–69
Veronica, 335. *See also* Speedwell
    description, **350**
    height contrasts and, 117
    staking, 300
Veronica grandis, 33
Veronicastrum virginicum, 166–69
Verticillium wilt, 321
Vervain, Brazilian, *56,* 119
Viburnum, 335
Vinca, overgrown, 331
Vinca minor. See Periwinkle, common
Vines, 223
Viola, **354**

Viola labradorica var. *purpurea,* 190–93
Viola × wittrockiana, **345**
Violet, *114*
    description, **354**
    Labrador, 190–93
Viruses, 308
Visualizing garden, 14, 28, 30, 32
    cutouts, 132
    drawing design, 108–9, 131, *131, 133*
Voles, 310, 311–12, *312,* 313
Volunteer plants, 326–27

W

Waldensteinia ternata, **357**
Walkways. *See* Paths
Wallflower, 78, *79*
Water features/ornaments, 217
Water gardens, 46, *47–48*
    sources, 358
Watering, 283–87. *See also* Moisture
    newly installed plants, 274
    roses, 38
    saving water, 284
    seedlings, 250
    outdoor, 252–53
Watering test for soil, 24
Watering tools, *285,* 286–87
Weak and yellowed plants, 332
Weeds
    controlling, 290, *291, 292,* 332
    groundcovers and, 206
    problems from, 289
    removing, 260
        back care and, 293, *293*
    soil analysis and, 22
    tilling and, 260
Whiteflies, 319, *319*
Wildflowers
    combination for hot and dry site, 96, *97*
    sources, 358
Wildlife, pools and, 190
Wildlife gardens, 46, 49
Wilt, 321
Wilting, 286
Windflowers, Grecian, 123

Winds, protection from, 18–19, *18, 19*
    with grasses, 134
    for seedlings, 250
Winston, Elizabeth, 312
Winter, shrubs for, 136
Winter protection, 200
Wishbone flower, **345**
Witch hazel, 136
Wolf, Bill, 270
Woodland garden, fencing for, 222
Woodruff, sweet, **355**
Woodyard, Cynthia, 174
Worms. *See* Cutworms; Earthworms

Y

Yarrow
    in color combinations, 82, *82,* 94, *95*
    in cool-colored garden, 100, *101*
    description, **346**
    fernleaf, 130, 202–5
    in island beds, 8
    in mixed garden, 178–81
    paths and, *227*
    Siberian, 198–201
Yellowed and weak plants, 332
Yellow flags, *118*
Young gardens, help for, 325–27
Young plants, care and shelter, 164, 204
Yucca, 130
Yucca filamentosa, 148–51

Z

Zajicek, Jayne, 280
Zebra grass, 202–5
Zinnia
    creeping, *126,* **343**
    in low-maintenance combination, 102, *103*
    in mixed garden, 178–81
    narrowleaf, **343**
    outdoor sowing, 251
    scale and, *110*
    staking, 300
Zinnia angustifolia/Z. linearis, 102, *103,* **343**